Thinking with Both Hands:

Sir Daniel Wilson in the Old World and the New

Thinking with Both Hands

Sir Daniel Wilson in the Old World and the New

Marinell Ash and colleagues

Edited by Elizabeth Hulse

UNIVERSITY OF TORONTO PRESS
Toronto Buffalo London

Printed in Canada

ISBN 0-8020-4443-3 (cloth)

∞

Printed on acid-free paper

Canadian Cataloguing in Publication Data

Ash, Marinell
    Thinking with both hands : Sir Daniel Wilson in the old world
    and the new

    Includes bibliographical references and index.
    ISBN 0-8020-4443-3

    1. Wilson, Daniel, Sir, 1816–1892.   2. University of Toronto –
    Presidents – Biography.   3. College presidents – Ontario –
    Toronto – Biography.   4. Educators – Ontario – Biography.
    5. Antiquarians – Scotland – Biography.   6. Anthropologists –
    Canada – Biography.   I. Hulse, Elizabeth, 1939–   II. Title.

    LA2325.W5A83 1999   378′0092   C98-932435-4

This book has been published with the help of a grant from the Humanities
and Social Sciences Federation of Canada, using funds provided by the
Social Sciences and Humanities Research Council of Canada.

University of Toronto Press acknowledges the financial assistance to its
publishing program of the Canada Council for the Arts and the Ontario
Arts Council.

Contents

Preface

MARGARET A. MACKAY

Thinking with Both Hands offers a comprehensive portrait of a nineteenth-century polymath. Daniel Wilson was born in 1816 into a city, Edinburgh, and a household which stimulated his intellectual development from early childhood. He began his working life as an engraver, was active as an author, critic, reviewer, essayist, poet, and historian, and turned to the pursuit of antiquarian interests in a Scottish and wider comparative context, before emigrating to Toronto in 1853. There, for close to four decades, until his death in 1892, he was engaged in university teaching and administration and in research which enabled him to make a formidable contribution to the disciplines of archaeology, anthropology, and ethnology.

The title deserves some comment. There is a literal reference, for Wilson was ambidextrous, writing with his right hand and drawing with his left. But more than this, he made the subject a focus for research and publication. It was his belief that by learning to use both hands, the human being could develop the two hemispheres of the brain more fully, a thesis eloquently illustrated in his own personality, with its amalgam of artistic, scientific, and other abilities.

Thinking with Both Hands reflects the diversity of Wilson's gifts and the range of dualities that marked his life. His family background was culturally diverse, both Highland and Lowland, Gaelic and Scots. Though he grew up in Edinburgh's neoclassical New Town, it was the medieval Old Town and the threats to it from civic development which early captured his imagination and led him to record its details as a pioneer of architectural conservation and restoration. His skill in organizing collections (he and his brother George played at creating museums as boys), such as that of the Society of Antiquaries of Scotland, now part of the new Museum of Scotland, drew on his capacity to perceive and demonstrate comparisons and contrasts in the study of human experience.

Wilson's career linked Old World and New, and intellectually and actually he never ceased to move between the two. To Canada he brought his Scottish, British, and European experience and contacts, while North America provided a fertile field for his investigations and data for *Prehistoric Man: Researches into the Origin of Civilisation in the Old and the New World*, the revised edition of *Prehistoric Annals of Scotland* (first published in 1851), and a host of other publications. The Industrial Museum of Scotland, presided over by his brother George, professor of technology at the University of Edinburgh, became home to Athapaskan and Inuit artefacts gathered through a scheme instigated with Scottish employees of the Hudson's Bay Company, while he was instrumental in the return to Scotland of the Crozier of St Fillan, a relic believed to have been in the tent of Robert the Bruce on the eve of Bannockburn and taken to Canada in the early nineteenth century by members of the Dewar family, its hereditary keepers.

Impetuous and quick of temper, Daniel Wilson was nonetheless known for his openness and flexibility, his skills as a mediator and conciliator, his sense of fun, his capacity for friendship, his charitable activities, and his ability to 'associate broad human sympathy with solid learning.' In him we find a figure who deserves his rightful place in the history of the two worlds of which he was a part.

This study of Daniel Wilson owes its genesis and original impetus to the vision of a scholar, Dr Marinell Ash (1941–1988), whose life and interests linked North America and Scotland in a similar fashion to his own. Born in Ventura, California, with ancestry that included emigrants from southwest Scotland, whose descendants moved across the United States generation by generation, Marinell Ash manifested in all her work a similar pioneering spirit. In a family memoir she once wrote, 'At the core of the western experience was always the belief in one's ability to make a new life, a belief in the possibility of possibilities. And that did not, and does not, require a specific place for its acting out, so much as the will that it should be so.' In many ways it is a suitable motto for this project.

Marinell Ash graduated from the University of California at Santa Barbara with a BA in 1963 and an MA the following year; she gained her PhD from the University of Newcastle in 1972 for a thesis completed under the supervision of the distinguished Scottish historian Geoffrey Barrow on the medieval diocese of St Andrews. Between 1967 and 1972 she lectured in Scottish history at the University of St Andrews, where Dr Ronald Cant had earlier stimulated her interest in medieval Scotland, and from 1972 to 1983 she was a radio producer with BBC Scotland, responsible for history output in the educational broadcasting department. From 1983 until her untimely death from cancer in 1988, she worked as a freelance, self-employed historian, creating in Scottish Historical Services a research bureau from which much valuable work emanated. Hers was a career devoted to making the past as accessible as possible to as wide an audience as possible, from the school pupil to the scholar, and to exploring the links between the Old World and the New.

Dr Ash's developing interests in Scottish historiography, archaeological thought, and professional scholarship were signalled by her 1980 publication *The Strange Death of Scottish History*, which has proved to be a seminal study in Scottish historiography. As an active fellow of the Society of Antiquaries of Scotland, she found in Daniel Wilson, elected secretary to the society in 1847, an individual whose impact had been profound, but whose achievements were imperfectly understood. His 1851 work *The Archæology and Prehistoric Annals of Scotland* was the first survey of a nation's archaeological remains in the English language, but his appointment two years later to the chair of history and English literature at University College, Toronto, took him into an entirely new milieu, where he spent the rest of his life, and this may in large measure account for the fact that on neither side of the Atlantic had his full story been told. In her 1982 article '"A Fine, Genial, Hearty Band": David Laing, Daniel Wilson and Scottish Archaeology,' in *The Scottish Antiquarian Tradition*, essays edited by A.S. Bell to mark the bicentenary of the Society of Antiquaries of Scotland, Marinell Ash began to address this situation in an eloquent way.

Her research into the career of Daniel Wilson was supported by the Leverhume Trust, the British Academy, the Society of Antiquaries of Scotland, and the Russell Trust. In 1984 she lectured at the Daniel Wilson Symposium, held at the University of Toronto to mark the 130th anniversary of the introduction of anthropological topics to the Toronto curriculum, a prelude to what may have been the first annual course on the subject offered anywhere in the world. In the face of failing health she continued to locate, collect, and identify relevant material, including the splendid collection of Daniel Wilson watercolours, then in family hands in Scotland, which has since been acquired by the National Archives of Canada. She retained her zest for the project to the end, but wrote only a portion of what she had planned.

As her friend and in due course one of her literary executors, along with Dr James Macaulay, I shared in Marinell Ash's exploration of Daniel Wilson from the very start, for University College was my alma mater and that of many members of my family. She took delight in seeing the prize volumes signed by Daniel Wilson won by a great-uncle (whose diary for 15 April 1878 recorded, 'Had last lecture in English. Dr. Wilson read the whole of the Nonne Preste's Tale') and hearing of the Wilson pictures that hung in UC in the 1960s, the display items from his collections, and the residence that carries his name, as a prelude to her research visits to Toronto.

Two other University College graduates have played a vital role in ensuring that this volume has come into being: Professor Bruce Trigger and Elizabeth Hulse, both of whom knew Marinell. We were guided towards potential contributors who could reflect the many facets of Wilson's life and career in Scotland and Canada, and, most significantly, we found in Elizabeth Hulse both an enthusiast for the subject and an expert editor. She painstakingly took in hand the drafts prepared by Marinell Ash, made her own contribution to the volume as an author, and coordinated the work of the other contributors.

It is right that readers should know the background to this volume and the reasons for the place of Dr Marinell Ash among the authors. Our debt to her is great, as it is to all who in a host of ways have ensured the appearance of this study. But she would certainly have wished it to be said that, for those who are fascinated by the time in which he lived and the disciplines he cherished and developed, it is Daniel Wilson, 'the man who invented prehistory,' to whom the greatest debt is owed.

Acknowledgments

I am most grateful to Dr Marinell Ash's executors, Margaret Mackay, James Macaulay, and Jane Ryder, for inviting me to assume responsibility for overseeing the completion of her work on Daniel Wilson and for their continued support during the years that it has taken to put this volume together. I met Dr Ash when she was researching Wilson in Toronto in the 1980s, and through her I came to know Dr Mackay and eventually the other executors, all of whom I now count among my friends. Margaret Mackay and her husband, John Gerrard, have shown me great kindness on numerous occasions, entertaining me both in Edinburgh and at their home in Glasgow and introducing me to Scotland's many cultural riches. Dr Mackay read the manuscript and made many helpful suggestions. She also looked after the Edinburgh illustrations for the volume. Jane Ryder has provided a base in Edinburgh by opening her flat to me during my visits to that city in 1992 and 1995.

To those who have contributed essays to this volume I owe a special debt. They have drawn on their varied backgrounds and specialized knowledge and have added a richness to the portrait of Wilson that it would have been difficult for one author to provide. In particular, I would like to acknowledge the assistance of Bruce Trigger, who met with Margaret Mackay and me in 1992 and helped us to plan the volume.

I also wish to thank the Institute for Advanced Studies in the Humanities at the University of Edinburgh and its director, Professor Peter Jones. A two-month fellowship at the institute in late 1992 allowed me to examine Dr Ash's papers and begin my own research into the Wilson family history. I remember fondly the office that I enjoyed in the institute's elegant eighteenth-century home and the kindness and help provided by assistant to the director Anthea Taylor, secretary Julie Dhanjal, and servitor Tam Jardine. In 1995 the School of Scottish Studies and its director, Dr Mackay, made available to me a most welcome office there.

My research into Wilson's family life has been much stimulated by access to papers in the possession of the Valentine family, which were lent to me during my fellowship in 1992. I am grateful to Danvers and James Valentine for allowing me to quote from manuscript material and to reproduce photographs from Wilson's album of family and friends. As well, Canadians and art lovers generally owe a debt of gratitude to the Valentines for arranging for the National Archives of Canada to purchase their magnificent collection of nearly two hundred Wilson watercolours in 1995.

Many individuals and institutions in Edinburgh assisted in my research. I would like to thank the staff of the National Library of Scotland for their unfailing courtesy, helpfulness, and efficiency in retrieving a vast array of material. I was also assisted by the staff of the Special Collections Department of the Edinburgh University Library, the library of the National Museums of Scotland, and the National Monuments Record of Scotland. Among individuals who supported the project in various important ways were Antoinette Watkins, Dale Idiens, and Andrew Martin of the National Museums of Scotland; Peter Freshwater, John Howard (now retired), and Murray Simpson of the Edinburgh University Library; Aileen Christianson of the Department of English Literature, University of Edinburgh; and Sheena and Alasdair MacDonald, who live in the Wilson family home, Elm Cottage. At an early stage of the project, Marinell Ash's good friend Joanna Bruning assisted by seeking out Wilson's papers.

In Toronto the staff of the Baldwin Room at the Toronto Reference Library and of the University of Toronto Archives answered numerous questions and helped to sort out many problems relating to the history of the city and the university and Wilson's published and unpublished writings. I would particularly like to thank Christine Mosser and Mary Rae Shantz of the Toronto Reference Library for their assistance. Harold Averill of the University Archives, as well as contributing an essay to this book, shared his extensive knowledge of the university with me and suggested illustrations for the volume. Maureen Morin of the University of Toronto Information Commons scanned a number of the images.

Among other Canadian friends of the project, I am grateful to Les Jones for showing me his fine collection of stereo views, which once belonged to Daniel Wilson, and for inviting me to address the Photographic Historical Society of Canada. Likewise, an invitation from Brian Land and the Ex Libris Association allowed me to interest others in the subject of this volume. Stephen Otto answered many questions about the buildings and history of Toronto. John Parry provided encouragement and support and read my essay at the copy-editing stage. And my niece Julie Fox suggested the book's title.

Research for this volume has led me down numerous byways. I am grateful to President J. Robert S. Prichard and Vice-President Michael Finlayson of the University of Toronto and the outgoing principal of University College, Lynd W. Forguson, for accepting my proposal to restore Daniel and Margaret Wilson's gravestone in St James' Cemetery and for sponsoring an application to the Ontario Heritage Foundation for a plaque to honour Wilson on the university campus.

Gerald Hallowell of the University of Toronto Press supported this project from the time that Marinell Ash first approached him in the 1980s with drafts of some early chapters. I would like to thank him for his continued interest and encouragement. Emily Andrew, formerly assistant editor at the Press, helped to smooth the bumpy road from submission of the manuscript to publication. And Darlene Zeleney supplied much valued advice as I donned the hat of copy editor for the volume.

Elizabeth Hulse

Abbreviations

AAS	American Antiquarian Society
AGO	Art Gallery of Ontario
AO	Archives of Ontario
APS	American Philosophical Society
BAAS	British Association for the Advancement of Science
BL	British Library
BLC	*The British Library General Catalogue of Printed Books to 1975*
CEM	*Canada Educational Monthly*
CJ	*Canadian Journal* (Canadian Institute)
CMNR	*Canadian Monthly and National Review*
DCB	*Dictionary of Canadian Biography*
DNB	*Dictionary of National Biography*
ENPJ	*Edinburgh New Philosophical Journal*
EUL	Edinburgh University Library
Hodgins	J.G. Hodgins, ed., *Documentary History of Education in Upper Canada* (28 vols., 1894–1910)
HUA	Harvard University Archives
JAI	*Journal of the (Royal) Anthropological Institute of Great Britain and Ireland*
ME1	*Memorials of Edinburgh in the Olden Time* (1848)
ME2	*Memorials of Edinburgh in the Olden Time* (2d ed., 1891)
MHS	Massachusetts Historical Society
MUA	McGill University Archives
NA	National Archives of Canada
NGC	National Gallery of Canada
NLS	National Library of Scotland

NMS	National Museums of Scotland
NUC	*The National Union Catalog: Pre-1956 Imprints*
PAAAS	*Proceedings of the American Association for the Advancement of Science*
PAAS	*Proceedings of the American Antiquarian Society*
PAS1	*The Archæology and Prehistoric Annals of Scotland* (1851)
PAS2	*Prehistoric Annals of Scotland* (1863)
PCI	*Proceedings of the Canadian Institute*
PM1	*Prehistoric Man* (1862)
PM2	*Prehistoric Man* (2d ed., 1865)
PM3	*Prehistoric Man* (3rd ed., 1876)
PSAS	*Proceedings of the Society of Antiquaries of Scotland*
PTRSC	*Proceedings and Transactions of the Royal Society of Canada*
RCAMS	Royal Commission on the Ancient Monuments of Scotland
RCI	(Royal) Canadian Institute
RMS	Royal Museum of Scotland
ROM	Royal Ontario Museum
RSC	Royal Society of Canada
SAS	Society of Antiquaries of Scotland
SIA	Smithsonian Institution Archives
TRL	Toronto Reference Library
UCA	University College Archives, Toronto
URL	University of Rochester Library
UTA	University of Toronto Archives
UTL(F)	Thomas Fisher Rare Book Library, University of Toronto

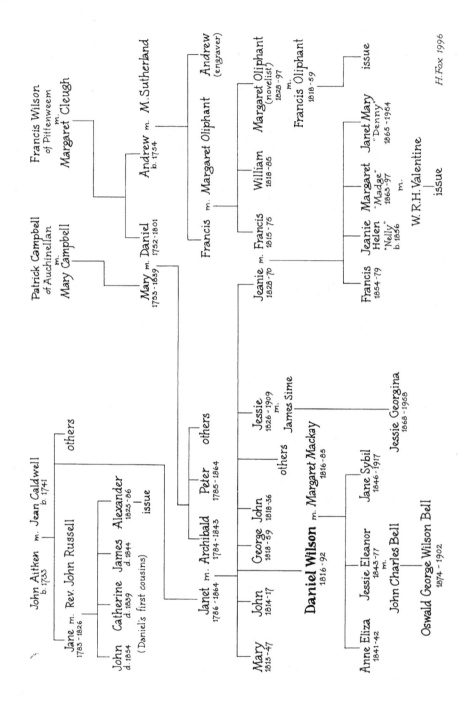

H. Fox 1996

Thinking with Both Hands:

Sir Daniel Wilson in the Old World and the New

Daniel Wilson: The Early Years

MARINELL ASH

'The Scene of All Our Youthful Years': 1816–1837

Daniel Wilson was a child of Edinburgh. The city of his birth bestowed much on him, and in return he gave it his scholarship and his devotion. He was born on 3 January 1816 in the family home at the base of Calton Hill. His birthplace was at the edge of Edinburgh's classical New Town, begun in the 1760s as a refuge for lawyers and lords who no longer wished to live in the crowded and dirty Old Town centred on the medieval High Street. In the New Town they built spacious houses and flats along straight streets and facing elegant squares, and they frequented the assembly halls, theatres, and shops that sprang up to serve their needs. Although Wilson would identify himself with the history of the Old Town, it was the New Town that shaped his earliest childhood. Among his first memories would have been the men and machinery at work on Waterloo Place and the Regent Arch, built to extend Princes Street and span Low Calton, just to the north of the family home.

Like many other citizens of the nineteenth-century Scottish capital, Daniel's father, Archibald, and his uncle Peter were incomers from the Highlands. They had been born in Strachur, a small, Gaelic-speaking parish on the eastern shores of Loch Fyne in Argyll. Their father, another Daniel, came from Pittenweem, in the Lowland county of Fife, but their mother was a Campbell of Auchinellan, and Archibald bore a characteristic Campbell name. The fact that he was tutored by a young theological student[1] suggests that the family had some social and financial status. When the brothers settled in Edinburgh is uncertain. A Peter Wilson, who may possibly have been Daniel's uncle, appears as the owner of wine vaults in Blair Street, to the south of the High Street, in the Edinburgh post office directory for 1808–9. Archibald Wilson, 'tea dealer,' is listed at 2 Greenside Street, at the top of Leith Walk, in the directory for 1810–11.

It was in Edinburgh on 12 June 1812 that Archibald married Janet Aitken, the daughter of John Aitken of Greenock, a prosperous land surveyor.[2] Unlike that of her husband, Janet's background was quintessentially Lowland. Her father's profession was a product of the mania for agricultural improvement that had transformed Lowland Scottish farming (and the landscape) in the later eighteenth century and made it the envy of Europe. Her grandparents were themselves farmers at Romanno Mains in Peeblesshire. Daniel Wilson thus combined the Highland and Lowland halves of Scotland: two cultures and at one time two totally distinct languages. Although there is little evidence to suggest that he was fluent in Gaelic, which his father almost certainly spoke, Daniel displayed throughout his life a sensitivity to Highland culture and traditions, and he took great pride in his part-Highland background. His mixed ancestry was not a division in his make-up but an enrichment, though it was the Lowland side of his heritage that was decisive.

The first child born to the young couple was a daughter, Mary, who suffered from heart trouble and would die in 1847 at the age of thirty-four. The second child, John, lived to 1817, a year after Daniel's birth. Of the eleven children born to the Wilsons, only five survived to adulthood. Daniel himself would recall 'dim visions of little sisters and brothers whose cradles I rocked and by whose sick beds I watched as they faded away in their early years.'[3] Doubtless this experience had its effect on him, perhaps explaining the affection, tinged with constant worry, that would mark his feelings for his own daughters. Nevertheless, he grew up in a happy household, loved by his parents and, as the eldest surviving son, cosseted by the family's elderly Highland nurse, Jeanie. He was devoted to his mother and loved his sisters and brothers deeply, especially the twins, George and a second John, who were two years his junior. John was always sickly, and when he died of lung disease at the age of seventeen, George transferred the unique feeling of twin for twin to his elder brother. Daniel became his 'dear brother and best friend.'[4] The bond between them would not be broken by Daniel's move to Canada or even by George's early death in 1859.

Janet Aitken Wilson was a talented woman, well educated and strong-minded. She had little time for the fripperies of fashion, and at about the age of thirty she invented a precursor of rational dress, a plain, but becoming style that she wore for the rest of her life. Her influence on her children was enormous, and others who knew her commented on her strong, attractive character. Her cousin by marriage, the novelist Margaret Oliphant, said of Janet Wilson, 'During my life I have known many clever and some able women, but I have met only one woman with genius.'[5] At the age of four, each of the Wilson boys was sent to an elementary school. They then attended a small private academy in George Street run by a Mr Knight, which prepared pupils for the High School. At the academy Daniel and his younger brothers made the first of their lifelong friends, among them the master's son, John Knight. But although they might have construed Latin sentences under Mr Knight, it is clear that to a large extent the Wilsons educated themselves under the loving tutelage of their mother. She was 'bright, vivacious ... a universal devourer of books, and with that kind of scientific tendency which made her encourage her boys to form museums, and collect fossils, butterflies, &c.'[6]

The home below Calton Hill was full of plants, geological and natural history specimens, and a dearly loved succession of pets: dogs, cats, mice, sparrowhawks, guinea pigs, rabbits, hedgehogs, tortoises, and owls. After the death in 1826 or 1827 of Mrs Wilson's older sister, Jane, widow of John Russell, the minister of Muthill in Perthshire, her orphaned children (and her husband's library) were added to the Wilson household. The arrival of John, Catherine, James, and Alexander Russell necessitated a move to a larger house at 26 St James Square. A special room was set aside by Mrs Wilson where her children and their cousins and friends could pursue their interests undisturbed by adults.

By contrast with his wife, Archibald Wilson appears a colourless figure. His children gave him the respect demanded of offspring, and Archibald doubtless reciprocated; but he remains a vague and shadowy personality who only occasionally intruded upon the lives of his children. Daniel was reticent about his father, in later years saying only that he was an 'amiable man who should have been a happy one, but the world did not prosper him; and he was not his own best friend.'[7] Yet Archibald also contributed to his children's development. Like his wife, he loved books, and in the 1820s he purchased a share in the Edinburgh Select Subscription Library, a move that had a decisive effect on his sons: 'there we were turned loose, like colts in a rich field of clover, to revel as we pleased in the wide range of English literature.'[8] The children's reading was broad and unsystematic, something that Daniel later saw as a positive advantage: 'it was invaluable for the healthful development of the innate intellectual powers of the eager youth, and for evoking whatever was original in his mind, by leaving him to follow out the bent of his tastes ... It is the grave

fault of some of our school and still more of our college systems of education, that a boy passes through them as if he had been put into a mould,
and comes out with the mere impress of the routine system and unvary-
ing standard of its tests, instead of having his own intellectual powers
quickened into healthful development.'[9]

Besides the richness of literature, Archibald Wilson gave his children
his deep religious faith.[10] Both he and Janet were Baptists, members of a
church that had grown up in Scotland in the late eighteenth century. It
stressed believer's baptism by immersion and the Lord's Supper as the
primary ordinances, together with an evangelical ministry and social
concern.[11] Archibald may have been converted to this faith while still in
Strachur, for there was a Baptist congregation there from about 1801,
presided over by the fisherman-evangelist Donald McArthur. In Edinburgh the family probably worshipped either at the Tabernacle in Greenside Place, established by the brothers Robert and James Alexander
Haldane early in the nineteenth century, or at Richmond Court Chapel,
presided over by Christopher Anderson.[12] The growth of the Baptist
Church in Scotland was stimulated by the Haldanes, who came from a
landed family near Stirling. They fell under the influence of the Independent minister David Bogue of Gosport, and by the late 1790s Robert had
sold his estate to finance a number of missionary projects. When a
scheme for a mission to India fell through, the brothers turned their
attention to the home mission field, undertaking long journeys throughout Scotland to hold revival meetings. In 1808 James Alexander's doubts
about infant baptism came to a head, and he became a Baptist.

From an early age the Wilson children were encouraged to exercise
private acts of charity to those less fortunate, thus expressing in practical
terms the Baptist emphasis on good works. The daily round of the household was regularly broken by small expressions of benevolence: 'it
chanced on one occasion that a poor, barefooted Italian boy, with his
hurdy-gurdy and white mice, became an object of compassion to us;
mother was readily induced to provide him with stockings and an old pair
of shoes, and in gratitude for these and other services, he presented us
with a pair of white mice.'[13] That such charity added to the children's
growing menagerie was, of course, an advantage, but it was also of a piece
with the Wilsons' humanitarianism. Politically, the family was strongly
whig, imbued with a belief in the equality of humankind and a distrust of
artificial distinctions of rank. Alexander Sprunt, a school friend from the
West Indies, recalled intense and heated discussions ranging over the politics of the day: 'the final struggle of the Poles, the French three days of

July, the Reform movement, etc. On all such questions George Wilson took the extreme liberal side. The subject of the immediate or gradual emancipation of the negro slaves in the colonies was keenly discussed about that time. Some of us being related to families of the colonists were familiar with the arguments for a gradual abolition of slavery. George was an unremitting advocate of immediate emancipation.'[14]

Janet Wilson encouraged discussion of such topics among her children and actively nurtured their love of literature. Daniel recalled the weighty theological volumes inherited from the Reverend John Russell's library, 'the very outsides of which had a learned, orthodox look about them. They were little likely to furnish the favourite reading of boys. Nevertheless, they were occasionally dipped into, and even the mere handling of such venerable tomes, and familiarity with their old type, quaint title-pages, or more curious colophons, were not without influence in the forming of tastes.'[15] Other books in the family home were of more immediate interest. These included Oliver Goldsmith's *Animated Nature*, the *Penny Magazine*, the *Encyclopaedia Britannica*, and the Library of Entertaining Knowledge. Begun in 1829 and issued in parts at two shillings each, the Library covered such diverse subjects as insect architecture, Egyptian antiquities, the Elgin Marbles, and Pompeii.[16] Daniel Wilson's introduction to antiquity may well have come from these pages. The series could also have provided his first acquaintance with the burgeoning world of cheap, mass-produced educational material for the rising artisan and middle classes of Britain, the sort of material that he himself was to write in the 1840s. The family copy of the *Encyclopaedia Britannica* began by being 'a mere child's picture-book' and changed, as the children grew, into 'an unfailing book of reference.'[17]

Because of Janet Wilson's predilections, storytelling and the reading aloud of poetry formed popular pastimes for the children. She introduced them to selections from *Paradise Lost* and the dramatic story-poems of Felicia Hemans's *Records of Woman*. The children took to heart what they heard. Once when she had read to them the anti-slavery passages in Cowper's *Task*, Daniel and George, 'in a fit of youthful enthusiasm, renounced sugar in our tea, as a practical protest against the slave-labour to which it was due ... but we were not sufficiently logical enthusiasts to feel at all aggrieved in conscience by the bargain we made that we were still to be allowed sugar with apple-dumplings!'[18]

This early introduction to poetry led to the reading for pleasure of Moore, Byron, Southey, Coleridge, Shelley, and Scott. From these authors it was a short step to the great literary love of Daniel's life, 'Shakspere' (the spelling he regularly used). With such a grounding the Wilsons and their cousins naturally wrote poetry themselves, and Daniel would remain a skilled versifier throughout his life. The household was a serious-minded, but not a solemn one. The children were allowed full rein to their imagination, which was nurtured on classic fairy tales – Jack and the Beanstalk, Cinderella, Bluebeard, and Beauty and the Beast – as well as the Arabian Nights and *Pilgrim's Progress*. All became lifelong favourites and contributed to the streak of fantasy and delight in language that Daniel and George displayed in adult life. From an early age they formed the habit of jotting down absurdities of language and behaviour, and these linguistic fancies spilled over into their writing and speech. As adults, both were known as witty writers and speakers, and the correspondence between the brothers is brimming with puns, extended verbal jokes, and linguistic oddities that had caught their fancy.

The children also kept notes from their natural history and antiquarian rambles, and Daniel began to draw. Many of his earliest efforts were illustrations of things seen or collected on their wanderings, but here too he allowed his imagination to roam widely. Years later George asked him: 'Do you remember a certain production of your schoolboy days, a painted procession of men of all nations, journeying towards some central goal, some mysterious and unpainted limit, which was left for the imagination to scheme out for itself, being too great to be squeezed into the narrow space of pasteboard dedicated to the marching of the wondrous host? I remember well the delight I used to feel in watching your deft (not daft) pencil designing, with a *curiosa felicitas*, the assembled hordes of all nations, and peoples, and kindreds and tongues.'[19] This 'painted procession' is the first evidence of Daniel's interest in the comparative history of peoples of the world, which would later so occupy him as an archaeologist and ethnologist.

Their father seems to have taken little part in the intense literary activity in his household, perhaps because he was preoccupied with business difficulties. The 1815–16 Edinburgh directory shows that Peter Wilson had moved his spirits shop to 45 Leith Street, a change that he may have made in order to be near his brother's family. From about the time of Daniel's birth in the latter year, Archibald Wilson's address is given in the directories without mention of an occupation, suggesting that his tea-dealer's business was no longer in existence. By 1820–1 Peter had moved again, to the newly completed Regent Arch, and Archibald joined him there within a few years. But although Peter prospered (he opened at least one other shop), Archibald seems to have been content to remain a subordinate figure in the Regent Arch business. Peter would come to occupy the dominant male position in the Wilson family, and he would take over as its father figure after his brother's death in 1843.

Both of Daniel's childhood homes were in the shadow of Calton Hill, the hard, black, basaltic plug of a long-extinct volcano which was just beginning to acquire the buildings and monuments that would make it the acropolis of the 'Athens of the North.' Old structures and those in progress are irresistible to small boys, and on Calton Hill they were present in abundance: the castellated Old Observatory, built by James Craig, designer of the New Town; the huge, inverted stone telescope of the Nelson Monument (completed the year before Daniel's birth); the severe Doric of the New Observatory, begun in 1818; and the fortalice of the Calton Hill gaol. In the 1820s, as the children were growing up, other buildings were being added: the incomplete memorial to the Napoleonic Wars, begun during George IV's visit to Edinburgh in 1822, and (of more immediate importance to the Wilson boys) the new High School of Edinburgh, rising on the south-facing slope of the hill.[20]

The Calton Hill and its buildings were fascinating enough, but from its summit a universe spread out at the boys' feet. To the north were the classical terraces of William Playfair's extensions to the New Town, stretching towards the port city of Leith, with the blue line of the Firth of Forth and the green land of Fife beyond. And farther still, on a clear day, they could see the distant outline of the Highlands, from where, only eighty years before, Prince Charles Edward Stuart had led his army to Edinburgh. To the east was the cultivated plain of the Lothian coast, ending in the twin basaltic heaps of North Berwick Law and the Bass Rock. This long, flat shore had been the favoured invasion route of Roman armies and of English forces in the days of William Wallace and Robert the Bruce. To the south were the dramatic lines of Arthur's Seat, its slopes covered with the patterns of fields ancient beyond imagining, and at its base the royal palace of Holyrood. Beyond the gap-toothed profile of the High Street were the Pentlands, with the faint outline of the Border hills beyond; to the west, the classical streets and circuses of the New Town, separated from the Old by the deep, empty space where once had been the waters of the North Loch. Towering above the town – both Old and New – was the dramatic thrust of the Castle Rock. It was a landscape to set the imagination afire – Scott's 'own romantic town,' every building and street replete with associations from his stories and poems. Years later Daniel Wilson would recall the time and place where his father had first pointed out Scott to him in the street.[21] But beyond such recent historical connections, the landscape of Edinburgh and Lothian spoke of long geological ages that had first been elucidated by the Scottish geologist James Hutton, whose work would be further advanced by Wilson's friends Robert Chambers and Charles Lyell.

As they grew older, the Wilson boys ranged farther afield. The royal hunting preserve of Holyrood, dating back to King David I in the twelfth century, was a favourite playground. It held not only the attraction of the ancient St Anthony's Chapel and its curative well but also the lure of danger. 'There we knew every accessible cleft and gully of the rocks, delighted in climbing the famous Cat-nick on Salisbury Crags, and preferred finding our way down from the top of the hill, as a goat might scramble down the cliffs, to taking the more leisurely and safer slope of the grass.'[22] From the heights of Arthur's Seat, their legs dangling from their eyrie atop its basaltic columns, Daniel and his brothers and friends watched the construction of the first railway into Edinburgh, a horse-drawn line from the town of Dalkeith.

The Old Town was a cherished haunt. It was associated with some of Daniel's earliest memories, such as the 1824 fire that destroyed the huge, dilapidated tenement in Parliament Close known as 'Babylon.'[23] As they grew older, the Wilsons and their circle relished the vivid life of the Luckenbooths beside St Giles' Church or the puppet shows in the timber-fronted tenements of the West Bow. Here, on one never-to-be-forgotten day, Daniel paid a penny to see a comic burletta entitled 'The King of the Cannibal Islands.'[24] Truly, as he later recalled, 'Edinburgh, our native city, was the scene of all our youthful years; and that itself was no unimportant element in life's training.'[25]

Family excursions into the Scottish countryside had begun when the children were still young. Summer holidays were spent in the small watering place of Corstorphine, to the west of Edinburgh. Daniel never forgot being taken into the church there to view the tomb of a crusader.[26] Trips were later made to the Perthshire village of Muthill, where John Russell was minister. On Sunday the children would be taken to the Norman church in the village to listen to the Presbyterian eloquence of their uncle. Other summer holidays were passed at the farm of Janet Wilson's grandparents in Peeblesshire and at the manse of Cumbernauld in Dumbartonshire, occupied by their father's former tutor, the Reverend John Watson. In the summer of 1831 Archibald Wilson took his sons to his birthplace in Strachur, and to their great delight the twins were able to sleep in the bed where their father had been born. On their return, the Wilsons called on Hugh Mackay, a Glasgow merchant who had befriended Jane Aitken Russell in her widowhood. Mackay had daughters the same age as Daniel and the twins, and they rapidly became friends. Later the younger daughter, Margaret, came to visit Mary Wilson, and a friendship began to ripen that would culminate in her marriage to Daniel.

By the mid-1820s he had left Mr Knight's academy for the Royal High School of Edinburgh, to be followed a few years later by George, John, and their cousins James and Alexander Russell. Dating from 1519, the Scola Regia Edinensis was redolent with historic associations. It had been built on the site of the thirteenth-century Blackfriars, immediately to the east of Kirk o' Field, where in 1567 Lord Darnley, the husband of Mary Queen of Scots, had come to an untimely end. The school was refounded in 1578, after the Reformation, and was briefly located in the former town house of Cardinal Beaton. This reorganization was part of the scheme of national education envisaged in John Knox's First Book of Discipline. In keeping with the Scottish tradition of democratic education, moderate fees meant that pupils at the school came from a wide social background. The playground in the High School Yards had seen most of the ornaments of Edinburgh's golden age as pupils: David Hume, William Robertson, Francis Jeffrey, Henry Cockburn, and Walter Scott. There was a sense of historic continuity about the High School Yards: 'the old school seemed a link between past generations and the living age.'[27] Further, Daniel's schoolboy trips between the New and the Old Towns were a journey between two cultures. The difference between them was symbolized and reinforced by the traditional 'bickers' between the 'blackguards' (the High School boys) and the 'puppies' of the Old Town, fought out on Saturday afternoons in the fastnesses of the Hunter's Bog on Arthur's Seat or at the town golf links.

Other historic continuities associated with the High School were perhaps less admirable. At the time that Scott had attended there in the late 1770s, Latin still formed the sole medium of study, and teaching was carried on, as it had been since the Reformation, by a rector and four masters. Yet already the steady rise in numbers of pupils and the shift of population to the New Town were creating problems for the school, which were only temporarily solved by its rebuilding on a larger scale in 1777. The real modernization of the High School began in 1810, when the town council of Edinburgh appointed James Pillans rector. Faced with a class of 144 boys, he spent his first year in office asserting his authority and wondering how to ensure that teaching could be carried out at all in the burgeoning school. The answer was to introduce a monitorial system. Each year's intake of boys (usually about 200) was carried through four years by a single master. The final two years were spent under the direction of the rector. Except for lectures by the masters or rector in 'general knowledge' (which included history, geography, and English grammar) or recitation before the whole class, each year was sub-divided into groups of about ten boys under a monitor, a member of the class who was chosen, on the basis of his academic performance, to lead the group. Learning was largely by rote, but a pupil's standing in the class depended on written work done at school.

Before he left to become professor of Latin at the University of Edinburgh in 1820, Pillans had expanded the study of Greek and introduced Latin verse composition to the curriculum. The High School of Edinburgh was virtually the only place in Scotland outside the universities where Greek could be studied. It was under Pillans's successor, Aglionby Ross Carson, another classical scholar, that Daniel Wilson was a pupil. In 1829 there were suggestions that the curriculum should be extended to include practical subjects, such as physics, chemistry, and natural history, in order to make the school a 'seat of useful as well as ornamental learning.'[28] At the time that Wilson knew it, however, the High School still betrayed its medieval origins, not least in the oral basis of its teaching; it continued to be the 'noisy mansion' that Scott recalled from his time under the rectorship of Dr Alexander Adam.[29] The inadequate rooms in the High School Yards were full of boys, huddled into little groups reciting their lessons under the direction of their monitor. Although the monitorial system was praised by visitors to the school (and widely copied elsewhere), the pupils had a different view of it. Scott recalled how he had 'glanced like a meteor from one end of the class to the other' as his standing fluctuated.[30] Wilson had similar criticisms: 'Those in the two front forms worked with more or less persistency under a somewhat coercive system; the remainder idled in the most flagrant fashion, and not a few of them looked back in later years on those dreary hours with an indignant sense of wasted time.'[31] Four hours a day were given over to Latin. By contrast, Greek (which began in the spring term of the third year) occupied only three hours a week and geography two hours. At the end of each academic year, a day was devoted to oral examinations and prize-giving in front of the civic dignitaries of Edinburgh.

For Daniel, rote learning was punctuated by repeated attempts to break him of his left-handedness. He became, he later said, 'ambidextrous, yet not strictly speaking ambidextrous,'[32] writing (as he was forced to do at school) with his right hand and drawing (as he naturally pre-

ferred) with his left. From this childhood experience developed a lifelong fascination with physiology that would culminate in his *The Right
Hand: Left-Handedness* (1891). His struggles with his left-handedness may
also have contributed to his lack of academic success. His friend William
Nelson was class dux and graduated with the gold medal in classics.
Daniel was not such a high-flyer, although he became a proficient classicist. Like his precursor Scott, he left the High School without any academic distinctions, but with fond memories of the place and its rector
and a group of friends that he would keep for the rest of his life.

An inner circle of friends, consisting of William Nelson, the son of an
Old Town bookseller, Alexander and James Sprunt, John Alexander
Smith, and others, in 1828–9 formed the Juvenile Society for the
Advancement of Knowledge, which met on Friday evenings at the Wilson
home. During these gatherings, papers were read and questions such as
'Whether the camel was more useful to the Arab, or the reindeer to the
Laplander'[33] were earnestly debated – perhaps the first ethnological
questions to which Daniel Wilson ever addressed himself. The members
also planned the excursions that occupied their Saturdays: to Dalkeith or
Duddingston Loch beyond Arthur's Seat, to the tidal pools of the Forth,
or to the Roman remains at Cramond. In a glass-fronted case supplied by
his mother, Daniel set up his first museum, which the members of the
society stocked with treasures brought back from their increasingly
adventurous wanderings: fossils, minerals, shells, insects, gallnuts. They
also had a small herbarium. A copy of the *Journal of James Fox*, perhaps a
relic of their uncle's library, was used as a blotter and press for botanical
specimens.[34] The Juvenile Society published its proceedings in a paper
with a heraldic motif designed by Daniel, and it also issued a regular journal under his editorship which contained news of natural history and
antiquarian interest. Outside the circle of the Juvenile Society, there were
other school friends who would help to shape the course of Daniel's life,
including the son of a prosperous linen merchant and draper in Edinburgh, George Brown. Their childhood friendship would later be reinforced by Brown's marriage to William Nelson's sister Anne. Another
schoolmate who would be Wilson's friend and colleague in Toronto was
George Paxton Young, also a couple of years his junior.

Daniel and many of his friends were present when, in 1829, the High
School flitted from its medieval seat to the new building at the base of
Calton Hill. By the early 1820s a decision about the school's future could
no longer be delayed. The Edinburgh town council was much concerned
that if two schools were built – one for the Old Town and the other for

the New – the social divisions between the two parts of the city would increase.[35] Eventually it was decided to build a single new school on the edge of the New Town, but with easy access from the Old over the North Bridge. Work began in the summer of 1826, after an impressive ceremony to lay the cornerstone.[36] The design by Thomas Hamilton was in the Greek-revival style: a severe temple of learning, colonnaded and with chaste friezes of laurel wreaths and stylized acanthus leaves surmounting its wall-heads and decorating its iron fences. The school was to contain five classrooms (one each for the rector and the masters) and a common hall, library, writing room, and large playground. After a number of delays, it was completed in early 1829 at a cost of £24,200.[37]

On Tuesday, 23 June, a grand procession formed in the High School Yards to march to the new building. Members of the parade carried suitably classical sprigs of laurel as they moved along Infirmary Street to the North and Regent bridges and Calton Hill. The procession was led by the mounted band of the 12th Royal Lancers, followed by the school janitor in his gown and bearing his baton. Next came the writing and mathematics masters and the year masters with their classes 'in fours, according to their size, the smallest in front.'[38] The scholars were followed by city officials, clergy, university dignitaries, and former pupils. At the new building the students lined up on either side of the entrance to allow the dignitaries to move through to the hall; they then went to their respective classrooms. Daniel Wilson remembered this 'bright, auspicious day' for the rest of his life, but he felt that the move somehow made the High School a less-interesting place.[39] Lucky Brown's 'laigh' pie shop in the old High School Wynd, a mecca for hungry boys where Scott had first tested his storytelling powers on his contemporaries, did not long survive the removal of its clientele. Old Blackie's toffee stall migrated with the schoolboys, but it seemed sadly out of place amidst the Grecian splendours of Calton Hill.

The fact was that Daniel had given his heart to the crowded, historic exuberance of the Old Town. In adult life he recalled the rational streets of the classical New Town as architecturally boring and unoriginal. 'The puny striplings of the eighteenth century were men of line and rule: feeble followers of precedent.'[40] It was otherwise with the Old Town, a place where 'sober matter-of-fact realities came into collision with the medieval elements which still struggled for perpetuity in an age for which they had grown obsolete.'[41] In addition to his daily trips to school, he had begun to know more of the Old Town in the course of his visits to the home of his friend William Nelson. The Nelson family lived in an ancient panelled and painted house in Trotter's Close on Castlehill, with a view across the Grassmarket to the Pentlands beyond. From the Nelson house the boys could explore the fairs in the Grassmarket and watch military parades by the castle garrison; they could play on the castle esplanade and wander the wynds and closes leading from the High Street. It may have been during these excursions in the picturesque and dilapidated Old Town that Daniel first began to think of art as a career.

But first there were his last years at the High School, spent under the rector, Dr Carson. The boys were drilled in geography, Greek, Latin, and composition, the works of Xenophon, Thucydides, Homer, Sophocles, Euripides, Virgil, Horace, Terence, Juvenal, Plautus, Livy, Cicero, and Tacitus, and 'antiquities.' The last named was a subject that they could easily relate to their own explorations. For example, during excursions to the Roman fort of Cramond, where the sculptured legionary eagle was still visible on the cliff at the mouth of the river Almond, it 'was an object-lesson, better even than the Roman altar dedicated to the goddess Epona ... which Dr. Carson, the Rector of the High School, produced to his class, and won their attentive admiration as he pointed to the focus in which the Roman horse-jockey was poured a libation; and adduced passages from the Satires of Juvenal in confirmation of his theme.'[42] This practical lesson in the conjunction of archaeological and literary evidence was not forgotten. After he left the High School, Daniel Wilson remembered his rector with affection, and when he was at work on his *Archæology and Prehistoric Annals of Scotland*, he called upon his knowledge of Roman Scotland for a number of debatable Latin inscriptions.

It was probably in the year before he left the High School that Wilson met Alexander Macmillan. One of his father's friends was the Irvine bookseller-inventor Maxwell Dick. The Wilsons apparently visited the small Ayrshire town about 1830. At that time Dick was attempting to raise funds for tests on a suspension railway he had conceived a few years before,[43] and he was content to leave the running of his bookshop in the hands of his young apprentice, Daniel Macmillan, the son of an Arran crofter who had brought his family to the mainland some years before. Daniel Macmillan was about seventeen years old at the time of the Wilsons' visit. He and his younger brother, Alexander, rapidly became friends with Daniel, George, and John Wilson and in time came to look upon the Wilsons as a second family.[44] The Macmillans had been educated briefly at the local grammar school and, like George and Daniel Wilson, were voracious readers. They had something else in common with the Wilsons: while still living on Arran, the Macmillans' parents had been deeply affected by a series of revival meetings held by the Haldanes, and the family had joined a Baptist congregation after they left the island.[45] Daniel Macmillan would soon go south to begin the remarkable career that would lead to the establishment of the great publishing house which bears the brothers' name, but his and Alexander's friendship with the Wilsons would be broken only by death.

By the time the two families met, Daniel and George were also thinking about their future careers. Daniel was fourteen and growing into a tall, rangy figure, with black hair, sparkling dark eyes, a beak of a nose, and prominent cheekbones. He was quick to anger and had a lively, vivacious, impulsive personality. George was small and fair; he was already determined on a professorship at the University of Edinburgh, even though he was not yet sure in what subject. Daniel seems not to have had such a strong sense of vocation. Perhaps the root of his indecision lay in the diversity of his gifts: which of his talents and interests could – or should – provide him with a career? It is not clear why he chose art and, more specifically, the highly specialized craft of engraving; but early in 1831, at the age of fifteen, he left the High School and began training in the studio of the engraver William Miller.[46]

Wilson's mentor had been born into a Quaker family in Edinburgh in 1796.[47] After training in London, he had returned to his native city in 1821 and established his workshop in the family home, Hope Park (later called Millerfield House), an eighteenth-century house in the open countryside south of Bruntsfield Links. The studio, with its north-facing windows, green baize–covered work table stained with acid and oil, and separate table for the apprentices, would be the focus of Daniel's life for the next six years.[48] He later recalled that the first thing he saw in the studio was a watercolour by J.M.W. Turner of the Tower of London from the Thames, which Miller was 'engraving on a large scale.'[49] Initially, the Turner sketches and paintings that came to Miller to be reproduced seemed like 'daubs' to the young apprentice, but in the course of watching the master turn 'the bedaubed scrap of coarse blue paper into the beautiful engraving,'[50] Daniel sharpened and refined his artistic sensibilities.

The work of engraving was in many respects a collaboration between the artist and the engraver, each with a different expertise to bring to the process, especially when the original was in Turner's highly atmospheric style. 'More slight or slovenly sketches of effect could not well be imagined; and as to detail that is due to the engraver, who in his effort at supplying the detail which his art rendered imperative was in danger of sacrificing the atmospheric effect and real beauty of the slight drawings.'[51] Turner was a brilliant retoucher of engravings of his own work, and as Wilson recalled, 'The arrival of a touched proof, especially from Turner, was always a subject of interest.'[52] He also remembered that William Miller taught not by precept but by example; this was as it should be: 'The lives of soldiers, of statesmen, or explorers and of adventurers of all sorts, furnish abundant material wherewith the biographer can enliven his pages with stirring incident; but the life of the author or the artist is in his works.'[53]

Daniel's time in the Miller household passed happily enough. The master and his wife were known for their kindness to their apprentices. Mrs Miller had been accustomed to invite the pupils for dinner on New Year's Day, but because this was a whole holiday and one of the few days when the apprentices were free of the studio, she changed it to Hogmanay (New Year's Eve) so that they could spend the next day on excursions. On 1 January 1836 Daniel joined his fellow apprentices James Giles and William Ballingall and a group of friends in a visit to the museum of the Society of Antiquaries of Scotland; it was his first recorded contact with the collection that he was later to organize.[54] The museum was open only intermittently, and visitors had to be accompanied or signed in by fellows of the society.

Not all of Daniel's life during this period was centred on William Miller's studio. His earliest surviving watercolour sketches of old Edinburgh buildings, later to form the basis of his *Memorials of Edinburgh in the Olden Time*, are probably from this period. He also attended lectures at the University of Edinburgh, although, since he did not intend to take a degree, he was never a matriculated student.[55] Nothing is known about the classes he attended, but his later writings on the development of human societies betray his debt to the Common Sense school of Scottish philosophy. He seems to have had some personal contact with John Wilson ('Christopher North'), professor of moral philosophy, whom he disliked, though it is not clear whether this acquaintance was through the university or *Blackwood's Magazine*.

Many of Daniel's extracurricular activities resulted from contacts made by his brother George, who in 1832 had entered the Royal Infirmary of Edinburgh as an apprentice surgeon. A number of their school contemporaries were attending the university, and on 4 April 1833 the Juvenile Society, after a period of decline, was reborn in new guise as the Edinburgh Zetalethic Society, again with Daniel as secretary.[56] The name seems to have been a mistranscription of the Greek word *zetetic*, meaning the search for truth through continuous enquiry. Certainly, the essays read before the society and its debates justified the epithet; they covered such worthy topics as the relative advantages of public and private education, compensation for the emancipation of slaves in the West Indies, the morality of duelling, the right and duty of resistance to tyrants, the moral influence of drama, and whether the married or the single life is happier.[57]

For both Daniel and his brother, however, the highlight of these student years was the meeting of the newly founded British Association for the Advancement of Science held in Edinburgh in 1834. The gathering was the first great scientific experience of their lives. It brought together not only such British scientists and savants as Sir Roderick Murchison, Sir Thomas M. Brisbane, Sir David Brewster, and Charles Lyell, but also foreign luminaries, including Louis Agassiz. Maxwell Dick came from Irvine to attend the meeting and stayed with the Wilson family.[58] Through his agency, George and Daniel were able to gain access to the chemical and other sections and were also admitted to an evening meeting in the New Town assembly rooms, when Dr William Buckland 'delivered one of his fascinating and piquant popularizations of geological science.'[59] Both returned from the meeting full of excitement, not just because of the lecture but also from a sense of having rubbed shoulders with the great figures of British science.

It was during these years of apprenticeship that the two brothers added a new group of friends to their circle, many of whom would themselves take their places in the front rank of science and the arts. Daniel may have been the first to meet the young artists George Harvey and David Octavius Hill; the latter, with Robert Adamson, would pioneer the new art of photography. Most of the extended circle, however, came through George's medical connections, among them James Young Simpson, the future discoverer of chloroform as an anaesthetic and a fine amateur archaeologist, to whom Daniel would dedicate the revised edition of his *Prehistoric Annals of Scotland* in 1863. Other friends included George Day, later to hold a medical chair at St Andrews, John Goodsir, future professor of anatomy at Edinburgh, and John Stuart Blackie, a young lawyer and *Blackwood's* writer. Blackie may have met the Wilsons through his friendship with D.O. Hill and George Harvey. He found the Wilson circle more congenial than his *Blackwood's* and legal friends and was especially attracted to George.[60] The Wilsons and their friends in turn enjoyed the older man's strong Scottish speech, his quirky personality, and his eccentricities, which included the wearing of checkered trousers and a plaid. His lodgings were the scene of many convivial evenings at which food and talk were followed by the singing of traditional songs. In return, Blackie zestfully joined in the Wilsons' more serious meetings and debates.

Daniel and George had lived at home during the first few years after they left the High School. The house at St James Square was still the centre of an active family circle, but one that was gradually thinning. In the spring of 1835 George's twin, John, died. His death had been expected for years, but George was devastated and compensated for it not only by drawing closer to his elder brother but by flinging himself more deeply into his studies. From the first he had found the suffering that he witnessed in his daily rounds at the infirmary almost intolerable. Within months of beginning his medical training, he knew that temperamentally he could never be a practising surgeon. Instead, he was increasingly attracted to chemistry. Here was a science, clear, clean, and unambiguous, which could help to make human lives better. He was drawn to it in part as a reaction to the haphazard horror that he saw in the Infirmary and in part out of a kind of intellectual idealism. He determined therefore that, after he qualified as a surgeon, he would begin studies in chemistry under Professor Robert Christison.

The year 1837 was one of endings and beginnings. George Wilson started his chemical studies, cousin John Russell married and sailed to Australia, and Daniel left Edinburgh to seek his fortune in London. He was now twenty-one, a trained engraver with some experience of literary reviewing in the Edinburgh journals.[61] He was already in love with Margaret Mackay and searching for a livelihood that would allow them to marry.[62] The time seemed propitious. The choice of London was probably the result of his friendship with the Macmillans. Daniel Macmillan had gone to England by way of the Wilson household in 1833. After working for a Cambridge bookseller, he had returned to Scotland for a brief holiday early in 1837, much of it spent in the Wilson household recovering from an illness brought on by the voyage from London to Leith. In the spring he had taken a position with the London publishing house of Seeley.

During his convalescence Macmillan must have discussed his experience in the south with the Wilson brothers. Here was a friend to stay with until Daniel Wilson found his feet and a source of information about the London publishing world. Much later he would choose to see his decision in terms of a gamble: 'I went to London ... eager, enthusiastic, sanguine, bent on winning some prize in the lottery of life ... I had left the old home with five pounds in my pocket, and all the world before me.'[63] In some senses it was a gamble, for he still had not found his true life's work; but behind the light-hearted quest that Wilson recalled in old age, it is not hard to discern a determination and a sense of purpose that sprang from the bedrock of his Edinburgh childhood.

'Fame, Fortune, and Futurity': 1837–1851

Daniel Wilson arrived in London in the autumn of 1837. It was a new
world, stranger even than Washington and New York would later seem.
He wandered the city, exercising his legs and his curiosity. However, he
had a living to make. Over the next months he was able to find some editorial and literary work, and he wrote a tragedy called 'Evelyne,' which he
submitted to the actor-manager William Charles Macready. But he wished
above all to follow his master, William Miller, and engrave a painting by
Turner. Soon after he had arrived in London, he gained his wish.

This commission and his other London adventures were duly reported
in letters home. In the days before the penny post, letters cost 13½ pence;
so he and his brother George made sure they got their money's worth in
long communications. George's letters are the only ones to have survived.
He was still grieving the death of his twin and the loss of Daniel to the
capital, but his missives are full of his usual high spirits and sense of fun.
'Mother says I don't write you proper letters, that instead of stuffing them
full of nonsense I should tell you about the family's doings; but ... I
thought I should be most likely to please you in my epistles if I just wrote
to you what I would have chatted to you had you been sitting over your
work, and I at my window with book in hand, surrounded by my bottles
and tubes.'[64] Almost as soon as Daniel was settled in London, George was
demanding to know if his brother had met his idol, Michael Faraday.

The correspondence alternates between light-hearted banter and
descriptions of the absurdities of Edinburgh and London and – on
George's part – news of family illness. By early 1838 the failing health of
their cousin Catherine dominates George's letters, while Daniel's contain
reports of his work on the Turner engraving. Soon after his arrival, he
had obtained an interview with Francis Graham Moon, who ran a print
shop in Threadneedle Street behind the Old Exchange. 'I found him a
wonderfully oily, fair-spoken gentleman, delighted to patronize a rising
talent, as long as he saw a reasonable prospect of coining his patronage
into gold!'[65] Wilson dined with Moon and 'had an uncomfortable sense
of being vulgarly patronized and condescended to.' They discussed
'Turner and high art, fame, fortune, and futurity; and it was finally
agreed that he was to secure the copyright of one of Turner's pictures
which I was to engrave on the largest scale for £100, and if successful it
was to be followed by another at £500.'[66] Wilson was so enthralled at
securing the commission that he failed to have the agreement put in
writing, an omission that was later to cost him dearly.

In the meantime, full of hope, he and Moon took a cab to Turner's 'dingy old mansion' at 47 Queen Anne Street West. From his time in William Miller's studio, Wilson knew something of the artist's eccentricities and his reputation as a miser, but nothing had quite prepared him for the reality.

His old housekeeper, a queer bundle of wrappages, opened the door and after some parleying ushered us into a room on the ground floor. The shutters were only partially open, and the window-panes, obscured with dirt, admitted very imperfectly the light of a gloomy November day. After what seemed a long delay the door was abruptly opened by an old, slovenly dressed, slouching little man, as remote from the ideal of artist or poet as could well be conceived. Yet even then I noted the wonderful flash of his keen grey eyes, which redeemed the otherwise vulgar and sensual look. They were very odd eyes, very partially opened, and shining through the two little chinks below his eyebrows in a very cunning and irate fashion ... he abruptly addressed Moon: 'Well, what do you want?' ... I trembled for my chances of success, but his manner to me was more gracious, and after inspecting some specimens of my handiwork he responded with an amiable grunt. I was introduced into the gallery cumbered with the treasures of art that now fill the Turner galleries at Trafalgar Square, and he indicated the picture he chose to let me have.[67]

The work was *Regulus*, one of Turner's 'Claude' paintings. Wilson did not regard it as among the master's great works, but for the sake of future success he was prepared to spend a good part of the next two years[68] in the painstaking task of transferring the image to copperplate, a process that he recalled as 'the art of extracting sunbeams from cucumbers.'[69] There were problems, too, caused by the artist's technique and materials. 'Turner would seemingly make any sacrifice to get the effect he aimed at. He had, moreover, worked so much and on so large a scale in watercolours that he was prone to resort to the same processes when painting in oils ... in making a slight attempt with the wet corner of a silk handkerchief to remove a spot of dirt, I made the discovery that if my operations were extended the whole clouds and tinting of the sky, with much else, would vanish, as they are all painted over an oil ground in mere size colours.'[70]

This was not the only problem that Wilson faced. The strict control that Turner exercised over the engraving process meant that all of Wilson's tact and self-control were required for him to survive his encounters with the artist as he took successive proofs to him for approval. The trouble began when he admitted to Turner that, in preparation for his work, he had spent a day in the British Museum studying the Claude engravings. 'To my surprise he assailed me in the wildest manner. Much good Claude would do me! What did I mean? Did I intend to copy his painting? What did I know of Claude? etc. etc.'[71]

Wilson was terrified that Turner might withdraw his permission and was careful never to mention Claude again. There was another outburst when he took his reduced drawing of *Regulus* to the artist. He went in the company of James Giles, his former fellow apprentice. They found Turner suffering from a cold and shabbily dressed, 'with dirty linen, a large coloured handkerchief tied like a poultice about his neck, ... a slouched hat drawn over his eyes.'[72] He at once declared that the dimensions of the drawing were incorrect, but by this time Wilson was wise in the artist's ways. He avoided contradicting Turner directly, but left the drawing with him. Nothing further was heard on the subject, and Wilson was able to start work on the engraving using his own dimensions.

George continued to write with news of home, questions about London, and accounts of student life and of his growing circle of friends, including the remarkable naturalist Edward Forbes. He had known Forbes since he was a medical student earlier in the decade. In the winter of 1834–5 Forbes had founded the *University Maga*, for which George wrote under the nom de plume Bottle Imp. The Barracks, Forbes's lodgings in Lothian Street, was a gathering place for the young scientists of Edinburgh: George Wilson, George Day, John Hughes Bennett, Samuel Brown, and John Goodsir. This group formed the nucleus of the Universal Brotherhood of the Friends of Truth, begun by Forbes in imitation of German student societies. Its manifesto stated: 'The highest aim of man is the discovery of truth; the search for truth is his noblest occupation. It is more – it is his duty. Every step onwards we take in science and learning tells us how nearly all sciences are connected.' The 'roseate band,' as the group was called after a distinctive sash that members wore across their chests, continued after student days were over and added congenial new members. Daniel Wilson would later be involved, attracted to the society not only by its ideals and membership, but also by its vision of science as a unified discipline and the pursuit of scientific truth as a moral obligation and the highest duty of humankind.

George's letters, full of his convivial life and academic work, seem to have contributed to a crisis of confidence in Daniel, who was struggling to establish himself in London, far away from Edinburgh. There is little doubt that both brothers were ambitious and impatient for the success which they felt their talents merited. By the late 1830s there are hints that

Daniel despaired of the course he had taken. It must have seemed to him that 'fortune and futurity' came all too slowly. In March 1838, after sending Daniel an account of his work on a chemical compound, George wrote: 'You must not contrast your situation and mine as you do – years of labour, and months rich in discoveries. Remember that you have fairly begun, have got all the machinery set in play, which can "lead on to fortune." You are engaged in purely professional labours, and the result is very much in your hands. Now, I have not even entered on the threshold of my profession.' He then added on a positive note, 'I read, with very great pleasure and sympathy, of your kneeling at the altar of St. Paul's.'[73]

Daniel had gone to pray in the cathedral as soon as the Turner commission was assured.[74] It is the first hint of the religious conversion through which he was to pass in the next few years. By the late 1830s he was probably attending St Peter's, Islington, a church established by a namesake, the evangelical clergyman Daniel Wilson.[75] The vicar at St Peter's was the young, Yorkshire-born Joseph Haslegrave, a forceful and popular preacher. The church was evangelical and strongly anti-Tractarian in its ethos.

Wilson was reticent about expressing his religious beliefs, but the events of his life show that they were deep and sincere, finding expression in regular church attendance and in acts of charity and Christian witness. Perhaps the nearest that it is possible to come to his religious feelings is *The Queen's Choir*, a poem written in 1851 and published two years later as a gift for his friends. It is about the demolition of the fifteenth-century Trinity College Church, which Wilson and his fellow antiquaries in Edinburgh had fought to save (see the following essay in this volume). But it is also a meditation on the spirit of his own times and the ways in which religious belief can – and cannot – be expressed in stones and mortar. Despite his historical and architectural interests, Wilson totally and violently rejected the Oxford Movement, which he saw as a betrayal of Reformation principles.

Rather than such emasculated faith
    As that half-monkish, ritualistic medley,
Preached, wolf-like, by sleek doctors, from beneath
    The gowns of brave old Latimer and Ridley,
    Should supersede God's truth, I'd witness gladly
Pillar, and clustering groin, and carven choir,
    Bow to fanatic axe,
And mad iconoclastic torch's fire.[76]

He viewed the Church of Scotland as one with the Oxford Movement in
the religious extremism that he abhorred, since it destroyed the unity of
faith and worship. He expressed the split as a divorce between the 'nobly
wedded pair' Truth and Beauty:

> Beauty alone, from manly truth divorced,
>   Is sensuous, prurient, and unnatural;
> Truth without Beauty, likens law enforced
>   Untempered by God's mercy; brimming full,
>   As thunder-cloud, of majesty a pall
> Of cloud unsunned, though heaven-born; so meseems,
>   My country, thy stern faith,
> Yet lacking sunshine more than lightning-gleams.[77]

There was no doubt in Wilson's mind that the Presbyterian choice of
truth was preferable to the empty ritualism ('Beauty') of the Tractarians,
but it was a cold and joyless thing, expressed in outward form by the
denial of the Christian year (for example, Christmas was not a holiday in
Scotland) and the severity of a ritual which rejected that 'kist o' whistles,'
the organ. Wilson respected Presbyterian principles and adherence to
form, but he felt that it was a church which denied internal spirituality.

In between these two extremes was a middle way where Wilson found
his spiritual home in these early London years and from which he never
deviated to the end of his days. His form of Anglicanism was historic, was
seemly in its ritual, followed the Christian year, was concerned with
beauty in its services and music, and was outgoing in its social concern. It
was a church of people and the spirit, not of stones and mortar, although
he appreciated the architectural and artistic context of worship which
called forth reverence:

> Reverent as in the golden rubied blaze
>   Of matin service, when the organ peals
> With its full-volumed hallelujah's praise
>   Through the o'er-arching vaults, then sudden stills,
>   And the strange silence all their echoes fills
> With the rapt pause, on smiling Christmas morn,
>   As beneath heaven's vault,
> When unto us th'incarnate God was born.[78]

Wilson's conversion to evangelical Anglicanism may also have been influenced by that of the Macmillan brothers. By 1842 they had joined the Church of England, attracted by the services and writing of the Reverend F.D. Maurice, author of *The Kingdom of Christ*. This work argued for a national church positioned between the excesses of the evangelicals and the Tractarians and allied to a strong social commitment that easily merged with the social conscience ingrained in Daniel and George Wilson since childhood.

By the middle of 1838 George's letters are full of his own plans to come to London, in order to study under Professor Thomas Graham and to meet Faraday. His trip was delayed at first because he did not wish to leave his sister Mary to deal with Catherine's increasingly severe illness, but in the autumn of the year he made the longed-for journey and joined his brother in his suburban lodgings at Stratford le Bow. In one of his letters home, he described a day spent with Daniel in Westminster Abbey. Half seriously, the brothers fixed 'on the corners we should be in when we are buried in that noble sepulchre.'[79] They were struck by the humble tomb accorded Sir Humphry Davy in contrast with the piles raised to lesser figures. George was offended by the comment of a friend who was with them: '"See, sir, he was a Baronet." That was all the merit he had in his eye.'[80] To the Wilsons, a man's worth came from what he did and not who he was. If the brothers were to win fame and fortune – and their places in Westminster Abbey – it must be because of their own abilities.

George had planned to stay in London only a few weeks, but just before he was due to return to Edinburgh, he was taken on as an unpaid assistant to Graham. The brothers moved to lodgings in Great Clarendon Street, Euston, so that George could be closer to the laboratory. His chemical equipment was sent from Edinburgh and set up in their rooms, and their landlady was given strict instructions not to touch the apparatus. The brothers settled into a pleasant bachelor existence. In their free time they walked in search of picturesque buildings and scenery for Daniel's pencils and paint,[81] and haunted the museums, galleries, theatres, and churches of London. In far-off Edinburgh Mrs Wilson worried about the moral danger that her sons faced in attending Anglican services. She was especially concerned about the quality of the clergy and their sermons. George sought to reassure her that there were pious and sincere clergymen in the Church of England: 'I attend the Church of England because it seems to me to conduct the public worship of God in the most befitting and devout way.'[82]

The brothers entertained themselves by continuing the tradition of the private magazine begun with the Juvenile Society; this time the manuscript volume, containing verses 'grave and gay' and with an emblematic design by Daniel on the title-page, was called 'Quips, Quirks, Quodlibets, and Quiddities, by Bottle Imp and Mynheer von Scratch.'[83] George began to learn the guitar, and the brothers enjoyed evenings of music and talk with Daniel's artistic and literary colleagues and the growing circle of friends from George's laboratory: the artists James Giles, John Wykeman Archer, and John Brown, the scientists Lyon Playfair and T.H. Huxley, and a young medical student named David Livingstone. In the spring of 1839, however, news of Catherine Russell's death forced George's early return to Scotland. That year he qualified as a physician. After attending the meeting of the British Association for the Advancement of Science in Birmingham late in 1839, at which he presented an abstract of his thesis, he paid a short visit to Daniel in London. He hoped that he might find a position there, but was unsuccessful, although he did finally achieve his ambition of a personal encounter with Faraday.

Daniel had at last finished the Turner engraving. As the work had progressed, he had thrown off successive proofs, which were taken to the artist for comments and touching up. His 'hints and touches on my proofs were very valuable. His skill in this respect was marvellous ... When my ambitious undertaking was finished, Turner expressed himself, in his gruff way, as pleased: – "Better than I expected of you" were his parting words: and so I saw my last of the strangely gifted artist.'[84] The engraving, entitled *Ancient Carthage – The Embarkation of Regulus*, which was published by Moon on 1 August 1840, was the beginning and end of Daniel Wilson's career as an engraver on a large scale. Thereafter he produced only pictorial work for his own books. It was not just that copperplate engraving was giving way to wood engraving and lithography[85] or because of the meticulous nature of the work that he changed course. For Wilson the Turner engraving had been a 'prentice piece' in the business of life. 'All I got for my laborious and successful work was £100. I had proved what I could do, and then made up my mind to seek my fortune by some other road. Happily, as it has proved, though not without troubles and cares in the transitional stage.'[86] He turned instead to writing, among other things reviewing prints that reproduced the work of contemporary artists and were sold in ever-increasing numbers to decorate middle-class homes. In some ways these prints were the visual equivalent of the popular reading material being produced by publishers such as the Edinburgh-based William and Robert Chambers and William Nelson, to which Wilson would turn his hand.[87]

When the brothers parted at the end of George's London visit in 1839, both must have known that their lives had reached a turning point. George was now qualified as a doctor; Daniel had proved himself and had the prospect of enough work to allow him to marry. Soon he would set up a household as a married man, and George would begin his career as a chemist. It was the end of their youth. Although they could not have foreseen coming events, these would test and change their lives in the next few years. There had been some sort of family crisis that autumn, perhaps to do with their father. Writing of it to Daniel, George merely said, 'We are men, and will strive to look things in the face; to bear is to conquer our fate.'[88] The Wilsons learned their stoicism in a harsh school, and in the next few years more difficult lessons were to come.

For a time, however, the family settled to a routine. George had so far been unsuccessful in finding work in Edinburgh, although in November 1839 he had been elected president of the Edinburgh Physical Society. He reconciled himself to staying at home for another winter of study, keeping his sisters, Mary, Jessie, and Jeanie, company. In the late spring of 1840 he wrote to Daniel to introduce Edward Forbes when his friend went south to London. Daniel was apparently working on some kind of scholarly project since his brother concludes his letter, 'We want to give you the red ribbon, as soon as your paper is done.'[89] But the subject of this project is unknown.

On 28 October 1840 Daniel married Margaret Mackay in Glasgow; he returned with her to London, where they established a household in lodgings in Camden Town. A few months earlier George and his cousin James Russell had gone on a walking tour around Stirling. During a long hike in a late summer storm, George had suffered a sprained ankle. Although the injury did not prevent him from attending the BAAS meeting in Glasgow, he became seriously ill after he returned to Edinburgh. In October he was subjected to leeching and poulticing, but the treatment failed and an abscess formed on his heel. The wound seemed to get better; then in December it again became inflamed.

Though active, George had never been physically strong. From the time of his walk near Stirling, he was never again to be well or free from pain. As a doctor himself, he could diagnose his own illness, and the prospect must have appalled him. Yet the tone of his letters to his brother remained cheerful, and among his friends he was a vivacious and popular figure. Indeed, to many his palpable fragility added to his charm. The historian John Hill Burton, who first knew the two brothers in the 1840s, recalled: 'Daniel was ... noticeable among men as tall, wiry, and erect. His brother the chemist was small, and so sickly and fragile in aspect that one had a nervous feeling, when he was present, as if some fit or worse might befall him; and yet, living, as if his existence and capacity for work demanded of him, a hermit's life of abstinence, in company the genial spirit within him shone forth and made him as full of pleasant talk as any Hercules of the table.'[90]

Despite the unfailingly cheerful tone of George's letters to Daniel, it must have been a worrying time for the brothers. From the summer of 1840 it was clear that their sister Mary's health was beginning to fail. As the months passed, the situation became even more anxious, but Daniel was tied to London by literary work and his wife's pregnancy. George's health was also becoming more precarious, and a visit to London in the autumn of 1841 did little to reassure Daniel, for immediately upon reaching the city, his brother came down with a severe eye inflammation.[91]

Soon after George's return to Edinburgh to begin a series of chemical lectures, news arrived of the birth on 9 October of a daughter, Anne Eliza, to Daniel and Margaret. He became the proud godfather, although his reading of the Book of Common Prayer convinced him that he could not carry out the spiritual duties required of a godparent by the Church of England. Soon he had more immediate problems to contend with. The inflammation returned with renewed force: 'I was twice cupped, blistered five times behind the ear, horribly sickened with colchicum, and severely salterated with mercury.'[92] He emerged from this 'fortnight of misery' weakened, but with some relief from his rheumatism.

In London, overwork – and perhaps worry about the health of his infant daughter – plunged Daniel into a series of severe and debilitating headaches. George wrote to his brother: 'I have at last seen in the "Athenæum" your work announced ... I hope things mend a little, and the clouds break up: still I fear you are like myself trading on the future.'[93] (Whatever the work announced in the *Athenæum*, it seems to have been published anonymously, for no article appears there with Daniel's name in 1841 or the first half of the following year.) Perhaps the growing precariousness of his brother's health, together with an opportunity to contribute to the popular series Chambers's Information for the People, published by William and Robert Chambers, began to turn Daniel's thoughts towards returning home.[94] In the spring of 1842 George's rheumatism returned in his knees and ankles. He leeched and bandaged himself and by March was able to report to Daniel that he was creeping along on a pair of crutches. He could, however, sleep only with the aid of morphia to dull the pain, and his eyes were affected by strong light. Further, he suffered a seizure during a lecture and was forced to cancel the rest of the series. It was clear that his foot was also growing worse. On 23 May George was told by James Syme, professor of clinical surgery at the University of Edinburgh, that he would have to undergo surgery.

During his convalescence, Margaret and his tiny god-daughter came to Edinburgh for a visit. George was entranced: 'Truly she is beautiful ... She is like nobody I know, though I daresay the lower part of her face will yet turn out Wilsonic.'[95] But within a few weeks, on 23 August, Anne was dead. Her death produced in Daniel a severe depression which can be traced in two poems that he later wrote. In the first, 'The Aster,' he seems prepared to consider the possibility of the universe as a godless void, redeemed only by a vision of Anne as one of God's angels:

> My babe, beloved one, didst thou come down
> > From inconceivable realties;
> Wert thou permitted – with my young life strown
> With thorns, – and thou so sweet a rose unblown,
> > The bitterest thorn; my closed eyes
> > To ope on Paradise?[96]

In the poem 'Wild Weeds' he achieves a more resigned tone as he considers the way that nature reverts to its original state of order and beauty after the violence of a storm:

> Bright things return with spring,
> But thou, my bright, my lovely one,
> Of thee, what doth it bring,
> But a new blossom to the weed hath grown
> Above thy grave, unsown![97]

About this time George wrote to Daniel: 'With all your sorrows I sympathize from my heart; I have learned to do so through my own sufferings. The same feelings which made you put your hand into your pocket to search among the crumbs there for the wanting coin for the beggar, lead me to search in my heart for some consolation for you ... A bankrupt in health, hopes, and fortune, my constitution shattered frightfully, and the almost certain prospect of being a cripple for life before me, I can offer you as fervent and unselfish a sympathy as ever one heart offered another ... God, who has supported both of us through cruel trials, will not desert us in our great need. My religious faith is feeble, because my light is dim, and my knowledge scanty, but I pray for more.'[98] It may have been the death of his child, together with the increasingly desperate state of his brother's health, that made Daniel decide to return to Edinburgh with his family towards the end of 1842.[99] His life in London had been full and increasingly successful. He had proved himself as an artist and had a wide circle of literary contacts who provided him with work. Wilson seems to have acted regularly as a bibliographical researcher in the British Museum for his friends the Macmillans, and he wrote for a number of journals. With the reputation he had established and his contacts with the Chambers brothers and the rising publishing house of his friend William Nelson, it would be possible to work in Edinburgh.

In some senses the move back to his native city was a new start, symbolized by the birth of a second daughter, Jessie Eleanor, in June 1843. Daniel would not limit himself to literary work. The business he chose to follow reflected his own expertise as an artist, engraver, and art critic. Daniel Wilson, 'printseller & artists' colourman,'[100] is first listed in the Edinburgh directory for 1843–4, living in Broughton Street near the top of Leith Walk and having a shop in West Register Street. He had returned to the part of the city in which he had spent his youth and near to the family home in Gayfield Square, where the Wilsons had lived since 1838. Daniel must have felt that, during a time of deepening crisis, his place was close to his family. At first the surgery on George's foot seemed successful, but the wound refused to heal. After it had been cauterized, his strength failed visibly. By the end of 1842 it was clear that his foot would have to be amputated. He asked only for a week's delay. In the days before anaesthesia he knew what he would have to face. He did not expect to survive and needed time to prepare himself for the ordeal. George did not tell his family of the impending operation, but spent the week rereading the New Testament. In the end, however, the truth could not be kept from the family, but he did attempt to lessen their apprehension on the morning of the operation by performing his 'toilet with peculiar pains and care' and by taking a normal breakfast of tea and toast.

Within six weeks the wound had nearly healed, and George was able to hobble around on crutches. Then, in March 1843, a new misfortune struck. Archibald Wilson had left the house and was returning with friends a few hours later when he suddenly dropped dead in the street of an aneurysm of the heart. The family were roused by a violent ringing of the doorbell. When they answered it, they were presented with the sight of Archibald's dead body in the arms of strangers. It was brought into the house and laid out. George limped into the room on crutches to see what the disturbance was about and discovered his father's corpse. Archibald's death led to changes. The family circle was shrinking, and probably with the help of Uncle Peter, the Wilsons moved to Brown Square on the south side of the city, to a house where George had kept lecture rooms since 1841.[101] After a summer spent recouping his health in the small village of Morningside to the southwest, he returned to Brown Square in the autumn to prepare a new course of lectures.

By this time James Russell was also ill. He had gone to the University of Glasgow to train as a minister, but in the winter of 1843–4 came back to Brown Square; he died there in April. George was devastated. James had been his favourite cousin, and the two had spent much of their youth together. The operation, followed so shortly by the deaths of his father and his cousin, produced a religious crisis in George. Like his brother, he had been attracted to the Anglican church, but after the operation he moved away from ritual, decorum, and historicity towards a more personal faith. In 1844 he accepted baptism by total immersion and joined the Congregational Church under Dr W.L. Alexander. James's death had an equally profound effect on his own younger brother. Alexander Russell had been set to a commercial career by his Wilson guardians; but following his brother's death, he too turned to religion. After attending a Baptist college in Stepney, London, for a year, he found himself increasingly drawn to the Church of England. Following studies in Edinburgh and at Trinity College Dublin, he was ordained deacon by the bishop of Winchester in 1850. As a curate in various parishes in the south of England, he too came under the influence of the Maurice circle. In 1854 he was offered the curacy of the cathedral church then being planned in Adelaide, Australia, and by the time of his death in 1886 would be dean of the cathedral.[102]

The years after Daniel's return to Edinburgh were ones of anguish in the Wilson family, and there is a sense that he himself was marking time. The print-seller's shop may have seemed a suitable occupation, but after the dreams of youth it must also have been an anticlimax. At best it was a means to an end – a way of making a living in a congenial occupation for which he had special skills – but little more. Yet from the print-seller's business came many of the contacts that were finally to determine the course of Wilson's life. Throughout the 1840s he would be increasingly preoccupied with his antiquarian interests (the subject of the two following essays in this volume), but there is evidence that he was a moderately successful businessman. By 1844–5 his shop had moved to a more central address in Hanover Street, just around the corner from the museum of the Society of Antiquaries of Scotland.[103] He was also active as a reviewer and what he himself called a 'professional literary hack.'[104]

Among the works Wilson later acknowledged from this period were reviews in the *British Quarterly Review*, founded in 1845 by the Congregational minister and historian Robert Vaughan. Daniel may have met Vaughan through his brother, George, who was also a contributor.[105] It is possible, however, that Daniel had been acquainted with Vaughan in London when the clergyman held the chair of history at University College there. He would certainly have known Vaughan's work *The Protectorate of Oliver Cromwell* (1839). Wilson's review of John Ruskin's *Modern Painters* in the *British Quarterly Review* of 1847 is especially interesting.[106] Not only is it the most assured and original of his early work, but it is also a kind of public summing-up of his artistic thought before he turned finally from art to archaeology. He was, of course, much in sympathy with Ruskin's attempt to prove the genius and 'truth' of the landscape painting of J.M.W. Turner. He agreed with Ruskin that art is not concerned with reproducing the detail of nature, but rather with capturing the spiritual essentials of the scene. Like Turner, Wilson believed that the truth of art was essentially religious: a successful painting was one that, like a successful church, made an integrated whole of the spiritual essence and the technique, the same fusion of form and spirit that he would explore in his poem *The Queen's Choir*.

There is less evidence of such elevated thought in some of Wilson's other work in this period. His *Spring Wild Flowers* (1845?), published under the pseudonym Wil. D'Leina, was reviewed in the *British Quarterly Review*: 'The materials are good; we wish we could speak of the execution as being equal to the conception. The author's style is not devoid of originality, and he displays often much vigour of thought, but his diction is frequently uncouth and obscure, and his versification remarkable for its ruggedness ... One of the sonnets, commencing "Great things were ne'er begotten in an hour," ably sets forth a truth which should teach Mr. D'Leina not to despise that care and patient effort which can alone make him to do justice to his own powers.'[107]

The same promise is apparent in the books *Oliver Cromwell and the Protectorate* (1848) and *The Pilgrim Fathers* (1849). Although Wilson later called it a 'pack of trash,'[108] *Cromwell*, which was published in Nelson's British Library series, grew directly out of hiss own beliefs. He never pretended that the book was a work of original scholarship, but it was written from a distinct and well-argued point of view. 'It is not from want of evidence that [Cromwell] has been misjudged hitherto, but rather, because

the evidence has been from the first so overlaid with extraneous prejudices and opinions, that it has required far more labour and ingenuity
than ordinary readers are in the habit of exercising, to separate the one
from the other.'[109] Wilson saw his hero as a great popular leader,
endowed with common sense and committed to genuine freedom of conscience. His duty as the author was to put the evidence, based on primary
sources such as the recently published *Oliver Cromwell's Letters and Speeches*,
edited by Thomas Carlyle, before his reader: 'the reader now has the
argument before him, and the evidence at his command. Truth, not victory, is the aim of the historian, and truth is the daughter of time.'[110]
'Truth' became one of Wilson's favourite words as a historian. Truth
came from the exercise of human intelligence upon evidence and
achieved its final form in the active partnership between writer and
reader: the former setting out all the evidence in an ordered and dispassionate manner, dictated not by personal bias but by the nature of the evidence; the latter using his or her own intelligence and perceptions to
understand what the evidence (and the author) had to say.

   Cromwell was respectfully reviewed, not least by the *British Quarterly
Review*: 'The style is simple and unaffected, which, considering how much
affectation has been thrown over the subject of late, is saying a good deal
... But the book itself presents a view of the life and character of Cromwell, upon the whole, as trustworthy as will be found in our language, and
very pleasant in style withal.'[111] Clearly, in the eyes of the *Review*, Wilson
had come a good way in the two years since the journal had reviewed his
book of poems. *The Pilgrim Fathers* is a lesser work. It was written as a
favour for his friend William Nelson, when the author originally con-
tracted to write this companion piece to W.H. Stowell's *History of the Puritans in England* had been forced to withdraw.[112] It is a typical example of
literary hack work, well organized and clearly written but totally lacking
in originality. Much of Wilson's writing during this period was for Nelson,
who had begun the series of thirty-two-page tracts, Nelson's British
Library of Tracts for the People, in 1846. These cheap monthly pamphlets were designed to contain interesting information and improving
tales with a Christian background, though they were not produced by a
religious body. Wilson appears to have been involved with the series from
its inception and wrote some of the earliest numbers.

   Reason and Instinct, the second in the series, is especially interesting,
not least because it deals with some of the same questions (and examples) later raised by Charles Darwin in *On the Origin of Species* (1859). The
work begins with the statement: 'The grand feature which distinguishes

man from the numerous tribes of living beings that share with him the productions of the earth is his intellect, or reasoning faculty.' It then goes on to trace examples of adaption in plants, insects, birds, and quadrupeds. Although most of Wilson's evidence comes from his wide reading in natural history sources, some of the most notable passages are from his own observations, such as his account of the solar eclipse of 1836:

> It was a warm and lovely day, and the hedge-rows were all astir with the hum of insect life, – the sharp note of the grasshopper, and the busy hum of the industrious bee. The trees were tenanted with their cheerful little songsters, and the sparrows, that, with their lively note, leapt forth in noisy flocks at the sound of approaching footsteps, only to alight as if in sport at a few yards further distance. But gradually as the light of the sun-beams became obscured, the sounds of life seemed to disappear, the sheep ceased to browse, and lay down together in their pastures, and a chilling silence sunk over the scene. [The writer] had seated himself on a bank to observe the eclipse, and when it was at the full, he was struck, on happening to glance at the turf, to observe a daisy with all its petals folded up, and this was found, on closer inspection, to be the case with them all.[113]

Wilson was especially concerned with distinguishing animal behaviour which could be attributed to genuine instinct and that which derived from something approaching a reasoning process, questions that were to resurface later in his archaeological and anthropological work. In *Reason and Instinct* there is a foretaste of his *Archæology and Prehistoric Annals of Scotland* (1851) and even more of *Prehistoric Man* (1862). He later called the work of this period potboilers: 'the good, bad, and indifferent; cheerful and useful; cheery, weary, dreary; droll, dull, stale and useless penwork.'[114] Wilson affected to see this activity as a regrettable prelude to the real and serious work that came after. But it is possible to glimpse, even in such genuine potboilers as *Tahiti and Its Missionaries* or the sentimental novella *The Curate's Daughter,* a training for the future both in the techniques of research, assimilation, and exposition of material and in the exercise of that much more necessary attribute, sheer persistence.

By the late 1840s, however, Wilson was clearly looking for an escape from the shop and his hack work. He hoped that his *Memorials of Edinburgh in the Olden Time* (which began to appear in parts in 1846; see the following essay) might help to pave the way to a job that would allow him to use his talents and provide him with some real security. University positions were out of the question, not just because of his lack of a degree, but because he, like his brother, was unwilling to take the oath required of holders of chairs in Scottish universities to support the tenets of the Church of Scotland. Increasingly, this oath was observed more in the breach than in the commission, but the Wilson brothers were not prepared to accept such a compromise with their conscience. George's accession to a chair at Edinburgh would be long delayed because of his reluctance to take the oath, and Daniel frequently referred to his brother's stand in terms that make it clear he shared George's sentiments.[115]

In 1848 Daniel sold his print and artists' supply shop. Perhaps he hoped to be able to earn his living from writing alone, or he may have had expectations of a particular appointment. That same year the aged Dr David Irving was persuaded to retire from his position as keeper of the Faculty of Advocates library, and Wilson became a candidate for the vacant office. In his printed application he stated his qualifications: while in London he had been a frequent visitor to the reading rooms of the British Museum; 'more recent studies have introduced me to the extensive field of literature, embracing history, topography, and archæological science; and I presume my engagements as Honorary Secretary of one of the oldest literary societies in Scotland, will not be considered inconsistent with the duties of Librarian of the Faculty of Advocates.'[116] His references included James Young Simpson, Robert Chambers, the Reverend Robert Vaughan, Charles Roach Smith, John Goodsir, the Reverend Joseph Haslegrave, the Macmillan brothers, and the Glasgow bookseller James Maclehose.

Wilson's candidature would seem to have been a strong one until, late in the day, fellow antiquarian David Laing decided to reapply for the post that he had failed to obtain in 1819.[117] His application seems to have taken Wilson by surprise, perhaps making him feel that he could not push his own claims against his older friend and patron. Then, equally suddenly, Laing withdrew his application. Francis Jeffrey wrote to George Wilson: 'Did Laing's retirement from the Library competition take him [Daniel] by surprise? or does he think that his own pretensions might have been made available, if he had known of it sooner?'[118] It was a confused and disappointing situation. The appointment went to another remarkable man, Samuel Halkett, a self-trained philologist with a wide bibliographical knowledge. In a characteristic attempt to appear totally fair, George had acted as one of Halkett's referees.[119]

His failure to gain the position at the advocates' library must have been a severe disappointment to Daniel, but characteristically his response was to plunge into intense activity. His antiquarian pursuits provided an outlet for his energies while he continued to write potboilers to earn a living. In his journal he later recalled how he finally broke out of this 'cheery, dreary' cycle. He had, for example, found the rewriting that he was forced to do on *The Hand of God in History*, by the American divine Hollis Read, particularly distasteful because he was so out of sympathy with its sentiments. 'Such a book is prepared for the British public by making the republican author say, not what he wrote, but what, in the judgment of his British editor and publisher, he should have written.'[120] Wilson had himself suffered such treatment when, in 1851, he compiled two booklets, *Old Edinburgh* and *Modern Edinburgh*, for the London-based Religious Tract Society. When the publishing secretary 'insisted on tacking on a moral of his own to sundry of the chapters,' Wilson refused to allow his name to be put on the title-pages and ended his dealings with the society.[121]

He was not immune from such revisions even by William Nelson. Before *Oliver Cromwell* 'could be presented to a select and religious British public,' certain changes were made that infuriated him: 'Perhaps the crowning reform of the faulty text was when, in reference to a modern disturbance, with more or less sacrilege, of the graves of Naseby battlefield, the words from the well known lines on Shakespeare's grave in the chancel at Stratford-on-Avon are quoted – "*Sweet friends, for Jesus'-sake forbear.*" The censor, missing both the source and application, erased the profane passage. Concerning which I had a passage of arms with the publisher on its discovery, rather amusing; but helping with other causes, to bring my engagement as a professional literary hack to an end.'[122]

NOTES

1 J.A. Wilson, *George Wilson*, 18.
2 Ibid., 1; Hannah, 'Sir Daniel Wilson,' 1.
3 Quoted in Hannah, 'Sir Daniel Wilson,' 2.
4 J.A. Wilson, *George Wilson*, 154.
5 Sime and Nicholson, 'Recollections of Mrs. Oliphant,' 37–8.
6 Oliphant, *Autobiography*, 28.
7 H.H. Langton, *Sir Daniel Wilson*, 12; quoting from Wilson's journal.
8 J.A. Wilson, *George Wilson*, 25.
9 Ibid.
10 H.H. Langton, *Sir Daniel Wilson*, 12.
11 Yuille, *History of the Baptists in Scotland*, 44–50. Donald Meek, now Professor of

Celtic, University of Aberdeen, provided information about Scottish Baptist history, upon which most of the discussion in this chapter is based.

12 The latter connection seems more likely because of the Wilsons' links with Strachur, Irvine, and the Macmillan family (see below). Donald Meek supplied information about this nexus of Baptist relations. See also Yuille, *History of the Baptists in Scotland,* 122–7.

13 J.A. Wilson, *George Wilson,* 19.

14 Ibid., 17.

15 Ibid., 13.

16 Altick, *The English Common Reader,* 269–70.

17 J.A. Wilson, *George Wilson,* 14.

18 Ibid.

19 Ibid., 237.

20 Youngson, *The Making of Classical Edinburgh,* 156–8.

21 Wilson, *Reminiscences* (1878), 1: 7.

22 J.A. Wilson, *George Wilson,* 10.

23 Wilson, *Reminiscences* (1878), 2: 313.

24 Ibid., 2: 98–9.

25 J.A. Wilson, *George Wilson,* 10.

26 Wilson, *Reminiscences* (1878), 1: 110–11.

27 Wilson, *William Nelson* (1889), 43.

28 *Letter to the Right Hon. the Lord Provost of the City of Edinburgh,* 29.

29 Scott, 'Memoir,' 29.

30 Ibid., 26.

31 Wilson, *William Nelson* (1889), 45.

32 Wilson, *The Right Hand* (1891), 126.

33 J.A. Wilson, *George Wilson,* 16.

34 Ibid., 13.

35 Edinburgh Town Council, *Minutes ... and Report ... respecting the Proposed New High School,* 11–13.

36 Edinburgh Town Council, *Address ... on the Subject of the New Buildings for the High School,* 5–8.

37 See Youngson, *The Making of Classical Edinburgh,* 158.

38 Steven, *The History of the High School of Edinburgh,* 232.

39 Wilson, *William Nelson* (1889), 44.

40 Wilson, Review of *Modern Painters* (1847), 470–1. This comment was made about the art of the eighteenth century generally.

41 Wilson, *Reminiscences* (1878), 1: 59.

42 Wilson, *William Nelson* (1889), 52.

43 See Dick, *Description of the Suspension Railway.*

44 Graves, *Life and Letters of Alexander Macmillan*, 16–18.

45 See Hughes, *Memoir of Daniel Macmillan*, 2–3; Graves, *Life and Letters of Alexander Macmillan*, 3.

46 Wilson later had difficulty recalling when he entered Miller's workshop; he thought that it was 1830 (see UTA, B65-0014/004(02), 153, 25 May 1889). But Miller family records reveal that he did so early in 1831 (see Miller, *Memorials of Hope Park*, 116). Further confirmation of this date comes from Wilson's signed alumnus ticket from the High School of Edinburgh ('Daniel Wilson Scholae Regiae Edinensis Alumnus Ann. 1830 31 N°. 340') pasted into 'Memorials of Auld Reekie,' his scrapbooks of drawings, engravings, maps, and broadsheets relating to Edinburgh and Leith, now in the NMS library.

47 Miller, *Memorials of Hope Park*, 85.

48 He was still there when another apprentice, James Giles, left in 1836 (see Miller, *Memorials of Hope Park*, 116, 156, 160). It seems likely that Daniel did not leave Miller's establishment until about the time he set out for London in the autumn of 1837.

49 UTA, B65-0014/004(02), 154 (25 May 1889).

50 Ibid., 155 (25 May 1889).

51 Ibid.

52 Miller, *Memorials of Hope Park*, 117.

53 Ibid.

54 NMS, SAS, Museum visitors' book, 1 January 1836.

55 Wilson does not appear in the matriculation rolls of the University of Edinburgh (EUL, Special Collections).

56 J.A. Wilson, *George Wilson*, 38.

57 Ibid., 39. It seems possible that this organization may have been the same as the 'Philo-Lectic Society of Edinburgh,' to which George Brown belonged (see Careless, *Brown of The Globe*, 1: 9).

58 J.A. Wilson, *George Wilson*, 41.

59 Ibid. See also BAAS, *Report of the Fourth Meeting ... 1834*, xliv.

60 See Blackie, *Notes of a Life*, 105, 107.

61 UTA, B65-0014/004(02), 155 (25 May 1889).

62 Ibid., 156 (25 May 1889).

63 Ibid., 155–6.

64 J.A. Wilson, *George Wilson*, 102.

65 UTA, B65-0014/004(02), 156 (25 May 1889). Wilson wrote two accounts in his journal about the engraving of the Turner work, both long after the experience; one was recorded in 1874 and the other in 1889.

66 UTA, B65-0014/004(01), 32 (13 April 1874); /004(02), 156–7 (25 May 1889).

67 Ibid., 157–8 (25 May 1889).

68 The meeting with Turner evidently took place in November 1837, and the finished print is dated 1 August 1840 (see Rawlinson, *The Engraved Work of J.M.W. Turner*, 2: 206, 334, no. 649). Wilson in his journal entry for 13 April 1874 notes that it was thirty-five years earlier that he completed the engraving, but the reference is apparently to the year and not the exact month (UTA, B65-0014/004(01), 31, 13 April 1874).

69 UTA, B65-0014/004(02), 159 (25 May 1889).

70 Ibid., 160 (25 May 1889).

71 Ibid., 161 (25 May 1889).

72 Ibid., 163 (25 May 1889); see also Giles's account of this visit in Miller, *Memorials of Hope Park*, 160.

73 J.A. Wilson, *George Wilson*, 134.

74 UTA, B65-0014/004(02), 158 (25 May 1889).

75 See Wilson, *Testimonials* (1848), 14; Daniel Wilson, vicar of Islington, *Two Sermons*, 8.

76 Wilson, *The Queen's Choir* (1853), 18.

77 Ibid.

78 Ibid., 17.

79 J.A. Wilson, *George Wilson*, 161.

80 Ibid., 162.

81 See Wilson, Review of *Modern Painters* (1847), 488.

82 J.A. Wilson, *George Wilson*, 170.

83 Ibid., 185.

84 UTA, B65-0014/004(02), 164 (25 May 1889).

85 See also Rawlinson, *The Engraved Work of J.M.W. Turner*, 1: lxi–lxix.

86 UTA, B65-0014/004(01), 32 (13 April 1874).

87 He later recalled reviewing prints by the Scottish-born engravers John Burnett and James Henry Watt in the *British Quarterly Review* in 1847 and acknowledged his review of an engraving of George Harvey's *First Reading of the Bible in Old St. Paul's* in the same journal in 1845.

88 J.A. Wilson, *George Wilson*, 220.

89 Ibid., 241.

90 J. Hill Burton, Review of *Memorials of Edinburgh*, in *Saturday Review*, 1 February 1873; copy in TRL, S65, vol. 3.

91 J.A. Wilson, *George Wilson*, 261.

92 Ibid., 263.

93 Ibid., 266.

94 In his journal Wilson listed 'Archaeology,' no. 93 in the series, among his early publications (see UTA, B65-0014/004(01), 20, 1865). However, that number in the 1842 edition is on architecture, and it had appeared at least as early as

1835; there is no article on archaeology. Though it seems unlikely that Wilson was mistaken about the series, it has proved impossible to determine what he wrote for it.

95 J.A. Wilson, *George Wilson*, 278.

96 Wilson, *Spring Wild Flowers*, 163. The quotation is taken from the 1853 edition, since no copies of the first edition appear to have survived.

97 Ibid., 168.

98 J.A. Wilson, *George Wilson*, 286.

99 H.H. Langton, in *Sir Daniel Wilson*, 37, says that he returned 'after little more than two years of married life in London.' At least one watercolour in the EUL collection is dated 1842.

100 'By the middle of the seventeenth century, an area of trade had come into being, the artists' colourman, who supplied prepared pigments, made brushes, prepared canvases and any other items required by the artist. The emergence of the trade may well have been stimulated by the increasing amateur interest in painting. Many professionals continued to assess and prepare their own pigments, possibly through fear of the adulteration of pigments by apothecaries or colourmen' ('The Trade of the Artists' Colourman,' 36; the editor is grateful to Robert Stacey for providing this quotation).

101 *The [Edinburgh] Post-Office Annual Directory, and Calendar, for 1841–42.*

102 See Russell, *The Light That Lighteth Every Man*, viii–xii.

103 *The [Edinburgh] Post-Office Annual Directory ... for 1844–45.*

104 UTA, B65-0014/004(01), 22 (1865).

105 J.A. Wilson, *George Wilson*, 338.

106 Wilson, Review of *Modern Painters* (1847).

107 *British Quarterly Review* 3 (1846): 264.

108 H.H. Langton, *Sir Daniel Wilson*, 38.

109 Wilson, *Oliver Cromwell* (1848), vii.

110 Ibid., viii.

111 *British Quarterly Review* 8 (1848): 289.

112 See Wilson, 'The Pilgrim Fathers' (1849), cccxl.

113 Wilson, *Reason and Instinct* (1846), 4.

114 UTA, B65-0014/004(01), 19 (1865).

115 See G. Wilson, *The Grievance of the University Tests*, and Daniel Wilson's comments on his brother's stand in *Address before the Select Committee of the Legislative Assembly* (1860), 10.

116 Wilson, *Testimonials* (1848), 3–4. He had been appointed a secretary of the Society of Antiquaries of Scotland the previous year.

117 See Goudie, *David Laing*, 50, 78–80. Wilson's application is dated 18 December and Laing's nine days later.

118 EUL, Special Collections, Dk.6.23/1, 56, Jeffrey to G. Wilson, undated (the year 1848 has been supplied in pencil).
119 Halkett, *Testimonials*, 10.
120 UTA, B65-0014/004(01), 20–1 (1865).
121 Ibid., 22 (1865).
122 Ibid., 21–2.

Daniel Wilson, Antiquarian of Edinburgh: A Sense of Place

MARINELL ASH, KITTY CRUFT,
AND ELIZABETH HULSE

In 1878 Daniel Wilson wrote a book of historical anecdotes about his beloved native city. In *Reminiscences of Old Edinburgh* every nook and cranny of the town was invested with events from his own life, from those of his contemporaries, and from Scottish history. It is a late example of the antiquarian impulse – a book of tales and gossip centred on a physical place and structural remains and arranged in an unsystematic and discursive way. It is also a tribute to the antiquarian Edinburgh that Wilson had known and loved in the 1840s and early 1850s, the world of Sir Walter Scott's antiquary, Jonathan Oldbuck, now 'as obsolete as Dr Dryasdust's powdered pig-tail.'[1] His artistic work and his historical interests had made it inevitable that Wilson would be drawn into the city's antiquarian circle, with its clubs and conviviality, and soon after his return in 1842 he was busy making watercolour sketches of ancient buildings in the Old Town and perhaps already contemplating his first major work, *Memorials of Edinburgh in the Olden Time*. It would start to appear in parts in 1846 and was published in book form two years later.

In the preface to the first edition Wilson states that the work 'was begun years ago, not with the pen, but the pencil' (*ME*1, 1: v). The idea for *Memorials* may have come from the work of Wilson's London friend and neighbour, the engraver John Wykeman Archer. Like Wilson, Archer had been affected by the decline of line engraving. His response was to turn to wood engraving and to painting watercolour sketches of the ancient buildings in the city. Eventually he was commissioned by a patron to produce twenty drawings a year of London scenes, and he would later be employed by the Duke of Northumberland on a regular basis each summer to make sketches of antiquities on his estates.[2] Archer's work culminated in *Vestiges of Old London* (1851). Immediately, however, his influence on Wilson may have been to inspire him to produce sketches of old Edinburgh in the hopes of finding a similar patron.

Shortly after his return to Edinburgh, Wilson met the antiquary and collector Charles Kirkpatrick Sharpe, who called at the shop in West Register Street. The scion of an ancient family, an eccentric, and a friend of Sir Walter Scott, Sharpe was a living link to the past. He had at first been destined for the church, but soon abandoned that career for a life of antiquarianism. He was an assiduous sketcher, writer, and collector of objects and gossip. Scott wrote in his journal: 'He has infinite wit and a great turn for antiquarian lore ... His drawings are the most fanciful and droll imaginable – a mixture between Hogarth and some of those foreign masters who painted temptations of St. Anthony and such grotesque subjects ... He is a very complete genealogist, and has made many detections in *Douglas* and other books on pedigree, which our nobles would do well to suppress if they had an opportunity. Strange that a man would be curious after scandal of centuries old!'[3] Sharpe throve on gossip and spared no one, but to those who could tolerate his eccentricities and not take his sallies to heart, he was a firm friend. Daniel Wilson became one such in the last decade of Sharpe's life.

By the time they met, Sharpe was over sixty. In *Reminiscences* Wilson painted a word portrait of the antiquarian: 'Peculiar in tastes, striking in personal appearance, and with a curiously-pitched falsetto voice, Mr. Sharpe would, under any circumstances, have attracted attention. But on some particular day, while all the world was moving along in its wonted way, he had suddenly paused; and there he lived on into a younger generation, with the huge Brutus wig of light-brown hair, the long blue frock-coat, the silk stockings and thin dress shoes with large bows of ribbon, the ample frilled shirt-breast, and plentiful breadth of linen neckerchief, in strangest antithesis to the usages of living men. Nor were his ideas more modern than his appearance.'[4] Doubtless Sharpe was attracted first by Wilson the artist, while the younger man may have seen the antiquarian as a patron after the Archer model. He certainly relished his friendship with Sharpe, not least because he was a survivor of earlier times. Sharpe gave the young artist access to his collections at his house in Drummond Place in the New Town and took great interest in Wilson's projected work on the antiquities of Edinburgh. As proof-sheets for *Memorials of Edinburgh* were thrown off, Sharpe read them over, made comments and corrections, and sometimes decorated the margins with his own drawings.[5]

Wilson had intended simply to prepare a number of sketches for engraving, many of them of buildings that had 'disappeared in the course of the radical changes wrought of late years on the Old Town,' and to supply 'a slight descriptive narrative to accompany them' (*ME*1, 1: v).[6] However, in the process he discovered that the information he needed was often lacking in other works, and he accumulated a 'good deal of curious material.' William Maitland's *The History of Edinburgh, from Its Foundation to the Present Time* (1753) contained much 'valuable, and generally accurate, but nearly undigested, information,' and Hugo Arnot's *The History of Edinburgh* (1779; 2d ed., 1788) was 'a lively and piquant *rifacimento* of his predecessor's labours' (*ME*1, 1: v). But both these historians lacked 'that invaluable faculty of the topographer, styled by phrenologist *locality*.' Thus they provided 'a large canvas,' rather than 'a cabinet picture of the Dutch school.' In striking contrast to these two works was Robert Chambers's *Traditions of Edinburgh* (1825), which in Wilson's view 'struck out an entirely new path.'

It was this work that had the profoundest influence on Wilson.[7] Robert Chambers and his brother William had founded the publishing firm of W. & R. Chambers, still extant today. William provided the business talent that made the firm successful, while Robert carried out his own literary projects and edited works to be published. His *Traditions* drew a picture of social life in the Old Town and the nascent New Town based on reminiscences and oral tradition – 'not without,' Wilson considered, 'occasional heightening touches from the delineator's own lively fancy' and still in the tradition of an eighteenth-century antiquary (*ME*1, 1: v).

In its organization and its balance between the physical remains and their human history, *Memorials* contrasts with Chambers's work. Many chapters in *Traditions*, particularly the early ones, are, like Wilson's book, structured around the principal buildings of the Old Town, but not in a way that follows so closely the layout of the city, and increasingly the focus is on personalities from the past. Indeed, the book is much like Wilson's later *Reminiscences*: gossipy and discursive. Yet this work, first published some twenty years before *Memorials*, with its emphasis on the buildings of Edinburgh and their inhabitants over the years, clearly inspired the organization of Wilson's two volumes. It provided the 'entirely new path' which he expanded and regularized.

In addition to Maitland, Arnot, and Chambers, Wilson made use of a wide range of sources, from medieval writers such as John of Fordun to the historians of the eighteenth century, including William Robertson, Lord Hailes, Alexander Kincaid, and Robert Keith, as well as such primary sources as the acts of the Scottish Parliament, the records of the Edinburgh town council, and 'hundreds of old charters, title-deeds, and records of various sorts, in all varieties of unreadable manuscript' (*ME*1, 1: vi).[8] He also read the work of such early travellers to Edinburgh as John Taylor, whose *Pennyles Pilgrimage* was published in 1618, and Fynes Moryson, who visited Scotland in 1598. Wilson's interest in scientific research led him to question the accepted sources for many of the traditional accounts of historic events in Edinburgh's past and aroused in him a corresponding interest in documentary research and a critical awareness of the importance of evidence and its interpretation, together with a strong concern for accuracy. At the same time, he recognized the importance of tradition, 'which is never to be despised in questions of local antiquity' (*ME*2, 1: 180).

Memorials of Edinburgh in the Olden Time is divided into two parts. The first, accounting for approximately a quarter of the work, provides a chronological history of Scotland from the 'earliest traditions' to the eighteenth century, particularly as it affected Edinburgh. The second part, which describes the city's historic buildings and the traditions associated with them, is arranged geographically, running from the Castle down Castlehill, the Lawnmarket, the High Street, and the Canongate to Holyrood Abbey and then treating the Cowgate, the West Bow and suburbs, and Leith and the New Town. The churches are brought together in a final chapter titled 'Ecclesiastical Antiquities.' The work is illustrated with forty-two full-page engravings and many smaller woodcut vignettes in the text, all reproduced from the author's own paintings and drawings. In the selection of illustrations, 'the chief aim has been to furnish an example of all the varieties of style and character that were to be found in the wynds and closes of old Edinburgh' (*ME*1, 1: vi).

Wilson, in his discussion of the city's historic structures, balances his detailed description of the buildings themselves, made from personal observation, with their human history. In this way, 'History becomes a living drama, instead of a mere bundle of dusty parchments; and the actors, who pass away in succession with its many changing scenes, appear once more before us what they really were, men of like passions with ourselves' (*ME*1, 2: 200). The buildings in which these individuals lived must be preserved because 'These relics of the past, however insignificant they may appear in themselves, assume a very different claim on our interest when thus regarded as the memorials of our national history, or the key to the manners and the habits of our forefathers. As such they acquire a worth which no mere lapse of time could confer; nor have our forefathers played so mean a part in the history of nations that their memorials should possess an interest only to ourselves' (*ME*1, 2: 200).

A theme running through *Memorials of Edinburgh* was the progress of 'improvements' during the early nineteenth century which had changed the face of the city and removed many of its historic features. Wilson repeatedly excoriates the 'Improvements Commission,' which, he was happy to note, had not succeeded in razing the 'haunted dwelling' of the notorious wizard Major Weir in the West Bow (*ME*1, 2: 115). He included as an appendix his own satirical tribute to the 'Hon. Board of Commissioners for City Improvements.' The eight-stanza poem concludes:

> Foul fa' the Commissioners wi' their improvements,
>> Their biggins, an' howkins, an' sweepins awa;
> May the Major, when neist bent on ane o' his movements, –
>> 'Tis the warst-waled retour that I wus may befa,' –
> Whisk his coach doun the Bow, just for ilk anes behovements,
> Wi' a team of Commissioners o' the Improvements.
>> Hurrying doun, stoiterin' an' stumblin,'
>> The gleger ye gang better luck against tumblin'! (*ME*1, 2: 214)

In discussing the New Town, whose 'regular array of formal parallelograms' was not to his taste, Wilson even imagined a 'twenty-second century Improvements Commission' whose first scheme would be the restoration of Gabriel's Road, of which only a fragment remained near the Register House (*ME*1, 2: 151–2).

Indeed, the demolition of historic buildings was very much a matter of public debate at the time. In the years just after *Memorials* appeared, the threatened destruction of two Edinburgh landmarks drew Wilson and his fellow antiquarians into fights to save them. The Society of Antiquaries of Scotland, of which Wilson had become a fellow in 1846 and one of its secretaries the following year,[9] had been involved in public campaigns before, notably the return of Mons Meg to Edinburgh in the late 1820s.[10] But that campaign could be seen as an exercise in old-fashioned antiquarianism: the restoration of an artefact to a place with which it had long historic associations. By the 1840s the need for such activism was more immediate, since much of Scotland's legacy was threatened by industrial development, the growth of railways, or simple neglect. In 1848 the SAS was successful in its efforts to prevent the demolition of part of the Edinburgh town wall[11] and to obtain the return of the Moray brass to St Giles' Church.[12] It also managed to stop the proposed demolition of the Flodden Tower.[13] As well, members did their best to persuade landowners to look after historic buildings in their care, such as Crichton Castle,[14] the royal vault at Holyrood,[15] and the ruins on Iona.[16]

Not all their campaigns were successful. There was, for example, the struggle to save the Collegiate Church of the Holy Trinity, commonly known as Trinity College Church, situated at the foot of Leith Wynd. It had been founded in 1460 by Mary of Gueldres, the widow of James II.[17] When she died three years later, she was buried in the unfinished building. Only the choir and transepts were ever completed, in a pure late Gothic style with rich carving and decoration that Wilson vividly recalled from the times when, as a boy, he had been taken to the church to hear his uncle the Reverend John Russell preach. By that time Trinity College Church was already in a state of decline, its congregation decimated by the removal of many of the buildings that had occupied the valley between the Calton Hill and the Old Town and the building of Waverley Station. After the completion of the station, the North British Railway Company decided to acquire the land where the church stood for a shunting yard. The Society of Antiquaries was galvanized into action in an attempt to save what Lord Cockburn described as 'not only the oldest, but almost the only remaining Gothic structure in Edinburgh.'[18]

The threat to Trinity College Church dominated Wilson's life in late 1847 and early the following year. He attended the last religious service held there on 14 May 1848, and both before and during the church's demolition he made numerous sketches of the building and its details. They are among the most assured work that he ever produced, perhaps indicating his sense of heightened consciousness as he watched the disappearance of this four-hundred-year-old Edinburgh landmark.[19] In a poem entitled 'The Provost and the Coal Bunker,' originally published in the *Scotsman* newspaper,[20] he pilloried the civic authorities for their role in persuading the minister of Trinity College Church to agree to the demolition, on the promise (as Wilson saw it) of a new church building in a richer and more fashionable neighbourhood.

O sican a Provost as Embrugh has got,
    An' sican a Council, an' Bailies, an' a'!
They wad wyle the auld lark frae the lift sae hie,
An' the swan frae the loch, and the gled frae the tree,
An' a minister's sell frae his pulpit sae slee,
    An' a' wi' a wink an' a blaw!

Wilson also used Scots in another poem to point up some of the comic aspects of the struggle. 'Ane Auld Prophecie, bot Doubte be Merlyne or Thomas of Erceldoune,' written in the style of a Border ballad, was composed as a *jeu d'esprit* for a conversazione held by the Society of Antiquaries. His verbal joke was later turned to visual effect: in 1849 he had it printed in suitably Gothic type with illustrations taken from his drawings of the church and sent copies to his friends.[21]

> An' years gaed bye, and changes wore,
>   An' times nane thought to see;
> There cam' a Demon, the Demon o' Steam,
> The Dragon o' Wantly was naething to him,
> He gobled doun churches like strawberries and cream,
>   Or a caup o'flummerie!
>
> ...
>
> But, as good luck would have it, there chanced the while
>   Ane pious Fraternitie,
>
> ...
>
> An' they vowed a vow, an' they sained a sign,
>   An' they sware fu' piouslie;
> An' never a man o' them a' was afear'd,
> For they grippit the Steam Demon by his beard,
> An' they howkit the Quene frae the mouldy yird,
>   All in the Sacristie.[22]

Despite all their efforts, however, the antiquaries failed to save the building and had to be content with a promise from the railway company that they could take a selection of decorated stones for their museum. The church was carefully demolished under the direction of the architect David Bryce, and the numbered stones stored on the Calton Hill, with the understanding that the church would be rebuilt elsewhere.[23] But when the North British Railway Company discovered that the cost of the reconstruction would be about £12,000, it began to have second thoughts.[24] The church was eventually re-erected in 1872, but by then the stones had been heavily pilfered for innumerable Edinburgh rockeries, and only the body of the choir, without aisles or transepts, was completed.

The railway proprietors had also agreed that if Queen Mary's grave were found, the remains could be reburied elsewhere. On 22 May 1848 officers of the Board of Works began the search in the chapel off the north aisle, and here a tomb was located. A group of antiquaries, including Wilson, Sharpe, Chambers, George Harvey, and David Laing, watched anxiously as a lead coffin was raised from beneath the floor of the lady chapel. Inside were the remains of a female. They were examined by Wilson's friend of student days John Goodsir, professor of anatomy at the University of Edinburgh, and pronounced to be those of a woman of about thirty with a distinct curvature of the spine.[25] The queen had been found. Arrangements were made for her reinterment in the royal vault at Holyrood on 15 July, and Wilson was given permission to take a cast of the skull.[26] There the matter rested until, as he recalled, a group of antiquaries gathered for supper at Laing's villa in Portobello on 20 September. They were startled to be told that, on that very day, 'another queen' had turned up, buried at the centre of the apse, a location that some felt was more in keeping with the patronage of a medieval religious foundation.

This 'second queen' was a sensation: 'It was like a bomb-shell among a bivouac party around the camp fire.'[27] Another report was commissioned from Goodsir and James Young Simpson, and its conclusions were most disturbing. The top of the skull had been sawn off, 'presumably in some ineffectual process of embalming,' a fact that Wilson felt helped to reinforce his dating of the remains to the late sixteenth century, when such practices were known.[28] Goodsir and Simpson found that the woman, aged between twenty and thirty, 'was of feeble or deficient intellect' and possibly subject to epileptic fits.[29] Laing accepted the 'new queen,' but Wilson could not, and he later recalled the occasion as the only time the two antiquarians had disagreed over anything.[30] It was a comic ending to a sad tale, as Wilson's 'moral' at the end of his poem makes clear:

> Now all you Antiquaries beware how you swear
>   To a Quene's identitie,
> Unless, in the case it should chance, indeed,
> That the ladye turns up well lappt in lead,
> With a crook in her spine, and a cleft in her haed,
> Which, as everybody knows, are the marks agreed
>   For a Quene in the North Countrie![31]

Despite the comedy of the two queens, the fate of Trinity College Church was a terrible one, and he reverted to the story throughout his life, not only as an example of history sacrificed to greed and technology, but because of the consequences for himself and his fellow antiquaries. Failure hardened their sense of urgency and also their sense of purpose, and it is from this famous defeat that the modern civic (conservancy) movement in Edinburgh originates.[32] Wilson looked back on the Trinity College Church campaign as in some ways a happy time. In a chapter of his *Reminiscences* devoted to this building and the fight to save it, he wrote, 'It is difficult to realise that upwards of a quarter of a century has transpired since those stirring times which seem but of yesterday.'[33]

Wilson's other conservation struggle at this time concerned John Knox's House in the High Street. Because of its bad state of repair, the house was condemned by the Dean of Guild Court in 1849; it was also considered to be an encumbrance to the street. The Society of Antiquaries, under Wilson's leadership, backed the life renter of the property, Frances Loch of Rachen, and a committee that had been formed earlier to collect money to purchase the building and neighbouring properties as a national monument to the reformer.[34] In order to gain support for the campaign, any questions about Knox's association with the house and the identity of the original owner had to be suppressed. Wilson's interest was in the preservation of the only extant example of a dwelling with timber galleries, once a common feature in the Old Town of Edinburgh. He was always sceptical about the traditional association with Knox, but if it had not been widely accepted at the time, the house would probably not have survived.

Raising funds proved difficult because the project was perceived to be in the interests of the recently established Free Church of Scotland, and it thus reflected the divisions caused by the split in the Church of Scotland of 1843. But the house was eventually saved and restored, though the adjacent buildings were pulled down. Religious sectarianism was always an anathema to Wilson, and the case of John Knox's House continued to haunt him for the rest of his life. Writing to Peter Miller in 1890, he lamented the fact that he had received many letters complaining that he was about to upset the cherished tradition of the house.[35] And when he published a paper on the subject the following year, he observed that it was 'with extreme reluctance that I venture on a reconsideration of the evidence' linking the house with the reformer.[36]

After he moved to Canada in 1853, Daniel Wilson had continued his interest in Edinburgh's historic buildings. He contributed a number of articles to the *Proceedings* of the Society of Antiquaries, most notably a long paper on Trinity College Church, read to the society in 1883; it was illustrated with more than twenty vignettes of the masks and grotesque figures that had ornamented the building, based on drawings that he had made before the church was demolished. In 1869 Wilson presented the society with two large volumes of drawings, engravings, photographs, and other illustrations of the city that he had collected while in Scotland,[37] and his *Reminiscences of Old Edinburgh* appeared in 1878.

It was always his intention to revise *Memorials of Edinburgh in the Olden Time*, and to this end he kept an interleaved copy of the first edition (now in the Toronto Reference Library). In it he wrote corrections and additions to the text and mounted clippings from the *Scotsman* and other newspapers and letters from individuals who sent him revisions or entered into correspondence about matters of mutual interest.[38] Also included in the interleaved copy are some draft revisions for the second edition. 'It was therefore with no less surprise than mortification,' Wilson later wrote, 'that I learned, in 1872, of the issue of a reprint of my work without my being even afforded the opportunity of amending the text. I had been for years in "another world," and my literary affairs were being administered as those of one who had died intestate' (*ME*2, 1: v–vi).[39] Not until 1891, forty-five years after *Memorials* had begun to appear in part publication and only a year before his death, did a true second edition incorporating Wilson's changes appear. Of this publication he wrote in the preface,

> The present edition has been carefully revised. Few pages remain without some emendation; considerable portions, embodying the results of later research, have been entirely rewritten; and additions of some interest have been made to the illustrations.
>
> In one respect, however, I have adhered to the old text. In most cases an author welcomes the opportunity of revision to bring down his work to the latest date. But any such attempt here would be little else than a tale of erasure and defacement. Some notice of such changes could not be avoided. But, as a whole, these volumes are the record of Old Edinburgh as it lives in the memory of a few survivors of the past generation. (*ME*2, 1: x)

While it is true that the changes Wilson made to the second edition were many, they are frequently minor, such as the correction of a name or date or the addition of a source published or discovered since the first edition. Some revisions are in the interests of style or to heighten the dramatic effect of a story. It is evident that he now had more confidence in his ability to present the material. He also added a series of 'Old-Edinburgh ballads,' which he had composed, to introduce each of the chapters in the first part.[40] But the basic structure of the work and much of the text remained unaltered. Whether this adherence to the character of the first edition reflected the fact that Wilson was removed in both time and place from the subject of his research, that he was now in his mid-seventies with failing eyesight and heavy administrative responsibilities at the University of Toronto, or even that he was essentially satisfied with the work as he had originally published it we cannot now know.[41] One of the buildings about which he was able to speak in a positive way was the 'venerable mother church of St. Giles,' which 'has, through the liberality of the late William Chambers, been restored internally to somewhat of its ancient beauty' (*ME2*, 1: xii).[42] The restoration of St Giles' had provided some new information about the historic structure, as had the research of other scholars. The account of the church in *Memorials* is one of the sections where Wilson made more extensive revisions. In the same chapter on 'Ecclesiastical Antiquities,' he related the very different fate of Trinity College Church, pulled down in the year that *Memorials* had first appeared in book form. In the second edition Wilson was able to describe the altarpiece (now in the National Gallery of Scotland), which had been returned to Scotland in 1857 and identified by David Laing as having come from the church.

The new edition also allowed Wilson to correct his own blunders. In the interval since the first edition he had had the experience of finding a 'fancy of my youth' accepted as 'well-accredited history' in no less a work than J. Cameron Lees's *St. Giles', Edinburgh – Church, College, and Cathedral* (1889). Wilson had been 'Beguiled by the conjecture of the arms of Robert, Duke of Albany, the son of Robert II, with those of Archibald, fourth Earl of Douglas,' on the same pillar in St Giles'. 'I was tempted to weave a romance, in which I gave the name of the Albany Chapel to the beautiful aisle with its two bays and finely groined roof; and suggested its origin as possibly an expiatory act of the two nobles for their reputed share in the murder of the Duke of Rothesay' (*ME2*, 1: vi–vii). Maturer reflection persuaded Wilson that such an explanation was not consistent with the known behaviour of the two noblemen; not only Lees, however, but also William Chambers in his lectures on St Giles' in 1881 accepted the 'legend of "The Albany Aisle,"' which, as Wilson notes, was no older than the year 1847 (*ME2*, 1: viii).

The 'restoration' of historic buildings by modern architects was an issue that had long preoccupied him. As early as 1852 he had engaged in an exchange of letters with architect Thomas Hamilton, who had been responsible for work on St Mary's Church, South Leith. About this restoration Wilson observed in *Memorials* that 'nearly every feature that was worth preserving' had been demolished, 'the architect having, with the perverse ingenuity of modern *restorers*, preserved only the more recent and least attractive portions of the venerable edifice' (*ME*1, 2: 194; emphasis in original).[43] In the 1880s, however, he had the opportunity to provide some advice on the restoration of buildings in Edinburgh. It was no doubt Wilson who drew the attention of his friend William Nelson to the state of dilapidation of St Margaret's Chapel, the Argyle or Portcullis Tower, and the Great Hall at Edinburgh Castle and helped him to initiate the schemes of restoration for which Nelson provided the funds. In correspondence with the Edinburgh architect Hippolyte Blanc, Nelson wrote that he 'has good news for him that he applied my friend Dr Daniel Wilson to Mr [Andrew] Ker, to see if he would recommend you as Architect for the restoration of St Margaret's Chapel and I have much pleasure in stating that he has done so con amore.'[44]

Wilson would have taken special interest in this project. In 1846, while he was working on *Memorials*, he had heard of a medieval font in a building used as a powder magazine at the Castle. When he went to investigate the small stone building with its iron-shuttered windows, he 'had to enter on stocking soles, and test its character more with hands than eyes.'[45] The structure had been divided into two storeys. On the ground floor Wilson found that the supposed font was, in fact, the empty socket of a pillar of the chancel arch; on the second floor he detected characteristic dog-tooth carving on the arch. He had rediscovered the tiny Norman chapel traditionally associated with St Margaret, wife of Malcolm 'Canmore' III, who lived in the eleventh century. The find was the subject of Wilson's first paper to the Society of Antiquaries, presented in July 1846.[46]

In 1885 Hippolyte Blanc sent him two series of photolithographs from his original drawings for the restoration, the first series representing the building as it then was and the second showing his (Blanc's) ideas for the repairs, 'with a view to harmonise our sympathies.' He intended to substitute a new door piece of two orders in the thickness of the wall, such as is found in St Oran's Chapel, Iona. He suggested a window in the north elevation, though he agreed that there was no sign of there having been one there; but more light was needed inside. What did Wilson think? Towards the east end of the north wall there were signs of a doorway, obviously, he wrote, a late insertion from the apse when the building was used as a powder store. On the inner surface of the west wall a doorway was built up; it seemed to record another opening for the master gunner's storeroom. However, Blanc proposed to obliterate it, and did Wilson agree to this step? He was in favour of stone from Forfar (Angus) for the roof covering and red paving slabs from Dunfermline inside to raise the floor.[47]

Replying on 5 December, Wilson saw no reason to question the correctness of the entrance door in the north side; 'internally,' he wrote, 'the original doorway was traceable in 1847.' He approved of the new doorway, but did not like the insertion of a window in the north elevation; 'the work of restoration of an ancient historical building such as this, might be carried out in the most conservative spirit. What is wanted is not a fine building, with all possible modern additions, but the original or a facsimile if it anyway effaced portions, as nearly as may be. There is nothing to indicate that a window existed on the north side.' Wilson considered in minute detail the building that might have been attached to the chapel. In answer to a question from Blanc, he urged retention of walling that was not obviously recent; it ought to be preserved as a memorial to some former condition. 'Excessive formality is to be avoided.' He did not like Blanc's drawing for a cross on the east gable, and included one of his own.[48] Unfortunately, his scholarly recommendations were not used. The Office of Works, which was responsible for the upkeep of St Margaret's Chapel, did not feel obliged to carry out Nelson's intentions to restore the chapel, for they 'looked with disapproval at his expenditure on a subject bringing in no return.'[49]

The Argyle Tower, erected to replace the Constable's Tower destroyed in 1573, had been rebuilt four years later and a new upper storey added in 1584. With a crenellated parapet, the flat roof was designed as a gun emplacement.[50] Hippolyte Blanc was again in charge of the 'restoration,' and in the course of researching the history of the structure, he visited the British Museum. William Nelson wrote to Blanc after the visit to ask him how the tower would look if restored according to the sketch that Blanc had found in the museum collection. His advice was to look at 'an engraving of Edinburgh Castle in Daniel Wilson's *Memorials* taken from a drawing by T. Sandby of about 1750, and in this the Argyle Tower is shown with a flat roof.'[51] Writing to Wilson on 15 November 1885, Blanc asked for some advice on his ideas for this restoration. 'Some say that was the original state of the structure while others maintain that over the flat top within the parapets, there must have been an additional apartment such as I presume we found at Borthwick Castle.'[52]

Wilson agreed with the restoration of the parapet 'somewhat as Borthwick Castle.' He considered that 'all that is genuine should be preserved, but at the same time the prominent position of this gateway tower in the general view of the castle, suggests the desirability of treating it in such a way as may best accord with the picturesque outline of the fine old fortress.'[53] This comment was pure nostalgia on Wilson's part, together with some romanticism, but particularly a continuing dislike, which he shared with Walter Scott and Robert Chambers, of the new barracks built in 1776. He asked Blanc if something could be done to bring the huge formal pile of the barracks on the west into harmony with the Castle. 'At present it looks like a cotton mill perched among the genuine buildings.' If the skyline could be broken up into some picturesque forms, it might 'fit with some harmony into the old.'[54]

One of Wilson's last acts for his friend William Nelson was to comment in 1888 on Blanc's designs for a memorial tablet for the family enclosure in the Grange cemetery. He considered the two sketches equally 'tasteful and pleasing to the eye,' and he was sympathetic to the idea of 'aiming at harmony with the other features of the burying ground of the family.' He also concurred with Blanc's idea of a pseudo-classical style of the seventeenth century. The tablet cut in red sandstone was to have a panel in white marble, which 'will have a pleasing effect on the ivy-covered wall,' though Wilson had doubts about the durability of marble in the Scottish climate and preferred sandstone. He provided a small ink sketch of a panel with an open pediment containing the Nelson shield, which he considered preferable, and 'consistent with the Scottish renaissance.'[55]

On 20 August 1891, in the Edinburgh council chambers, Sir Daniel Wilson became a burgess and guild brother, and was presented with the freedom of the city 'in recognition of his distinguished literary services in historical and literary research.'[56] In his speech to the gathering, he described how his feelings and sympathies had been 'intimately identified with all the ancient associations and historical memories of the capital of his native land.'[57] Edinburgh was to him what Jerusalem was to the old royal Hebrew or the city of the violet crown to the Athenian. Its greatest charm lay in its historical associations, which Wilson had explored with such assiduity in his younger days.

NOTES

This article is based in part on a chapter drafted by Marinell Ash. The discussion of Wilson's involvement in saving John Knox's House and his ideas regarding the restoration of historic buildings, as revealed in his correspondence with Hippolyte Blanc, was provided by Kitty Cruft. Elizabeth Hulse supplied material on *Memorials of Edinburgh*, particularly that drawn from Wilson's working copies of the first edition and other manuscript sources now in the TRL (ed.).

1 Wilson, *Reminiscences* (1878), 2: 155.
2 'Archer, John Wykeman,' in *DNB*, 1: 544.
3 Scott, *Journal*, 1: 3.
4 Wilson, *Reminiscences* (1878), 1: 15.
5 These proofs survive in TRL, S65, vol. 5. Some of Sharpe's anecdotes and a few of his sketches were incorporated into *Reminiscences* and the 1891 edition of *Memorials*.
6 The early nineteenth century had seen the publication of a number of such works on Edinburgh. J. and H.S. Storer had issued *Views in Edinburgh and Its Vicinity*, with text and plates by William Home Lizars, in 1820 (Wilson's copy is now in the TRL), and Lizars's own *Picturesque Views of Edinburgh*, containing fifty-one engravings after drawings by J. Ewbank, was published in monthly numbers in 1825.
7 Wilson's interleaved, annotated copy of the 1825 edition of Chambers's *Traditions of Edinburgh* is now in the TRL. The manuscript notes are in several different hands, and it is not clear which, if any, are Wilson's. The two volumes may have been given to him by another student of Edinburgh history, possibly Charles Kirkpatrick Sharpe. Some of the comments written into this copy are consistent with what Wilson says about Sharpe's habit of enriching his books with marginal notes (see Wilson, *Reminiscences* [1878], 1: 24).
8 Many of Wilson's copies of his sources were purchased from his library after his death by the Toronto Public Library and are now in the TRL. However, he was evidently not in the habit of annotating books in his library, and apart from the interleaved copies of two works by Chambers, which he may have acquired from someone else, none of the sources contain marginal notes.

    In the interleaved copy of the first edition of *Memorials*, in which Wilson recorded additions and corrections, he made a number of references to Andrew of Wyntoun's *Orygynale Cronykil of Scotland* (see TRL, S65, vol. 3, *Memorials*, vol. 1), a source that he had evidently not used, since it is not cited in the first edition; perhaps it was not easily available until David Laing's edition of the 1870s. These references were added in the 1891 edition.
9 Wilson's involvement with the SAS is discussed in greater detail in the following essay; see also Ash, '"A Fine, Genial, Hearty Band."'
10 See Stevenson, 'The Return of Mons Meg from London, 1828–1829.'
11 NMS, SAS, Communications, vol. 8, letters dated 12 and 14 March 1848.
12 NMS, SAS, Minute book, 1840–53, 13 March 1848, 212ff.
13 Ibid., 5 March 1849, 276–8.
14 NMS, SAS, Correspondence, letter from Wilson to William Burn Callendar, 6 November 1849.
15 NMS, SAS, Minute book, 1840–53, 243–5.

16 Ibid., 349, 311.

17 The date of 1460 for the foundation of the church is from RCAMS, *Inventory*, 36; Wilson cites 1462 in his publications.

18 Cockburn, 'A Letter to the Lord Provost on the Best Ways of Spoiling the Beauty of Edinburgh,' 330.

19 Wilson's account of the richly carved and decorated interior of the church in *Memorials* would be recognized by the Royal Commission on the Ancient Monuments of Scotland in its 1951 inventory of the city of Edinburgh as probably the most comprehensive (see RCAMS, *Inventory*, 36). A number of the watercolours and drawings are in the Special Collections Department, EUL.

20 The poem was reprinted in Wilson, *Reminiscences* (1878), 2: 36–8. A copy, possibly clipped from the *Scotsman*, is bound into a volume commemorating Trinity College Church that Wilson put together with the title 'Memorial of the Collegiate Church of the Holy Trinity' (now in the TRL). It also contains *Ane Auld Prophecie* (1849) and *The Queen's Choir* (1853), as well as a number of extra illustrations of the church and portraits of James I, II, and III.

21 The poem was reprinted in Wilson, *Reminiscences* (1878), 2: 26–32. It is quoted here from the original pamphlet.

22 Wilson, *Ane Auld Prophecie* (1849), vii–viii.

23 Gifford et al., *Edinburgh*, 171.

24 NMS, SAS, Correspondence, 19 November 1849: Wilson and J.A. Smith, 'Memorial to the Rt Hon. the Lord Provost and the Hon. the magistrates and Town Council of Edinburgh,' 14 June 1852, and Wilson, 'Letter respecting the rebuilding of the Trinity College Chapel to David Cousin, Esq., Architect, City Chambers,' 5 July 1852.

25 Wilson, *Reminiscences* (1878), 2: 17, 19. An account of the discovery is also given in Wilson, 'Notes of the Search for the Tomb of the Royal Foundress of the Collegiate Church of the Holy Trinity at Edinburgh' (1862).

26 NMS, SAS, Minute book, 1840–53, 1 June 1848, 241–3, 246.

27 Wilson, *Reminiscences* (1878), 2: 20.

28 Ibid., 20, 23.

29 Ibid., 21, 22.

30 When in 1862 Wilson published an account of this affair in the *PSAS*, it then recorded, 'In reference to the preceding communication, Mr DAVID LAING said, he regretted that his friend Dr D. Wilson should have revived this subject' (*PSAS* 4 [1862]: 565). Laing's own 'Remarks' on the affair, originally presented to the SAS in 1848, were printed following Wilson's paper.

31 Wilson, *Ane Auld Prophecie* (1849), xii.

32 See Bruce, *Some Practical Good*.

33 Wilson, *Reminiscences* (1878), 2: 41.

34 See NLS, MS 1956.

35 Ibid., no. 138, 28 November 1890. See also Wilson, 'John Knox's House, Netherbow, Edinburgh' (1891). It is now accepted that the association of the house with Knox is no older than the late eighteenth century; see RCAMS, *Inventory*, 96–7.

36 Wilson, 'John Knox's House, Netherbow, Edinburgh' (1891), 155.

37 Wilson was one of the first Scottish historians to collect an archive of illustrative material in this way, enabling him to analyse the architectural history of a building. Among the important items in these scrapbooks are photographs of a model of St Giles' Church and environs made about 1805, before the tenement buildings and shops huddled around it were pulled down, and a copy of James Craig's plan for the New Town (1768), printed from the original plate, which subsequently disappeared.

38 Among these was Peter Miller, who in 1890–1 was much preoccupied with the question of where John Knox had lived in the last years of his life. Wilson's letters to Miller concerning 'James Mosman's House at the Netherbow' were printed for private circulation in 1897, presumably by Miller himself.

39 It may have been the publication of this edition that inspired Wilson to write *Reminiscences*. Another 'new edition' of *Memorials*, also without any input from Wilson, was published in 1886.

40 In writing these ballads he was evidently inspired by the mock-medieval poems of Chatterton, whose life he had written in 1869; see *ME*2, 1: viii.

41 In one of the few references to the revised edition in the surviving excerpts from his journal, Wilson recorded on 11 March 1890, 'The writing of them [the Old Edinburgh ballads] has been a relief to me amid the strain of work and worry which this dire conflagration [the fire that gutted University College on 14 February] has involved' (UTA, B65-0014/004(02), 181).

42 Wilson was able in the preface also to pay tribute to the liberality of his lifelong friend William Nelson for the restoration of St Bernard's Well, the Argyle Tower, and the Great Hall at the Castle. On the restoration of the Argyle Tower, see below in this essay.

43 The exchange of letters with Hamilton was published in the *Scotsman* on 4 August 1852 and reprinted as a four-page leaflet. A copy is inserted in TRL, S65, vol. 4, between pp. 194 and 195; there is also a copy in the scrapbooks that Wilson presented to the SAS in 1869, now in the NMS library.

44 NLS, MS 1734/12, William Nelson to Hippolyte Blanc, 14 September 1885.

45 NMS, Daniel Wilson Scrapbooks, vol. l, p. 6a. A sketch of the arch is dated 27 February 1846 (ibid., p. 7).

46 NMS, SAS, Minute book, 1840–53, 151; SAS, Communications, vol. 8, 27 July 1846.

47 NLS, MS 1734/74–87, Hippolyte Blanc to Wilson, 4 November 1885.

48 NLS, MS 1734/99–110, Wilson to Hippolyte Blanc, 5 December 1885.

49 Quoted in Gifford et al., *Edinburgh*, 88.

50 Ibid., 91.

51 NLS, MS 1734/38–9, William Nelson to Hippolyte Blanc [undated].

52 TRL, S65, vol. 1: 278, Hippolyte Blanc to Wilson, 15 November 1885. This letter shows two sketches in the margin, one with the tower as it then was, with crenellations sketched in, and the other indicating Blanc's suggested arrangement with a pitched roof.

53 NLS, MS 1734/128–9, Wilson to Hippolyte Blanc, 12 December 1885.

54 NLS, MS 1737/21, Wilson to Hippolyte Blanc, 16 December 1890.

55 NLS, MS 1736/98, Wilson to Hippolyte Blanc, 13 August 1888.

56 Quoted in Hannah, 'Sir Daniel Wilson,' 16.

57 Ibid.

Old Books, Old Castles, and Old Friends: The Making of Daniel Wilson's *Archæology and Prehistoric Annals of Scotland*

MARINELL ASH

Daniel Wilson is frequently credited with the invention in English of the word 'prehistoric,' first used in his *Archæology and Prehistoric Annals of Scotland* (1851).[1] But the work has a wider significance: it introduced to the English-speaking world the Danish three-age system in its practical applications, and it set Scottish archaeology on a modern course, freed from the classical and English biases that had characterized much archaeological enquiry in the previous centuries. Wilson's achievement as a systematizer of Scottish archaeology can only be understood against his Scottish background. His childhood had been permeated by the influence of Sir Walter Scott, and both men benefited from older traditions, especially the tenets and methodology of the eighteenth-century Scottish social philosophers.

Newtonian induction underlay the work of the early philosophers of the Scottish Enlightenment. They owed other intellectual debts to English philosophy, most notably the question of epistemology, which developed out of the work of John Locke. Another major influence derived from the nature of Scots law, which, unlike the English system, was one of general principles and not built up from precedent and specific cases. Many figures of the Enlightenment were trained (if not practising) lawyers, and the shape of Scots law had considerable bearing on their philosophic thought, human activities being placed within an overall theoretical context. Thus the development of law and legal institutions came to be a major preoccupation of the Scottish philosophers, who saw them as essential evidence of human social development.

These threads came together in the work of Francis Hutcheson, professor of moral philosophy at the University of Glasgow from 1729 onward, who was the intellectual precursor of the Moderates in the Church of Scotland. He was much concerned with the question of the origins and purpose of moral feelings and their bearing on the creation of human institutions. The natural condition of humankind was one of 'innocence and beneficence toward all' (a condition that Hutcheson did not necessarily see as tied to a knowledge of God or divine grace). Nations and their attendant institutions were necessitated by the imperfect nature of human beings: 'mankind cannot be preserved without a sociable life.' 'In the first state constituted by nature itself ... there are many sacred rights competent to men, and many obligations incumbent on each one toward his fellows.'[2] The starting point for all human actions and the creation of institutions, according to Hutcheson, was this moral sense.

His certainty was challenged by the epistemological scepticism of David Hume, who doubted the basis and certitude of all human knowledge and held that social groups had been forced to establish common standards of justice and morality, not from an innate moral prompting, but on the basis of random and imperfect perceptions of the world. Reaction to Hume's ideas provided the foundation for the Common Sense school of Scottish philosophy. Among the first to take up the challenge was Thomas Reid, from 1764 professor of moral philosophy at Glasgow, whose *Inquiry into the Human Mind* (1764) was a direct response to Hume's *Treatise of Human Nature* (1739). Reid made a distinction between the existence of phenomena in the natural world and human beings' perception of them, which in turn could be divided into two parts, natural signs and acquired perceptions: 'we need not surely consult Aristotle or Locke, to know whether pain be like the point of a sword.'[3] Human judgment might be faulty, but that did not negate or deny the human capacity to form judgments and act upon them.

These philosophers provided later social thinkers with two essential tools with which to conduct their enquiries into the origin and purpose of social groups. The first was the methodology of perceptions, rooted in the Common Sense school of philosophy and centred on the mind of the individual. Secondly, they built up the outline of a theoretical framework for understanding the growth of human societies and their constituent institutions. 'Natural' or 'philosophical' history in Scotland was based firmly on the work of these early philosophers, who provided the starting point for later thinkers to chart human progress by 'consulting nature herself' for evidence of real life, past and present. Lord Kames, Adam Smith, Adam Ferguson, William Robertson, and John Millar, to name a few, were all in their debt, as Daniel Wilson was also later to be. Like them, he began from a general assumption of human progress from rudeness to refinement, but he borrowed particularly from the ideas of Adam Ferguson, who felt that the progress of a social group should be judged by that group's standards rather than according to terms imposed from outside. Implicit in the work of such writers as Adam Smith and John Millar was what came to be called in the nineteenth century the comparative method. It derived ultimately from Montesquieu's *L'Esprit des lois* (1748), in which comparative references were brought to bear on the study of government and its relationship to economy, climate, manners, and social institutions. A major feature of the Scottish comparative method was reference to the growing body of information about North American Native peoples, but the social thinkers used a wide range of other sources as well: travellers' accounts of journeys within Britain and to remote corners of the world, the Bible (as both an anthropological and a historical source), classical writers, and medieval charters and chronicles.

Besides these sources, the Scottish social philosophers had the Highlanders of their own country, whom they saw as evidence of a society in a more primitive stage of development. Until the middle of the eighteenth century, it was possible to speak of two distinct societies in Scotland. The Lowlands were modern and up to date, benefiting from the wider world opened up by the parliamentary union of 1707. This was the milieu in which the philosophers moved. Just beyond the dark hills of the Highland line, however, and visible from Edinburgh and Glasgow was another world, that of the Gaelic-speaking Highlander, still seen as essentially primitive in its organization and ethos, clinging to ancient social forms based on real or implied kinship between clansmen and the chief, and centred on ancestral clan lands.

Highland society provided valuable evidence for the philosophers' attempts to work out a progression of social forms in human development. Smith, Millar, and Robertson saw savages as the first stage of such evolution, with the nature of every subsequent human state being determined by the economic base of society. But the first philosophical attempt to deal with the stages of human progress was concerned with the law; Sir John Dalrymple's *Essay towards a General History of Feudal Property in Great Britain* (1757) argued for three stages in the development of property ownership. The next work to discuss this question was *Historical Law-Tracts* (1758), by Henry Home, Lord Kames, which postulated four stages of social development linked to the evolution of legal institutions. Both works may, however, have been anticipated by the lectures that

Adam Smith was delivering at the University of Glasgow throughout the 1750s.

For Smith the four stages of development were hunting, herding, agriculture, and commerce. The age of the hunters could barely be said, initially at least, to have an economic basis: 'Their sole business would be hunting the wild beasts or catching the fishes. The pulling of a wild fruit can hardly be called an employment.'[4] Eventually the growth of the hunter population would make dependence on hunting too precarious, and society would have to move towards domestication of animals to augment its diet: the age of shepherds had arrived. Smith, like other social philosophers, mentioned the rather puzzling instance of the North American Native peoples, who had 'no conception of flocks and herds,' although they had 'some notion of agriculture.'[5] After a time, most societies were forced to supplement their flocks and herds with agriculture. This stage of social development led to a diversification and separation of jobs. Trade in labour and goods resulted ultimately in Smith's fourth age, that of commerce.

Within this theoretical framework the role of individuals in society was subordinate, as Adam Ferguson recognized. 'Mankind are to be taken in groupes, as they have always subsisted. The history of the individual is but a detail of the sentiments and thoughts he has entertained in the view of his species: and every experiment relative to this subject should be made with entire societies, not with single men.'[6] Individuals should not be ignored, however; rather, they should be studied in order to understand the whole. Thus Smith and his pupil John Millar (once tutor to Lord Kames's son and from 1761 professor of law at Glasgow) both saw little use for theories about the original state of nature or social contracts, even as explanatory devices or to deal with periods of human experience beyond direct knowledge or analogy. Instead, at the centre of their studies they placed certain universalities of human behaviour. According to Millar, 'a disposition and capacity for improving his condition' was a constant factor in the human being. The 'similarity of his wants, as well as the faculties by which these wants are supplied, has every where produced a remarkable uniformity in the several steps of his progression.'[7]

Adam Ferguson modified this concept by his concern to understand societies on their own terms, and his sympathy with the reality of human experience forms a marked contrast to the economic determinism of Adam Smith. Ferguson may have come by his sympathetic stance from his own Highland background: he was born in Perthshire and was a Gaelic speaker. Among his pupils at Edinburgh was Walter Scott, and it was this concern with the human basis of past societies that Daniel Wilson acknowledged as his greatest debt to Scott. But to understand Scott and Wilson it is necessary first to look at the second source from which they both drew: the Scottish antiquarian tradition.

By Wilson's time this tradition was nearly two centuries old. The first important Scottish antiquary was Sir Robert Sibbald (1641–1711), a friend and correspondent of many English antiquaries, physician and geographer to Charles II, and first professor of medicine at the University of Edinburgh. His antiquarian work was closely tied to his scientific interests and displayed an interest in classification and close description of natural phenomena.[8] Sibbald and the best of his Scottish contemporaries were concerned to describe field monuments and to understand their physical and social contexts; nevertheless, the placing of structural and artefactual remains in some sort of social context was difficult for them. The problem was epitomized by the question of stone arrowheads. By the end of the seventeenth century, English antiquaries, using the analogies provided by the Native peoples of the New World, were satisfied that these were human products and not supernatural 'elf-bolts.' But in Scotland belief in the reality of the supernatural lingered longer. When he was twenty-one, Sibbald had witnessed a trial for witchcraft, and it seems that he was never completely able to put by the feeling that stone arrowheads might be of supernatural origin.[9]

It is no accident, therefore, that the first Scottish anthropological treatise should deal with the supernatural as a regular part of natural phenomena. In 1691 the Reverend Robert Kirk, the Gaelic-speaking minister of the Perthshire parish of Aberfoyle, wrote *The Secret Commonwealth of Elves, Fauns & Fairies*, a serious work of systematization that was to have a profound effect on Scott, especially in his *Letters on Demonology and Witchcraft* (1830). Kirk himself was in no doubt about the supernatural origins of arrowheads, as he wrote to Robert Boyle: 'I have had Barbed arrowheads of yellow flint, that could not be cut so smal [*sic*] and neat, of so brittle a substance, by all the art of Man.'[10]

Unlike Kirk, however, most Scottish antiquaries of the seventeenth and eighteenth centuries were concerned primarily with Roman remains. Sibbald himself produced *Historical Inquiries, concerning the Roman Monuments and Antiquities in the North-Part of Britain Called Scotland* (1707), published in the year of the union of the Scottish and English parliaments. The date was not entirely fortuitous, because the proposed union had led to a flowering of literary antiquarianism as the ancient records of Scotland were searched for documents that would support arguments for and against it.

The union of 1707 was a major antiquarian problem. Unlike the English, the Scots took the concept of union between parliaments seriously and looked forward to the day when Scotland and England would be as culturally unified as they were constitutionally. For example, when in 1780 it was proposed to found a Society of Antiquaries of Scotland (modelled on the London Society of Antiquaries), there were objections to the idea because, as William Smellie observed, 'till we were cordially united to England, not in government only, but in loyalty and affection to a common Sovereign, it was not, perhaps, altogether consistent with political wisdom, to call the attention of the Scots to the ancient honours and constitution of their independent Monarchy.'[11]

Thus for many, an interest in Scottish history was politically and culturally retrograde. Adam Ferguson certainly felt this to be the case. Political realities could produce tensions and intellectual doubts for Scottish antiquaries. The most extreme example was Sir John Clerk of Penicuik, who had been a fervent supporter of the union, but who was also the greatest antiquary of his age. Now that Scotland and England were one, how could he justify continuing to study the Scottish past? Roman walls, for example, represented not only Roman genius and might but also the suppression of the freedom-loving tribes of Caledonia, his own ancestors. Increasingly, structural remains were raising questions about the nature of the societies that had produced them. The growth of philosophical generalizations about progressive stages of society were aids to the interpretation of these field monuments, as was the increased availability of historical texts, especially classical ones. But the centuries after the Roman occupation were dark ages as far as literary evidence went. To fill this vacuum, the Scots over the years had invented legends ascribing the origins of their people to Scota, the eponymous daughter of the pharaoh, and had also developed long king lists tracing the royal line back to Fergus MacErc. Then at a stroke nearly half this list of kings was, in Scott's phrase, 'conjured down' by the Catholic priest and antiquary Thomas Innes in his *Critical Essay on the Ancient Inhabitants of the Northern Parts of Britain or Scotland* (1729).[12] The essay was a rigorous survey of the primary and secondary sources for early Scottish history, but it had little immediate impact, largely because of the author's Catholicism and Jacobitism.

A good deal of Scottish antiquarian enquiry in the eighteenth and nineteenth centuries was bedevilled by such political and religious antagonisms. Whole periods of history were ignored. The Middle Ages were abandoned by Presbyterians as a time of spiritual darkness, and the greatest of eighteenth- and nineteenth-century scholars of the medieval period were, almost without exception, Catholics and Episcopalians. Father Innes's work was only accepted by dispassionate scholars, and his greatest successor, Sir David Dalrymple, Lord Hailes, (who was an Episcopalian) caused deep offence when his *Annals of Scotland from the Accession of Malcolm Canmore to Robert I*, with its devastating critique of some of the most dearly held historical beliefs of the Scots, appeared in 1776. It was accepted only because of Hailes's impeccable social and political standing, and criticism of the work caused him to abandon it before his originally intended termination date.

By the end of the eighteenth century, the work of antiquaries had resulted in an agreed chronology for Scottish recorded history. Extensive fieldwork had produced records of many surviving historic structures, especially of the Roman period, but the Middle Ages tended to be ignored. About the earlier structures, such as hill forts, brochs, and souterrains, speculation was rife. Following the lead of the English antiquaries John Aubrey and William Stukeley, the study of field monuments had come to be an important aspect of the work of Scottish antiquaries. Nevertheless, these monuments were still viewed primarily in textual terms. Largely as a result of the writings of Julius Caesar and Stukeley's published accounts of his Wiltshire fieldwork, the dominant literary association was with the 'Celtic' Druids. But the increasing availability of published texts of ancient Scandinavian literature led to some field monuments being reinterpreted along Scandinavian lines.

Thus by the later eighteenth century there was an increased popular and scholarly interest in archaeological remains seen in terms of associations – real or imagined – with events and personalities in the past. A stone circle would be a 'Druid's temple' in the popular mind, but to serious antiquaries it was evidence of a stage of social development: religion organized on a massive scale involving the whole community. Gradually, structural remains came to have a human or social context expressed in terms of social organization and progress. The man responsible for popularizing this new spirit was Walter Scott.

Scott, in fact, stands at the synapse between the world of the eighteenth-century social theorists and antiquaries and the systematization of archaeology and ethnology in the nineteenth century. In his own life he brought together various intellectual threads from the past and wove them into new patterns which were to change the practice of both history and archaeology. It was not just that his mind could encompass the huge range of historical and literary knowledge which he used in his work; it was also that he lived in an antiquarian milieu where it was still possible to have interests and expertise across a wide spectrum of historical and literary concerns. For Scott, and all Scots of his age, the past was imminent in a way that was true of few other European societies. During his childhood at his grandfather's Border farmhouse at Sandyknowe, in the shadow of Smailholm Tower, he had heard tales from eyewitnesses of the execution of Jacobites at Carlisle after the failure of the rebellion of 1745. His first novel, *Waverley* (1814), dealt with this event and bore the significant subtitle ''Tis Sixty Years Since.'

Scott was distinguished from the rest of his contemporaries by his amazingly retentive memory, a ragbag of a mind that stored up information in an unsystematic way. He was eventually able to give this mental collection of fable, lore, and fact some shape and force by applying the concepts of the Scottish social thinkers, although he recalled that learning to use these concepts was a difficult business. 'The philosophy of history, a much more important subject, was also a sealed book at this period of my life [early teens]; but I gradually assembled much of what was striking and picturesque in historical narrative; and when, in riper years, I attended more to the deduction of general principles, I was furnished with a powerful host of examples in illustration of them. I was, in short, like an ignorant gamester, who kept up a good hand until he knew how to play it.'[13]

In his first major published work, *The Minstrelsy of the Scottish Border* (1802), Scott showed how well he could play this hand. For this compilation he wrote an extended introduction describing the social and historical background of the Border ballads. It is a fine account based on a variety of sources, including written material and Scott's own fieldwork in the Borders collecting ballads and viewing antiquities. In *The Minstrelsy* he painted a picture of a patriarchal, clan-based society whose primary activities were warfare and cattle raiding. In Border society those laws that existed were regarded as sacrosanct. Fidelity to clan and kin was valued above all other virtues. Many of the ballads dealt with the social mechanisms of this society. It was a community largely without conventional religion, but with a strong belief in the supernatural. 'The fact at least is certain ... that the character of the Scotish [sic] fairy is more harsh and terrific than that which is ascribed to the elves of our sister kingdom.'[14] The capriciousness of fairy disposition reflected the precarious nature of Border society. Scott cites as an example of this generalization the popular belief that stone arrowheads were of supernatural manufacture. 'The triangular flints, frequently found in Scotland, with which the ancient inhabitants probably barbed their shafts, are supposed to be the weapons of fairy resentment, and are termed *elf-arrow heads*.'[15]

There are marked theoretical and methodological parallels between Scott's non-fiction and his novels, which may be illustrated by a brief consideration of his use of Scandinavian literature and antiquities to create an imaginative reconstruction of past societies. He had been fascinated by Scandinavian literature since his student days.[16] In the summer of 1814 he set out on a cruise to the northern isles of Scotland on a yacht belonging to the Commissioners for the Northern Lights (the body responsible for Scottish lighthouses). The prehistoric and Viking remains that Scott saw on his trip he viewed very much in the light of his extract from the Eyrbyggja Saga, which had appeared a few months earlier in *Illustrations of Northern Antiquities*, edited by Robert Jamieson. The trip would influence and shape his later work, most notably his poem *Harold the Dauntless* (1817), his novel *The Pirate* (1822), and to a lesser extent *Ivanhoe* (1820).[17] The party visited a number of major sites in both Shetland and Orkney: in Shetland the Iron Age brochs at Clickhimin and Mousa and the ting (open-air parliament) site at Tingwall and in Orkney the Romanesque cathedral and medieval bishop's and earl's palaces in Kirkwall, the chambered tomb cut from a single rock called the Dwarfie Stane on the island of Hoy, and the complex site centred on the henge ring of Brogar at Stenness.

Scott was well aware that contemporary knowledge did not allow the dating of these sites with any certainty; so in his notes he was careful not to draw chronological or historical conclusions unless he felt that the evidence justified them. At Stenness, however, all his techniques and concerns came together. His reading of the sagas had already led him to the belief that these henge sites were not Druidical temples but Scandinavian judgment seats. 'The idea that such circles were exclusively Druidical is now justly exploded. The northern nations all used such erections to mark their places of meeting, whether for religious purposes or civil policy; and there is repeated mention of them in the Sagas. See the Eyrbiggia Saga for the establishment of the Helga-fels, or holy mount.'[18] Scott was right in his reading of the saga but wrong in his attribution of Stenness to the Vikings. Nevertheless, he was careful to describe the physical appearance of the site, and he asked engineer Robert Stevenson to make careful measurements. He also enquired of the factor whether he knew of any local traditions regarding the site. The reply was negative, but Scott knew that that was probably a result of the factor's lack of interest rather than the absence of local tradition. Nearly forty years later it would, in fact, be local tradition that would establish the pre-Viking date of Stenness.

There was another legacy from Scott in Daniel Wilson's later work: his concern with the dynamics of change. In Shetland, for example, Scott had been much struck by the mutations to traditional Scandinavian forms of life resulting from the influx of Scots in the three and half centuries since the islands had been pledged to Scotland by Norway. He could see that this change was continuous, and so he felt that in order for the present-day islanders to enjoy a better way of life, they would have to make a further evolution from their traditional life as 'fishermen with crofts' (smallholdings) towards a division of labour between full-time fishermen and full-time crofters. Change was essential and desirable in order to ensure the maximum human happiness, but in the midst of all such change there were certain constants of human character, as Scott had stated in the introductory chapter to *Waverley*:

> By fixing then the date of my story Sixty Years before this present 1st November, 1805, I would have my readers understand that they will meet in the following pages neither a romance of chivalry, nor a tale of modern manners ... From this my choice of an æra, the understanding critic may farther presage, that the object of my tale is more a description of men than manners ... [I have thrown] the force of my narrative upon the characters and passions of the actors; – those passions common to men in all stages of society, and which have alike agitated the human heart, whether it throbbed under the steel corslet of the fifteenth century, the brocaded coat of the eighteenth, or the blue frock and white dimity waistcoat of the present day.[19]

Waverley appeared in 1814. When, thirty-seven years later, Daniel Wilson published his *Archæology and Prehistoric Annals of Scotland*, he made his intellectual debt to Scott clear in the first paragraph of the book: 'The zeal for Archæological investigation which has recently manifested itself in nearly every country of Europe, has been traced, not without reason, to the impulse which proceeded from Abbotsford. Though such is not exactly the source which we might expect to give birth to the transition from profitless dilettantism to the intelligent spirit of scientific investigation, yet it is unquestionable that Sir Walter Scott was the first of modern writers "to teach all men this truth, which looks like a truism, and yet was as good as unknown to writers of history and others, till so taught, – that the bygone ages of the world were actually filled by living men"' (*PAS1*, xi).[20] This passage might seem merely a form of *pietas*, expected of a true son of Edinburgh, Scott's 'own romantic town.' But such is not the case, for throughout his life Wilson's work was pervaded by the influence of Scott in a number of diverse ways, such as his use of literary source material, the careful observation of field monuments, the use of folklore and linguistic material collected in the field, and the application of Enlightenment social theory.

Wilson had joined the Society of Antiquaries of Scotland in February 1846, some months before his first major antiquarian publication, *Memorials of Edinburgh in the Olden Time*, would begin appearing in parts. In November the following year he was appointed one of the society's secretaries. The SAS had experienced a period of relative prosperity in the 1820s, but its finances had then fallen into confusion. In the winter of 1836 David Laing was appointed treasurer, with the task of sorting them out. It would take almost a decade, and during this time the nature of the society changed fundamentally, to a large extent because of the efforts of Laing and a group of like-minded fellows. The librarian of the Signet Library and a noted book collector and editor of historical texts, David Laing was the son of the bookseller William Laing. His father's shop was a favourite meeting place of men such as Scott, the antiquary George Chalmers, and the Icelandic scholar Grimur Thorkelin, who was probably responsible for the Laings' link with Scandinavia. Both David and his father travelled to Scandinavia to buy books for Scottish libraries and collectors, and had strong contacts with scholars in those countries. By 1823, when at Scott's suggestion he became secretary of the Bannatyne Club, David Laing was already recognized as a formidable literary scholar, so that, although he had been blackballed by the Society of Antiquaries in 1820, he was elected without his knowledge four years later. Other members who helped to reform the society included the painter David Octavius Hill, John Mitchell, a Leith merchant who was deeply learned in Scandinavian archaeology and languages, and Wilson's physician friend James Young Simpson. All these men brought their special gifts to the society and in so doing changed the face of Scottish archaeology.[21]

By the 1840s Laing was leading a campaign to persuade the British government to take over the antiquaries' museum as the basis of a national collection. The society's requests were initially refused, and it became clear that if the antiquaries were to be successful in transferring their museum to government control, they would first have to put their house in order. They had reorganized their archaeological collections on several occasions in the past, and as early as the mid-1820s were looking to Scandinavian models, particularly to the work of C.J. Thomsen in Copenhagen. In April 1828 members had heard a short notice on the collections in the Copenhagen museum, of which Thomsen was director.[22] The Scottish antiquaries were struck not only by the simplicity and flexibility of the Stone, Bronze, and Iron Age system of archaeological classification used by Thomsen and J.J.A. Worsaae, but also by the enlightened Danish laws concerning treasure trove. In the 1840s John Mitchell and publisher Robert Chambers made journeys to Scandinavia to study archaeological collections there.[23] Worsaae himself came to Edinburgh in 1846. He had been sent by the Danish king to study Viking remains in Britain and Ireland,[24] and he arrived with a letter to the Society of Antiquaries' secretary announcing that part of his mission was 'to unite the efforts of the British and Scandinavian antiquaries more than has hitherto been the case.'[25] He was elected a corresponding fellow of the society and left in its library an inscribed copy of his *Danmarks Oldtid oplyst ved Oldsager og Gravhøie* (published in English in 1849 as *The Primeval Antiquities of Denmark*), the work in which he had set out Thomsen's three-age system.

By the time of Worsaae's visit, Wilson was already working on his *Prehistoric Annals*, and there can be no doubt that, although the two did not meet on this occasion, the visit was a major influence on Wilson's thinking. During his travels in Britain and Ireland the Danish scholar had been struck by the correspondence between archaeological material in Britain and Scandinavia, and he had developed this theme in an account of the formation of the museum of antiquities in Copenhagen that he gave to the Royal Irish Academy in November 1846.[26] A copy of his paper was sent to the library of the Scottish antiquaries. Worsaae saw Ireland as the closest parallel to Scandinavia since it too had been barely touched by Roman influences and its prehistoric development before the Iron period was largely indigenous. He argued, following (whether he knew it or not) the Scottish social philosophers, that societies in similar stages of development produced similar artefacts and structures.

Another Scandinavian influence was the Norwegian historian P.A. Munch, who came to Edinburgh in 1849 to seek sources for the early history of his country. He became a close friend of Wilson's, and from their fireside discussions developed some of the most illuminating and original passages of *Prehistoric Annals*, especially Wilson's arguments against the classical and literary biases of so much earlier Scottish archaeological thought and the common attribution of every non-Roman prehistoric structure or artefact to the Danes: 'while the artless relics of our primeval Stone Period were generally assigned to native workmanship, whatever evinced any remarkable traces of skill distinct from the well-defined Roman art, was assumed of necessity to have a foreign origin, and was usually ascribed to the Danes. The invariable adoption of the latter term in preference to that of Norwegians or Norsemen, shews how completely

Scottish and Irish antiquaries have abandoned themselves to the influence of English literature, even where the appropriation of its dogmas was opposed to well-known historical facts' (*PAS1*, xiv).

In the year that Munch visited Scotland, Wilson completed his *Synopsis of the Museum of the Society of Antiquaries of Scotland,* which as one of the society's secretaries he had helped to reorganize.[27] This small compilation is in essence a sketch for *Prehistoric Annals.* In the *Synopsis* he used the tripartite system in its 'freest signification' and rightly saw it as a guide, not an absolute; its outlines could be applied to local conditions and employed as a framework for the discussion of the social and cultural context of artefacts. Wilson's work as a comparative ethnologist in later life is foreshadowed in his preface to the *Synopsis,* when he makes comparisons between the Stone and Bronze ages in Scotland and analogous societies in Assyria, Egypt, and Mexico. The reorganized museum reflected this comparative approach. The first case contained British and Irish stone arrowheads and axes, labelled with their provenance, donor, and date. In the next case were Danish stone artefacts, part of a gift from the Royal Society of Northern Antiquaries and the Danish crown prince, who had visited the Edinburgh museum in 1844. Other cases contained Amerindian, African, and South Sea exhibits 'for the purposes of comparison.'

The range of the society's museum revealed in the *Synopsis* showed that the antiquaries' claims to be the possessors of a collection of national scope and significance were justified. By 1850 it was clear that the government was going to agree to take over the collection; final terms were reached the following year. Wilson and his fellow antiquaries could now turn their attention to making their museum and the society more accessible. They introduced longer opening hours for the public, arranged for regular meetings and excursions, and continued to take a lead in campaigns to preserve threatened historic structures. Wilson's other great legacy to the society was the commencement of a regular journal, the *Proceedings of the Society of Antiquaries of Scotland,* in 1852.

The Archæology and Prehistoric Annals of Scotland, published the year before, represents a profound shift in the methodology of antiquarian thought. For a start, 'prehistoric,' the term that Wilson used to describe history before written sources, implied that literary antiquarianism was to be 'but little avail [to] us in reaching the desired point' (*PAS1*, 16). In its place, other tools and disciplines would have to be used, most notably ethnology, which had developed rapidly in the 1840s, largely as a result of the work of James Cowles Prichard. The third edition of his *Researches into the Physical History of Mankind* had appeared in five volumes between 1836 and 1847. Wilson was strongly influenced by this work, as well as by Prichard's *On the Relations of Ethnology to Other Branches of Knowledge,* published in Edinburgh in 1847.

Unlike his mentor, however, he had no doubt about ethnology's position as a scientific discipline, 'the youngest of all the recognized band of sister sciences' that included archaeology, chemistry, and geology (*PAS*1, xvii). Despite his philosophical differences with Prichard, Wilson's debt to him is clear throughout *Prehistoric Annals* in his use of comparative linguistics, physiological studies, historical evidence, and comparative analyses of other historic or contemporary societies. The older writer's influence is most obvious in passages dealing with monogenesis and craniology (for a fuller discussion of Wilson's views in these areas, see Bennett McCardle's essay in this volume). Wilson's first public statement on craniology was a paper that he gave at the meeting of the British Association for the Advancement of Science held in Edinburgh in 1850: 'Inquiry into the Evidence of the Existence of Primitive Races in Scotland prior to the Celtae.'[28] This paper became part of chapter 9 of *Prehistoric Annals,* 'Crania of the Tumuli,' which is explicit in its debt to Prichard. Although Wilson apparently accepted his mentor's arguments for monogenesis, he was aware that continental ethnologists 'have set aside the idea of one primitive stock' (*PAS*1, 164). But by the time the second edition of *Prehistoric Annals* appeared in 1863 he would have been led – largely as a result of his experiences in North America – to accept at least the possibility of 'the independent creation of numerous distinct races of men' and had excised all references to Prichard's 'Adamic history' from the work (cf. *PAS*1, 164; *PAS*2, 1: 234).

Prichard's thought helped to shape *Prehistoric Annals* in other ways. There was, overall, a general acceptance of his 'evolutionist approach' to human development, along with a reluctance to place religion within a similar context.[29] But this similarity may be more apparent than real. Wilson, like his English colleague, was an evangelical, with the significant difference that he was a Scottish Episcopalian. In the highly charged period after the disruption in the Church of Scotland in 1843, Episcopalians were regarded with suspicion as near-Catholics. Religiously based attacks on Episcopalian and Catholic historical scholars, most of whom Wilson knew personally, were commonplace and could cost both reputation and position.[30] Therefore, while not disguising what he felt to be the truth, he knew that he had to tread carefully.

In the opening passages of *Prehistoric Annals,* in a cautiously worded exposition, Wilson discussed the work of geologists and biblical scholars in pushing back human chronology beyond Bishop Ussher's conventional date for the creation of the world. He had been a close friend of publisher Robert Chambers, the author of *Vestiges of the Natural History of Creation* (1844), from at least the early 1840s, and during the course of an evening walk, had listened to 'glimpses of Lamarckian and Darwinian views, now very familiar to all.'[31] Wilson saw the Bible as part history and part model. The Old Testament contained episodes that were close to history, but it was silent about untold generations. Job, for example, was 'one pregnant scene of primitive social life ... while all the rest are swallowed up with the centuries to which they belonged' (*PAS1*, 2).

Nevertheless, there is a religious element to *Prehistoric Annals*. Wilson unquestionably saw the cultural development that he described in his book as a progression towards a revealed Christian religion, an attitude well illustrated in his passage comparing the tumuli and medieval recumbent effigies: 'Perhaps no work of the period is more characteristic of the change from the age of the tumulus builders than the recumbent effigy of the Christian knight. It is one of the most significant memorials of the mild influences of a purer faith on the arts and sepulchral rites of the race' (*PAS1*, 648). Wilson ends his book with a statement that seems to place archaeology in a kind of teleological great chain of being: 'Man ... feels himself no isolated being, but one link in a vast chain ... he discovers in the preadamite periods of creation a preparatory dispensation, he recognises in his own period a more perfect one, not because he conceives it to be final, but because he knows it to be probationary, and the preliminary to that which is perfect' (*PAS1*, 701–2).

It is difficult, however, to take all this implied piety totally at face value. What Wilson wrote must be seen, in some measure, against the particular religious background of Scotland at the time. One of his most striking characteristics is his open-mindedness and his ability to accept new ideas and change (although not without much genuine soul-searching), such as the implications of the work of Boucher de Perthes or the publication of Darwin's *On the Origin of Species*.[32] What he hated was dishonest or incorrect use of new ideas, not the ideas themselves. In 1877 he would state as his lifelong credo: 'Truth has nothing to fear in the long run from the researches of such men as Darwin and Huxley. I think it suffers from the shackles with which orthodox zeal would hamper enquiry, with the most honest intentions ... Truth has everything to gain from the most absolute freedom of enquiry.'[33] By that time he could speak from a position of considerably more authority than in 1851, but his feelings were substantially unchanged.

The opening and closing passages of *Prehistoric Annals* were to a large extent nods to prevailing orthodoxy, designed to ensure a favourable reception for the work. The book is informed throughout with Wilson's religious attitudes, but these are more usually implicit than explicit. They appear in two main guises: in his assumption of the growth of humankind towards the 'true GOLDEN AGE OF MAN [which] lies before him, not behind' (*PAS*1, 698), and in the role of the individual in effecting this progression. Change, like salvation, is not bestowed, but must be worked for. The link between this view and the emphasis placed on individual salvation in Anglican theology is clear.

Wilson's methodology and the setting out of his evidence is similar in all four sections of *Prehistoric Annals*: an opening exposition of the historical background (which in the Stone, Bronze, and Iron Age sections is largely geological or based on inductive reasoning and analogy), leading to a consideration of the structural and artefactual remains and culminating in a sketch of social organization. The opening passages of what he calls 'The Primeval or Stone Period' display yet another borrowing from Prichard: the placing of human history within a strong geographical context.[34] From the most obvious geographical feature of Britain – its insularity – Wilson was able to draw his first historical conclusion about the arrival of the earliest settlers, a change that he termed 'the primal transition': they had to have been able to construct some kind of boat and to have had some knowledge of navigation (*PAS*1, 29). His survey of this period is based on random finds of such objects as the hollowed log canoes of the first arrivals, burial sites, grave finds, souterrains, and stone artefacts, including hatchets, hammers, awls, vessels, and items of personal adornment. Comparisons are made between these objects and existing Stone Age cultures, such as the 'Esquimaux,' African bushmen, and the Polynesians. The commonality of human experience at analogous stages of development is illustrated by the comparison of burial sites, temples, and memorial stones, all indicative of a common belief in an afterlife and the instinct to mark important physical sites such as battlefields and boundaries. The concept of 'instinct' would reappear in Wilson's survey of American prehistory in *Prehistoric Man* (1862) as the common denominator for humankind's cultural advancement.[35]

His treatment of the complex structures around Brogar and Stenness in Orkney illustrates not only his debt to scholars of the past but also the practical working out of the 'legitimate induction' that he wished to introduce into archaeological enquiry. His chapter on 'Temples and Memorial Stones' begins with a wide-ranging survey of Scottish examples of stone markers on battlefield and law-giving or oath-taking sites. An important example was the Odin Stone, associated with the henge monument at Stenness. It had stood about eight feet high and was perforated by an oval hole, through which hands were clasped to exchange vows or oaths. The stone had been seen by Scott, but shortly afterwards it was thrown down. While recognizing Scott's importance in condemning the Druidical interpretation of henges and standing stones, Wilson was at pains to show that all the Orcadian monuments were incomparably older than Scott and other antiquaries had believed.

Wilson had never been to Orkney, and so his descriptions depended on another antiquarian practice – information provided by local correspondents, who included the naval surveyor F.W.L. Thomas, the Orkney antiquary George Petrie, and other scholars. Using literary evidence provided by his friend Munch, Wilson was able to establish finally that Stenness was pre-Viking. After meeting Wilson in Edinburgh, Munch had visited Orkney, armed with a letter of introduction to Petrie. During his stay he had made particular enquiry about old place names for the area around Stenness. Petrie later wrote to Munch that he had been able to ascertain that there was a place named Hourston, near the loch of Harray.[36] Munch identified this site with Havardsteigr, scene of the murder of Earl Havard in 970, which was mentioned in Olaf Trygvesson's saga: 'Havard was then at Steinsnes ... The place is now called Havardsteigr' (PAS1, 112).[37] In order to establish the even older origins of Stenness, however, literature and place-name evidence were not enough. Wilson fell back on analogy, particularly the work of Sir Richard Colt Hoare in Wiltshire. Indeed, his debt to the English antiquary is manifest in the name that he applied to Orkney, 'the Wiltshire of Scotland,' and the direct comparison that he made between the lack of evidence for metal working on the stones of Stenness and Avebury, which allowed him assign Stenness to the Stone Age for the first time.

The next section of *Prehistoric Annals* deals with what Wilson termed 'The Archaic or Bronze Period.' The technological process involved in smelting implied a more settled and complex social structure than that of the Stone Age. Unlike Worsaae, however, Wilson did not see the Bronze Age revolution as contemporaneous or uniform throughout Europe, or even within Scotland. The Society of Antiquaries of Scotland had commissioned Wilson's brother George to carry out a chemical analysis of a number of bronze objects from Fife, Midlothian, and Berwickshire, 'selected solely as furnishing a comprehensive diversity in the elements of comparison.'[38] The results of these and other tests, showing different ratios of alloy, led Wilson to the conclusion that it was impossible to determine a common source for bronze- and metal-working technologies. He also disagreed with Worsaae's belief that the introduction of bronze implied an influx of new peoples; at least, such a thesis could not be supported on the evidence available.

Wilson termed the third era 'The Teutonic or Iron Period.' Once again he saw the technological change implied by the introduction of iron as a gradual one, not deriving from a common source. At this point the divergence between Scottish and English archaeology became manifest. The Scottish Iron Age was the era of invasions: Romans, Teutons, Angles, Scots, and Vikings. In Scotland the Romans had been able to effect little more than a military occupation of the Lowlands. Thus Wilson, using both literary and archaeological sources, was at pains to play down the inordinate attention paid to the Romans by previous Scottish antiquaries and archaeologists and the general assignation of many field monuments to the Danes. Evidence for the uniqueness of Scottish archaeology was the remarkable range of Iron Age structures in Scotland: hill forts such as the Caterthuns in Angus and the mysterious vitrified forts and brochs, neither of which had any European parallels.

At this point in *Prehistoric Annals*, Wilson leaves the tripartite system and enters an era when remains were more numerous and there began to be written evidence, an era that he calls 'The Christian Period.' It was an age with an essentially different character, since from the arrival of the first Christian missionaries in the fifth century, Scotland was increasingly drawn into the mainstream of European culture. There were now clear and direct links with, for example, Ireland, not least the arrival of the Scots themselves from that country in the sixth century. More and more, too, Scotland was drawn into the European-wide religious unity which was, in Wilson's view, the salient feature of the Middle Ages (*PAS*1, 696). With the possible exception of the Pictish Norrie's Law silver hoard, all the artefacts and artistic styles covered in this section had European connections and resonances. This attempt to place the Catholic Middle Ages in direct continuity between the Dark Ages and the present was dangerous ground in mid-nineteenth-century Scotland. Wilson felt it necessary to make the disclaimer 'It is no part of the plan of this work to embrace ecclesiastical controversies' (*PAS*1, 603).

There is a definite sense of a falling off in imaginative sweep and synthesis in this final section of *Prehistoric Annals*, and Wilson has been criticized for ending his book with a discussion that apparently falls outside the synthesis which he had built up for the truly 'prehistoric' Stone,

Bronze, and Iron Ages. Yet this is to misunderstand his purpose. This closing section, in fact, forms an integral part of his overall plan, since he believed that his own time and culture were part of a continuum with the past. It also allowed him to arrive at a definitive conclusion about the relative places of archaeology and ethnology in the 'circle of the sciences.' Ultimately, Wilson felt that archaeology alone was essential and indispensable: 'The researches of the ethnologist carry us back somewhat beyond that epoch [the Middle Ages], and confirm many of those conditions, especially in relation to the close affinity between the native arts and Celtic races of Scotland and Ireland, at which we arrived by means of archæological evidence ... the conclusions of the ethnologist receive not only confirmation but much minute elucidation from archæological research' (*PAS*1, 695–6).

The Archæology and Prehistoric Annals of Scotland was enthusiastically received on publication. Wilson hoped that its success might lead to a position in a Scottish university, library, or museum. Although he was awarded an LLD *honoris causa* from St Andrews, however, he failed to gain his wish. Instead, in 1853 he was appointed to the chair in history and English literature at University College in Toronto. For a man who had become so closely identified with the history of Scotland, such a move to a new world – in every sense of the term – could have been intellectually devastating. But soon after he reached his landfall at Philadelphia, he saw about him the materials for a new, but related study of humankind in the New World. Here he would find living examples of the social and cultural changes that he had postulated for the long-vanished peoples of Scotland. By the summer of 1855 he was able to write to his old friend David Laing, describing a field trip to the Great Lakes region. On the unspoiled shores of Lake Superior

> it was my great good fortune to see the red Indian savage, painted and adorned in his genuine native condition; and to observe thus the manners and habits of a people probably closely resembling those of Scotland's primitive eras, which contributed one of the themes on which I used to bore you at our S.A.S. meetings. Here, however, we have no black letter tomes, parchment chartularies, or ancient MS.S. and one must be thankful for such materials as offer. At one point on the Ontonagon River, on the south shore of Lake Superior, where Ancient Indian workings of native copper have been brought to light, I was greatly interested by the sight of a collection of curious antique copper tools and weapons, dug up at some depth under the roots of some lofty and aged pines. They were hammered copper; and pre-

sented some curious analogies in the mode of making a socket by means of bevelled edges turned in, to the bronze axe heads, etc., both of Denmark and Scotland. But indeed the analogies between the primitive arts of the New World and the old, are remarkable and highly interesting ... Altogether the opportunities I have already enjoyed of examining the Red Indian in his Native State, and exploring the traces of his primitive Arts, appear to me of great value as throwing light on the Ancient arts of Prehistoric Britain. I shall try and write a paper for the Antiquaries this winter ... There is not a luxury you enjoy in Edinburgh that is not to be had in Toronto, – always excepting old books, old castles & Abbeys, and above all, Old friends.[39]

NOTES

1 The word had appeared first in French, but Wilson was unaware of this fact, and in a letter written to Sir Charles Lyell in 1865, he claimed to have invented the term (EUL, Special Collections, 1/6083, Daniel Wilson to Sir Charles Lyell, 13 December 1865). Throughout his life he took a proprietary interest in 'pre-historic.' In April 1880, for example, he wrote to William Dawson, thanking him for a copy of his book *Fossil Men and Their Modern Representatives*. 'By the bye, why do you break off prehistoric with a hyphen? The word is a bantling of my own, and it offends me to see it reduced to pre-historic, with no reason at all! It is as good a word as predisposed, preposition, or a score of other words that dispense with any hyphen' (MUA, Acc. 927). Wilson was equally offended by John Lubbock's use of the hyphen in *Pre-historic Times* (1865).

2 Hutcheson, *A System of Moral Philosophy*, 2: 280–1.

3 T. Reid, *An Inquiry into the Human Mind*, 106.

4 Glasgow University Library, MS Gen. 94/1, Adam Smith, MSS notes of his lectures on jurisprudence, vol. 1, 24 December 1762; quoted in Rendall, *The Origins of the Scottish Enlightenment*, 141–3.

5 Rendall, *The Origins of the Scottish Enlightenment*, 142.

6 Ferguson, *An Essay on the History of Civil Society*, 8.

7 Millar, *The Origin of the Distinction of Ranks*, 3.

8 Piggott, *Ruins in a Landscape*, 19, 135–8.

9 Ibid., 139.

10 Kirk, *Secret Commonwealth of Elves and Fairies* (1691; ed. S. Sanderson, Folklore Society, 1976), 51, 107; quoted in Piggott, *Ruins in a Landscape*, 138–9.

11 Smellie, 'An Historical Account of the Society of Antiquaries of Scotland,' iv.

12 See Ash, *The Strange Death of Scottish History*, 32–3.

13 Scott, 'Memoir of His Early Years,' 33.

14 Scott, *The Minstrelsy of the Scottish Border,* 2: 213–4.

15 Ibid., 214; emphasis in the original.

16 J.M. Simpson, 'Scott and Old Norse Literature,' 303.

17 See Ash, '"So Much That Was New to Us."'

18 Scott, *Northern Lights,* 71–2.

19 Scott, *Waverley,* 4–5.

20 The source given by Wilson for this quotation is Thomas Carlyle's *Miscellanies* (2d ed.), 5: 301.

21 For a detailed account of the role played by Laing and Wilson in the Society of Antiquaries of Scotland, see Ash, '"A Fine, Genial, Hearty Band."'

22 NMS, SAS, Minute book, 1827–40, 32.

23 Mitchell's report is recorded in NMS, SAS, Minute book, 1840–53, 131, 134.

24 Klindt-Jensen, *A History of Scandinavian Archaeology,* 71.

25 NMS, SAS, Communications, vol. 8, 3 November 1846.

26 Royal Irish Academy, *Proceedings* 3 (1845–7): 310–15.

27 There is some disagreement about the extent to which Wilson was responsible for the reorganization of the SAS museum. It has been argued by R.B.K. Stevenson that he was presented with a half-finished job when he took over work on the collection; see Stevenson, 'The Museum, Its Beginnings and Its Development.'

28 Wilson, *Reminiscences* (1878), 2: 140.

29 See Stocking, 'From Chronology to Ethnology,' lxxxvi.

30 See Ash, *The Strange Death of Scottish History,* 119–23, 129–32.

31 Wilson, *Reminiscences* (1878), 2: 147.

32 In 1849 C. Roach Smith sent Wilson a parcel of books by 'my friend M. Boucher de Perthes to whom I mentioned your Society' (NMS, SAS, Correspondence, vol. 8, 18 April 1849). Boucher de Perthes continued to send the society his publications throughout the 1850s.

33 UTA, B65-0014/004(01), 39 (3 May 1877).

34 See Stocking, 'From Chronology to Ethnology,' lxxvii.

35 Wilson considerably modified his use of 'instinct' in the revised and enlarged third edition of *Prehistoric Man,* which appeared in 1876.

36 Munch, *Lærde Brev,* 1: 395.

37 This identification has been questioned by more recent scholars, such as J.S. Clouston in *A History of Orkney* (1932), 24n, and Alexander Burt Taylor, editor of *The Orkneyinga Saga* (1938), 146, 356n4.

38 NMS, SAS, Minute book, 1840–53, 331; *PAS1,* 245–7.

39 EUL, Special Collections, La.IV.17, no. 5, Wilson to David Laing, 8 September 1855.

Prehistoric Man and Daniel Wilson's Later Canadian Ethnology

BRUCE G. TRIGGER

In later life Daniel Wilson must often have wondered how his career as an archaeologist would have developed had he remained in Scotland. Like many other Scots before and after, he arrived in Toronto in 1853 driven by hopes of economic advancement and planning to return to his native land as soon as possible. Yet, since he had failed to obtain an academic post in Scotland, it must have come as a relief when the Canadian government appointed him professor of history and English literature at University College. He was luckier than the young T.H. Huxley, who had just been turned down for the chair of natural history at Toronto in favour of William Hincks, the brother of the Canadian premier. Many of Wilson's Scottish friends feared that he would not be able to pursue his prehistorical studies in the New World.[1] Although he expressed the desire to become a Canadian antiquary, there were no substantial collections in Canada for him to study, and the Natives, who had continued to live in the 'Stone Age,' were not suitable subjects for applying the Scandinavian three-age scheme.

Yet, as Marinell Ash's essay has suggested, Wilson's Scottish research had already aroused his interest in a variety of general anthropological issues. Moveover, in *The Archæology and Prehistoric Annals of Scotland* he had discussed the prehistoric cultures of the Mississippi valley, Mexico, and Central America, his curiosity about them having been stimulated by artefacts in the collections of the Society of Antiquaries of Scotland. He appreciated the value that a broader anthropological approach to the New World might have for understanding European prehistory (*PM*1, 1: 1–4). For him, the European settlers who were pushing back the forests constituted a society that in many ways resembled that of northern

Europe in the Dark Ages, while contact with Natives familiarized him 'with a condition of social life realizing in the living present nearly all that I had conceived of in studying the chroniclings of Britain's prehistoric centuries' (*PAS2*, 1: xv). In the European colonization of the New World Wilson also saw an unparalleled opportunity to study the interaction of peoples from Europe and Africa with new environments and the processes by which different cultures came into contact with each other under widely varying circumstances. He believed that a study of contemporary changes in the New World would result in a more general understanding of the nature of cultural contact, racial mixing, and adaptation to environment. He later observed that through the study of such issues 'some difficult problems of ethnology have been simplified to my own mind; and opinions relative to Europe's prehistoric races, based on inference and induction, have received striking confirmation' (*PM3*, 1: 5).

Over the next eight years Wilson would use his summer vacations and other time free from teaching and administrative duties to carry out a massive research project that would culminate in 1862 in the publication of *Prehistoric Man: Researches into the Origin of Civilisation in the Old and the New World*, one of the most important works of anthropological synthesis produced in the nineteenth century. No doubt he was partly motivated by the hope that a second major publication would help him secure an academic or museum appointment in Scotland. His brother George, who by now was Regius Professor of Technology at the University of Edinburgh and director of the Industrial Museum of Scotland, continued to hope that Daniel might one day return to Edinburgh as a professor of archaeology.[2] The urgency of this task may also explain why Daniel Wilson decided largely to synthesize existing data rather than to try to collect substantial amounts of new material.

The questions about human history that intrigued Wilson were similar to those that already had been addressed by English ethnologists such as J.C. Prichard.[3] Yet Wilson's approach to answering these questions was grounded in his general familiarity with the literary and intellectual culture of the Edinburgh of his youth. Scottish culture remained broadly humanistic and philosophical, regarding the general as more important than the particular and the whole as more than the sum of its parts.[4] While the English intellectual establishment, in an effort to defend traditional social values against French revolutionary ones, espoused Newton's reluctance to enquire into 'ancient causes,' Scottish intellectuals continued to ponder how social institutions had evolved and where they might be headed. These interests were in turn grounded in the philosophy of the French Enlightenment, which had become deeply rooted in Scotland in the eighteenth century. Both in France and in Scotland the ameliorationist principles of the Enlightenment corresponded with the aspirations of the rising middle class, and in Scotland they appealed especially to landed advocates, university teachers, the moderate clergy, and literary men.[5]

Enlightenment philosophy was dominated by the belief that cultural progress typified human history. In agreement with official Christian doctrine, it was accepted that all groups of human beings shared a common origin, as a result of which they had a similar nature and were equally capable of benefiting from intellectual progress. Human groups in different parts of the world were believed able to develop along generally similar lines independently of one another, although it was recognized that knowledge could also spread from more-developed nations to their less-advanced neighbours. Progress might be retarded by unfavourable environmental settings; but where it occurred, it resulted in improved social and political institutions, ethical standards, and intellectual life, as well as in a more-evolved technology.

The main force bringing about cultural evolution was believed to be rational thought. This not only enabled human beings to control nature more effectively, but also perfected human nature by eliminating ignorance, superstitions, and antisocial violence. The Enlightenment was the first philosophy in modern times to ascribe to human beings the power to control their own destiny. It was also based on a belief in the decency and good sense, rather than in the sinfulness, of human beings.[6]

The Enlightenment philosophers of the eighteenth century lacked archaeological evidence to support their theories. Yet they believed that, if all human societies had developed from simple to complex along essentially similar lines, it should be possible, by arranging existing societies from around the world in the same order, to illustrate the general stages through which western European nations had evolved. This procedure had been adumbrated as early as 1689 in John Locke's claim that 'in the beginning all the World was America.'[7] In 1777 the Scottish historian William Robertson had applied these ideas in his *History of America*, where he argued that, despite the absence of sustained contact between the eastern and western hemispheres prior to 1492, human societies in both parts of the world had evolved from 'savagery' to 'civilization.' He emphasized, however, that the Native American civilizations had not achieved the same high levels of development as had those of the Old World before being destroyed by European conquest. Like other Enlightenment philosophers, Robertson attributed the slower and more limited cultural development of the New World to what he regarded as its inferior natural environment.[8] By emphasizing the developments that produced irreversible social and intellectual changes, this sort of 'conjectural history' helped to lay the basis for the development both of social, as opposed to dynastic, history and of ethnology.[9]

Wilson was also deeply influenced by the Common Sense philosophy of Thomas Reid and his followers. These Scottish thinkers sought to make good the limitations of pure reason as an explanation of human behaviour by demonstrating that all human customs and social relations were grounded in specific aspects of human nature. In opposition to John Locke's idea that the human mind is simply a tabula rasa on which sensations are recorded, they argued that human beings are born with innate moral and intellectual faculties, comparable to those of seeing and hearing. These faculties included capacities for making moral and aesthetic judgments. Such judgments were thought to resemble language, which was grounded in an innate capacity that permitted speech but did not determine the specific form of any particular language. Yet the universality of such faculties suggested that all humans would tend to judge matters in a similar fashion; this view provided an explanation for the parallelisms noted in cultural development.[10] Wilson had considered these issues in his pamphlet titled *Reason and Instinct*, published in 1846.

In Toronto a number of prominent people were interested in Canadian prehistoric archaeology and the customs, languages, and lore of living Natives. These included the engineer Sandford Fleming, the painter Paul Kane, the explorer Henry Youle Hind, Captain John Henry Lefroy of the Royal Engineers, and the financier and collector George William Allan. With their support, Wilson expanded the scope of the *Canadian Journal*, the magazine of the recently founded Canadian Institute, to include regular items on archaeology and ethnology.[11] He also participated in the exploration of various Native sites in what is now southern Ontario, although he did not produce any detailed accounts of this work. He did, however, have some Native copper artefacts found near Brockville scientifically examined in order to dispel the widespread belief that such implements had been artificially hardened (*PM1*, 1: 260–2). He and his brother George, with help from Sir George Simpson, initiated a scheme for Scots employed by the Hudson's Bay Company to collect artefacts for the Industrial Museum of Scotland. Between 1858 and 1863 almost three hundred Native artefacts from the subarctic and a large number of Inuit ones made their way to Edinburgh.[12]

As Ash has mentioned in the preceding essay, Wilson in 1855 made a 'summer ramble' to the west end of Lake Superior. There he examined prehistoric copper mines along the south shore of the lake, visited prosperous, racially mixed communities, and briefly encountered a few Native bands (*PM*1, 1: xiii). The following summer he journeyed to the Ohio valley to view the prehistoric earthworks for which that part of the United States was famous. Over the years he also visited various Native communities in southern Ontario, and in 1858 he travelled down the St Lawrence River past Quebec City. He was disconcerted to find that, because of what he viewed as their superstitious fears, most Natives were reluctant to have their heads measured (2: 259). With the support of Sir Edmund Walker Head, governor of the Province of Canada, he distributed a questionnaire to Indian agents and missionaries enquiring into the effects of racial mixture (1: xv–xvi).

The most serious problem that Wilson faced was the nearly total lack of research facilities in Toronto. Most of his research for *Prehistoric Man* was carried out in the course of visits to libraries, public museums, and private collections in Washington, Philadelphia, New York, Boston, and Albany. He examined many archaeological and ethnological collections and measured human skulls gathered from various parts of the Americas. He noted with surprise and gratitude the willingness with which American institutions and individuals put their collections at the disposal of visitors (*PM*1, 1: xiv). He also had opportunities to discover and read many books that were not available in Toronto.

In the United States, anthropology was largely identified with the study of the Amerindian. Its four branches, although variously named, were ethnology, which sought to record the rapidly disappearing traditional cultures of the Natives; anthropological linguistics, which investigated their languages; physical anthropology, which studied their physical types; and archaeology, which examined their prehistoric remains. These four branches had begun to constitute a single discipline in the 1840s, as an interest in amassing and classifying information about Native languages and cultures, which had begun in the eighteenth century, became linked with a growing curiosity about prehistoric archaeology and a physical anthropology that sought to account for human behaviour in biological terms.[13] By the 1850s substantial amounts of data had accumulated in each of these subfields, including that found in such distinguished works as Lewis Henry Morgan's *League of the Iroquois*, published in 1851.

In the late eighteenth and early nineteenth centuries the nascent American anthropology had been shaped by Enlightenment concepts similar to those with which Wilson was familiar. This influence was especially apparent in the writings of Albert Gallatin.[14] But by the mid-nineteenth century these views had given way to more racist explanations of human behaviour under the influence of polygenists such as Samuel G. Morton, J.C. Nott, and George R. Gliddon. They maintained that each of the major human races had been created separately and differed radically not only in appearance but also intellectually and emotionally. This theory was used to oppose the emancipation of Blacks and to provide a scientific gloss for the widespread conviction (despite much evidence to the contrary) that Amerindians were incapable of adopting a European style of life.[15]

Wilson, who, as we have seen, had grown up in a family that vehemently opposed slavery, had been shocked in 1853 to encounter educated people in Philadelphia who denied that Africans and Europeans were derived from the same stock.[16] For the rest of his life, he was more often critical than approving of the contemporary 'native school of American ethnologists,' whom he judged to be racist in their views of Amerindians and Blacks. Because of this antipathy, while Wilson corresponded with Morgan and other American anthropologists, he never developed close personal ties with them. At the same time, he was cut off by distance from direct contacts with British anthropologists. He could keep abreast of what was happening in England and Scotland only through books and occasional visits. Wilson's anthropology thus developed in considerable isolation. He was keenly aware of 'the clearly marked line which the broad Atlantic has drawn between those early years and later Canadian experiences.'[17]

In the late 1850s Wilson published various papers on specialized topics, such as Native use of tobacco and craniometry. Yet the prospectus of a series of lectures titled 'Primitive Sources of Historical Truth' that he gave to the Mechanics' Institute of Toronto late in 1856 indicates that the broad outlines of *Prehistoric Man* were already clear by then.[18] The following year he began a course in 'Ancient and Modern Ethnology' at University College that he was to teach annually for the rest of his life. This may have been the first university course dealing exclusively with anthropology taught anywhere in the world.[19] The first edition of *Prehistoric Man* was in the hands of his British publisher by January 1861, but it did not appear until a year later (*PM*1, 1: xvi).

In *Prehistoric Man*, Wilson sought to use new data to reconsider the comparisons that William Robertson had drawn between the development of human societies in the Old and New Worlds in an effort to gain a deeper understanding of the essential characteristics of human beings. *Prehistoric Man* was the first comprehensive anthropological synthesis of New World data viewed from a global perspective to be published in the nineteenth century. Like Robertson, Wilson assumed that there had been little, if any, direct contact between the Old and New Worlds after the original settlement of the Americas. Hence the parallel development of cultures in the two hemispheres resulted from common human instincts. These parallels extended to items as detailed as the Middle Woodland (c. 500 BC – AD 500) Native pottery unearthed in what is now Ontario, about which Wilson wrote to a Scottish friend in 1855 that if it were 'mixed with what you find in Scottish barrows, it would puzzle you to say which was American and which Scottish.'[20] He argued that, in addition to reason and moral sense, human instincts included specific propensities for religion, language, toolmaking, the construction of buildings, art, the use of fire, and even boat-building. Thus every human being possessed the rudimentary drives and abilities that could be used to construct increasingly more elaborate cultures.

Prehistoric Man was shaped to a large degree by Wilson's opposition to polygenism. On both religious and philosophical grounds, he believed that all human beings were descended from a single pair of ancestors and that differences in skin colour and other physical traits had arisen more recently as relatively minor, and reversible, adaptations to environmental differences. In the following essay Bennett McCardle discusses in detail how he set out to refute Morton's claim, promoted by Nott and Gliddon, that the Amerindians represented a uniform and separately created species. He did this by demonstrating craniometrically that, contrary to Morton, there was considerable variation both between and within American Native populations.

Wilson believed that the ancestors of the Amerindians consisted of varied ethnic groups that had reached the New World by travelling in boats across both the Pacific and the Atlantic oceans, as well as on foot across the frozen Bering Strait. In postulating transoceanic migrations, he was following Alexander Bradford, who in 1841 had derived the high civilizations of Mexico and Central America from southern Asia by way of Polynesia, as well as still earlier ideas of the quixotic American polymath Constantine Rafinesque.[21] Wilson believed, however, that the first arrivals were few in number, had failed to bring any domesticated plants and animals with them, and as a result of this and their subsequent dispersal across an uninhabited continent, had soon lost whatever skills they initially possessed. Hence they had had to start again at a primitive level and slowly create the civilizations of the New World in isolation from those of the Old. Ironically, despite Wilson's belief in transoceanic voyages in early times, his Enlightenment desire to view the New World as a laboratory for the study of independent development motivated him to maintain that, after the initial arrival of various groups of human beings, the Americas had remained isolated from outside influences. He spent considerable time refuting the many claims being advanced in the mid-nineteenth century in support of Hebrew and Phoenician visits to the New World and of Norse penetrations deep into North America (*PM*1, 2: 155–98). Wilson had a rare talent for detecting fakes and rejecting fantastic notions, as a result of which these chapters are still regarded as being among the best in his book.

Influenced by William Robertson and by the New York State writer Robert A. Wilson, who in 1859 had published *A New History of the Conquest of Mexico*, in which the Aztecs were treated as a simple tribal people, Daniel Wilson concluded that William Prescott and other historians had grossly exaggerated the cultural achievements of the Incas and the Aztecs. Yet he decided that these peoples had reached the same cultural level as had the earliest civilizations of the Old World and that, if there had been more time for them to develop, they might have equalled or excelled the achievements of western Europeans (*PM*1, 1: 423). He maintained that civilizations initially developed in mild climates and, for reasons that are still acceptable today, judged the Mayas of Central America to have created not only one of the oldest, but also the most advanced, aboriginal civilizations in the New World. He pinpointed Peru as a centre for the development of metallurgy, but rightly surmised that neither the Aztec nor the Inca civilization was a particularly old one.

Wilson argued that, because of the easy conditions under which tropical civilizations developed, they tended towards despotism, pomp, and 'sensuous display' rather than seeking to promote the mental and moral progress of the majority of their citizens (*PM*1, 2: 63–4). More-progressive civilizations developed only later and in harsher climates, and so far had come into existence only in the Old World. He suggested that the mound builders of the Ohio and Mississippi valleys probably had made some progress in that direction before they had perished and that, if they had been left to evolve longer, peoples such as the Micmacs and Iroquois might have become the French and English of the New World (2: 86–7). These ideas were strongly influenced by the British historian Henry Buckle's eulogy of the beneficial effects of colder climates, in the first volume of his *History of Civilization in England* (1857). The idea of the propitiousness of northern climates for cultural and moral development was to play a major role in nationalistic thinking in Canada in the late nineteenth century.[22]

Daniel Wilson denied the popular belief that degeneration constituted the overall pattern of human history, but he accepted it as something that happened not infrequently to individual peoples. Like many earlier believers in Enlightenment philosophy, including Antoine-Ives Gouget, Lord Kames, and John Millar, he squared a belief in cultural evolution with the biblical account of early human history by maintaining that, as human groups had moved away from the Middle East, they had lost their knowledge of metallurgy, agriculture, and many intellectual refinements, which they had to reinvent in the course of later cultural development.[23] For Wilson, the Stone Age was not simply an early and primitive stage in cultural development but a base level to which human societies from time to time declined and from which they then had to reascend (*PM*1, 1: 144, 183). This concept is very similar to the cultural history of the New World that the Spanish Jesuit José de Acosta had outlined in 1589 in his *Historia natural y moral de las Indias*.[24] Because Wilson saw the earliest newcomers to the New World falling to this level, degenerationism played a more prominent role in *Prehistoric Man* than it had done in *The Archæology and Prehistoric Annals of Scotland* (*PM*1, 1: 92–3).

In accordance with Enlightenment beliefs, Wilson maintained that human nature was God-given and could not be permanently altered by the influences of the natural environment or by changing levels of cultural development. Yet the extent to which powers inherent in human beings were realized could be enhanced by cultivation or diminished by abuse. He allowed that both intellectual development and brain function might be influenced for better or worse by factors such as climate, social class, diet, education, and state of health. Since the potential that was inherent in human nature was most completely realized in a civilized society, an adult European could soon learn to hunt better than a North American Native who had hunted all his life (*PM*1, 2: 411, 434). Civilizations provided an opportunity for developing the potential of human nature to its fullest, just as growing up made possible the realization of the potential inherent in an individual.

Wilson did not confuse inherent ability with cultural development. He pointed out that under propitious circumstances Anglo-Saxons, Hungarians, and Arabs had evolved from barbarism to civilization in only a few generations. He further argued that ferocity and aggressiveness probably did more to facilitate such progress than docility would have done. He observed that European scholars often interpreted the most savage customs of their ancestors as evidence of 'primitive vigour' (*PM*1, 1: 10). On these grounds, he denied that the practice of cannibalism or human sacrifice indicated any lack of potential for nineteenth-century tribal peoples to become civilized (1: 209, 301). Wilson believed, as did all nineteenth-century cultural evolutionists, that cultural progress quickened as human beings acquired more leisure to use their intellects to devise ways in which to control nature more effectively. He also cautioned that hunter-gatherers appeared unintellectual only because so much of their time had to be spent trying to stay alive.

When peoples at radically different levels of development encounter one another, Wilson observed, the result was frequently the rapid degeneration and collapse of the less-evolved society and the integration of its surviving members into the more advanced one (*PM*1, 1: 229; 2: 333–63). He believed that this process of contact and of cultural and biological mixing was one of the most important ways in which cultural progress comes about. Wilson has been accused of failing to distinguish clearly between the biological and cultural factors involved in these processes. Yet he realized more fully than most anthropologists of his time that it was necessary to deal separately with race, language, and culture. He maintained that the conditions which were destroying North American Native societies would have killed off any European group that found itself in a similar situation (2: 388).

Wilson viewed all human races as temporary and believed that new races came into existence as a result of interbreeding among existing ones (*PM*1, 2: 418–20). He looked forward to the creation of a new North American people, in whom the 'blood' and cultural achievements of Natives and Blacks, as well as Europeans, would be represented. As evidence of what Afro-Americans had already accomplished, he pointed out that, even though they had been deprived of education and treated like domestic animals, former slaves had established a modern nation state in Haiti (2: 413). Wilson also insisted on the normality, and probable superiority, of 'half breeds' such as the Métis of western Canada and maintained that interbreeding between Natives and Europeans had gone on in eastern North America to a much greater extent than was generally acknowledged (2: 340–54). As he reminded readers, it was agreed that, in the course of British history, progress had resulted from new peoples invading Britain and mingling with its previous inhabitants. In his opinion, only the most 'primitive' peoples remained sufficiently isolated to stay 'pure-blooded,' and this isolation largely accounted for their retarded cultural development (2: 451).

These views have been condemned in recent years as constituting a justification for the expropriation of aboriginal lands by the Canadian government,[25] although only two minor treaties involving cessions of Native lands were concluded between 1850 and 1871. It is true that in *Prehistoric Man* Wilson greatly exaggerated the amount of warfare among aboriginal groups prior to the arrival of the Europeans, ignored the oppression of Natives by European settlers, and exaggerated the tolerance of Euro-American society towards intermarriage with aboriginals. It was also contrary to fact for him to suggest that the barrier between Natives and European colonists was one that most Natives had themselves erected as a result of their desire to resist change (*PM*1, 2: 327–8). Yet Wilson repeatedly stressed the need to treat Natives without prejudice and provide them with employment if amalgamation were to proceed (2: 434). He also tried to secure justice for specific aboriginal groups, especially those who he believed were trying to adapt to modern conditions. His concern with adaptation may explain why he was so much more interested in acculturated Natives and 'half breeds' than in those who continued to live in a traditional fashion.[26] Like other anthropologists of that period, Wilson did not realize to what a great extent the demoralization of Native people and their subordination to Euro-Canadian control resulted from massive population declines brought about by epidemics of various European diseases against which Natives had no immunity, as well as from losses of vital resources.[27]

If Daniel Wilson is to be judged fairly, it must be by the standards of his own time, not our own. In the mid-nineteenth century most American anthropologists and historians viewed Amerindians as being biologically inferior to Europeans and unable to adopt a European style of life even if they wished to. Hence they believed the Native peoples to be doomed to extinction as European settlement spread across North America.[28] This view was already prevalent in the United States by the late eighteenth century, and polygenism – and later, Darwinism – merely provided it with apparent scientific legitimacy.[29] Reserves were viewed as places where Natives could live until most of them had died out and those who survived had integrated as best they could into the lower echelons of Euro-Canadian society. Wilson's vision was more generous. His goal in advocating biological and cultural assimilation was that of the Enlightenment: to enhance the potential for personal development that was present in all human beings. It was for this reason that he opposed keeping Natives on reserves and under Euro-Canadian tutelage, just as he opposed separate schools for Native and Black children (*PM*3, 2: 325). He did not doubt, however, that many individual Native people would fail to make this transition.

Wilson continued to adhere to a biblical chronology, as he had done in *The Archæology and Prehistoric Annals of Scotland*. He maintained that human beings had existed for only a few thousand years, although he accepted geological evidence which suggested that the world was much older. Although he was aware of the important Palaeolithic finds that had been made in France and southern England in the late 1850s, he ignored the challenge that the geological context of these finds offered to a biblical chronology (*PM1*, 1: 49–52; 2: 475). Wilson also rejected a Darwinian view of human origins. While he praised Darwin's scholarship and welcomed his detailed studies of variations within animal species as contradicting polygenism, he refused on the basis of existing evidence to accept the idea of biological evolution, especially as it applied to human beings.[30] He continued to maintain that basic human nature was fixed, rather than evolving over time, even though he believed that it could be perfected by increasing knowledge or lapse, as a result of moral failures, into savagery (2: 410–11). He accepted an Enlightenment scheme of cultural evolution that ran from hunting and gathering societies through pastoralism and agriculture to civilization, but he was unwilling to abandon a creationist view of human biological origins, even though his friend, the publisher Robert Chambers, had already provided the concept of biological evolution with a certain degree of respectability by portraying it as governed by divinely ordained laws in his anonymously published *Vestiges of the Natural History of Creation* (1844).[31] Yet despite these views, in his discussions of evolution, Wilson insisted that Darwin's theories deserved further investigation, maintained that scientific questions could only receive scientific answers, and condemned all theological constraints on scientific debate (2: 456).

His refusal to embrace Darwinian evolutionism made *Prehistoric Man* appear conservative and even old-fashioned by comparison with the Darwinian-inspired anthropology that was initially expressed in John Lubbock's *Pre-historic Times* (1865). This new anthropology was based on the belief that human intelligence and human nature, no less than the human body, had slowly evolved from an ape-like prototype. There was also no place for the vestiges of degeneration theories that had featured prominently in Wilson's book. Throughout his life, Wilson would remain convinced that an unbridgeable gap separated human beings, both morally and intellectually, from all other animals. He believed that the chief distinguishing feature of human behaviour was an 'inner world of thought,' by means of which human beings alone were 'capable of searching into the past; anticipating the future' (*PM2*, 121). Such thought was essential for humans to reason and make moral judgments. Archaeologists and anthropologists who accepted Darwin's views were dedicated to eliminating this gap.

Lubbock reviewed *Prehistoric Man* in the *Natural History Review* of January 1863. He concluded that Wilson's book was 'very readable, and may be recommended as an introduction to more special works on Archaeology.'[32] In particular, he commended Wilson's treatment of aboriginal tobacco use, the Scandinavian discovery of North America, and Amerindian physical anthropology. But he objected to the distinction that Wilson drew between the 'instincts of the inferior orders of creation' and the 'devices of man'[33] and to his belief that 'the date of our creation has been revealed to us [in the Bible].' More generally, Lubbock protested what he interpreted as Wilson's attempt 'to fix a stigma of irreligion on the theory of Natural Selection.' Taking unfair advantage of Wilson's open-mindedness, he expressed astonishment that someone who believed the biblical account of human creation 'should still regard the Age of Man as a fit subject for "Guesses."'[34]

Later, following a visit to Europe in 1864, in the course of which Wilson was able to examine several large collections of Palaeolithic artefacts in France and England, he accepted the great antiquity of human origins and the likelihood that the human body had evolved from that of an ape-like higher primate (*PM2*, 27; *PM3*, 1: 21–63). He also removed all references to a biblical chronology and many allusions to cultural degeneration from the third edition of *Prehistoric Man* (1876). As a result, that edition looked more like a standard work of Darwinian-inspired cultural evolution than the first one had. Wilson still relied, however, on biblical genealogies as a source of information about early racial and ethnic history.

He also continued to object to the Darwinian assumption that human beings were little different from apes. He insisted that the transformation from ape to human had been an instantaneous one, in which a soul had been infused into an animal body. His description of this process left open the question of whether he viewed this as a natural or supernatural event. Wilson also maintained that there had to be, not one missing link, but a long series between the bodies of apes and humans and that what (still using degenerationist terminology) he continued to call 'degraded' Australian Aborigines and Andaman Islanders did not suffice to fill that gap.[35] His was clearly a belated and much qualified acceptance of an evolutionary explanation of human origin, closely resembling that held more recently by many Roman Catholic scholars.[36] In matters relating to biological evolution and the origins of culture, Wilson was, from 1859 on, a follower, not a leader. Because of his cautious attitude towards biological evolution, he seems to have been widely read by liberal Christians who were troubled by Darwinian evolution but were willing to consider new ideas. Lubbock and others who accepted Darwin's ideas believed that, by adopting this position, Wilson had forfeited his place on the cutting edge of the scientific thought of his day.

His position was not arrived at without careful thought, and in retrospect his caution seems to have been largely justified from an intellectual point of view. Darwin's belief in slow, incremental changes in the natural world challenged him and his followers to provide evidence of an easy transition between apes and humans. Lacking all but the most rudimentary fossil evidence, they attempted to do so by arguing, among other things, that the difference in cranial capacity between the most-advanced apes and the least-evolved humans was less than between the largest and smallest brained human beings. Lubbock sought to demonstrate that modern human societies ran the gamut from nearly bestial hunter-gatherers to civilized communities. He pictured primitive peoples as invariably few in number, unintelligent, dirty, unable to control their emotions or to follow a fixed course of action, and addicted to abusing wives, children, and weaker individuals, murdering aged parents, eating human flesh, and offering human sacrifices.[37] These differences were attributed to the operation of natural selection, which, it was believed, had made Europeans biologically superior to all other human groups. Lubbock treated cultural evolution as a process that was irreversible as well as biologically grounded.

Alfred Wallace, the co-discoverer of the theory of natural selection, was, like Wilson, unable to accept Darwin's claim that primitive peoples were biologically, as well as culturally, inferior to Europeans. Four years' work in the tropical forests of South America and another eight in the Malay archipelago had brought him into close contact with Native peoples and convinced him that they had the same emotions and powers of reasoning as did civilized human beings. In 1855 he wrote, 'The more I see of uncivilized people, the better I think of human nature and the essential differences between civilized and savage men seem to disappear.'[38] Likewise, all the information that Wilson collected about the behaviour of peoples of African, European, and Amerindian origin in the New World appeared to confirm his belief in the essential similarity of human nature and human abilities.

No one realized in the late nineteenth century how long human evolution had taken and hence how wide was the gap between all living apes and humans. It is now accepted that what human beings are today, both intellectually and emotionally, has been shaped by natural selection operating for millions of years on scavengers and hunter-gatherers who lived together in small groups. Hence it is no surprise that the biological basis of all human behaviour is very similar, even if peoples in various parts of the world have come to look different as a result of natural selection adapting them to dissimilar natural environments.[39] Both Wilson and Wallace recognized this behavioural similarity and rejected a Darwinian explanation for the origin of human intelligence and morality. Darwin, in his effort to make an evolutionary origin for human beings seem plausible, maintained that peoples with less-complex cultures were biologically inferior to civilized ones and hence could be used to narrow the gap between apes and humans.

The arguments of Darwin and his followers, although positing a single origin for humanity, lent credibility to the polygenist contention that human races were significantly different from one another behaviourally by replacing polygenism's discredited concept of multiple creations with an explanation of differentiation based on natural selection. These ideas influenced the thinking of many late-nineteenth-century anthropologists, including Augustus Pitt Rivers and Lewis Henry Morgan. Even Edward B. Tylor, who had initially believed in the uniformity of human nature, embraced a racial explanation of cultural differences.[40] Darwinian-inspired anthropology was based on a highly selective reading of the ethnographic evidence available at that time, one that ignored the judgment and creativity of hunter-gatherers and unduly stressed their violence and brutality.

Wilson, guided by his religious beliefs and by the Enlightenment and Common Sense ideals of his youth, interpreted evidence about human behaviour in a way that is more in accord with modern thinking than are the racist views of Darwin and Lubbock. Yet racist thinking, rationalized within the framework of natural selection, was to pervade scientific thought in western Europe and North America from the 1860s until the 1940s.[41] Hence, in historical terms, Wilson's ideas must be regarded as being, not ahead of his time, but behind it.[42] Yet, while he failed to appreciate the full explanatory potential of an evolutionary view of human origins, his old-fashioned beliefs allowed him to ascribe enduring meaning to much that he observed, while Darwinian evolutionists were led by their very different perspective to ignore or misinterpret the same evidence.

In 1863 Wilson published a revised *Prehistoric Annals of Scotland*, into which many parallels with New World data were incorporated. After that time he continued to teach anthropology, and in 1882 he was officially appointed professor of history and ethnology at the University of Toronto. Yet, while anthropology may have remained 'his favourite study,'[43] the pace of his anthropological research and publications slackened. In 1861 his bid to become professor of history at the University of St Andrews failed, as two years later did an attempt to be appointed professor of English literature at the University of Edinburgh. Gradually he and his wife, Margaret, became reconciled to remaining in Canada, and problems of college and university administration increasingly occupied his time. He also began to publish more in the field of English literature, including his biography of Chatterton (1869), which he once described as his favourite book,[44] and *Caliban* (1873), a quasi-anthropological study of fantastic creatures in the works of Shakespeare. (For a fuller discussion of his work in English literature, see the essay by Heather Murray later in this volume.)

Nevertheless, Wilson continued to pursue anthropological research. In 1871 he produced the first of a series of studies of right- and left-handedness that laid the basis for his book *The Right Hand: Left-Handedness* (1891; see also McCardle's essay). Beginning in 1872, he wrote a series of articles on Indian policy, and two years later revisited the Ohio mound country in preparation for a third, much revised edition of *Prehistoric Man* (1876). In 1882 he published the first of a series of six major articles in the *Proceedings and Transactions* of the newly founded Royal Society of Canada. Together with two papers on physical anthropology, they constituted his quixotically titled book *The Lost Atlantis and Other Ethnographic Studies*, which was published the year he died.

These elegant essays were largely reflections on Wilson's earlier work and together covered the full range of his anthropological interests. He restated his belief in the indigenous nature of cultural development in the New World prior to 1492, a development that was little affected even by genuine contacts with the Norse. An article on aboriginal trade argued that a division of labour beyond that of the household had evolved at an early stage in human development. Other essays dealt with the aesthetic faculties of aboriginal peoples, changes in Native cultures in prehistoric times and after European contact, the social and biological benefits of racial mixture, and how brain weight does not correlate with ability among modern humans. Yet in his chapter on the Hurons, whom he presented as a 'typical race of American aborigines,' archaeological data were scarce and used only to illustrate historical and ethnographic sources. Despite his former pre-eminence as an archaeologist, Wilson did not excel other American anthropologists of this period in his use of archaeological data to understand Amerindian cultures and history. While *The Lost Atlantis* contained less original material than Wilson's earlier works, it reaffirmed his belief in the unity of humanity, in the possession by all peoples of the same basic abilities, and in the capacity of all peoples to attain the highest possible level of development. His essays are not blemished by the tendency of many of his contemporaries to try to explain cultural and linguistic differences in terms of racial variations.

Yet in his later years, even in Ontario, Wilson was being surpassed as an anthropologist by two more committed scholars. The systematic study of Ontario archaeology was begun by David Boyle, a Scottish teacher and bookstore owner who in 1884 became the archaeological curator of the Canadian Institute museum, incorporated into the Ontario Provincial Museum in 1897. During a career that lasted until his death in 1911, Boyle amassed a collection of 32,000 Native artefacts from across the province, and beginning in 1887, he edited the *Annual Archaeological Report* for Ontario, which was the first Canadian anthropological journal. He established a close working relationship with professional archaeologists at the Smithsonian Institution in Washington, DC, and trained a small group of amateur archaeologists to carry out fieldwork across Ontario. Yet, although Boyle lived in Toronto and must have been influenced by Wilson's books and public lectures, there is no evidence of significant interaction between them.[45]

In ethnological research Wilson was similarly outstripped by Horatio Hale. Born in New Hampshire in 1817 and educated at Harvard University, Hale had done important linguistic and ethnographical research in Oregon and Polynesia between 1838 and 1842 as a member of the United States Exploring Expedition under the command of Captain Charles Wilkes. In 1856 he had moved to Clinton, Canada West, where his energies were long absorbed by a successful law practice. Then in the late 1860s he began to study the languages and traditions of the Six Nations Iroquois reserve near Brantford. This research culminated in 1883 in the publication of *The Iroquois Book of Rites*, the major scholarly achievement of his career. A product of the long-extinguished American Enlightenment, Hale saw in the oral traditions of the Iroquois evidence of noble feeling, political wisdom, and literary skill that long pre-dated any European influence. He maintained that, although a tribal people, they were neither intellectually nor morally inferior to any other historically recorded nation. When the young German scholar Franz Boas was hired as an ethnologist by the committee of the British Association for the Advancement of Science that had been established in 1884 to carry out research among the Natives of British Columbia, Hale rather than Wilson was appointed to supervise him, no doubt in part because of his own previous experience on the west coast.[46] Hale also exerted more of an influence than did Wilson on a younger generation of Canadian amateur anthropologists and anthropological popularizers, most notably the missionary John Maclean.[47]

Wilson is known to have inspired only one of his students to become a professional anthropologist. Alexander F. Chamberlain, who had been born in England, completed an MA at Toronto in 1889 and then attended Clark University in Worcester, Massachusetts, where, under the supervision of Boas, he earned the first PhD in anthropology in the United States. His doctoral thesis was an ethnographic study of the Mississaugas of Ontario. Following Boas's departure, Chamberlain succeeded him at Clark University, where he remained for the rest of his career. Thus even this one recruit to anthropology was lost to Canada.[48] Despite his personal eminence in the field, Wilson failed to establish a lasting tradition of anthropological research at the University of Toronto.

Prehistoric Man was one of the great anthropological syntheses of the nineteenth century and proof that Wilson was far more than the dilettante anthropologist he was often thought to have been (this was the view at the University of Toronto when I was a student there in the 1950s). Yet because he believed in the similar nature of all human beings, he opposed the racism that coloured contemporary anthropological thinking. As a result, he tended to be dismissed after 1862 as an old-fashioned scholar who had failed to appreciate the significance of Darwinism for understanding human behaviour. Today, because they support pluralism and multiculturalism, most anthropologists generally dismiss as a rationalization of colonialism Wilson's vision of a homogeneous new race and a new civilization being created in North America.[49] There is no doubt that he promoted in Canada an understanding of Native people as able to adapt to changing conditions that was very different from the racist fantasies of Francis Parkman and many American anthropologists. Whether that led the Canadian government to inflict more or less suffering upon Native people is an open question. Yet however Wilson's specific ideas may be judged, his anthropology is of lasting interest precisely because, at a time when it would have been professionally fashionable to do so outside Canada, he refused to divorce the study of humanity from the universalistic moral principles of the Enlightenment, which he correctly viewed as having become an essential element of civilized life.[50]

NOTES

Portions of this essay draw heavily on Trigger, 'Daniel Wilson and the Scottish Enlightenment,' which was based on a lecture sponsored by the Society of Antiquaries of Scotland and the Ash Trust for Scottish and North American Studies.

1 Wilson, *Reminiscences* (1878), 2: 148–9.
2 McCardle, 'The Life and Anthropological Works of Daniel Wilson,' 35, 56–7; George Wilson to Daniel Wilson, cited in Ash, 'New Frontiers,' 51.
3 Prichard, *Researches into the Physical History of Man.*
4 McKillop, *A Disciplined Intelligence*, 24–5.
5 Stocking, 'Scotland as the Model of Mankind,' 65.
6 Bryson, *Man and Society*; Meek, *Social Science and the Ignoble Savage.*
7 Quoted in Slotkin, *Readings in Early Anthropology*, 174.
8 Hoebel, 'William Robertson'; Keen, *The Aztec Image*, 275–85.
9 The term 'conjectural history' (he also called it 'theoretic history') was introduced by Dugald Stewart; see Slotkin, *Readings in Early Anthropology*, 460.
10 Stocking, 'Scotland as the Model of Mankind'; McKillop, *A Disciplined Intelligence*, 25–58.
11 Berger, 'Wilson,' 1109–10.
12 Bunyan et al., *No Ordinary Journey*, 96–7.
13 Gruber, 'Horatio Hale,' 5–9.
14 Bieder, 'Albert Gallatin,' and *Science Encounters the Indian*, 16–54.
15 Horsman, 'Scientific Racism and the American Indian,' and *Race and Manifest Destiny*; Stanton, *The Leopard's Spots.*
16 Berger, 'Wilson,' 1110.
17 Wilson, *Reminiscences* (1878), 2: 41.
18 'Course of Lectures to be Delivered in the St. Lawrence Hall, during the Winter of 1856–7' (copy in TRL).
19 McCardle, 'The Life and Anthropological Works of Daniel Wilson,' 22.
20 Wilson to David Laing, 8 September 1855; cited in Piggott and Robertson, *Three Centuries of Scottish Archaeology*, item 71.
21 Bradford, *American Antiquities*; S. Williams, *Fantastic Archaeology*, 101.
22 Berger, *The Sense of Power*, 128–52.
23 Bowler, *Theories of Human Evolution.*
24 Pagden, *The Fall of Natural Man*, 146–200.

25 McCardle, 'The Life and Anthropological Works of Daniel Wilson,' 129–31.
26 Ibid., 20–1.
27 Dobyns, 'Their Number Become Thinned'; Crosby, Ecological Imperialism; Ramenof-sky, Vectors of Death.
28 Bieder, Science Encounters the Indian, esp. 97–9.
29 Vaughan, 'From White Man to Red Skin.'
30 Wilson, 'The President's Address' (1861); McKillop, A Disciplined Intelligence, 99–110.
31 Desmond, The Politics of Evolution, 7.
32 Lubbock, Review of Prehistoric Man, 28.
33 Ibid., 27.
34 Ibid., 30.
35 Wilson, Caliban (1873), 13–38.
36 Ewing, 'Current Roman Catholic Thought on Evolution.'
37 Lubbock, Pre-historic Times (2d ed., 1869), and The Origin of Civilisation; Bowler, 'From "Savage" to "Primitive,"' 726.
38 Cited in Eiseley, Darwin's Century, 303.
39 Carrithers, Why Humans Have Cultures, 34–54.
40 Bowler, 'From "Savage" to "Primitive,"' 726.
41 Barkhan, The Retreat of Scientific Racism.
42 Trigger, Natives and Newcomers, 42; Berger, 'Wilson,' 1111.
43 Sybil Wilson in Wilson, The Lost Atlantis (1892), vi.
44 Berger, 'Wilson,' 1111.
45 Killan, David Boyle.
46 Gruber, 'Horatio Hale'; William N. Fenton, 'Hale, Horatio Emmons,' in DCB, 12: 400–3.
47 Maclean, The Indians.
48 Cole, 'The Origins of Canadian Anthropology,' 40.
49 Towards the end of his life, Wilson was aware that, as a result of racial preju-dice, this new civilization was not going to happen; see Wilson, The Lost Atlantis (1892), 336–8.
50 Dunn, Western Political Theory.

'Heart of Heart':
Daniel Wilson's Human Biology

BENNETT McCARDLE

Daniel Wilson's career spanned two of the three major phases of international social science in the nineteenth century: the pre-Darwinian period of conflict between monogenism and polygenism up to 1860 and the rise of evolutionism in biological and social theory from the 1860s to the 1890s. The third phase – the eclipse of evolutionism by historical particularism in North America from the 1890s onward – was just under way at the time of his death. As Bruce Trigger has noted in the preceding essay, however, Wilson's own approach remained rooted in a biologically oriented variety of monogenism that had prevailed in the first half of the century. Its principles included a belief in the development of all humankind from a single stock, the uniform distribution of intellectual capacities among the various races, and the tendency of all human forms to change in response to their environment.

Wilson's research was essentially synthetic in nature and dependent on an extremely wide variety of sources, many of them secondary, but it also drew on some unusual experimental material. Much of his writing on human biology was an attack on racial-determinist polygenism: the doctrine that the human races are different, fixed, and incompatible species. Nevertheless, he did accept 'race' as the basis of study, in spite of its known shortcomings as a scientific category. Like the polygenists, he maintained – in opposition to extreme Christian fundamentalism – that it was possible to apply empirical science to human phenomena. Conversely, his defence of religion and the imagination, most notably in his study *Caliban* (1873), was intended to prevent the intrusion of rationalism into the metaphysical sphere by tracing the common divine origin of both scientific and religious inspiration.

In Scotland Wilson's work had allowed him to use skeletal remains, in conjunction with artefactual and documentary evidence, to reconstruct ancient populations. Both his special preoccupation with skulls and his techniques of measurement were derived from a relatively old anthropometric tradition, beginning with the schemes of universal classification established by German physiologist and comparative anatomist Johann Friedrich Blumenbach in the 1770s and continuing through the craniological works of Louis-Jean-Marie Daubenton, Pierre Camper, and James Cowles Prichard to the more specialized studies of Samuel G. Morton and Anders Olof Retzius in the 1830s and 1840s. Wilson devoted an entire chapter of *The Archæology and Prehistoric Annals of Scotland* (1851) to the analysis of early British crania.[1] He used as one of his most concrete proofs for the existence of pre-Celtic peoples an unusual type, the 'kumbecephalic,' or boat-shaped, skull, but he also took into account the unique artefacts associated with it.

In North America, where three different 'racial' groups and their 'intermediate forms' were available for observation, Wilson's craniological interest expanded. Yet the unexpected outcome of his lifelong study was, paradoxically, to cast doubt on the relevance of head and brain dimensions to sociological study, thus invalidating his own earlier claims for craniology as the 'key' to a scientific understanding of humankind. Soon after he arrived in 1853, he found himself at the centre of a battle between two well-entrenched camps of scholars, in North America called simply 'monogenists' and 'polygenists.' In Europe their counterparts can be more broadly identified as, on the one hand, 'ethnologists' of historical-particularist leanings, who belonged to the Ethnological Society of London, and, on the other, the biologically oriented 'anthropologists' of the kind who were later members of James Hunt's Anthropological Society of London.[2] Wilson shared the ethnologists' unitarian, pro-Christian ideology, but he was also attracted by the polygenists' claim to greater scientific objectivity. Though basically a monogenist, he continued to work on questions of racial ethnology more commonly the preserve of the opposite side.[3]

In Daniel Wilson's day the most cogent spokesman for the monogenist position was the British ethnologist and psychologist J.C. Prichard, a writer to whom, as Marinell Ash has demonstrated in an earlier essay in this volume, Wilson owed a good deal in his early ethnological research. Prichard derived the underlying 'psychic unity' of humankind from the Christian doctrine of divine creation through a single human pair and supported this premise with cross-cultural examples of common physical, mental, and 'moral' features. He attributed the diversity of existing races, not to original separate creation, as the polygenists did, but to the shaping forces of the environment. To express this idea, Prichard compared human races to animal subspecies or varieties; both in his view were environmentally determined categories that were internally diverse, mutable, and capable of interbreeding across varietal lines.[4] The monogenists did hold that some races might, at any given moment, be inferior in some degree to others on a scale that led upward to the level of European civilization. They believed, however, that such states were impermanent, and any group had the potential to rise to the highest possible level of human existence.[5]

Their position was opposed by the polygenist, or 'multiple creationist,' school. This group accounted for existing differences between human beings by proposing a separate divine creation of several different types. The strength of this approach was the major weakness of the monogenists' argument – the shortness of the biblical chronology of some 6,000 years to account for the age of the earth, within which it was clearly difficult to place the diversification of one creation into many races. If ancient Egyptian frescoes, nearly as old as the world itself, depicted human beings in all the colours known in the mid-nineteenth century, and if change was now so slow as to be invisible, how – unless God had created them so – could the races have been differentiated? And if God had so ordered them, was it not both logical and a fact confirmed by observation that the human races continued to be both naturally separate and, like animal species, incapable of intermixture? Moreover, did these qualities not satisfactorily account for the continuing segregation of races in America, to the benefit of the white race? Thus one could come to the comfortable conclusion that the other races were of lesser capacities than Europeans, physically, mentally, and morally, regardless of the effects of differing environments.

The problem of chronology remained unanswerable until after 1860, when Darwin's work demonstrated that the natural diversification of species could be proved through biology, thus disposing of the simple beliefs in divine creation held by both monogenists and polygenists.[6] But the *definition* of physical differences between races, as opposed to their *origin*, was a problem that could be attacked by either side. The polygenists therefore produced evidence (often derived a priori from existing conditions and their own wishes) for the existence of distinct, homogeneous, and physically incompatible human types. This evidence they used to argue for the impossibility of mixing types or the futility of attempting to civilize or improve the condition of the inferior races. In political and ideological, as well as scientific, reaction to this position, the monogenists were forced to seek evidence for the non-uniformity of physical types and their mutability as a result of environment and physical intermixture.

Thus the first half of the nineteenth century saw the development of studies that were to be the foundation of modern physical anthropology: the systematic identification and classification of somatic features (at first only the most easily observable and quantifiable ones), together with research into their origin and effects on non-somatic capacities. The means that these researchers employed were the crude metrical techniques of anthroposcopy and anthropometry, with some excursions into the quasi-psychological practice of phrenology. Instead of the complex calibrated measurements and carefully controlled liquid or optical volumetric tools employed today, Wilson and his contemporaries used plain rulers, artists' callipers, and loose particles, such as lead shot, mustard seed, and sand, to measure the capacity of skulls. Entire articles could be, and were, devoted to such problems such as how to prevent shot from rolling out of eye sockets or how to ensure that seed was of a standard diameter so as not to invalidate the statistics on which American science's view of a race's level of civilization or a gender's intelligence depended. These methods were at the same time unstandardized enough to permit gross distortion of results for non-scientific ends and rigorous enough to be capable of yielding some objective data. Thus the early anthropometrists aspired to, though they did not always attain, a greater degree of accuracy and more-complex quantitative methods for the physical study of human beings.

Even before Daniel Wilson left Britain, he had read Samuel Morton's great craniological compendium *Crania Americana* (1839) and had discussed it, together with his British materials, in *Prehistoric Annals of Scotland*.[7] In 1852 he had been in contact with the British craniologist J. Barnard Davis, who wanted to make use of Wilson's Scandinavian colleagues to acquire skull samples and patronage for a British counterpart to Morton's American work.[8] In September the following year Wilson landed in Philadelphia on route to Toronto, and (apparently on the advice of either Davis or J. Aitken Meigs) he visited George R. Gliddon, a disciple of Morton's and, with his co-author Josiah Clark Nott, one of the most notorious proponents of the American polygenist school. Nott had recently modified his views on the homogeneity of races, and he had just published a paper whose thesis would certainly have attracted Wilson's attention. It put forward the notion that the hybridization of races –

within strict limits and among certain peoples only, according to an arcane theory of 'proximate' and distant types – produced offspring that were hardier, better adapted, and more fertile than their parent stocks. Nott also made much of the threat to honest scientific enquiry ('facts, and the laws of God as revealed in his works') posed by the doctrinaire rigidity of the 'theological naturalists,' whom he depicted as being eager to suppress freedom of thought for illegitimate and anti-scientific purposes.[9]

Both the subject matter and, to some extent, the anti-fundamentalist tone of Nott's paper appealed to Wilson, but his hackles were raised by the portrayal of Christianity and Prichard's views on human unity as 'irrational.' However, Nott and Gliddon's first major monograph, *Types of Mankind*, would not appear until 1854, and the extent of their contempt for monogenism and their manipulation of scientific data were not yet evident. Thus Wilson travelled on to Toronto convinced that racial ethnology (reduced in craniology to its biological minutiae) would provide an answer to the problem of how human types differed and what their relation to culture was. Nevertheless, he did not wish to pursue the study in the company of his Philadelphia hosts for emotional, as well as scientific, reasons. After all, he had absorbed anti-slavery views literally at his mother's knee.[10] In his journal he describes with some dismay how, when he was in Philadelphia, a Black woman had curtsied to him when he made room for her, out of common courtesy, on the sidewalk. He had not expected such behaviour in a scientific centre and was grieved 'to find that Ethnology is here made to subserve the vulgarest prejudices, and the idea that the black man is sprung from the same stock as the white is counted as ridiculous.'[11] Almost without thinking, he had joined the monogenist camp. He was to spend the rest of his career maintaining a precarious – though from his point of view, successful – accommodation between such deeply felt beliefs and the demands of science, represented first by the polygenists and later by the far more formidable Darwinians.

During his first year in Toronto, Wilson's time was taken up amassing facts about the history of the New World and discovering parallels between it and the pattern that he had uncovered for the Old World.[12] At the same time, he began to adopt Nott's idea that some types of racial mixture, even if they involved mixing 'superior' with 'inferior' groups, might contributed in some way to 'national' success.[13] This approach represented a distinct change in tone from his previous, more descriptive treatment of hybridity. Seeking a foothold in the wash of assertions flowing around the few hard rocks of data, Wilson lit upon a simple idea: skulls. After he reread Morton's work, his enthusiasm for crania as the measure of human development increased. They were, he proclaimed, the very 'heart of heart' among the relics of vanished humanity. Complex, durable, and mensurable, skulls would ultimately reveal not only the 'differing cerebral organization' of superseded races, but also their 'intellect and feelings,' even preserving 'a vivid outline of their very features and expressions.'[14] He had at last found the basis for a purely scientific answer to the frustrating riddles of prehistory, until then understood only indirectly through tools and tombs. Beyond doubt or vulgar prejudice (such as he had observed in Philadelphia), skulls would dictate the ranking of races in a uniform 'scale of civilization' according to quantitative analysis of both physical and mental traits. In an ambitious moment he proposed a plan, never fulfilled, of forming a master collection of 'Canadian' skulls to match those of Morton in the United States and Davis in Britain.[15]

It was perhaps fortunate that there were fewer political and social pressures in Canada than in the United States, or Wilson might have clung harder and longer to these naive assumptions. Fortunately, too, they did not distract him from the less-exciting duties of local archaeology. In urging other researchers to collect skulls, he was careful to recommend systematic procedures for the excavation, preservation, and recording of all aspects of burials, including orientation and associated artefacts. He cautioned researchers in Upper Canada (Ontario) to try to keep ahead of the province's spreading settlement and railway construction. These 'hints,' probably the earliest outline of archaeological method published in Canada, were clearly intended for the general public, though it is impossible to tell how widely they were distributed.[16] Other attractive problems intervened, and for several years Wilson concentrated on ethnological topics. He acquired crania and excavated burials during a few modest digging expeditions, reports of which were published in the *Canadian Journal.* These apparently constitute the earliest formal archaeological accounts ever to be published in Canada, though for several years the *Journal* had carried occasional notices of accidental finds.[17]

Meanwhile, in 1854–5 Nott and Gliddon's *Types of Mankind* had appeared. This controversial work brought together the assertions that Wilson had pondered in 1853 and, with its argument for the great age – and therefore the separate creation – of the different races, delivered a paralysing blow to monogenist theory. But the issue that caught Wilson's eye was the authors' assertion (derived from Morton) that the Amerindian race's essentially separate nature was proved by its uniform cranial shape across all populations in both North and South America, regardless of environment.[18] He saw and seized on this key argument as a weak point that he had the resources to refute. Not until further provocation was published did he act, however. The opportunity came after two more years of miscellaneous ethnological writing and desultory skull collecting. Nott and Gliddon's last major work, *Indigenous Races of the Earth*, a large anthology of polygenist essays assembled around Gliddon's stridently anti-theological tracts, appeared in 1857. It repeated the authors' earlier arguments for the existence of separate races from the beginning of humankind and for the persistence of races as homogeneous groups, even where they had migrated to different environments or had dwelt in close proximity to one another for long periods of time. Once again, Nott and Gliddon used their work to pillory the monogenists for their supposed unscientific methods.

Wilson was ready to respond. He had received early warning of the publication when Gliddon, in his usual unctuous manner, had asked for his help in getting 'celebrities' to sponsor the book.[19] Wilson assembled the results of his four years of collecting and contemplation in order to make an attack, not on doctrinal or theoretical grounds, but on the factual data that Nott and Gliddon had themselves claimed as their ultimate authority. His answer to *Indigenous Races* was characteristically inductive – and destructive. The essay, published in the *Canadian Journal* in 1857,[20] re-examined the same cranial specimens cited by Nott and Gliddon, tested and revised their measurements, and performed calculations on newer material, all to establish the very opposite of their conclusions – that the supposedly 'pure,' uniform, and immutable Amerindian racial type displayed such a great range of dimensions that, whatever 'Indians' were, they could not be called a single homogeneous group.

Wilson remarked on his opponents' failure to define the terms 'race,' 'family,' and 'species' in any consistent manner, thus preventing anyone from comparing their data with other samples or analyses. Further, he denounced the narrow focus of Nott and Gliddon's raciological studies and urged that racial ethnology be broadened to take account of cultural factors, specifically philology (what we now would call historical linguistics) and material culture. Only with this enlarged foundation of human information could firm definitions of human groups, their origins, and their boundaries be established on a 'commonly recognized scientific basis.' Nothing could be founded exclusively on somatic type and still less, he implied, on the raciologists' own irrational biases. Turning Nott and Gliddon's own words against them, he observed: 'It is facts we want at present; carefully, accurately and unprejudicedly noted facts. These, once accumulated, will fall into their order in due time, and the legitimate conclusions they point to, whatever they may be, will carry conviction to all honest seekers after truth, and will find no lack of adherents "morally brave enough to avow them.""[21] The assertion that facts would speak for themselves is, of course, untrue in the absence of an accepted theoretical structure, but it is an interesting echo of contemporary developments in European social thought.[22] Moreover, in this specific argument Wilson was seeking only to demonstrate the negative point that even within their own frame of reference, Nott and Gliddon's data did not support their conclusions. He claimed to do no more, and given the limited anthropological knowledge of his era, he perhaps could have accomplished nothing more constructive than this critique of method.

After this first attack, Wilson pursued and expanded his argument in several articles that introduced more cranial data and cited additional measurements that diverged inexplicably from Morton's and Gliddon's 'uniform racial types.'[23] He eventually forced members of the American raciological school to concede that they had not proved the existence of originally separate, uniform races,[24] although not all historians of the idea of race have given him credit for this achievement. The fact that he published his findings in an obscure Canadian intellectual journal did not help. Scientific research was rapidly advancing in the more prominent centres of learning, and by the early 1860s other scholars had duplicated Wilson's conclusions, either independently or in light of his findings. Moreover, polygenism, at least in its creationist form, became virtually a dead issue in the scholarly world after the introduction of the theory of evolution.[25] Perhaps the greatest internal defect of Wilson's work was its failure to present any alternative description of and rationale for racial types and, specifically, any proposal for the relationship, if any, of cranial variation to other distinguishing racial traits. As even his sympathetic contemporaries complained,[26] his invalidation of the homogeneous Amerindian type offered no new directions for research.

Having disposed of skull measurement to his satisfaction, Wilson shifted immediately to another craniological enthusiasm: the study of artificial skull deformation, that is, the cultural processes by which the skulls of living humans are moulded into unusual shapes, either by design or as a by-product of child-rearing customs. This subject, which may now seem a bizarre novelty, in fact provided him with another useful angle from which to attack American typological schemes. His interest in the subject had been aroused when he learned that the phenomenon, already documented in prehistoric eras in the Old World, existed in the

New, even among living peoples, but had not been recognized by scientists as a factor affecting cranial typology. Prichard and Retzius had already raised it as a topic of ethnological interest,[27] but no one had yet studied its incidence or looked systematically at its cultural context.

From original and secondary research, Wilson identified three factors affecting normal cranial form: the deliberate (artificial) moulding of infants' skulls into forms prescribed by local culture, accidental deformation caused in living persons by abnormal and persistent pressure, and posthumous stresses on skeletal remains. He amassed evidence of an unexpectedly high incidence of deliberate deformation in the Old World and speculated on the possibility of early cultural diffusion between the two continents, via the Bering Strait, as an alternative to independent invention. The evidence in this study for the plasticity of skull form – specifically, for the artificial origin of the flat occiput, one of Morton's 'typical' Amerindian traits – again helped to undermine the rigid typologies on which the doctrine of a hierarchy of immutable races was based.[28] Wilson extended this conclusion even to tentative remarks on possible correlations between the variations within samples and such factors as social class, income, and level of nutrition.[29] Environmentalism in anthropometry, or at least an early and crude form of the approach, can thus be dated to a somewhat earlier period than is usually cited: Franz Boas's post-1900 studies in craniological variation among immigrant populations.[30]

As Bruce Trigger has noted in his essay, in 1855 and 1856, soon after his arrival in Canada, Wilson had made field trips to aboriginal copper-mining sites around Lake Superior and the 'mound-builder' remains in Ohio.[31] These trips stimulated his interest in the parallels in New and Old World metallurgical invention and in the supplanting of supposedly 'high' cultures by 'barbarian' invasions, subjects that he would address in *Prehistoric Man* (1862). They also allowed him to see briefly, but at first hand, the then racially mixed and prosperous settlements of the Great Lakes frontier; the experience left him with a favourable impression that coloured all his later writing on race in North America. But Wilson's only known research expeditions after the 1850s were a second 'mound-builder' tour in 1874, a few visits to American skull and artefact collections, occasional digs for crania in the Ontario countryside, and one isolated late tour of archaeological sites in Europe in 1878.[32] However, he corresponded with Americans such as Lewis Henry Morgan and the Scandinavian archaeologists for the exchange of information and the assembling of artefacts or cranial samples.[33] After a hiatus of some years spent on other studies, he returned to craniology in connection with ethnological work, in an attempt to carry out his own exhortation that scholars should enrich physical studies of race with relevant cultural data.[34] Craniology and racial ethnology ('racial' or population movements, hybridity, and environmental influences) are among the subjects discussed in a series of loosely connected essays that conclude *Prehistoric Man*. In his later writings he modified, though he never quite neutralized, the determinist tendencies of his views on race in general. His conclusions on the interrelationship of race, culture, intelligence, brain dimensions, and the environment require us to look at his anthropological work as a whole (for another perspective, see Bruce Trigger's essay in this volume).

Later in his life Wilson indulged an old personal interest by researching and publishing several lively papers on the question of dexterity. Why most people favour use of the right hand over the left, what leads to this choice, what if anything are the consequences of left-handedness and ambidexterity, and what scientific experiments could be done to test dexterity hypotheses were questions that he pursued and attempted to answer in a monograph, *The Right Hand: Left-Handedness* (1891), that is still of interest today. This topic was yet another avenue that allowed him to explore the innate versus culturally determined nature of distinctive physical traits. As Marinell Ash has noted, Wilson himself had been left-handed as a child; but in line with nineteenth-century practice, he had been obliged against his will to learn to work right-handed. He went further and developed his skills with both hands in various combinations for different kinds of work, impressing acquaintances with his ability to sketch separately with each hand or draw with one while writing with the other. Curious as to the origins of these specializations and their possible effects on intellectual and artistic performance, he not only pursued his usual extensive secondary research, but also performed experiments on students at the University of Toronto. These focused on such questions as the statistical incidence of left-handedness, the sensitivity of the preferred hand to various stimuli, and variations in task performance among persons using right, left, or both hands. Wilson even ventured into what we would now define as neurobiology when he speculated that the evidence he had collected supported recent medical theories that dominance of one hemisphere of the brain determined dexterity.[35]

In *The Right Hand* he admitted that his motivation for this work was activist as well as scientific. He had a specific practical purpose in writing the book: to convince the public of 'the folly of persistently striving to suppress an innate faculty of exceptional aptitude' and of 'the advantages to be derived by all from the systematic cultivation of dexterity in both hands.'[36] For present-day readers, this injection of his personal experience and his gusto in describing what were, even in the 1880s, 'curious' studies enlivens his analysis of both popular and highly specialized information. Wilson ranges from the literary through the ethnological to the purely biological. Though he introduces relatively little new material, he offers a broad synthesis and a rich source of references for further research. However, few serious modern studies of dexterity – social or neurobiological – refer back to this readable book, well stocked with references to abstruse primary materials. As in other fields, his is an admirable work without offspring. We can enjoy it, like *Caliban*, as a bracing expression of his wide-ranging mind and agreeable personality; but as a minor work from an isolated scientific community, it sank with few ripples into the widening pool of North American science.

Was Daniel Wilson a pioneer in what we would now call population studies, rather than a minor contributor to the inevitable downfall of deterministic, race-based theories of human biology? A learned critic, Aleš Hrdlička, argued in 1915 that Wilson's craniometric methods, though good for their day, were never detailed or accurate enough to supply adequate proof for his conclusions.[37] It is certainly true that by modern standards of mechanically elaborate, multivariate craniometry, Wilson, like most other nineteenth-century scholars, used techniques that provide statistics of doubtful value for direct comparative purposes today. Whether his methods were much more rigorous than those of his contemporaries deserves closer analysis. It can, however, be argued that this is not really the issue. When we look back on what Wilson and his contemporaries themselves knew and did, we can determine that he indeed advanced the understanding of this controversial science in its adolescence. His practice of reduplicating measurements, on the original samples with similar tools, was appropriate and sufficient to test and evaluate the results produced by other analysts. At least by the end of his career, he was fully aware that non-standard tools or conventions of measurement lowered the value of findings. But he maintained that his use of similar or identical methods within a single, relatively large cranial series yielded acceptable comparative results.[38]

The more valid criticism of Wilson's work is that his cranial measurements were not varied enough to define fully either a skull type or all the possible significant variations shown by a single specimen. Like the craniologists on whose work he based his findings, he relied on a far smaller number of variables per skull than is normal in modern multivariate analysis. Compare his eight linear measurements without indices, after Morton,[39] with the twenty-odd linear measurements and nine composite indices used in J.E. Anderson's standard guide, *The Human Skeleton.*[40] Further, Wilson at times turned back to increasingly old-fashioned and imprecise anthroscopic terms, as when he coined a new descriptive type – the 'kumbecephalic,' or boat-shaped, skull – to describe a quantitatively distinct set of samples. Inadequate as this approach is from our perspective a century later, it served Wilson well enough, allowing him to argue that the polygenists' proposed skull typology was not justified by the inaccurate, irreproducible measurements performed by its inventors.

Not surprisingly, Wilson's years of craniological study were soon overshadowed by the work of European scholars and the rapid development of human evolutionary biology after the mid-century. His original lines of argument were picked up or independently developed by – and celebrated as the discovery of – other scholars.[41] In particular, John Lubbock's concise, popular summary of findings in evolution of the human body provided a more readable text, set in the language of current theory, than even the most accessible of Wilson's specialist publications. By the end of the century, racial studies had been 'cleaned up' – had adopted more rigorous, objective, and analytically complex approaches that focused more narrowly on physical phenomena. To modern scientists, the data derived from Wilson's years of measurement and comparison, using many thousands of skulls, are almost entirely useless except as an illustration of 'the bad old days' of benighted raciology. His suggestions as to possible environmental influences were buried in hard-to-find publications and never followed up as he shifted his interest from one specialty to another.

From the perspective of today, Daniel Wilson's greatest achievement in craniology was in a sense more political than scientific. Against a forcefully mounted attack on the position for racial unity, he succeeded in maintaining the primacy of true scientific method. Despite his strong feelings, clearly expressed in his private writings, that the raciologists were morally wrong and their views of humanity repugnant, he did not fall back on merely doctrinal criticism. His destructive assault on the polygenist school was against their methods, not their conclusions – on the pretended accuracy of their statistics and the supposed uniformity of their racial types. But the positive effect of these attacks on the course of biological ethnology was made more or less redundant by the rise of evolutionary biology, beginning with Darwin's first great publications.

NOTES

This essay has been adapted from my thesis, 'The Life and Anthropological Works of Daniel Wilson (1816–1892).'

1 Wilson, *The Archæology and Prehistoric Annals of Scotland* (1851), 160–89.
2 Stanton, *The Leopard's Spots*, 155–60; Burrow, *Evolution and Society*, 118–27.
3 Stocking, 'What's in a Name?' 378.
4 Prichard, *Researches into the Physical History of Man*, 1–7.
5 Weber, 'Science and Society in Nineteenth Century Anthropology.'
6 Stanton, *The Leopard's Spots*, 184–8.
7 Wilson, *The Archæology and Prehistoric Annals of Scotland* (1851), 160–89.
8 TRL, S65, vol. 2: 3b, 3e.
9 Stanton, *The Leopard's Spots*, 159–60.
10 J.A. Wilson, *George Wilson*, 14–17.
11 UTA, B65-0014/004(01), 2 (10 September 1853).
12 Wilson, 'Remarks on Some Coincidences between the Primitive Antiquities of the Old and New World' (1854).
13 Wilson, 'Remarks on the Intrusion of the Germanic Races on the Area of the Older Keltic Races of Europe' (1854).
14 Wilson, 'Hints for the Formation of a Canadian Collection of Ancient Crania' (1855).
15 Ibid.
16 Ibid.; TRL, S65, vol. 2: 2; Davis and Thurnham, *Crania Britannica*, preface.
17 Wilson, 'Discovery of Indian Remains, County Norfolk, Canada West' (1856); Noble, 'One Hundred and Twenty-Five Years of Archæology,' 3–22.
18 Stanton, *The Leopard's Spots*, 39, 156–75.
19 TRL, S65, vol. 2: 4a–4c.
20 Wilson, Review of *Indigenous Races of the Earth* (1857).
21 Ibid., 214.
22 Burrow, *Evolution and Society*, 82–3.
23 Wilson, Review of *Catalogue of Human Crania* (1857); 'Supposed Prevalence of One Cranial Type throughout the American Aborigines' (1857); Review of *Crania Britannica* (1857); Review of *Crania Britannica* ..., decade III (1859); *Prehistoric Man* (1862), 2: 199–288.
24 Tylor, 'American Aspects of Anthropology,' 222; Dallas, 'On the Primary Divisions and Geographical Distribution of Mankind,' 326; Hunter, 'The Semi-Centennial of "Prehistoric Man,"' 18; Trigger, 'Sir Daniel Wilson,' 25.
25 Darwin, *The Descent of Man*, 38–9; Stanton, *The Leopard's Spots*, 184–8; Wilson,

'Brain-Weight and Size in Relation to Relative Capacity of Races' (1876), 199–200.

26 Dallas, 'On the Primary Divisions and Geographical Distribution of Mankind,' 326.

27 Wilson, *Prehistoric Man* (1862), 2: 298; Darwin, *The Descent of Man*, 888.

28 Wilson, Review of *Description of a Deformed Fragmentary Skull* (1859); 'Notice of a Skull Brought from Kertch, in the Crimea' (1860); 'Illustrative Examples of Some Modifying Elements Affecting the Ethnic Significance of Peculiar Forms of the Human Skull' (1861); 'Ethnical Forms and Undesigned Artificial Distortions of the Human Cranium' (1862); *Prehistoric Man* (1862), 2: 336; 'Ethnology and Archæology: Artificial Occipital Flattening of Ancient Crania' (1863); 'Illustrations of the Significance of Certain Ancient British Skull Forms' (1863); 'Indications of Ancient Customs, Suggested by Certain Cranial Forms' (1863); 'Physical Ethnology' (1863); 'The Long Peruvian Skull' (1874); *Prehistoric Man* (1876), 2: 212–7.

29 Wilson, *The Archæology and Prehistoric Annals of Scotland* (1851), 170–89; *The Lost Atlantis* (1892), 367–8.

30 See, for example, M. Harris, *The Rise of Anthropological Theory,* 99.

31 Wilson, 'Antiquities of the Copper Region of the North American Lakes' (1856); 'The Ancient Miners of Lake Superior' (1856); 'The Southern Shores of Lake Superior' (1856); see also Hunter, 'The Semi-Centennial of "Prehistoric Man,"' 15–17.

32 Wilson, *Prehistoric Man* (1865), 27; Hunter, 'The Semi-Centennial of "Prehistoric Man,"' 15–17; Trigger, 'Sir Daniel Wilson,' 22.

33 TRL, S65, vol. 2, passim.

34 Wilson, Review of *Indigenous Races of the Earth* (1857), 212.

35 Wilson, *The Right Hand* (1891), chap. 11; Trigger, 'Sir Daniel Wilson,' 17–18; H.H. Langton, *Sir Daniel Wilson,* 204.

36 Wilson, *The Right Hand* (1891), vii–viii.

37 Hrdliœka, 'Physical Anthropology in America,' 160.

38 Wilson, *The Lost Atlantis* (1892), 344–5.

39 Wilson, *Prehistoric Man* (1862), 2: 220–80.

40 Anderson, *The Human Skeleton,* 102.

41 See Lubbock, *Pre-historic Times* (4th ed., 1887), esp. 530–1; Darwin, *The Descent of Man,* 38–9, 80–1, 270, 888–9; Tylor, 'American Aspects of Anthropology,' 224.

'Merchants of Light':
The Culture of Science in Daniel Wilson's Ontario, 1853–1892

SUZANNE ZELLER

But thus, you see, we maintain a trade, not for gold, silver, or jewels, nor for silks, nor for spices, nor any other commodity of matter, but only for God's first creature, which was *Light*, to have *light* (I say) of the growth of all parts of the world.

Sir Francis Bacon, The New Atlantis (1627)

Daniel Wilson's career as professor of history and English literature (and later president) at the University of Toronto between 1853 and 1892 paralleled the remarkable rise to authority, in Canada as elsewhere, of both science and schools in Victorian society. His Edinburgh background in the afterglow of the Scottish Enlightenment had shaped his appreciation both of science and technology in attaining Enlightened progress and of public education in disseminating the Enlightened values that underpinned so much of Victorian culture.[1] He thus arrived in Canada prepared to welcome and promote this dynamic transformation in some very particular ways.

Although he did not complete a degree at the University of Edinburgh, Wilson witnessed its heyday as an exciting centre of scientific debate and training – not only for specialized physicians and scientific explorers, but for many others who disseminated the results of their Edinburgh education in myriad activities throughout Britain's expansive empire. Edinburgh's Regius Professor of Natural History, Robert Jameson (1774–1854), cultivated a worldwide network of contributors to assemble the collections of what later became the Royal Museum of Scotland. More particularly, he was succeeded in 1854 by Edward Forbes (1815–54), a

leading British naturalist whom Wilson much admired and whose biogeographical theories helped to frame his approaches to ethnology. In 1855
Wilson's brother George attained Edinburgh's newly created Regius
Chair of Technology, further affirmation of science's pivotal role in modern progress. For his part, Daniel Wilson promoted science in Canada in
multiple capacities as educator, administrator, and scholar, guided by the
light of his early Victorian values long after younger colleagues had
turned to other priorities.[2]

Wilson admired science as a part of a widespread Baconian revival in
early Victorian culture. He imbibed the conviction that the natural world
could best be known rationally, through observation, experiment, and
the application of inductive reasoning to 'facts' thus accumulated. Baconian philosophy promised important utilitarian benefits, including material prosperity and social order. Extolled during an age of revolution as
an attractive alternative to political and social upheaval, this born-again
Baconianism defended the dislocations and inequities entailed by industrialization as short-term pains for long-term gain. Its nineteenth-century
followers hoped to realize Bacon's utopian *New Atlantis*, with peripatetic
'Merchants of Light' assigned to accumulate scientific knowledge from
all over the world; in turn, this knowledge would be processed in various
stages as it passed through 'Salomon's house,' a public clearing house for
the new learning and its applications. The British Association for the
Advancement of Science, founded at York in 1831, with its division of
labour and published transactions to accumulate and disseminate scientific knowledge, represented the Victorian quintessence of this Baconian
project.[3]

The progress of Victorian science also demanded increasingly standardized observations and statistical analyses, qualities sometimes characterized as Humboldtian. Alexander von Humboldt (1769–1859), the
influential Prussian scientific traveller, was inspired by reports of Captain
James Cook's circumnavigations during the 1770s to advocate a 'cosmi-
cal' approach to the study of nature. Tracing patterns of natural phenomena over the earth, including geographical distributions of species, he
aspired to understand the 'cosmos' with all the precision and predictive
powers of Isaac Newton's universal laws of motion. His example activated
collectors of natural specimens and investigators of climate and resources
to search the world over for information about the earth and its workings.
Especially after the peace of 1815, the British government supported
now-underemployed military officers, who advanced their careers
through science in this manner. Fur traders in the North American wilds,

too, responded to the Humboldtian tug of their cultural metropolises in London and Edinburgh, participating in scientific exploration.[4]

Science also served important social purposes in Victorian culture. A long-standing amateur naturalist tradition stimulated aesthetic, as well as intellectual tastes for nature and natural objects among the British upper and middle classes, including the Wilson family. Walks to observe the seasonal cycles of flora and fauna, journal records of specimen sightings and weather conditions, and classified collections of ferns, insects, and fossils all manifested this naturalist tradition. It inspired Gilbert White's enormously popular *Natural History of Selborne* (1788), echoed in Catharine Parr Traill's *Backwoods of Canada* (1836), P.H. Gosse's *Canadian Naturalist* (1840), and other literary works. Natural history gained popular currency by encouraging mental and physical discipline, and in fortifying religious faith by protecting idle minds from worldly temptations. By finding in nature evidence of God's creative and beneficent Design, natural theology in turn legitimized outdoor activities, even for women, even on the Sabbath. It lent a common context to most scientific enquiry, in Canada until the 1870s and beyond.[5]

The New World to which Daniel Wilson applied this cultural outlook easily met his expectation that science held keys not only to material and social progress, but also to the very measure of 'civilization' itself. Shortly before his arrival in 1853, John Henry Lefroy (1817–90), director of the Toronto Magnetic and Meteorological Observatory, highlighted Canada's unusual vantage point on the cultural ladder: 'We have, so to speak, side by side, in this extensive country, the twelfth and nineteenth century. The rude beginnings of settlement, where man shares the soil with the wildest natives of the forest, and nothing has as yet occurred to affect the physical conditions of the state of nature; and the fully developed empire of his industry, where all the local changes likely to occur are already wrought out.'[6] Surely, Lefroy suggested, a land in the throes of such dramatic transformation invited scientific enquiry. In just such colleagues Wilson found a nascent cultural community, fellow Merchants of Light dedicated to illuminating the greater cosmos through spotlight applications of their scientific gaze.

Institutions

At mid-century the United Province of Canada (later Ontario and Quebec) was making rapid strides to promote science and education, establishing institutional structures including public school systems, and attracting individuals who shared these cultural goals. The achievement of 'responsible government' in 1848 diverted public attention, temporarily at least, away from political uncertainties to railway building and economic progress. Government Grand Trunk and Great Western lines linked commercial and industrializing centres to agricultural hinterlands and a population that now exceeded one million in Canada West alone. Electric telegraphs followed these iron pathways, quickening communications to virtual instantaneity. As 'space and time' were being 'annihilated' apace, at least along the major axes of transportation and communication, a reciprocity treaty with the United States in 1854 acknowledged an increasingly continental scale of trade patterns. Wilson interpreted these thoroughgoing changes as a revolution of the 'whole relations of commercial and social life.'[7]

Accompanying this modern reconfiguration of economic spaces, he found Canadians justifiably proud of their scientific institutions. Since its inception in 1842 the Geological Survey of Canada had earned international recognition through its director, William Logan (1798–1875), a native Montrealer, Edinburgh-educated and reputed for his scientific explication of the *in situ* formation of coal. Logan applied to Canada Charles Lyell's 'uniformitarian' *Principles of Geology* (3 vols., 1830–3), which had synthesized geological theory in modern form. Armed with impressive credentials, he downplayed disturbing scientific evidence that the province was unfortunately bereft of coal, that much-sought prerequisite fuel of industrial nationhood. After showcasing more positive aspects of Canada's geological structures and mineral resources to win awards at London's Crystal Palace Exhibition in 1851, Logan was poised, just as Wilson arrived, to clinch his scientific authority at the Paris Exposition of 1855. There his splendid geological map of Canada earned him induction into the Legion of Honour, a knighthood, and the Geological Society of London's Wollaston Medal. Logan was widely fêted as the first Canadian so highly honoured in international scientific circles.[8]

So effectively did the Geological Survey repay public trust that the Canadian government accepted responsibility for Toronto's Magnetic and Meteorological Observatory after the British government recalled Lefroy, a Royal Artillery officer, in 1853. Established in 1839 among a worldwide chain of similar imperial institutions engaged in Humboldtian science, the observatory had flourished through Lefroy's contributions to investigations by his superior officer, Edward Sabine (1788–1883), of terrestrial magnetism. Lefroy also linked the observatory to the Smithsonian Institution in Washington, cooperating with Joseph Henry to analyse

North American weather patterns and coordinate continental storm watches.[9]

Before leaving Toronto, Lefroy persuaded Egerton Ryerson, chief superintendent of public schools in Canada West, to extend these observations through a network of county grammar schools. Ryerson required headmasters to record daily meteorological readings using standardized instruments provided by the Toronto observatory. Lefroy dedicated such valuable evidence, from 'that great epoch in the physical history of a country' when it became settled, to 'a number of refined enquiries of the greatest interest' to society at large. For example, he pointed out, scientists could now address more effectively the crucial questions 'whether we can bring about changes of climate by human agency; whether such changes are always beneficial, and therefore in harmony with the design of the Universe; or sometimes noxious, and therefore in favour of the opinion that there are pre-ordained bounds to the extension of civilised man over the Globe.'[10] He hoped accordingly to be able to document as well the 'gradual disappearance of whole classes of the animal kingdom' that was expected to occur in newly settled lands. While in the long-settled Old World, scientists (including Daniel Wilson) pursued just such evidence with considerable difficulty, Lefroy explained, Canada remained a precious living laboratory of these transformative processes.[11]

Logan and Lefroy served as first (and, in Logan's case, long-distance) presidents of the Canadian Institute in Toronto, a leading local scientific nexus. Founded in 1849 by Sandford Fleming (1827–1915) and others as a professional association for engineers and surveyors, the institute succeeded where several of its short-lived predecessors had failed. In an age when knowledge was often communicated through conversation, Quebec had enjoyed its Literary and Historical Society since 1824, Montreal its Natural History Society since 1827, and Pictou, Nova Scotia, its Literary and Scientific Society since 1834. In Toronto the Canadian Institute now took root by broadening its constituency to embrace both science and practical arts. It also supported the fledgling *Canadian Journal of Industry, Science, and Art*, edited by Henry Youle Hind (1823–1908), science lecturer at the Toronto Normal School. In lobbying the government to help investigate the province's natural history, resources, and aboriginal inhabitants, the institute held out hope of determining whether settlement and cultivation were actually modifying Canada's climate.[12]

While the Canadian Institute's material survival benefited from its absorption of the Toronto Athenaeum in 1855, its transition from professional to scientific association was also well served by the establishment of the University of Toronto as a non-denominational institution in 1850. University College appointed several professors of science, along with Daniel Wilson, to join Henry Holmes Croft (1820–83), professor of chemistry and experimental philosophy there since 1842: John Bradford Cherriman (1823–1908) in mathematics and natural philosophy; the Reverend William Hincks (1794–1871) in natural history; and Edward John Chapman (1821–1904) in mineralogy and geology. In addition, H.Y. Hind became professor of chemistry and geology at Trinity College; George Paxton Young (1818–89), professor of logic and metaphysics at Knox College; and George Templeman Kingston (1816–86), director of the Toronto observatory. Their membership strengthened the Canadian Institute with councillors, editors, and contributors who also practised science, a pattern repeated locally at Kingston, Montreal, Fredericton, and Halifax with the expansion of Queen's, McGill, New Brunswick, and Dalhousie universities during those same years. As substantial additions to Salomon's house in British North America, these institutions accommodated the incoming Merchants of Light who defined the contours of Canadian science in their time.[13]

Ideas and Influences

Although the new University of Toronto officially emulated the modern example of the University of London, within this framework Wilson and his colleagues approached scientific issues through individual perspectives shaped largely by their own training and experience. In physical sciences, J.B. Cherriman adopted the curriculum of the University of Cambridge, where he had excelled in the mathematical tripos. He taught natural philosophy (including heat, optics, electricity, magnetism, mechanics, hydrostatics, pneumatics, acoustics, and astronomy) through its classical Newtonian foundations in mathematical analysis. In contrast, H.H. Croft imparted his training from the University of Berlin, with experimental chemistry in the laboratory using his own practical manual for students. E.J. Chapman drew upon more varied experiences at the universities of Göttingen and London to teach mineralogy informed by crystallography and chemistry, including pioneering methods in blowpipe analysis.[14]

Life sciences at Toronto reflected idealist offshoots of Cambridge's neoplatonist revival and German romanticism's *Naturphilosophie*. On the one hand William Hincks, a philosophical naturalist from Queen's College, Cork, organized natural history according to quinarian theory.

Quinarians had filled a critical gap in British taxonomy some twenty years earlier, organizing their investigations around the assumption that a general plan structured the natural world in discernable groups of five; yet Hincks did his students no favour in continuing for some twenty more years thereafter to impose these anachronistic tenets upon them by rote.[15] On the other hand, Daniel Wilson's archaeological studies (in which he included anthropology, ethnology, and comparative philology) derived useful insights from the biogeographical approaches of yet another philosophical naturalist, Edward Forbes.[16]

A leading naturalist educated at Edinburgh, Forbes epitomized a renewed 'idealistic impulse' in British biology during the 1840s and 1850s. His untimely death shortly after acceding to the chair of natural history in 1854 shocked Wilson, whose brother published a memoir of his lamented colleague. Eight years earlier Forbes had published a groundbreaking essay, 'On the Connexion between the Distribution of the Existing Fauna and Flora of the British Isles,' in which he explored these patterns in terms of successive geological changes. His work advanced significantly the scientific discussion – and investigation, by Canadian naturalists among others – of various means by which species could have dispersed from centres of origin where, it was assumed, they were created.[17]

Forbes's biogeographical approach to the understanding of species and their dispersal in turn inspired Wilson to consider the historical ebb and flow of human populations in terms of similar distribution patterns. 'In all ages,' observed Wilson in 1855, 'history discloses to us unmistakeable evidence ... of the fundamental differences whereby a few highly favoured races have outsped all others; triumphing in the onward progress of the nations, not less by an innate constitutional superiority, than by an acquired civilization, or by local advantages.'[18] In his view, British society's powerful dynamism in the nineteenth century stemmed from a fortuitous ancient amalgam of diverse peoples. For him, the example illuminated processes still at work in North America, where native populations seemed naturally destined, through contact with Anglo-Saxon culture, to absorption if not outright extinction. As Bennett McCardle has described in the preceding essay, Wilson called upon the Canadian Institute, the Hudson's Bay Company, and other institutions to assemble a Canadian collection of ancient human crania for further ethnological research.[19]

Following Forbes, he identified geographical factors as one source of hope for the survival of native cultures against 'the fatal influences of our triumphant progress.' Had not the complex landscapes of Scotland and

Wales, he noted, preserved pockets of Celtic settlements in isolation until well into the eighteenth century? Wilson went on to outline the impact of continental landforms in explaining notable historical differences between American and European patterns of distribution and development, even among the same peoples.[20]

Neither Hincks nor Wilson undertook extensive fieldwork at Toronto, the former preferring localized strolls in the amateur naturalist tradition and the latter consulting larger collections of specimens abroad. In contrast, McGill College in Montreal appointed John William Dawson (1820–99), a highly regarded Nova Scotian geologist, and James Barnston (1831–57), a Canadian botanist; while Queen's College in Kingston engaged George Lawson (1827–95), a Scottish botanist. All three had imbibed the importance of natural history fieldwork at the University of Edinburgh. Like William Logan, Dawson based his outstanding analysis in *Acadian Geology* (1855) on Lyellian uniformitarian principles. Barnston and Lawson honed their organizational, field, and laboratory skills under the guidance of the Edinburgh botanist J.H. Balfour (1808–84), and set out to appreciate and explore Canadian vegetation well beyond the bounds of settlement, with particular attention to northern species. Barnston founded the Botanical Society of Montreal on the model of the Botanical Society of Edinburgh in 1856, but his untimely death the following year left both McGill's chair of botany and Montreal's botanical society stillborn. Also on the Edinburgh model, Lawson established the popular Botanical Society of Canada at Kingston in 1860, raising hopes from Red River to Prince Edward Island, and even Europe, that North America's vast botanical unknown between the American boundary and the Arctic Circle would at last be revealed.[21]

Expansive themes in Canadian science after mid-century meshed closely with a rising expansionist movement in politics. Eyeing the great northwest, long monopolized by the Hudson's Bay Company, whose charter was about to expire, territorial expansionists clustered mainly in Toronto sought an outlet for land pressures as agricultural settlement encountered the physical limits imposed by the Canadian Shield. They also hoped to neutralize the disappointment of mounting evidence that clearing and cultivation had not substantially moderated Canada's climate after all. In 1857 the Department of Crown Lands, an expansionist hotbed, published an official map of the northwest criss-crossed with Humboldtian isorithms – cartographic lines through places of equal value – to emphasize its climatic and agricultural similarities with prosperous settled regions farther south in Canada. That same year the British and Canadian governments also directed scientific exploring expeditions, led respectively by John Palliser and George Gladman (with H.Y. Hind), to assess the territory's viability for agriculture, settlement, and transportation facilities. Although Canadian prognostications waxed more positive than British ones did, the fate of the HBC's monopoly was sealed by the use in both reports of geological, botanical, meteorological, and other scientific evidence to reinterpret the great northwest as key to the development of a future British North American empire.[22]

In other ways, too, Victorian science empowered Canadians to broaden their horizons. William Logan and J.W. Dawson induced the American Association for the Advancement of Science to meet in Montreal in 1857, and thus to venture for the first time outside the United States. Both scientists had suffered the disillusionment of apparent neglect from British mentors and had turned increasingly to American colleagues, as Daniel Wilson did for ethnological consultations. Logan, in particular, illustrated Canada's scientific maturity at the meeting by presenting his definitive analysis of the Precambrian Shield, whose Laurentian and Huronian divisions he named as prototypes for analogous geological formations elsewhere. The publication, soon thereafter and in rapid succession, of no less than four major Canadian works seemed to support widespread optimism that an era of remarkable productivity in Canadian science had dawned.[23]

Issues of Species

It had indeed, but not without some irony. For, perhaps more accurately, William Bovell's *Natural Theology* (1859), Dawson's *Archaia* (1859), Wilson's *Prehistoric Man* (1862), and Logan's *Geology of Canada* (1863) combined instead to mark the close of an age of comforting certainties. As A.B. McKillop has explained, it was clear within the context of early Victorian culture what could (and could not) legitimately be asked of science. Those days were now numbered. Even as Wilson's book went to press, the appearance of the respected British naturalist Charles Darwin's *On the Origin of Species by Means of Natural Selection* (1859), with its arresting mastery of broad and detailed evidence, laid claim to startling evolutionary conclusions. Darwin reopened for scientific discussion some fundamental issues, not only of humanity's place in nature, but also of the very means of attaining truth through scientific method.[24]

Important challenges to long-standing convictions about science were hardly new to Wilson. As McCardle has related, he had drawn attention in the *Canadian Journal* in 1855 to a recent public furore in the United

States and Britain over racial theories, by Louis Agassiz of Harvard University and Samuel Morton at Philadelphia, that humanity comprised several separate species. Wilson patiently conceded that, notwithstanding the authority of biblical accounts of human descent from a single pair, studies of the geographical distribution of plants and animals had recently 'revived inquiry into the tenability' of the scriptural view of human origins. Indignant resistance to such discussions from a religious correspondent elicited his further admonition that the 'profoundly difficult question' of the unity of the human race 'is not ripe for controversy. It is open only, as yet, to earnest inquiry; and it will be well for the cause of religion if our divines and theologians seek to master it in all its bearings ... before it do ripen into a controversy which will only be characterised by danger in so far as it is stamped with the intolerant spirit of ignorant assumption.'[25] Wilson, meanwhile, harboured every confidence that the biblical interpretation would ultimately withstand the scrutiny of modern science.

In 1860 he silenced challenges from another direction in his testimony before a select committee investigating the University of Toronto under its charter as a public institution. Against Egerton Ryerson's criticism of a new curriculum in which traditional classics gave way to science and modern language options, Wilson unleashed a venomous defence of the university's commitment to impart to 'the youth of Canada' not only 'intellectual culture' but also the ability to undertake 'the practical duties of life.' 'The old Classical Course of Oxford,' he hissed, might suffice in an institution 'understood from vague tradition to have owed its origin to a meeting of three monks in a barn, some time in the good old times of the Saxon Alfred.' But since theology and philosophy, let alone science, were no longer communicated in Latin, Oxford's tradition clearly failed to satisfy 'the advanced requirements of this age' in a modernizing country such as Canada. Still, he argued, it was important to rein in the urge towards educational reform, in contrast to American colleges that were devising radical new professional courses and degrees; if Masters were making room for 'Mistresses' of Arts, he mused, would Bachelors soon be followed by 'Spinsters' of Science?[26]

Yet Darwin's challenge was unlike these others; it was deeply rooted in first-hand scientific knowledge. In the earliest published responses to *The Origin of Species* by Canadian naturalists, Wilson, Dawson, and Chapman in 1860 collectively exhibited a 'moral imperative' that is said to have circumscribed intellectually an immature colonial society. For Dawson, this apparent cultural consensus precluded questions of origin from the domains of both natural law and the inductive method of enquiry. For all three, Darwin had failed to demonstrate the evolution of even one species, his argument weakened by a reliance instead upon gaps in the fossil record to suggest their gradual transmutation.[27]

Beneath this formal ideology, however, Chapman acknowledged 'the visitation of sundry hauntings' over traditional demarcations between varieties and species, and allowed that Dawson's entrenched position went too far. Wilson, moreover, recognized in Darwin's scientific achievement an outgrowth of Edward Forbes's reasoning from geographical distribution patterns. These connections made it impossible for him to ignore *The Origin*'s positive bearing upon the important problem of human racial classifications, as 'alike descended of one primal stock.' Wilson drew the line, however, at the evolution of the human mind, which he could not conceive as anything but specially created. As president that year, he nonetheless ensured the Canadian Institute's immediate purchase of *The Origin* for the library.[28]

Among naturalists, perhaps the greatest beneficiaries of the strong biogeographical roots in Darwin's research were botanists, whose enquiries quickly blossomed into a modern cluster of ecological and palaeobotanical disciplines. Darwin's theory refined answers to important biogeographical questions raised by Forbes, whose approach also inspired one of Darwin's earliest supporters, the eminent botanist J.D. Hooker (1817–1911) of the Royal Botanic Gardens at Kew. Hooker's 'Outlines of the Distribution of Arctic Plants' (1862) applied Darwin's theory of 'creation by variation' to explain the circumpolar distributions of northern plant forms in terms of the migrations of their ancestors from Scandinavia to northern Asia and America during the glacial age. The position of British North America, bordering two of Hooker's five regions of Arctic floras, stimulated Canadian collectors to seek out further botanical evidence without having to declare themselves openly on the controversial question of evolution by natural selection.[29]

Among Canadian botanists galvanized by Hooker's Forbesian-Darwinian theoretical framework, George Lawson, who moved from Queen's to Dalhousie University in 1863, recast his botanical researches over large northern expanses in terms of the variation, adaptation, and survival of plants under changing climatic conditions. Ever the organizational catalyst, he mobilized a network of British North American botanists to contribute to his growing geographical and ecological collations of plants. Among them, A.T. Drummond (1844–1923) adapted this model to analyse Canada's own botanical subregions. Abbé L.-O. Brunet (1826–76) of Laval University also collected plants in remote places, contributing to Asa Gray's Darwinian efforts at Harvard University.[30] In this context, British North America provided a field for more botanical work than any few people could hope to accomplish in a lifetime. As J.M. Buchan of Hamilton confessed to the Canadian Institute in 1874, 'Our knowledge of the distribution of Canadian plants is indeed so limited, and geographical botany is so important a subject in its relations on the one hand to climate, and on the other to the vexed question of the origin of species, that one may be excused for feeling, and pardoned for endeavouring to excite, an interest in it.'[31]

By the 1870s these geographical approaches found parallels among entomologists. William Couper (d. 1886), who had for years investigated the role of wind and water in the geographical distribution of plants and insects, addressed the Entomological Society of Montreal in favour of Darwin's theory in 1875. Allen Pringle (1834–96), a freethinking beekeeper from Selby, Ontario, had expressed similar support at least a year earlier. The Toronto entomologist William Brodie (1831–1909), a dentist who became a renowned specialist in insect galls, followed suit with his ecological studies of insects and, later, insect consciousness.[32]

Ironically for Wilson, the biogeographical dimensions of politics also intensified public interest in ethnology. Canada's expansionist program clashed openly with the lives of aboriginal inhabitants in the great northwest, culminating in the Riel resistance of 1869, shortly before Darwin's long-awaited second volume, *The Descent of Man* (1871), made its appearance. 'One after another,' Wilson conceded, 'of the assumed specialties of man, and his claims to a distinct classification in animated nature, is being ruthlessly swept away, in the marvellous revolutions of modern science.' He questioned the wisdom of government force and duplicity towards Native peoples in these lands and hoped to enhance understanding through increased precision in ethnological classification. Wilson idealized these struggles on the frontier as part of a long-term natural interblending of peoples, 'a series of undesigned yet exhaustive ethnological experiments carried out on the grandest scale,' ultimately to produce unpredictable new ethnological alloys, especially 'in the new provinces now forming in the great North-West.'[33]

Ideals and Reforms

Confederation in 1867, and the transcontinental nation-building process that followed, thus lent Canadian dimensions to structural changes

already under way in the culture of Victorian science. As science cut loose
from its moorings in both the amateur naturalist and natural theology
traditions in an age of industrialization and urbanization, it became
increasingly professionalized and specialized. The most obvious examples
of the former were the rise of professional schools of practical science at
Toronto, Queen's, and McGill and the growing popular movement for
technical education across the country.[34]

The experience of the Canadian Institute offers a case study in the
effects of specialization. In the wake of recent regional crop infestations,
in 1862 a sub-group of the Institute, including H.H. Croft, William
Hincks, and Daniel Wilson, formed the Entomological Society of Canada,
which soon sprouted regional branches in London and Quebec City.
When the dominion's new federal structures not only disrupted the institute's traditional sources of public funding, but also separated the provincial jurisdictions of Ontario and Quebec, Hincks expressed a further
organizational dilemma: should the institute aspire to extend its influence nationally, or instead remain provincially or even locally bound? He
for one preferred a provincial scope, as both more feasible than the federal and more desirable than the local options. Still, the growth of scientific knowledge to unmanageable proportions necessitated a continual
process of organizational mitosis: the Institute's botanical section, created
in 1874, gave way in 1885 to separate biological, geological, and other sections. The need for further splintering was intensified by the institute's
absorption that year of the Natural History Society of Toronto, founded
by William Brodie in 1877. By 1891 the biological section was again subdivided to accommodate microscopy, ornithology, and botany.[35]

Additional developments after 1870, both within Canadian society and
abroad, inaugurated a period of restless questioning that challenged the
traditional cultural consensus more deeply than Charles Darwin alone
could have done. The growth of urban middle classes and the prolifera-
tion of national literary magazines, including the *Canadian Monthly and
National Review*, promoted public discussion of broader scientific issues
and their implications for Christian morality. The rise of 'materialism' in
the physical sciences, epitomized by John Tyndall's notorious Belfast
address to the British Association for the Advancement of Science in
1874, which traced the origins of life to inorganic compounds and even
single atoms, made Darwin appear positively moderate in comparison.
University students flocked to the lectures of philosophers and others to
ease growing tensions caused by myriad doubts visited upon them as a
result.[36]

In an interesting counterpoint to the ultramontanism that predominated as a formal ideology in French-Canadian Catholic thought (and which constructed the national identity upon traditional foundations of faith, language, and the land), English-Canadian thought by the 1880s, too, manifested a powerful philosophical idealism. Derived from Scottish adaptations of Kantian and Hegelian ideas, this Protestant outlook attempted to reconcile Christian faith with evolutionary science. An important result was the popularization in English-Canadian society of a 'practical idealism' that updated the traditional 'moral imperative' through evolutionary principles designed to rechannel the materialist path of modern science. Repelled by the rampant individualism generally associated with social Darwinism in the United States, universities and public schools in Canada emphasized commitment to community for the moral evolution of society, nation, and empire.[37]

Moreover, traditional 'moral imperatives' no longer permeated the outlooks of a younger generation of Canadian scientists, who had imbibed much that was modern in their professional training. At Toronto, James Loudon (1841–1916), the university's first Canadian appointee as professor of mathematics and physics in 1875, openly challenged Daniel Wilson's traditional assumptions and hesitations. He denied scientists' responsibility to reconcile their work with overarching religious or metaphysical principles. In 1877 he apprised the Canadian Institute of his commitment instead to the German research ideal of pursuing knowledge for its own sake. Loudon was joined at Toronto by Robert Ramsay Wright (1852–1933), in the chair of natural history. In 1876 Wright, an Edinburgh-trained zoologist, told the institute that he considered the 'theoretical nature of species,' including humankind, to have been 'definitely settled' by Darwin. He set about teaching modern biology and developing a research laboratory with a program designed accordingly.[38]

Loudon and Wright would have found a kindred spirit in George Mercer Dawson (1847–1901), a son of J.W. Dawson, who made his career with the Geological Survey of Canada. Dawson returned from Britain in 1872, a star graduate of the Royal School of Mines. The prize student of Darwin's bulldog, T.H. Huxley, in natural history, he trained in a modern evolutionary approach that informed the ethnological and other studies which made him a leading figure among the second generation of professional Canadian geologists. In general, the new contingent introduced Darwinian concepts openly into university curricula during the 1890s, as the older incumbents left the scene.[39]

While Daniel Wilson continued to emphasize cautious inductive reasoning in archaeological progress, both Darwinian evolution and the research ideal penetrated the field through younger advocates and institutional means during the 1880s. The Canadian Institute's new curator, David Boyle (1842–1911), championed a revisionist program of archaeological research and a public museum in Ontario because, he judged, 'hitherto absolutely nothing has been done methodically or scientifically.' Boyle in Ontario was echoed on a national level by the younger German anthropologist Franz Boas (1858–1942), whose researches among Native peoples in North America rejected as quaintly anachronistic the primacy of 'anthropogeographical' factors in determining the origins of aboriginal cultures.[40]

Both Wilson and Boas found a forum beyond the Canadian Institute for their scientific publications, not only abroad but also in the transactions of the Royal Society of Canada, an elite and most un-Baconian national academy of sciences and letters founded by Governor General Lord Lorne in Ottawa in 1882. The society's creation effectively limited the Canadian Institute's advisory role on important new issues, including forestry and wildlife conservation, to the provincial level of government. When the British Association visited Montreal in 1884, it collaborated with the Royal Society of Canada in sponsoring large-scale joint anthropological surveys, as well as tidal and astronomical observations. In response to these organizational reconfigurations, David Boyle and others suggested peripatetic meetings of the Canadian Institute throughout Ontario in order to serve its provincial constituency more effectively.[41]

Nor did the Royal Society of Canada simply provide a venue for fine-tuning the established science of its charter members. Its emphasis on original research also 'introduce[d] a style of work,' exemplified by Ramsay Wright's biological analyses of fishes, which Daniel Wilson acknowledged had little precedent in Canada. Indeed, George Lawson agreed, the society echoed 'a great, if somewhat silent, change' that had 'been brought about in recent years in the character of our higher education': 'pupils are now subjected to actual training in observation and experimentation and reasoning upon facts observed, instead of being merely furnished with book knowledge of such facts, and exercised in figures, formulae and phrases ... Thus willing hands are secured for working out unsolved problems, and otherwise contributing to the general stock of knowledge, and the physical sciences, instead of being regarded as merely useful for certain kinds of professional training, have acquired high educational value, and science itself, as a profession, has come within reach of our youth.'[42] The growth of the research ideal in late-Victorian science shifted its focus away from natural history societies altogether and into universities and government departments.[43]

Still, Wilson's second round as president of the Canadian Institute, from 1878 to 1881, facilitated one last impressive display by the Merchants of Light. In 1878 the institute's founder, Sandford Fleming, a fellow Scot and the civil engineer responsible for surveying the Intercolonial and Canadian Pacific railways, presented a proposal to standardize public time-reckoning. Like Wilson and many others, Fleming recognized the revolutionary impact of the 'extraordinary sister agencies' of steam and electricity in the modern age. He decried the resulting incongruities between traditional local time and the demands of transportation systems that extended trans- and even intercontinental travel beyond the 'pillars of Hercules.' Under his and Wilson's active leadership the institute evinced an extraordinary drive to universalize a phenomenon of everyday life that had for centuries remained locally determined.[44]

Fleming's intentions as well as his rhetoric reflected both classical Newtonian assumptions of linear time characterized foremost by its unity and continuity and more general Victorian presumptions linking civilization and progress. His outlook was also Humboldtian, aiming telegraphic precision towards a 'cosmic' time-reckoning system governed by the earth as its chronometer. Twenty-four time zones would mark the hours away from a designated prime meridian, with minutes past the hour to be synchronized across all zones; local time – true noon, for example – would effectively be 'absorbed' by the cosmic system. Fleming hoped to number the hours of the day accordingly, eliminating a.m. and p.m. divisions, and to define a universal 'cosmopolitan time' calculated at the prime meridian. He urged the continuity and feasibility of his new system by designing a double-dialled timepiece, which Wilson exhibited at the meeting.[45]

Fleming's pivotal role in the adoption of standard time zones, first in North America and gradually beyond, is well known. Less frequently noted has been the actual extent of his universalizing intentions. As with Wilson's ethnological utopianism, Fleming envisioned a future, perhaps only 'a generation' away, in which a 'radical change' in time-reckoning would be so 'imperatively demanded by the new conditions of the human race' that cosmopolitan time would see all present means of time-reckoning 'fall into disuse.' In contrast, the astronomer Simon Newcomb (1835–1909) of the Nautical Almanac Office in Washington dismissed it as a 'capital plan for use during the millenium. Too perfect for the present state of humanity'; he saw 'no more reason for considering Europe in the matter than for considering the inhabitants of the planet Mars.' Even the systematizing British Association prevented Fleming from presenting his radical proposals at its annual meeting in 1880. Yet he at least acknowledged with some sympathy the 'shocked public sentiment' that had accompanied the French Revolutionary calendar almost a century earlier; the younger W.J. Loudon (1860–1951), James Loudon's nephew and a demonstrator in the department of physics at the University of Toronto, in 1885 proposed a still more radical 'decimal' system of time with all units, including minutes, hours, days, and weeks, divisible by ten instead of twelve. Fleming, meanwhile, worked through provincial educational systems to disseminate his time-reckoning principles in the schools, among those as yet not irrevocably attached to traditional time-reckoning systems. He also induced the Royal Society of Canada to begin developing a specialized nomenclature for his proposed new units of time.[46]

Daniel Wilson's death in 1892 in many ways marked the sunset of the era of the Merchants of Light, a generation of Victorians whose Baconian and Humboldtian ideals once blazed a straight and narrow – albeit broadening – path through science to knowledge and certainty. But no longer. In an age of intellectual transition, with knowledge branching out wildly in so many directions, it was perhaps telling that James Loudon not only preceded Wilson's last presidential term at the now Royal Canadian Institute, but also succeeded him as president of the University of Toronto. Among Loudon's and Ramsay Wright's own students, A.B. Macallum (1858–1934), a biochemist, had already arrived at the fore. More concerned than they had ever been to publish or perish, and to establish priority of discovery, Macallum could hardly imagine a time when thermodynamic energy, luminiferous ethers, and Darwinian evolution had *not* held scientific sway. He confessed himself part of a generation that took such developments 'more or less for granted.'[47]

And while the exact nature of scientific truth might remain unclear, the accepted method for its encounter had truly come full circle. 'The years gather,' Wilson confided to Fleming in 1890, 'on an old survivor outliving the generation to which he properly belongs, as it is my fate to do.' In a regular meeting of the Royal Canadian Institute two years later, Arthur Harvey, a former government statistical clerk and now the society's president, listened patiently as William Houston, a legislative librarian and public school inspector, declaimed on the benefits of studying Canadian society using social science methods. 'The inductive method,' Harvey reminded Houston, had indeed been 'the most successful for the past 300 years.' Yet he hesitated to 'think that we should neglect the deductive method' of enquiry. For 'the former,' he had concluded, 'was the best when we were young, the latter when we were old.'[48] In the view of Daniel Wilson and his fellow luminaries, it might be preferable not to grow old.

NOTES

The author gratefully acknowledges both financial support for the research and writing of this paper (through a grant from the Wilfrid Laurier University operating funds and an SSHRCC institutional grant) and the helpful comments of Bruce Trigger, Elizabeth Hulse, Ken Dewar, Cynthia Comacchio, and Graeme Wynn.

1 Trigger, 'Daniel Wilson and the Scottish Enlightenment'; Daiches et al., *A Hotbed of Genius*; Wilson, 'The President's Address' (1860); Wilson's testimony in 'Proceedings ... of the Select Committee,' in Hodgins, 15: 214–15.

2 Zeller, 'Nature's Gullivers and Crusoes,' 193–5; H[enry] C[roft], '"What is Technology?" An Inaugural Lecture by George Wilson,' *CJ* 3 (1855–6): 53–8; [Wilson], 'Professor George Wilson' (1860), 62–3. For an overview, see also Zeller, *Land of Promise, Promised Land*.

3 The specific task of the Merchants of Light was to 'sail into foreign countries, [and to] bring us the books and abstracts and patterns of experiments of all other parts'; the various processors of this knowledge included Pioneers, Compilers, Benefactors, Lamps, Inoculators, and Interpreters of Nature, each with their designated tasks; from Francis Bacon, *The New Atlantis* (1627), reprinted in *Francis Bacon: A Selection of His Works*, ed. Sidney Warhaft (Toronto, 1965), 455–6. Cf. also Richard Owen's presidential address to the British Association for the Advancement of Science (1858), reprinted in *CJ*, n.s., 5 (1859–60), esp. 64–5, in which Owen singled out the Merchants of Light and identified 'this latter feature of the Baconian organisation' as 'the chief characteristic of the British Association.' See also Berman, *Social Change and Scientific Organization*; Yeo, 'An Idol of the Market-Place.'

4 Humboldt, *Personal Narrative of Travels* and *Cosmos*; Cannon, *Science in Culture*, 73–110; Nicholson, 'Alexander von Humboldt and the Geography of Vegetation'; Zeller, 'The Spirit of Bacon'; UTL, James Hargrave Papers (mfm), George Barnston to Hargrave, 14 December 1852, p. 5239. See also Lindsay, *Science in the Subarctic*.

5 R.M. Young, 'Natural Theology, Victorian Periodicals, and the Fragmentation of a Common Context'; Allen, *The Naturalist in Britain*; Berger, *Science, God, and Nature in Victorian Canada*; McKillop, *A Disciplined Intelligence*, chap. 3.

6 J.H. Lefroy, 'Remarks on Thermometric Registers,' *CJ* 1 (1852): 30.

7 'Supplement to the *Canadian Journal*: Statistics of Upper Canada,' *CJ* 2 (1854): 285; Wilson, 'The President's Address' (1860), 124; Careless, *The Union of the Canadas*.

8 Zeller, *Inventing Canada*, part 1; 'Proceedings of the Canadian Institute, 1854–5,' *CJ* 3 (1854–5): 135, 404–6.

9 Zeller, *Inventing Canada*, part 2; Thomas, *The Beginnings of Canadian Meteorology*; Cawood, 'The Magnetic Crusade'; T.H. Levere, 'Sabine, Sir Edward,' in *DCB* 11: 798–800.

10 J.H. Lefroy, 'Remarks on Thermometric Registers,' *CJ* 1 (1852): 29.

11 Ibid., 30; Wilson, 'Early Notices of the Beaver, in Europe and America' (1859), and 'An Ancient Haunt of the Cervus Megaceros' (1879); Zeller, *Inventing Canada*, chap. 12. See also Crosby, *Ecological Imperialism*.

12 Bender, *New York Intellect*, 39; *CJ* 1 (1852): 1, 25–6, (August 1853): 1; 'The President's Annual Address,' *CJ* 1 (1853): 123; n.s., 4 (March 1857): 148. Various meteorological projects were discussed; see *CJ* 2 (1854–5): 154–5; 2 (December 1855): 406–10; 3 (1854–5): 123–4; n.s., 4 (1857–8): 177–80, 361–4.

13 UTL(F), MS Collection 193, RCI, box 36, Minutes of council, 1849–63, 6 May 1854, p. 153; *CJ*, n.s., 5 (1859–60): 337. For background and context on the growth of universities in Ontario, see McKillop, *Matters of Mind*, part 1.

14 See *DCB* for Cherriman, Chapman, Croft, and Young, who contributed to mathematical theory; Young, 'A New Proof of the Parallelogram of Forces,' *CJ* 3 (1855–6): 357–9; 'Resolution of Algebraical Equations,' n.s., 5 (1859–60): 20–40; and many other articles in *CJ*. See also Croft, *Course of Practical Chemistry* (Toronto, 1860); Chapman, *Examples of the Application of Trigonometry to Crystallographic Calculations* (Toronto, 1860); review in *CJ*, n.s., 5 (1859–60): 299–302.

15 Cunningham and Jardine, *Romanticism and the Sciences*; Rehbock, *The Philosophical Naturalists*, 26–8; Zeller, 'Nature's Gullivers and Crusoes,' 211, 238; 'The Late Professor Hincks,' *CJ*, n.s., 13 (1872): 253.

16 On Forbes, see [Wilson], 'Professor George Wilson' (1860), 62; Wilson, 'The President's Address' (1860), 125–6, and 'The President's Address' (1861), 108; Chapman's review of James Bovell, *Outlines of Natural Theology*, in *CJ* n.s., 6 (1861): 202; Desmond, *Archetypes and Ancestors*, 104; Rehbock, *The Philosophical Naturalists*, 171–5, 186–90. Forbes's influence upon Wilson was directly evident in Wilson, 'An Ancient Haunt of the Cervus Megaceros' (1879), 210, and persisted in Wilson, 'The Lost Atlantis,' in *The Lost Atlantis and Other Ethnographic Studies* (1892), 1–36.

17 G. Wilson and Geikie, *Memoir of Edward Forbes*; Forbes, 'On the Connexion between the Distribution of the Existing Fauna and Flora of the British Isles'

(1846); Rehbock, *The Philosophical Naturalists*, 98–9, 131, chap. 5; Browne, *The Secular Ark*, 116–17; Mills, 'A View of Edward Forbes, Naturalist'; Zeller, *Inventing Canada*, 205–6, 243–51.

18 Wilson, 'Displacement and Extinction among the Primeval Races of Man' (1855), 4.

19 Wilson, 'Ethnology and Archæology ... Value of Natural History to the Archæologist' (1856); 'Remarks on the Intrusion of the Germanic Races on the Area of the Older Keltic Races of Europe' (1854), 246–7; 'Hints for the Formation of a Canadian Collection of Ancient Crania' (1855); 'Supposed Prevalence of One Cranial Type' (1857); 'Ethnology' (1859), 232. See also Berger, 'Wilson,' and S.G. Morton, *Crania Americana*.

20 Wilson, 'Some Ethnographic Phases of Conchology' (1858), 408–9; Review of *The Sandwich Islands Monthly Magazine* (1858), 458; 'Early Notices of the Beaver' (1859), 387. See also his review of *Crania Britannica* (1859), 145; 'Illustrative Examples of Some Modifying Elements' (1861), 417–18; 'Illustrations of the Significance of Certain Ancient British Skull Forms' (1863); 127ff; 'The Huron Race and Its Head-Form' (1871); *Prehistoric Man* (1876), 1: 39–40; 2: 384–6.

21 'Local' collections were kept to specimens found within six miles of city limits; see Thomas McIlwraith, 'List of Birds Observed in the Vicinity of Hamilton,' *CJ*, n.s., 5 (1859–60): 385; cf. also Hincks, 'Specimen of a Flora of Canada,' *CJ*, n.s., 6 (1861): 165–6, and 'Materials for a Fauna Canadensis,' *CJ*, n.s., 7 (1862): 446–7; Zeller, 'Nature's Gullivers and Crusoes,' 236–8; Connor, 'To Promote the Cause of Science,' 3–33. The Canadian Institute did not organize such fieldwork until 1874; see UTL(F), MS Collection 193, RCI, box 37, Minutes of council, 14 February, 7 March, 4 April 1874, pp. 335, 338, 342.

22 AO, map B-24, 'Map of the North West Part of Canada[,] Indian Territories and Hudson's Bay'; Palliser, *The Journals*; Hind, *Narrative of the Canadian Red River Exploring Expedition*; G.W. Allan, 'The President's Address,' *CJ*, n.s., 4 (1859): 91–2; Hincks, Review of Hind, *A Sketch of an Overland Route to British Columbia* (1862), *CJ*, n.s., 7 (1862): 200; Wilson, 'Science in Rupert's Land' (1862). See also review of Hind, *Reports of Progress* (1859), *CJ*, n.s., 7 (1862): 187–95, and Hind, 'A Glance at the Political and Commercial Importance of Central British America,' *CJ*, n.s., 8 (1863): 409–27. Zeller, 'Nature's Gullivers and Crusoes,' 230–5, and 'Classical Codes'; see also Owram, *Promise of Eden*; W.L. Morton, *Henry Youle Hind*.

23 Zeller, *Inventing Canada*, 100–1, and 'Mapping the Canadian Mind'; Eagan, 'Reading the *Geology of Canada*,' 154–64.

24 McKillop, *A Disciplined Intelligence*, chap. 1–3; see also McKillop, *Matters of Mind*, chap. 4–5.

25 Wilson, 'The Unity of the Human Race' (1855), 229; T.H.M.B., 'The Unity of the Human Race,' *CJ* 3 (1854–5): 284–5; Wilson, 'The Unity of the Human Race,' 303. Wilson took up these same issues from a scientific perspective in 'Supposed Prevalence of One Cranial Type' (1857).

26 Wilson, in 'Proceedings ... of the Select Committee,' in Hodgins, 15: 208–11; see also his review of *On the Course of Collegiate Education* (1856), esp. 178. For the larger context, see McKillop, *Matters of Mind*, 41–3 and chap. 6; Berger, 'Wilson'; and Ainley, *Despite the Odds*.

27 McKillop, *A Disciplined Intelligence*, 99–110; Dawson, in *Canadian Naturalist and Geologist* 5 (1860): 100–22; Wilson, 'The President's Address' (1860), 116–26, and 'The President's Address' (1861), 113–19; Chapman, *CJ*, n.s., 5 (1860): 367–87. Hincks responded similarly in his 'President's Address,' *CJ*, n.s., 12 (1870): 355–8. See also McKillop, *Matters of Mind*, chap. 5; Berger, *Science, God, and Nature in Victorian Canada*, 69–70; and Roome, 'The Darwin Debate in Canada: 1860–1880.'

28 Chapman, review, *CJ*, n.s., 5 (1860): 368, and his review of Dawson, *Archaia*, *CJ*, n.s., 5 (1860): 61; Wilson, 'The President's Address' (1861), 118–19; 'Annual Report of the Council,' *CJ*, n.s., 6 (1861): 201.

29 Rehbock, *The Philosophical Naturalists*, 169, 184–7; Browne, *The Secular Ark*, 127–34; Zeller, *Inventing Canada*, chap. 13.

30 Hooker, 'Outlines of the Distribution of Arctic Plants'; Drummond, 'Observations on Canadian Geographical Botany'; Zeller, *Inventing Canada*, 243–49. See also Chartrand, Duchesne, and Gingras, *Histoire des sciences au Québec*, 167–79, and Zeller, 'George Lawson,' 54–67. This discussion is derived from Zeller, 'Environment, Culture, and the Reception of Darwin in Canada.'

31 J.M. Buchan, 'Notes on the Flora of Hamilton,' *CJ*, n.s., 14 (1874): 282.

32 Chartrand, Duchesne, and Gingras, *Histoire des sciences au Québec*, 166. See also Cook, *The Regenerators*, 48–52; Pringle, 'A Little Afraid of His Own Logic,' and 'Those Bee Glands and Evolution'; Suzanne Zeller, 'Brodie, William, in *DCB*, 13: 112–14.

33 Wilson, 'Righthandedness' (1871), 229; 'Remarks on the Wisdom of Our Government with Regard to Their Treatment of the Indians,' reported in UTL(F), MS Collection 193, RCI, box 37, Minutes of council, 22 February 1868, p. 154; and 'On the Present State and Future Prospects of the Indian Race in British North America,' ibid., 25 February 1870, p. 236. Wilson, 'Race Head-Forms and Their Expression by Measurements' (1869); 'Hybridity and Absorption in Relation to the Red Indian Race' (1875), 452; 'Some American Illustrations of the Evolution of New Varieties of Man' (1879), 1, 21–2. Later he included Chinese immigration as an additional factor in creating new peoples; see 'Pre-Aryan American Man' (1883), 35; 'The Huron-Iroquois of Canada' (1884).

34 McKillop, *Matters of Mind,* 166–76; see also Richardson, *Queen's Engineers,* 1–23.

35 *CJ,* n.s., 7 (1862): 525; n.s., 8 (1863): 313; UTL(F), MS Collection 193, RCI, box 37, Minutes of council, 25 January 1868, p. 151; Hincks, 'The President's Address,' *CJ,* n.s., 12 (1869): 103–4; *PCI,* ser. 3, 3 (1884–5): 122–3; 4 (1885–6): 1. The others were photographic, architectural, and philological; see *PCI* 5 (1886–7): 206; n.s., 2 (1890–1): 61. See also Connor, 'Of Butterfly Nets and Beetle Bottles,' 127–50; Zeller, 'Brodie, William,' in *DCB,* 13: 112–14.

36 Irving, 'The Development of Philosophy in Central Canada,' 264; see also Cook, *The Regenerators,* chaps. 2–3; McKillop, *Matters of Mind,* 111–19; Johnson, *Science and Religion,* 6; Dalhousie University Archives, William Lyall, address in *Halifax Reporter and Times,* 4 November 1874 (clipping), and Charles Mac-Donald, 'Evolution' [1883], and 'Old Lesson in Metaphysics' [n.d.] (MSS).

37 Zeller, 'Environment, Culture, and the Reception of Darwin,' nn 30, 43, 45–6; the philosophical idealists included John Watson (1847–1939) at Queen's, George Paxton Young at Toronto (1818–89), John Clark Murray (1836–1917) at McGill, and Jacob Gould Schurmann (1854–1942) at Acadia University. See also McKillop, 'The Idealist Legacy,' in *Contours of Canadian Thought,* 96–110; McKillop, *Matters of Mind,* 119–24, chaps. 8–9; Wood, *Idealism Transformed,* 26–9.

38 McKillop, 'The Research Ideal and the University of Toronto,' in *Contours of Canadian Thought,* 85; McKillop, *Matters of Mind,* chap. 7; Loudon, 'The President's Address,' *CJ,* n.s., 15 (1876–8): 369, 380; Wright, 'Haeckel's Anthropogenie,' *CJ,* n.s., 15 (1876–8): 235–6; McRae, 'The "Scientific Spirit" in Medicine,' chap. 3. Cf. also J.M. Buchan, 'The President's Address for the Session 1882–3,' *PCI* 1 (1879–83): 364.

39 Suzanne Zeller and Gale Avrith Wakeam, 'Dawson, George Mercer,' in *DCB,* 13: 257–61; Zeller, 'Environment, Culture, and the Reception of Darwin,' nn 53–4.

40 Wilson, 'Address of Professor Daniel Wilson, Chairman of the Subsection of Anthropology' (1877): 334. UTL(F), MS Collection 193, RCI, box 37, Minutes of council, 2 December 1882, p. 534; the collections eventually formed the Royal Ontario Museum. David Boyle, 'The Archaeological Outlook,' *PCI,* ser. 3, 4 (1885–6): 2–3, and 'The Persistence of Savagery in Civilization,' *PCI,* ser. 3, 4 (1885–6): 130–1; see also Killan, *David Boyle,* esp. 47–9, 59–61. Franz Boas, 'The Indians of British Columbia,' *PTRSC* 6 (1888), sec. 2: 47. On Boyle and Boas, see also Bruce Trigger's essay in this volume.

41 Daly and Dufour, 'Creating a "Northern Minerva,"' 3–14; W.H. Van der Smissen, 'The President's Address,' *PCI* 5 (1886–7): 7–9; R.W. Phipps, 'Forestry, and the Necessity for Its Practice in Ontario,' *PCI* 3 (1884–5): 109–12; J.B. Williams, 'The Destruction of Wild Animals and the Means That Should Be

Taken for Their Preservation,' *PCI* 4 (1885–6): 142–6; *PCI*, n.s., 1 (1889–90): 4; J.W. Dawson, presidential address, *PTRSC* 1 (1882–3): vi–xi; Berger, *Honour and the Search for Influence.*

42 George Lawson, Address of the vice-president, *PTRSC* 5 (1887): xxiii. Cf. Robert Bell, 'Presidential Address: The Huronian System in Canada,' *PTRSC* 6 (1888), section 4: 3–14; Wilson, Address (1886), xix. See also Levere, *Research and Influence*, and 'The Most Select and the Most Democratic.'

43 De Vecchi, 'Dawning of a National Scientific Community,' and 'Science and Scientists in Government,' parts 1–2.

44 UTL(F), MS collection 193, RCI, box 37, Minutes of council, 25 January and 8 February 1878, pp. 453–4; Sandford Fleming, 'Time-Reckoning,' *PCI*, n.s., 1 (1879–83): 97–137, and 'Longitude and Time-Reckoning,' *PCI*, n.s., 1 (1879–83): 138–49; Wilson, 'Cosmopolitan Time and a Prime Meridian' (1880). Wilson undertook an unusually frequent correspondence with Fleming on the subject of the latter's 'ingenious solution of the question of a Common Prime Meridian,' and declared himself 'fully alive to the Credit which would result to the Canadian Institute and to the Dominion of Canada at large, if your excellent solution of this International difficulty were successfully adopted.' He even offered to take the institute's memorial to Ottawa personally: see NA, MG 29, B1, vol. 54, folder 273, Wilson to Fleming, esp. 11 and 23 November 1878, 14 January, 19 February 1879, 19 and 25 April, 13 and 21 May, 4 July 1879, 1 April 1880.

45 UTL(F), MS Collection 193, RCI, box 37, Minutes of council, 25 January and 8 February 1878, pp. 453–4; for Fleming's descriptions of time, see 'Universal or Cosmic Time,' *PCI*, n.s., 2 (1884–5): 74, and 'Reforms in Time-Reckoning,' *PCI*, n.s., 2 (1890–1): 133–4. Cf. Creet, 'Sandford Fleming and Universal Time.'

46 See, for example, O'Malley, *Keeping Watch*; Kern, *The Culture of Time and Space.* NA, MG 29, B1, vol. 6, folder 39, BAAS to Fleming, 18 May 1878; Fleming to BAAS, 26 May 1878. Fleming, 'Time-Reckoning,' *PCI*, n.s., 1 (1879–83): 119, 122, and 'Longitude and Time-Reckoning,' *PCI*, n.s., 1 (1879–83): 145; Loudon, 'The Decimal System Applied to Time,' *PCI*, n.s., 2 (1884–5): 118–20; an interesting discussion afterwards suggested that the human mind was 'musically' organized and hence would insist upon the continuation of units divisible by twelve. Fleming, 'Universal or Cosmic Time,' *PCI*, n.s., 2 (1884–5): 60–77; Newcomb (1882), quoted in 'Supplementary Papers,' *PCI*, n.s., 3 (1885–6): 64; *PCI*, n.s., 6 (1887–8): 54–5; Fleming, 'Presidential Address: The Unit Measure of Time,' *PTRSC* 8 (1890), section 3: 3–6; 'Nomenclature in Time-Reckoning,' *PTRSC* 9 (1891), section 3: 19–26.

47 A.B. Macallum, 'Extract from the Annual Address of the President,' *PCI*, n.s.,

1 (1895–8): 1, and 'The Semi-Centennial of the Origin of Species,' *PTRSC*, ser. 3, 8 (1909), section 3: 535–47.

48 NA, MG 29, B1, vol. 54, folder 273, Wilson to Fleming, 14 April 1890; report on William Houston, 'Economic Science for Canadian Students,' *PCI* 3 (1891–2): 13. Harvey (1834–1905) was a former chief statistical clerk in the auditor general's department of the Province of Canada; Houston (1844–1931) was librarian of the Legislative Library of Ontario and from 1892 a public school inspector; see Wallace, *The Macmillan Dictionary of Canadian Biography*, 339–40, 367. On Houston, see also the following essay by Averill and Keith.

Daniel Wilson and the University of Toronto

HAROLD AVERILL AND GERALD KEITH

The Provincial University

On 1 January 1850, by act of the legislature of the Province of Canada, the University of King's College in Toronto was abolished. Created in 1827 with a strong Anglican bias, it had proven unsatisfactory to a majority of the citizens of Canada West (present-day Ontario), and it was replaced by the non-denominational University of Toronto. Most of King's faculty transferred to the new institution, including the president and classics professor, Dr John McCaul. Five new chairs were created, and in July 1851 the university's Senate advertised in the *Athenæum* for applicants.[1] It was for the chair of history and English literature that Daniel Wilson applied. As a professorship would provide him with both pecuniary peace of mind and the relative leisure to continue his anthropological studies,[2] his friends recommended him for an LLD to the University of St Andrews. Only later was he informed that it had been intended as a 'service to you in reference to the Toronto chair.'[3]

The university's non-denominational status was a principal attraction for Wilson. Passing the 1849 act had been a bold step by the Reform government of Robert Baldwin, after years of strife between the denominational factions of Canada West, to resolve the 'university question.' The government's view was that the only way to create a university for all its citizens was to exclude religion altogether. King's royal charter of 1827 and its endowment of 226,000 acres of Crown land had also been assigned to the University of Toronto. This move enraged the denominational colleges that had been founded in the previous decade in response to the exclusive nature of King's. Victoria College (Methodist) in Cobourg and

Queen's College (Church of Scotland) in Kingston, representing large portions of the colony's population,[4] were particularly hostile.

A non-denominational university was, in fact, ahead of its time. Although it was supported by liberal secularists such as George Brown, of the *Globe*, and William Hume Blake, soon to be elected the university's second chancellor,[5] the majority of the people in Canada West were not ready for the idea of non-sectarian higher education, and the cry of 'godless institution' thundered from the pulpits. 'There were ... too many people who believed that it was "essential for a teacher in arithmetic to hold orthodox views upon the doctrine of the Trinity."'[6]

The clause that required 'no religious Test or qualification whatsoever' of any student or employee of the university was roundly attacked. To remove doubts 'as to the Christian character' of the university, the act was amended in 1850 to provide for 'opportunities of religious instruction and attendance upon public worship.'[7] This change, however, satisfied no one, and in 1853 the 1849 act was repealed. Two corporate bodies, the University of Toronto and a new University College, emerged as the basis for a proposed federated system. The purpose of the 'Hincks Act' was to encourage the denominational colleges to federate under the umbrella of the University of Toronto, now considered to be the 'provincial university.' The model, as stated in the act, was the University of London, though Wilson himself believed it was really Queen's University in Belfast with which the premier, Sir Francis Hincks, was familiar.[8]

The new act retained the non-denominational feature of the 1849 act in University College and did not divide the endowment with the sectarian colleges, as they had wished. Rather, they had to federate to be entitled to a share of any surplus that might be available *after* the prior needs of the university and University College had been met.[9] The University of Toronto was limited to conducting examinations, awarding degrees, and managing the endowment. It was governed by a Senate, chaired by a vice-chancellor, which included the heads of all the denominational colleges. This arrangement, Wilson afterwards wrote, 'to a large extent handed over the government of the institution, at a most critical period in its history,' to those who wished the extinction of the institution itself.[10]

University College was the teaching wing of the university, in the arts alone, law and medicine having been 'privatized' under the act (though the university continued to examine in these subjects). It was governed by a Council, which was headed by the college president and composed of its professors through virtue of their occupying academic chairs. As only the president had a seat on the university Senate, the professors 'had no voice in determining the system of study on which their whole teaching depended.[11] University College was open to anyone who could pass its matriculation examinations and pay the nominal fees. Though dubbed 'godless' by its enemies, it was a thoroughly Christian institution. 'Lecture rooms are provided, and suitable hours will be set apart for the religious instruction of undergraduates by Ministers of their respective denominations,' and prayers were read 'on each lecture-day in the College hall at 10:00 a.m.'[12] From the beginning it attracted a body of students of diverse faiths. In 1863 they included Anglicans and Canada (Free Church) Presbyterians, who together formed the majority, Church of Scotland adherents, Methodists, Baptists, Congregationalists, and even Catholics, Lutherans, and Jews.[13]

Wilson was appointed to the chair of history and English literature at University College in the summer of 1853. In applying for the position he utilized his Scottish connections, which including fellow antiquarian Lord Elgin, governor of the Province of Canada and visitor to the university. Being Anglican, he also introduced himself to Bishop John Strachan, the founder of King's College, who had recently been in England to obtain a charter for his new Anglican institution, Trinity College.[14] Wilson relied heavily on his testimonials, which emphasized his high moral character, his industry, his acquaintance with his subjects, his communication skills, and his standing as an author. They praised, in particular, his ability to impart knowledge 'with eloquence and clearness' and 'the judgement and excellent method with which you turn your materials to account.' Most important of all was his ability 'to associate broad human sympathy with solid learning.'[15] Over the years this was to emerge as one of Wilson's greatest gifts for his tasks as administrator.

His unwavering belief in non-denominational education was reinforced by personal experience. For many years his brother George, an eminent scientist, was denied 'honours justly his due, and many Students were deprived of his instruction in his favourite science,' because he was not a Presbyterian.[16] When, in 1877, Daniel Wilson declined the headship of the new Anglican college being founded at London, Ontario, he gave as the reason his deeply held beliefs as an educationalist:

> I need not assure you of my sympathy in reference to all that pertains to the clear setting forth of evangelical truth ... But I must also inform you that I no less strongly desire to see the untrammelled freedom of scientific and philosophical research. Truth has nothing to fear in the long run from the researches of such men as Darwin and Huxley. I think it suffers more from

the shackles with which orthodox zeal would hamper enquiry, with the most honest intentions.

One of the grand blessings of the Reformation was the emancipation of the human mind from ecclesiastical authority; and the leaving it absolutely free in the exercise of private judgment and of the most unrestrained search into all truth ... Truth has everything to gain from the most absolute freedom of inquiry.

... Holding these opinions I conscientiously prefer such as that of the University of Toronto to any Denominational institution.

He concluded, 'The pecuniary inducements which you offer are considerably more than I enjoy at present. But if they were much greater they would exercise no influence on my decision.'[17]

The New Professor

Wilson's initial reaction to his new home was optimistic and positive. He wrote to his family, 'as to the place, people and the duties of the College, I like them all'; as he got to know them better, he would poke fun at those for whom he developed little regard.[18] The college had inherited many features of Scottish university education that were familiar to him: the giving of lectures by the professors themselves rather than, as in the English system, by tutors and the emphasis on the classics, mathematics, and philosophy. Attendance was at first not required, but examinations were integral to the system.[19] As Wilson was quick to note, this meant 'a vast deal more work to professors than our plain-sailing Scottish system.'[20] The new professor had some of the largest classes in the college, and his initial confidence that, 'if I stay here I shall after a year or two find it both easy and pleasant,'[21] was in time replaced by a wry admission that 'my duties are much more laborious than those of a Scottish History Chair. I have three lectures daily, besides examinations and other extra work.'[22]

Wilson found the bizarre, bifurcated structure of the college and university to be a recipe for conflict and soon discovered that few people, including ministers of education and premiers, fully understood how it functioned.[23] Thus the government, which had ultimate authority over university affairs, often did not comprehend the impact of its decisions and, being also susceptible to outside pressure, could not be guaranteed always to act in the university's best interests. It could influence internal statutes, for it could change the composition of the Senate at will, and it controlled the appointment of its officers – the chancellor and, initially, the vice-chancellor, who was thereafter elected to two-year terms by the Senate. Any statutes, passed either by the Senate or the College Council, that it did not like could be disallowed through the governor in his capacity as visitor to the university.

The Senate set the curriculum in arts and examinations in arts, law, and medicine and appointed all examiners, officers, and servants of the university, subject to government approval.[24] It could petition for increases in the salaries of the faculty and the creation of new positions, but all academic appointments remained the jealously guarded prerogative of the government until after the end of the century.[25] As the latter did not have to consult university or college officials when making appointments and disgruntled professors could also appeal directly to the minister of education or the premier, the result was endless intrigues within the university, which Wilson commented on with asperity over the years. The College Council, which was responsible for all aspects of the work of the college, was also vulnerable, especially to interference in matters relating to student discipline and the college buildings, including the residence.

The provision in the act for the affiliation of denominational colleges placed the university in a minority position in its own Senate. In 1853 the university and its college had only two seats out of twenty-three: the chancellor and the president of University College, who was also vice-chancellor. Half the remainder were the prerogative of its political masters; the others – ex officio the heads of the sectarian colleges, representatives of the professional schools (law and medicine), and the provincial superintendent of education, Egerton Ryerson – were potentially its enemies. John Langton, a government appointee and chair of the provincial Board of Audit, described the glaring deficiencies in the system: 'The heads of these other colleges, who bear us no love and, if they attend at all, do it only to obstruct ... the really important body, University College, has been thrown entirely into the hands of its President and only representative in our Senate ... The professors, who are a body of as good men as any country need wish to possess, are extinguished and Dr. McCaul is University College.'[26]

For his part, Wilson initially was willing to give McCaul full benefit of the doubt, declaring him to be a 'shrewd fellow and a good scholar, very well fitted for his post.'[27] But with experience and because he disliked sham and intrigue,[28] he came to deplore the president's methods. His opinion of him was to decline by degrees until, twenty-six years later, at the end of McCaul's presidency, he described him thus: 'at his best he has always been a ridiculously over-estimated man, and never out of some mean trick or other.'[29] Wilson was determined not to be bullied by McCaul. He wrote home about an anticipated 'fight about my Chair. He wants to make it a Chair of Ancient History, being imbued with all the old scholastic exclusive preference for everything classical. But I have not the slightest intention of being dictated to by any one as to what or how I shall teach.'[30] Besides stonewalling on issues in which he did not see a clear advantage to himself, McCaul kept professors in the dark on policy matters and maintained personal control of discretionary funds.[31]

Wilson quickly discovered him to be 'a bit of a martinet in all matters of College discipline'[32] with a penchant for ceremony that was often as comical as it was unnecessary. The university's matriculation examinations were 'managed with all becoming pomp and formality and at the same time with a degree of strictness such as would rather frighten some of our Scottish students.' He described a spectacle in which 'the examining professor enters in full costume preceded by the College Beadle bearing the mace, and is received by all the students standing, uncovered.' Wilson was not allowed to forgo this ritual even 'where *one* poor solitary student awaited my arrival! It cost me some difficulty to preserve my gravity under my silk tassel.'[33] In contrast, he strove to put his own students at their ease, as a question that he posed for the 1856 matriculation examinations illustrates: 'Write a short essay on the statement that examinations are more of a bugbear in anticipation than in reality.'[34]

Wilson had ample opportunity to observe the impact of politicians on faculty appointments. In 1853 only two of the four other new chairs were filled on the basis of merit, and in one of these, the chair of mathematics and natural philosophy, not with the best candidate. John Bradford Cherriman, a Cambridge mathematician of some standing, was selected over John Tyndall, a man with a much greater reputation.[35] Mineralogy and geology was awarded to Edward John Chapman, who had held the chair of mineralogy in the University of London. The other appointees relied on their close connections to the premier, Sir Francis Hincks.[36] Modern languages was filled by James Forneri, who presented an excellent testimonial from the premier's father. Natural history went to William Hincks, who, although his ideas and methods were antiquated and his teaching left much to be desired,[37] had the virtue of being the premier's brother. This connection outweighed the application of T.H. Huxley, whose career was already showing considerable promise and whose testimonials included one from Charles Darwin.[38] The troubled issue of political influence in faculty appointments was to continue throughout Wilson's career, driving him in the end to seek relief in retirement.

Daniel Wilson soon after his arrival in Canada in 1853 (UTL[F], Sproatt
Collection)

Above left: Wilson's mother, Janet Aitken Wilson, the remarkable woman who encouraged her children in their intellectual pursuits (Valentine collection)

Below left: Wilson's brother George, the first director of the Industrial Museum of Scotland; sepia drawing by ——— Fox (1839/40) (Scottish National Portrait Gallery, PG 2628)

Above: A photograph believed to be of Wilson's wife, Margaret Mackay (Valentine collection)

An engraving by Wilson after George Dodgson; probably done while he was working for William Miller or during his years in London (TRL, S65, vol. 6)

John Knox's House, Edinburgh, before its restoration; watercolour by Wilson dated April 1843 (EUL, Special Collections)

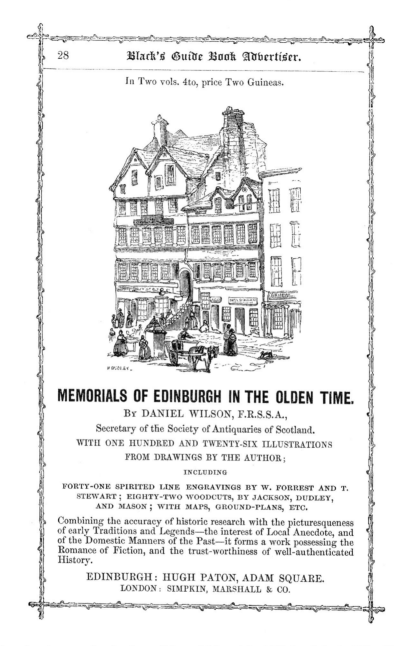

An advertisement for the first edition of *Memorials of Edinburgh in the Olden Time*; from *Black's Guide through Edinburgh* (1848) (National Monuments Record of Scotland, C76580)

Picts House at Wideford Hill showing the inclosing wall 2 feet high. From the upper edge of this to the top it is covered with stones lying flat, and over these the turf is laid. It appears as if the slope of the roof had afterwards been continued in front of the encircling wall, continuously with the slope of the hill by stones and rubbish care-fully laid in front of the wall, thus:-

The large stone forming the lintel of the opening of the western passage leading to the exterior, is placed about three feet within the front of the enclosing wall, as shown in the sketch.
O, the lintel.
X the encir-cling wall.
The dotted lines show how the line of the slope is continued by stones and rubbish carefully disposed outside the wall.

From Notes furnished by Mr Geo. Petrie Jr of Kirkwall, to Captain Thomas. R.N.

Wilson's drawings and notes on a 'Picts' house' in Orkney excavated in 1849 by George Petrie; Lieutenant F.W.L. Thomas's plans of the site were reproduced in Wilson's *Prehistoric Annals of Scotland* (TRL, S65, vol.1: 55)

Elm Cottage, Blackford Road, Edinburgh, the pair of houses built for the family by Uncle Peter Wilson in the 1850s, where Wilson always hoped to retire (photograph by Ian MacKenzie, School of Scottish Studies, University of Edinburgh)

St Paul's, Yorkville (Toronto), in July 1848, a few years before Wilson and his family moved to a cottage just out of sight to the left; watercolour by William Arthur Johnson (TRL, T10800)

Daniel Wilson and his younger daughter, Sybil, about 1854 (reprinted from H.H. Langton, *Sir Daniel Wilson*, courtesy of UTA)

Wilson's Cousin Maggie, the novelist Margaret Oliphant (Valentine collection)

University College, Toronto, under construction in the 1850s (UTA, A77-0049/002[181])

Daniel Wilson, *The Saguenay* (undated); watercolour (NGC, acc. 2014)

Daniel Wilson, *Landing in a Mist, Nipigon Gut* (13 July 1866); watercolour over pencil (NA / C-40206)

Daniel Wilson, *West Cliff, Nipigon* (27 July 1866); watercolour over pencil (NA / C-40220)

Daniel Wilson, *Camp Fire, Trading Lake* (22 August 1870); watercolour (AGO, acc. 744)

THE MARTYRS OF THE "REFORMATION."

AS THE LEARNED PROFESSOR *MIGHT* HAVE ILLUSTRATED IT.

Wilson defending the principles of the Reformation against the inroads of
Tractarianism; cartoon by J.W. Bengough in *Grip*, 19 February 1875 (UTL)

The Crozier of St Fillan, which Wilson was able to return to Scotland in 1877;
a lithograph, based on his own drawing, in Wilson, *The Quigrich* (1859) (TRL)

The graduating class in modern languages at University College in 1880, the year
that Wilson became president; he is seated second from the right (UTA, B97-0027)

Daniel Wilson (seated left) and William Nelson (standing left) with their families,
holidaying at Philiphaugh in the Scottish borders in 1880; Sybil Wilson is seated at
the far right (Valentine collection)

Wilson's last home, Bencosie (right), at the corner of St George and Russell streets; demolished in the 1960s; the house to the left is still standing (private collection, Toronto)

The University of Toronto convocation of 1890, held in tents on the lawn after fire gutted University College in February that year (UTA, A76-0002[17])

Sir Daniel Wilson in old age (UTA, A75-0026/517[99])

Familiar with the richness of student life at the University of Edinburgh, Wilson was convinced that an organization for students would give those at Toronto 'a fresh and more lasting interest in the College, a thing greatly needed here.'[39] In February 1854, only months after arriving, he initiated the founding of a literary and debating society, mediating between the students and McCaul, who 'very nearly knocked the whole on the head by some of his stupid martinet interference, just for the pleasure of exercising a little brief authority.'[40] Wilson invited the students to tea at his home. 'My college janitor, a very nice obliging fellow, came and acted as my waiter ... I feel well assured the young gentlemen won't get on a bit the worse with me, or treat me with the less respect for the pleasant evening they spent with me.' The response was positive. 'I have promised,' Wilson wrote, 'to take the chair at the first meeting.'[41] His relationship with the students had already achieved a level of geniality and an absence of stuffiness that was to mark his career. After his death, a friend observed that 'the students found him easy of access and were always welcome in his home.'[42]

So began the University College Literary and Scientific Society, the first student organization of the college. It had its own reading room, which it stocked with periodicals, but it was best known for its Friday night meetings and periodic public debates; the latter quickly became a feature of the Toronto social calendar. The evening meetings of the 'Lit' involved readings by its members, debates, and essay competitions. Wilson was in regular attendance, often chairing the debate. On one of the rare occasions when the usually terse minutes were expanded, 'Dr. Wilson in a few remarks stated that "it would have been interesting to have seen the views of William III, the great originator of the alliance against France to know what would have been his views when the King of Spain was no longer Archduke of Austria, but Emperor."'[43] Wilson's support for the students and the Lit never wavered, as its newspaper, the *White and Blue*, acknowledged in 1879: 'The Society is not to be discouraged. He who has long been its guide, mentor and friend ... has magnanimously promised it that mild but impartial criticism, and that unobtrusive but ever-welcome advice which has so long been its reliance and support.'[44]

In 1853 Wilson had no seat on the Senate and thus a very limited say on the curriculum and related matters. Hence he sought out senators with whom he might establish a rapport. John Langton and Frederic W. Cumberland, an architect, became friends and allies, but one man proved a huge disappointment. Years later, Wilson wrote that, because of Egerton Ryerson's reputation in establishing the non-sectarian public school system, 'I welcomed his advances when I first came to Canada, and communicated with him on College matters, in full belief that he, as one of the then members of the University Senate ... was peculiarly worthy of reliance. I learned to know in him the most unscrupulous and jesuitically untruthful intriguer I ever had to do with ... his ideas scarcely rose above the requirements of the common school.'[45] Ryerson's interests were incompatible with the welfare of the university. He wanted to limit its functions and subordinate it to the common schools,[46] and he championed the Methodists in the despoiling of the university's endowment. A distinct enmity grew between the two men that climaxed during the 1860 inquiry into the university.

Internal college politics of the early years focused around the intractableness of President McCaul. John Langton spent three very trying years attempting to instil order in the institutional finances, fretting that 'the monetary system or rather no system' was 'radically bad, the limits of the College and University almost undefined.' He added that McCaul 'was absolutely deficient in the talent of order.' Langton enlisted the assistance of Wilson and other professors who, he observed in his characteristically strong language, 'from hatred of McCaul stick to me like bricks, but without much power.'[47]

All university funds were invested in the Crown, but the university had to ask permission to utilize them. As the endowment then also provided 'more money than we could or the Government would let us spend,' political meddling was inevitable. Between 1853 and 1856, for example, the university was forced to make bad loans, sell land for less than market value, and agree to a portion of the University Park being fenced off for an insane asylum in the old King's College building, which was insultingly named the 'University Asylum.'[48] The university also infuriated the denominational colleges by ensuring that there was no surplus of funds to share. Langton observed of those first years, 'We spent in some things most lavishly, granting scholarships and prizes without limit, so that it was the exception rather than the rule if a student had not a scholarship or half a dozen prizes.'[49]

Wilson arrived just as the curriculum was about to undergo a major revision, the first of many over the years. It had become so overloaded with subjects that the undergraduate program followed the Scottish example[50] of being extended from three to four years. The principle of 'options' was introduced, which allowed new courses, such as modern languages, to be substituted for core ones in certain years.[51] Wilson strongly supported this development as contributing to the educational needs of the future. He argued that 'the old Classical Course of Oxford is not fitted to accomplish that object,'[52] a view that had been expressed years before by fellow Scot John Strachan.[53]

McCaul, however, stalled on discussions over much needed changes to the examination system, bringing on a challenge to his authority. In May 1856 Langton defeated him in the first Senate election for vice-chancellor.[54] The president was not to be counted out, for, when William Hume Blake resigned as chancellor the following month, McCaul campaigned furiously for the post. Langton warned darkly that his getting it 'would effectually finish the University.'[55] He used his access to the governor (a new chancellor was not designated until December) to press for the appointment of college professors to the Senate. In February 1857 Wilson, his friend Henry Croft, professor of chemistry, and J.B. Cherriman were chosen. The resulting power shift in the Senate enabled the reform of the curriculum to go forward. Statutes relating to examinations in arts, law, medicine, civil engineering, and agriculture, moved by Langton and usually seconded by Wilson, were passed by the end of April. McCaul was reduced to retaliating in small ways, such as voting against certain of Wilson's projects.[56]

Wilson's reputation was further enhanced with the construction of a building for University College. In 1853 the government had expropriated the former King's College building and its 'very fine, and extensive, beautifully planted' grounds, in what is now Queen's Park, for the future site of the legislative buildings. Wilson had begun lecturing in the college's temporary quarters in the former Parliament Buildings.[57] Over the next five years the college was relocated as many times, with corresponding disruptions to its work and morale. Chancellor Blake argued that it brought what ought to be the foremost educational institution in the country 'into public contempt' and left it 'dependent on public charity for the means of carrying out its necessary business.'[58] Matters were in such a troubled state that in 1852 and again in 1855 there was no commencement (as convocation was then known).

A new governor and former professor at Oxford, Sir Edmund Walker Head, signalled his support for the proposed building. Years later Wilson described him as 'a Governor-General of the old type, who in that transitional stage of Canadian history, claimed to rule when he saw fit, as well as to govern.'[59] As visitor to the university, Head pressured the government to authorize the drawing of £95,000 from university funds for a new building, library, and museum. On 7 February 1856 the Senate appointed a building committee and an architect, Frederic Cumberland,

recently resigned from the Senate. Shortly afterwards, with the resignation of Blake as chancellor and the refusal of the chief justice to play an
active role, Langton became a one-man committee. An ad hoc committee
was struck, which included Wilson and McCaul, to serve as an advisory
body to, but not to share authority with (as McCaul wished), Langton's
building committee. In meetings with the architect, Wilson happily drew
on his background as an artist and antiquarian. He furnished drawings
for capitals, corbels, many of the gargoyles, the great double-lit window in
the tower with the rich and elaborate ornament surrounding it, and the
three finials on the corners of the tower which balance the turret at the
northeast corner.[60] The result of their collaboration was a Norman
Romanesque style 'with traces of Byzantium' proudly summarized by
Langton as 'the Canadian style.'[61]

On 4 October 1856 the cornerstone of University College was laid by
Langton, Wilson, and Croft. Exactly two years later, at a banquet attended
by the governor on the very public occasion of placing the coping stone
with the tower, Wilson, fittingly, gave the toast to the architects. In a lively
speech laced with humour, he contrasted the laying of the cornerstone to
the present public occasion: 'We rather proceeded in it, something like the
returned captive Jews of old, who wrought with swords in their hands,
dreading the enemy. (laughter) Secretly as if we were engaged almost in a
deed of shame, we laid that stone, full of hope, but full also of fear ... it is
an emblem and an evidence of what is to be the character of this institution
and of its alumni in future times – that they are not to boast as they who lay
hold of the sword, but are to wait for the hour of triumph when the work
is accomplished.' Wilson concluded with the hope that the lesson taught
by Cumberland – not to be a slave to precedent – would be remembered.
'He has finished a beautiful structure, consistent in all respects with the
style he has adopted, but has in no one point sacrificed its wise and fitting
adaption to the modern purposes to which it is to be devoted.'[62]

Wilson's metaphoric references to swords, armour, and fields of battle
were apt. The building's magnificence, so contrasting to the more modest structures of the penurious denominational colleges, would bring on
another round of attacks against the 'godless' university. But the expenditure had been deliberate and wise, for, as John A. Macdonald commented
humorously, 'even Methodists can't steal bricks and mortar.'[63] In the
Senate the professors were now in a position to exercise considerable
influence,[64] and to use their talents effectively, Langton created five
standing committees.[65] To rein in McCaul, who had indirectly controlled
the Senate's discretionary funds, each committee now had its funds voted

directly by the Senate and was accountable to it for how the moneys were spent.[66]

These standing committees and ad hoc ones created later served as Wilson's training ground in university administration and politics. He tackled his new duties with determination, skill, and good humour. Even the committees on which he served briefly, such as those devoted to Upper Canada College and buildings and grounds, gave him valuable experience, especially in the hiring of academic staff,[67] managing the divided responsibilities between the college and university, and dealing with legal issues.[68] One of his first tasks as a member of the Senate was to help negotiate with the city the thorny issue of the University Park. Wilson also sat on the museum committee, which seldom had a budget of more than $50 per year. He spent many hours writing letters to individuals and institutions to ask for specimens.[69]

As well, Wilson poured much energy into the library committee, on which he sat continuously, except for four years, from 1857 until his death.[70] He firmly believed in the central role that a library played in a university, having arrived in 1853 to a pitiful collection of books in his subject areas.[71] His pressure resulted in the Senate's committing more funds[72] – the book budget reached £2,500 in 1856. By the following year the library's overwhelmingly classical bias had been reduced, and one-sixth of its 6,900 volumes related to courses that Wilson taught.[73] After it moved into the East Hall of the new building in 1859, however, the era of financial largesse came to an end. Wilson had to fight annually even for modest sums, and in some years he despaired of finding any funds.[74]

The financial management of the university and the college was vested in the bursar, who reported to the government independent of the Senate.[75] The latter, before 1866 and the creation of a standing committee on finance,[76] had little fiscal authority. The impetus for change was the report of an ad hoc committee, set up in 1863 to review the university's finances and chaired by Wilson. His report recommended changes in accounting procedures and confirmed that expenditures had been exceeding revenues for some time. As an economy measure, it urged that the professors in meteorology and agriculture have their salaries paid from non-university sources. But it insisted that annual allotments be made for books and periodicals for the library.[77]

Formal duties aside, Wilson had many ideas for the improvement of the university. The adoption of official symbols, he argued, would help to facilitate a much needed sense of pride and place for the institution. Two statutes were introduced in the Senate in 1857, one respecting a corporate seal for the university, which was opposed by McCaul and Ryerson, and the second for a coat of arms that Wilson had designed. The first proposal apparently did not progress past second reading, but the second received unanimous support.[78]

Enemies within the Gates

The university and college had not yet moved into their new home when the sectarian colleges resumed their attack. It began at the Conference of the Wesleyan Methodist Church in November 1859, and President Samuel Nelles of Victoria College made no apologies for a lack of tact, arguing that 'the rich and well-fed are known to be delicate; hungry palates are not so nice.'[79] The Conference's memorial was referred, early in 1860, to a select committee of the Legislative Assembly in Quebec City. The Methodists and their allies, led by Egerton Ryerson, levelled charges of abuse of the terms of the 1853 act, extravagance, and lowering the standard of higher education. Unfortunately for them, they faced an unsympathetic commissioner in George Brown and strong rebuttals from John Langton, representing the University of Toronto, and Daniel Wilson, selected by the University College Council as its representative. McCaul, who would normally have defended the college, acknowledged that he was too closely identified with former colleagues now at Trinity College.[80] But the choice of Wilson was an acknowledgment of the ascendancy that he even then exercised among his associates.[81]

No recommendations came from the proceedings of the select committee, only an exhaustive record of every charge and defence. Wilson's testimony was a brilliant tour de force and consolidated his reputation both as an educational reformer and as a spirited defender of the university. He countered Ryerson point for point, castigated him for 'characterizing us as a pack of scoundrels,' and stated the case for modern languages as the key to modern philosophy and science. He refuted Ryerson's championing of the English model of education, arguing that the university had 'tried to mature a system of study adapted for Canada; neither taking Oxford, nor Dublin, nor the Scottish Universities, nor the Queen's University in Ireland, as our sole model; but trying to get from each what was specially fitted for the requirements of this new country which occupies a position different from all.' He reiterated the then 'startlingly novel' view that the program of matriculation examinations should be adjusted to the educational level of the province and that the whole academic program should be flexible in its application. The course of study should 'prove an effective source, not only of intelligent culture, but would prepare the youth of Canada for the practical duties of life.'[82]

When the committee issued no report, Wilson, anticipating further trouble, moved for the establishment of a Senate committee to defend the university against any attempt to divide its endowment.[83] Among this committee's members was James Patton, a tool of the Methodists, but not Langton, who was now involved in politics at Quebec. The latter's absence weakened the pro-university forces, and before Wilson's committee could accomplish anything, Ryerson and his friends moved to take over the Senate. When Langton stood for re-election as vice-chancellor in December 1860, he was defeated by Patton despite being stoutly defended by Wilson.[84]

With the enemy now occupying the chair of the Senate itself, an avalanche of pamphlets on the 'university question' descended on the public from both camps.[85] Ryerson used his influence with the government to get a royal commission, stacked with enemies of the university, to review the evidence of the 1860 committee and present a report. Its recommendations were both predictable and regressive: the university was to be reconstituted as the University of Upper Canada, with two-thirds of the members of the Senate representing the affiliated colleges. University College was to be renamed King's College and limited to $28,000 a year. As well, a liberal provision was to be made for any institution agreeing to affiliate with the university, including a permanent endowment.[86]

The report set off a series of events that would change forever the political landscape regarding education in Canada West. Over the years, increasing numbers of students had been graduating from the provincial university. Dedicated to the defence of their alma mater, these young men were led into battle by lawyers Edward Blake and Adam Crooks, both former students of Wilson's and recent appointees to the Senate, who shared their professor's ideals on non-sectarian education. Alarmed by the reactions to their report, Patton and Ryerson manoeuvred desperately to prevent the Senate from acting against it, but Crooks and Blake took the matter to a public meeting on 3 March 1863. It 'consisted mainly of determined undergraduates seated in a solid block. They were in no mood for formalities, they had no ears for their opponents, and their series of resolutions were simply bellowed through.'[87] Ryerson's grand scheme for the destruction of the university died with Robert Sullivan, a prominent graduate, proposing from the platform at Convocation an appropriate acknowledgment of the mole, Patton: 'three groans for the Vice-Chancellor.'[88] In December 1864 Patton stood down as vice-chancellor, and Adam Crooks was elected in his stead.[89] Wilson later wrote, 'It is very doubtful if the men of our own day realize how narrowly their University escaped extinction.'[90]

The events of these three years had two immediate results, one being the entrenching of Wilson's belief in the perfidy of the denominational colleges. 'In Senate, College Council, and wherever I have any influence I protest against all compromise ... I came out here under a totally different and nonsectarian system, which all my experience and observation satisfy me is the wise and true one for the province. Compromise is a mere staving off of the evil, especially with men so utterly unprincipled as I have found the Methodist leaders to be.'[91] The immediate threat of extinction was removed, however, for 'from that date the representatives of the denominational colleges ceased to take any active share in the administration of the provincial University.'[92]

The Rise of Convocation

The new power created was that of the graduates of the university themselves, collectively known as Convocation. Young and self-confident, Crooks and Blake represented a new element in educational politics, that of 'nativism' – the belief that Canadian, even Torontonian, was best. Given impetus by their role as saviours of the university, it emerged by the mid-1870s as a rallying cry whenever academic posts became available. With the annual number of graduates rising from seventeen in 1853 to sixty-one in 1867, provided with a standard of education second to none, they not surprisingly wanted to see members of their own select class become leaders, not only in society and politics, but in teaching within the college itself.

Confederation in 1867 diverted public interest away from the 'university question.' In the new Canada, education was designated a provincial responsibility. One of the first acts of the government of Sandfield Macdonald in the new province of Ontario was to stop providing annual grants from the public purse to the denominational colleges, forcing them to rely entirely on voluntary subscriptions. The provincial university, with enrolment rising rapidly and facing new demands for a broader curriculum, was also hard pressed to survive on its endowments alone. It had no alternative; Macdonald stated categorically that 'the Government had nothing to do with the University and did not want to have anything to do with it.'[93]

Crooks, an advocate of 'a strong, central provincial university, with control shared by faculty and graduates,'[94] was representative of a group of recent graduates that included William Mulock, Thomas Moss, and James Loudon, all of whom would soon play significant roles in the university.[95] They began to press for the election of graduates to the Senate. Wilson was sympathetic, for in Quebec in 1860 he had stated that one measure of Senate reform was for graduates to elect some members from among their own.[96] But he was wary of the ideas of the Toronto-based Canada First movement, which gained influence when the Reformers under Edward Blake took power in December 1871.[97] He viewed its promoting of Canadians whenever academic positions opened up as antipathetic to the principle of getting the best minds for the money offered. At stake was the very standard of education that he had defended in 1860.

The supporters of nativism were not yet strong enough to mount a challenge in 1871, when two chairs became vacant with the forced retirement of James Beaven,[98] the unpopular professor of metaphysics, and the death of William Hincks. George Paxton Young, professor of mental and moral philosophy in Knox College and previously grammar school inspector for Canada West,[99] applied for Beaven's position. He asked his long-time friend and fellow Scot Daniel Wilson for a reference. This Wilson gladly gave, but in spite of Young's credentials, 'frankly added that, on general principles, he was in favour of advertising the vacancy, and then selecting the best candidate who might offer himself.' Premier Macdonald thought otherwise and appointed Young without advertising.[100] The university, in Wilson's words, got 'a really good man,' who proved to be the best lecturer of his era.[101] It also got a 'new, young Natural History professor,' Henry Alleyne Nicholson, another Scot, to replace Hincks.[102] He was both vigorous and innovative, but stayed only three years, much to Wilson's regret, for he proved a stalwart ally on the College Council.

Adam Crooks had joined the Blake government in 1871, and through the 'Crooks Act' passed two years later, graduates finally got a real say in the government of the university (Convocation elected fifteen senators for five-year terms and the chancellor). The government's direct influence (nine appointees for three-year terms) was reduced and that of the denominational colleges was removed entirely, as only affiliated ones were permitted representatives.[103]

Of the leading Convocation senators, only James Loudon, dean of residence with a seat on the College Council, combined administrative experience with an academic position. Mathematical tutor since 1863 and a lecturer in the new School of Technology, he championed disinterested scientific research, the total separation of science from metaphysics, and a commitment to the German-led principle of research within universities.[104] He was in disagreement with Wilson, who, like most of his contemporaries, 'chose to subordinate both "pure" and "practical" forms of research to the pursuit of "culture" – indeed to "high culture" ... to forge a compromise between empirical investigation and metaphysical necessity, between the imperatives of nature and culture.'[105] Nevertheless, Wilson had encouraged Loudon in his academic advancement and hoped for his support on the College Council. But Loudon, ambitious, proud, and easily offended, saw himself not 'belonging to any party in the Council, but intended to act independently on all questions that came before it.'[106] The testing of wills between the older professoriate and the younger members of the Senate began immediately over the issue of a separate science degree. Loudon's minority report, which advocated maintaining the arts degree as the universal one, carried when he was able to convince the waverers that the DSc proposed by Wilson would suffice as a distinctive science degree.[107]

In April 1874, when Nicholson's impending departure was announced, the nativists teamed up with McCaul to launch an attack on Wilson and his supporters. Wilson discovered, much to his surprise, that Crooks 'had been recommending the abolition of the chair and the President working like a mole underground.'[108] While this attack did not succeed – the chair remained and was filled by another Scot, Robert Ramsay Wright – the battle lines were drawn. The following year, Cherriman resigned from the chair of mathematics and natural philosophy. He recommended that it be divided into a lectureship in experimental physics (Loudon's speciality), to be filled immediately, and a senior appointment in mathematics and natural philosophy, to be filled later with a Cambridge man.[109] When the government demurred, the nativists seized their chance.

Loudon represented the first opportunity for a graduate of University College to be appointed to one of its chairs. He later claimed that he applied only after receiving an 'insulting message from Dr. Wilson' that he 'need not go to the expense of printing testimonials ... as the matter had already been decided' against him.[110] Loudon was certainly not Wilson's choice,[111] but the latter's testimonial was gracious and his covering letter offered additional information 'if you are printing.'[112] Loudon's friends, fearing Wilson's influence on Oliver Mowat, who had replaced Blake as premier, insisted that he apply. One wrote, 'I *advise* you to *move* – don't *wait* to receive the office – or be offered it – but see your friends – especially *Moss* [double underlining] ... Have written Mowat and Moss.'[113] Loudon quickly gathered in no fewer than fifty-five testimonials.[114]

Wilson's position in favour of outside candidates stood little chance before the enormous pressure now brought to bear on Mowat. Moss and Blake both wrote to him,[115] the issue might be raised in the legislature, and George Brown was said to be favourably disposed.[116] Most of Loudon's colleagues were supportive, none more so than Paxton Young, who had 'much pleasure in bearing testimony to your eminent fitness for the position,' and President McCaul, who saw a chance to thwart Wilson.[117] The issue of excellence versus a 'nativist' appointment was argued to the highest level of the administration. While Mowat agreed with Blake 'that as between two applicants of nearly equal ability the Canadian should be selected and without hesitation,' he asked, 'would you go further than that, in favour of nativism, as regards college professorships?' While the premier was 'a little inclined' to recommend Loudon's appointment without advertising, he retreated under pressure from Wilson and the other professors, who argued that 'a much superior man might happen to be among the applicants' and that advertising was 'a check against inferior appointments – a check which some future government may need even if we do not.'[118] Mowat compromised by keeping the closing date for the competition so short that Wilson remarked, 'we have been treated with scant courtesy in getting such tardy notice of the vacant chair.'[119]

The growing influence of the nativists was also being reflected in the Senate. In the election for vice-chancellor in 1874, Thomas Moss, who had been registrar of University College from 1861 to 1873, won easily.[120] He was a popular choice, being, as Wilson put it, 'a man of clear intellect, sound judgment, and sterling integrity,'[121] as well as great charm. Beginning in 1875, McCaul's participation in the work of the Senate began noticeably to decline. Despite heavy commitments elsewhere, Moss devoted a great deal of time to his position. He and Wilson piloted many measures through the Senate, with Wilson taking on more committee work than ever.[122] He moved Moss's re-election as vice-chancellor in 1877 and was devastated when he died in 1881 at the early age of forty-four.

Growth and Change

The rise in the status of the vice-chancellor under Moss's stewardship had been aided by the election of Edward Blake as chancellor in 1876 in succession to the ineffectual Joseph Morrison. Blake 'bestrode the narrow world of university politics like a colossus'[123] and shared Moss's philosophical and political views. Together they began to institute a number of changes that had an immediate impact. Two developments in 1878 were of particular importance for the future. First, a School of Practical Science, advocated by Loudon and others and supported by Moss and Blake,[124] replaced the School of Technology. This move, also strongly encouraged by Adam Crooks, who had became minister of education the previous year, brought the study of engineering into a close relationship with University College.[125] While funds for its costly scientific equipment were met largely from government revenues, an additional financial burden was placed on the university,[126] and the teaching load of the professors was increased.

Wilson was directly involved with filling the school's chair of engineering, for he urged Crooks to appoint William Bell Dawson, a son of his old friend at McGill, John William Dawson. The minister seemed amenable and invited Dawson to Toronto to look over the facilities in the new school building. Dawson arrived after Wilson had left for Edinburgh and just as the professors were finalizing their selection of offices. With Crooks's approval, he began making his own arrangements, to the intense annoyance of the other professors. Ramsay Wright, in a letter to an absent James Loudon, stated: 'I was rather flabbergasted when I came back [from Muskoka] to find he is to be retained for consultation till the appointment is made ... I was most astounded however to find that Crooks had been out to the School with young Dawson ... and have appropriated the large room, reserved as I understood for your apparatus.'[127] The letter also reveals that, contrary to Loudon's later assertions, Crooks meant to advertise the position from the beginning. He then asked Loudon to recommend the most appropriate applicant. Loudon chose John Galbraith, a University College graduate with solid practical experience.[128]

In May the finance committee of the Senate was replaced by a Board of Management headed by the vice-chancellor. Its other members were two nominees from the Senate, one from the College Council – who did not have to be members of either, to encourage the inclusion of businessmen – and the president of University College. More members were added later, and in 1884 the name was changed to the Board of Trustees.[129] The board advised on the management of the endowment and the sale or lease of property and monitored internal university expenditures. While the bursar retained ultimate control, the board, by bringing in financial expertise, was expected gradually to expand the university's contacts in the business community and ultimately to tap private sources of funding. It also provided another power base for the vice-chancellor, for it was much more easily controlled than the Senate.

During the last few years of the 1870s, the strains on the university's resources increased. Its fixed revenue could not accommodate the demands for more teaching staff, books for the library, and equipment for the laboratories as the numbers of students continued to grow. The scarcity of funds increased tensions in the College Council, where professors quarrelled over departmental funding allocations. The School of Practical Science and James Loudon, with their insatiable demands for expensive scientific equipment, merely added to the problems.[130] For its part, the Senate had to address demands for new programs and for fundamental changes to the curriculum.

Meanwhile, two of Wilson's nemeses left the scene. The first to go was Egerton Ryerson, who had retired as superintendent of education in 1877. Four years earlier, when the position was still a civil service appointment and Ryerson had toyed with retiring, Wilson had been offered it. But, he observed, 'Old E. changes his mind; so I don't change my place.'[131] In 1875, in anticipation of Ryerson's final departure and as a sign of Wilson's stature as an educator, Mowat offered to make him minister of public instruction with a seat in the cabinet. Wilson stated that he could not accept the offer, 'reserving the reversions of one or other of the two offices, worth $4000 per ann. placed at my option, without risking the chances of finding myself in a very invidious position, in which I should peril my independence and self-respect.'[132]

The second departure was President McCaul, whose attended his last Senate meeting in June 1876, though he regularly appeared at the Board of Management meetings until 1879. With Moss's appointment as chief justice of Ontario in 1878, a vacuum began to emerge in the leadership of the college. News, in July 1879, of McCaul's retirement raised Wilson's hopes. He noted that 'we have much need of a little new blood. Things have been drifting of late in a fashion that has made me wonder at times how we escaped the shoals and sunken rocks.'[133] The news was premature, however, for in October the college reopened 'with McCaul reinstated as President ... Rumours of what is to be are of the most contradictory and conflicting kind: probably because the minister does not know his own mind.'[134] Crooks had been unable to find a replacement for McCaul, there were unresolved differences over his pension,[135] and he now proved more difficult than ever. Wilson observed grimly that 'the President is now in that stage of touchy irritable senility which makes him an obstruction in every way.'[136] McCaul would not leave office for another year.

Among the press coverage of his impending departure was a comment on the nature of president's office. The *Mail* noted that it was not necessarily an adjunct to any chair and that it could be conferred on 'one of the present members of the faculty, on one of the new appointees [to the chairs of chemistry – Croft was also retiring – and classical literature], inasmuch as the duties are onerous enough in themselves, upon someone who is charged with no particular department of college work.' Its comment that 'the office is, comparatively speaking, of less consequence than the other appointments' underlined the challenges any incumbent faced. The paper argued that the appointee 'should be possessed of good administrative ability ... a careful economizer' of the college's income, and 'a prudent director of its expenditure.'[137]

That Wilson would succeed McCaul was by no means certain. The government had no intention of making an appointment that was not linked to a chair. McCaul's had been the senior chair, and the government, with an eye to tradition and to saving money, was inclined to fill both it and the presidency with the same person. Wilson opposed Crooks's 'one idea the getting of an eminent classical scholar' and his being 'prepared to place in the office of president any good first class Oxford or Cambridge classical man. I must confess I look forward to it with no little apprehension. A man from any of the Scottish Universities would have a vast deal less to unlearn.'[138]

The imminent retirement of Croft, Wilson's junior by four years, on two-thirds salary after thirty-seven years prompted Wilson to reflect on his own situation in January 1880 (he had just turned sixty-four): 'Getting old. Pair of glasses for reading at night ... Who knows if even three years lie at the bottom of the yet undrained cup. What a luxury would an independent competency be now. On the wrong side of sixty; though with no great consciousness of failing energy as yet.'[139] As for the possibility of his being passed over for the presidency, Wilson wrote to William Dawson: 'If a really efficient administrator, in sympathy with non-sectarian education and having faith in the moral and religious element, as a thing perfectly compatible with a non-denomination college, – if such a thing is found for the President, I for one shall be delighted to serve under him, and loyally help him in all ways.'[140]

Ten months passed with no decision coming from the minister. In March 1880 Wilson wrote to Dawson, 'We are no nearer any settlement of College matters than we were months ago; and are meanwhile accumulating cares for the new head, whoever he may be, that will render his office no sinecure.'[141] Crooks, notoriously indecisive, was becomingly more erratic as his mental and physical faculties declined. His behaviour during the search in England was odd enough to cause comment among academic circles there, and it was not long before the stories reached Toronto.[142]

The first potential candidate, a recent Oxford honours graduate chosen by Crooks and Moss, hurriedly declined the offer when his visit to Toronto was greeted with hostile comments in the press.[143] In subsequent negotiations, Wilson rejected Crooks's promise that, if a classical professor was also made president, he would receive the post of vice-president with a suitable increase in salary.[144] Crooks finally made him an offer of the presidency in a letter of 6 May 1880, only to withdraw it.[145] At the end of term, Wilson and his family left on holiday for Scotland. Before sailing, he wrote to Crooks 'asking him "to inform me on what terms you will allow me to retire." I left Toronto in the belief that I had delivered my last lecture; and when in Edinburgh revisited my old "Elm Cottage" with the thought and hope of recovering it and ending my days there. Maggie was contented; and I was more than reconciled to the prospect, when on July 29 came a cable message from the Minister of Education "Council will advise your appointment as President" and instructing me to proceed at once with efforts to find a fit successor for the classical chair. So here I am, President of University College, with a new lease of Canadian life.'[146] Crooks had run out of options, and in Toronto the editor of the *Canada Educational Monthly* trumpeted, 'We have Professor Wilson at last as President.'[147]

The New President

His vacation ruined and with the minister in Toronto, Wilson tackled the problem of selecting a successor for the chair of classics, a tutor in classics, and a new dean of residence.[148] With the last two positions being combined as an economy measure, choosing a new dean proved particularly challenging, for 'correspondence has been impossible, except through the Ocean Cable; and that does not admit to a detailed discussion of principles.'[149]

Meanwhile, back in Canada, the Young Canada Party railed in the press against Crooks over the appointment of non-natives to these positions.[150] The temperate *Canada Educational Monthly* conceded that, while an English appointment to the chair of classics could be supported, such was not the case for the other positions. Moreover, 'the arrangement under which the classical professor comes out is understood to give great offence to the faculty.' It concluded that more was expected of Crooks than 'to set the Faculty by the ears and to estrange from himself and the institution every *alumnus* of the College.'[151] When Wilson returned to the university, he found 'students, graduates, professors and all in a state of intensest irritation ... so I shall enter on my duties as president with abundant need for all possible tact, prudence and judgment.'[152] In addition, the university faced the greatest turnover of staff in a decade. 'I am likely to find myself with a new visitor, a new vice-chancellor, College Registrar, and Dean; just when any kind of old experience would be valuable.'[153]

Wilson was placed in the difficult position where 'the champions of my appointment as President have me now thrust in their teeth as the culprit who went to Oxford and did the deed of selecting both classical professor and tutor there!'[154] He took up his pen to defend his choices and, by implication, his minister. In a letter to the *Globe*, 'suggested by myself, though professedly in reply to one written by the Provincial Secretary,' he made no apology for the standards by which he had measured his actions. His primary concerns were administrative continuity and the maintenance of high academic and moral standards. These, he said, had been met in Maurice Hutton, the new classics professor, who had impressive academic credentials, and in Frederick Vines, the new college dean, 'a thoroughly high-minded man, impressed with the responsibilities involved in undertaking the oversight of the Residence students.' Wilson disarmed the critics further by reminding them that the best Canadian candidate for the deanship had declined the post.[155] The furore in the faculty was the result of Hutton's salary being $600 more than the other professors received. Their appeal to Crooks merely exacerbated the problem, since he raised the salaries of only two of the five. Moving quickly to defuse the situation, Wilson persuaded those with higher incomes to give a portion to the other three and promised Hutton a quid pro quo later on.[156]

The first staff appointment to be filled was that of university registrar, where Wilson faced 'a canvass of the keenest and most unscrupulous kind to force an unqualified man on the University for the sake of the salary.'[157] This was William Henry Van der Smissen, whose appointment as librarian he had opposed eighteen years earlier and whose backers were Convocation electees. Alfred Baker, already college registrar and the choice of both the president and the professors, got the position, much to Wilson's relief.[158]

These modest victories were accompanied by a defeat that was to be a thorn in his side for an entire decade. Vice-chancellor Moss, prior to his resignation on 1 November 1880 and with Chancellor Blake's support, suggested as his successor William Mulock,[159] a wealthy local businessman and politician who was 'shrewd, drivingly ambitious ... brilliant and witty, ruthless and intriguing, and as foul mouthed on occasion as any carter beating a lagging horse.'[160] But Moss, finding those whom he canvassed 'unfavourable to Mulock's claims had failed to press them.' Even Mulock's friend, James Loudon, thought that the offices of president and vice-chancellor should be combined. 'A non-Academic Vice-Chancellor never did, and never would, discharge the full duties of his office, but either neglected them or unloaded them on the President.'[161]

Mulock very much wanted the position, but with Wilson elected pro vice-chancellor, he had to await Moss's death before making his move. Then Wilson, who discovered his intentions by accident, found himself 'taking steps I should not otherwise thought of' and stood as a candidate himself.[162] He had little hope of winning, but in Mulock he found much to fear and dislike. As a politician he was suspect; moreover, he demanded total loyalty from his supporters[163] and lacked the social graces that Wilson deemed so important to a man in a position of authority: 'the fellow does not so much mean to be insolent as he is so devoid of the instincts of a gentleman that he unconsciously achieves perfection in the process.'[164]

Mulock was elected vice-chancellor in January 1881,[165] confirming his ascendancy in the power structure of the university, especially with Blake preoccupied with politics in Ottawa. Mulock chaired and directed the proceedings of both the Senate and the Board of Management. He was never above using his money to curry favour in private deals or on public occasions, as Wilson's description of one evening of opulence demonstrates: 'Dinner at the Club. The Vice-Chancellor entertained the University Senate, Professors, Ministers, Judges, etc. – a party of sixty. Everything on the most liberal scale; the guests asking for what wines they pleased.'[166] However, Mulock was to discover that even he could not always control the Senate. His earliest defeat was his proposal in 1884 for a committee of management in the Faculty of Arts that, in Wilson's words, would have 'reduced the professors to a mere set of hired lecturers with no interest beyond their individual work and pay.'[167]

The president faced an early challenge in the School of Practical Science. He needed leverage to balance the demands of the college professors, who were expected to teach students at the school with no extra remuneration, against the escalating costs of the science programs in the school and the college. He got himself appointed as chair of the school board, even though this move incurred some resentment and a sharp personal outburst from Edward Chapman.[168] The worst conflict was a two-year dispute over the nature of the school's chemistry program, during which Wilson maintained a conciliatory, but firm course. His skill and patience were rewarded when his solution was adopted as policy by the minister of education.[169]

In the university and college world, where the will of the government was supreme, Wilson knew the value of putting his case to the public. At commencements, convocations, and inaugurations he addressed the issues of the day, with full knowledge that his comments would be printed in the local papers and read by politicians and voters alike. His address at the University College convocation in October 1883 was 'too long for the audience in the Hall, but it was not meant for them but for readers outside.'[170] A typical example was his inaugural address as chairman of the School of Practical Science in November 1881, written to herald a new development in education that had been a decade in the making – the introduction of evening lectures for working men. Wilson himself had organized these lectures in spite of 'strong opposition at first, and the persistency with which it was upset last winter.' He melded the broad sweep of history and science into a high-Victorian appeal to the value of scientific knowledge. And his references to the newest field of study, electricity, enabled him to emphasize the costs of developing new scientific programs.[171]

Annual reports were another vehicle for educating both his political masters and the public. Wilson's presidential reports for University College and the School of Practical Science were clear, containing overviews of the principal issues and references to requirements for the future, and were often respectfully critical of the government.[172] By contrast, his predecessor, McCaul, had typically produced a page consisting largely of statistical tables, and the vice-chancellor's reports on the university continued to follow that model.

Wilson's public addresses and writings were part of his campaign to improve relations between the university and the wider community, including the city of Toronto. For years he had been concerned about the income derived from the University Park and other fees from the 'avenues' (College Street and University Avenue, then called the Yonge Street Avenue and the Queen Street or College Avenue), which the university owned. It had long jealously guarded its prerogatives by locking gates on the avenues, so that access to them, including the crossing of them, was at its sufferance, much to the chagrin of the city.[173] The attitudes of the university officials had not helped, as Wilson noted in his journal. David

Buchan, the recently retired bursar, had been 'one of the most unconciliatory of men; and in his intercourse with the City authorities developed the maximum of possible friction. Mr. Crooks ... was the opposite of conciliatory. Nevertheless he was a gentleman, which could not be said of Mr. Mulock, when he became Vice-Chancellor and united the rudeness of Buchan to the high-handedness of Crooks.'[174]

The impasse over the park, which had been leased to the city in 1859, came to a head in 1888 when the university sued, claiming forfeiture of the lease. There was pressure to settle on both sides, for, while some thorny issues, such as the fate of Taddle Creek, had recently been settled,[175] others, including running an access road through the campus to the new legislative buildings then under construction, remained. The Board of Trustees was left to resolve the matter, with Mulock remaining aloof in hopes that the negotiations would fail. But Wilson worked closely with a new member of the board, lawyer John Hoskin, whose sagacity he respected. The resulting compromise pleased both parties, and Wilson had the satisfaction of Mulock's apologizing to Hoskin for the way he had behaved.[176] The president was particularly gratified that, as a part of the settlement, the city agreed to endow two chairs, one in English literature and the other in mineralogy and geology.[177]

When Wilson assumed office, the university had been preparing for a major expansion in its curriculum, especially in the science and honours programs. The Senate struck a committee that included Wilson, Blake, Mulock, and Loudon[178] to review the income and expenditures of the university and University College and to make recommendations to accommodate these changes. While it gathered evidence throughout 1881, Wilson made the best of the financial system already in place. Though there were many constraints on what he could achieve through the Board of Management, he rarely missed a meeting, for it was Mulock's most secure power base within the university. Always pragmatic, Wilson sought Mulock's cooperation since he could accomplish little without it – as the latter's treatment of Professor William Pike demonstrated. Mulock loathed Pike, a College Council representative and an authority on investments, and blocked him from attending more than one meeting. He routinely tabled the professor's requests for funds for his chemical laboratory[179] while quickly approving those from James Loudon.[180] Mulock enjoyed putting Wilson on the spot,[181] and the president therefore strove to ensure that every financial matter in which he was personally involved had the vice-chancellor's consent before it was submitted to a vote.[182]

The Senate committee's report of January 1882 advocated new programs in constitutional law, political science, and physiology, a substantial increase in the faculty, with separate professors or lecturers in no fewer than seventeen subjects, and additional demonstrators, tutors, and fellows 'as the number of certain classes render necessary.' Also mentioned for the first time was the matter 'of providing facilities for the higher education of women.'[183] Wilson hoped to implement some of these recommendations through a professorship of history, constitutional law, and jurisprudence that would also lighten his own teaching load. He got the Senate on side, 'not without difficulty';[184] more important was the support of the board, which would have to find the $2,000 salary, and the chancellor. Wilson wrote to Blake that the post 'may be a great attraction to men looking forward to the legal profession, and may prove of great value if properly filled. But names have been already suggested, who would simply fill the gap and draw the salary!'[185] The man Wilson had in mind was Jacob Gold Schurman, a native of Nova Scotia.

His hopes were compromised by college intrigue and an impending provincial election. Though supported by both the premier and the minister of education, he was, he complained, 'undermined in a way that vexes me, fully as much by the underhand way in which it has been done by J.L. [James Loudon] as by the failure of a scheme from which I really hoped greatly more for the College than myself.'[186] He was finessed by Mulock, who argued that 'the Board has no jurisdiction to approve any recommendation concerning the teaching staff' (a disingenuous statement since the board had been doing so for years), and Loudon, self-righteously indignant over Wilson's request to the Senate.[187] Wilson was determined to maintain standards, in spite of this personal rebuff. 'Rather than having a temporary appointment at $800. as proposed with the chances of some incompetent slipping in by the side door, I shall hold on at all risks and do the work myself.'[188]

In the fall of 1882, with some urgency, he returned to the issue. His first year as president had left him exhausted – 'I was like a man staggering under too heavy a load. A mere pebble was enough to trip me up' – and in the spring he had suffered from a severe attack of pleurisy. He realized that he could not 'afford to wait till another breakdown. As things go at present it is a mere alternative of suicide or resignation.'[189] Wilson's dream of a separate chair was quickly dashed by the board in a less-than-courteous manner.[190] He expressed his disappointment in a letter to Blake,[191] for in David Reid Keys, a local graduate, he got what he had always tried to avoid: an intellectual lightweight who gained the respect of neither the president nor his colleagues.[192] But at $1,000 a year, the assistant was cheap, and Wilson typically made the best of it. 'Lectured three hours to-day – which, with a good deal of correspondence and other work after it, comes to be somewhat exhausting. But with Mr. Keys now to assist me, and take at least one lecture per day off my hand, I can get along famously.'[193]

These events greatly exasperated Wilson, and his pent-up frustration spilled over into the pages of his journal, where he began applying animal labels to his most insufferable opponents. Loudon became the Mole or sometimes the Snake, who worked with his allies, such as the Echo (J.M. Gibson), the Donkey (Galbraith), and even the Gorilla (William Houston), 'like so many moles in the dark. But their noses will peep out at times, even when trying wire-pulling from behind.'[194] Wilson must have felt that his caricatures were justified when, only months later, Mulock easily found the funds for a lectureship in French and Italian at $2,000 a year.[195]

The president was an earnest Christian who 'carried his religion into his daily life.' To this characteristic was added his generosity and 'his warm sympathy for those in trouble, his ready assistance in cases of distress, his unfailing kindness to dependents and employees ... such acts were always unostentatious, and known to few besides those concerned.'[196] Wilson's altruism, combined with a Scottish pragmatism, was reflected in his attitude towards the faculty and staff. He always balanced the well-being of the college against his own dislikes and allowed for differences in temperament and philosophical approach.

He expended more effort in maintaining a workable relationship with James Loudon than with anyone else. Their different temperaments meant that they often clashed at meetings. Wilson, open and flexible, supported discussion and opposed 'any rigid rule applied to prevent ... consultation among professors. I think it is a thing to be encouraged, not repressed.'[197] Loudon, who was rigid, paranoid about plots, and sensitive to perceived insults, preferred a tightly controlled approach. But Wilson respected his colleague's work (Loudon was an expert on the curriculum) and relied heavily on him. He went to considerable lengths to mollify him, as this letter in 1882 demonstrates: 'Let me beg you to dismiss from your mind any personal feeling. There is no member of the College Council on whom I rely more than yourself for taking a hearty general interest in the business that comes before us; and I should regret your absence at any meeting.'[198]

Wilson also actively supported Loudon's scientific projects, personally raising funds for his electrical laboratory,[199] and defended his interests in university appointments. In 1887 he stopped the minister of education from unloading an incompetent physics lecturer from Victoria College on Loudon (who was in Europe) in the political horse-trading accompanying the approval of university federation.[200] But the following year, when Wilson would not countenance additional laboratory space in the college at the expense of the residence, which occupied its west wing, Loudon was furious and nursed a grievance for years.[201]

The president advocated periodic salary increases for faculty, both to counter the rapidly rising cost of living in the 1880s and to keep the university from losing its best men. He also regarded a satisfactory retiring allowance 'as of utmost importance to the successful working of any university.'[202] The need was underlined after Paxton Young's death, when Wilson learned that his nieces had been left 'very badly off indeed'. He approached both the minister of education and the Board of Trustees, which made a generous provision for them.[203] Privately, Wilson thought that Blake's 1891 retirement scheme discriminated 'cruelly against the older men.' He empathized with the 'particularly sensitive and irate' reaction[204] from Ramsay Wright, who, he discovered after discreet enquiry, had family members back in England to support. In the hope of persuading the chancellor to modify his scheme, he tried to blunt the edges of Wright's sharp attack.[205]

Nor did he neglect advocating salary increases for the staff, knowing from personal experience what it was like to be poor. He pushed hard for those with low wages, such as the bedel, whose $700 a year after twenty-six years of service the president judged 'inadequate and much below salaries now paid for similar services.'[206] Wilson was particularly generous when personal misfortune struck, pressing upon one college servant 'a cheque for one hundred dollars, which he was to return only in the event of his being able to afford it.'[207] On the other hand, he was unforgiving to those who betrayed positions of trust and pushed for their dismissal.[208]

The Arrival of Women

In the 1860s, in England, the United States, and even Ontario, the question of higher education for women was part of the controversy over their role in a changing society. More and more women had been availing themselves of the opportunity for an education in the province's public schools, for there they could find employment as teachers, though at significantly lower wages than their male colleagues. To middle-class

Victorians, women were the angels of the household, and their fitness, both mentally and physically, to endure the rigours of higher education was hotly debated.[209]

As early as 1869 Wilson had been involved in a local movement for the higher education of women. At its inauguration ceremony he spoke of the need 'to secure for ladies facilities for training in the higher departments of mental culture in some degree corresponding to those already available for young men.' He recognized that 'the need for something more cannot be doubted. To what extent the want is as yet felt among ourselves the present movement is designed to test.'[210] With the assistance of the other college professors, 'systematic courses of lectures, and written examinations, were carried on for eight years, to large and annually increasing classes of lady students.' Then for some reason the movement failed. 'When we thought the scheme had been thoroughly organized we transferred the management to a committee of ladies, undertaking to continue our services as lecturers. To my great disappointment it was speedily dropped.'[211]

Wilson envied the access that William Dawson in Montreal had to private donations to found a college for women. 'But I presume you have a class of lady students, the daughters of your wealthy families, seeking education for its own sake; and not as a means towards preparing them as teachers. We have not this class.' Of course, 'with sufficient money, all difficulties will vanish.'[212]

The trend in higher education in Ontario towards readying young men for positions in local industry and the professions Wilson dubbed 'a mere trafficking with knowledge.' In his convocation address in 1884, he painted an ideal situation where women might counter this trend. 'Education in its higher sense means something distinct from this. It means education based on the love of knowledge for its own sake; and widely diffused, so that it shall leaven the whole community and make us an educated people. For this purpose we stand particularly in need of highly educated women, through whom we may look for intellectual culture extending its refining influences even into the stormy arena of political contention, while it places before the rising generation a humane and ennobling standard such as we can very partially lay claim now.'[213] Clearly, Wilson's view of the purpose of higher education for women remained firmly within the Victorian 'angel' paradigm. Not so with another member of the Senate, journalist and subsequently legislative librarian William Houston (elected by Convocation in 1882). Two years earlier he had written passionately in the new college paper, the *Varsity*, of the desperate plight of 'that large class of girls in this country who are compelled to earn their own living, many by teaching. Without a University training they cannot hope to win any of the prizes of their profession. They cannot take charge of High Schools or become even acceptable assistants in them.'[214] It followed, therefore, that women should be admitted to University College.

In 1877 Wilson had helped to open the examinations of the University of Toronto to women.[215] This change, however, did nothing to provide instruction for women students, as teaching was the prerogative of University College alone. While he strongly supported higher education for women, Wilson did not approve of coeducation. Lecturing to mixed classes offended his Victorian sense of propriety, his gentlemanly sensibilities. He confided to William Dawson that 'as to the reading carefully, with critical analysis,' of certain of Shakespeare's plays, 'even with young men it is a work I should prefer to avoid: but with mixed classes of young men and women it would be a painful ordeal to some: and a source of mischievous jest to others.'[216] He had earlier expressed similar sentiments to his friend over troubles at the Queen's University medical school. 'In truth the lecturing of young men, in the presence of young women, on some of the subjects that must be dealt with, appears to me one of the most trying ordeals I can conceive of, both to teacher and student.'[217]

In the autumn of 1881 three female matriculants of the university wrote to the college asking for admission to lectures. Henrietta Charles, noting that 'this right has hitherto been denied to women,' put her case eloquently and forthrightly: 'Permit me to ask if that is quite just? The examinations of the University are open to us, but at no other institution can we obtain tuition that will enable us to compete in those examinations beyond First Year; consequently we have either to employ private tutors or trust to our own unaided exertion.' She stated that she would submit to 'whatever rules and regulations may be imposed' and hoped to receive 'your favourable consideration.'[218]

The president replied personally, courteously, and at length, explaining both his sympathy with the cause of higher education for women and his view that coeducation was unacceptable. He cannily anticipated that the government would bow to pressure and publish any correspondence it received on the matter;[219] so he 'kept it in view' when penning his responses, 'which parliament is welcome to peep into now if it has a mind.'[220] Wilson explained that, while he saw 'many grave objections' to coeducation, he believed that the higher education of women would be 'most successfully prosecuted in institutions exclusively set apart for them, with modifications specially adapted to their requirements and aims in life, as well as to the physical and intellectual differences that distinguish the sexes.'[221] His aim was the establishment of a 'Provincial College for Women, erected on the University grounds, placed under the charge of a Lady Principal and instructors of its own; but also where the Professors and Lecturers of this College might take some part in the instruction.'[222]

The pressure to admit women increased inexorably. They were not only passing the matriculation examinations, but were winning prizes and scholarships as well. The Senate's reaction was to get around the implied contradiction in its rules by passing a statute allowing the scholarships 'won by females be paid without requiring attendance on lectures.'[223] Presumably, the money could be used for private tutoring. Although the Senate's 1882 report on university revenues alluded to 'the consideration of the question of providing facilities for the higher education of women,' it seemed in no hurry to act; it pleaded poverty and asked for government funds to carry out any changes.[224] The issue was raised in the Senate at various times over the next two years, but always by Houston, who got few of his motions on any subject past first reading. The last time was in January 1884, when he presented a motion to provide 'for the female undergraduates of the University of Toronto tuition throughout the Arts courses of a quality equal to that of the tuition provided by University College, and at no greater cost to students.' He withdrew the motion in May.[225] Clearly, the Senate did not take coeducation seriously, partly because it had not the funds to act on the matter.

As public interest grew during 1883, there was a provincial election, summarized pithily by Wilson as 'Politics! Yesterday was election day, the choosing of our masters.'[226] When George W. Ross shortly afterwards replaced Crooks as minister of education, the president reacted uneasily, 'Know little about him – not a college bred man, an old school teacher and school inspector.'[227] Several months later, on 4 March 1884, he recorded, 'At the Legislative Assembly to-day debate on co-education. The assembled wisdom of the Province decides in favour of it.'[228]

Wilson's response was a fifteen-page letter of tightly woven eloquence, covering all of the points against coeducation as he saw them. It was 'addressed to the Minister of Education, but really designed as an answer to the debate in the legislature on the question of co-education,'[229] and so he had it printed for distribution to all members. He cited American and British authorities and pointed out that, as the college building was designed for men only, it would require 'very considerable and costly alterations.' He compared the college with the collegiate institutes in Toronto, which separated the sexes as much as possible, and stated that 'increasing numbers of thoughtful parents' had confided in him that they preferred the idea of a ladies' college rather than 'risk the doubtful experiment of sending their daughters to "refine, and bring under wholesome female influences," some three to four hundred stranger youths, as their fellow-students of the rougher sex.' Wilson added his own dark opinion of young ladies being 'thrown into more or less familiar intercourse' with vast numbers of young men.

He concluded, adroitly, 'having thus fulfilled my duty in endeavouring to lay the case clearly before you, I have only to add, that whatever the Government or Legislature shall determine, it will be my earnest endeavour to carry out with all possible efficiency.'[230] He learned to his satisfaction several days later that this final paragraph had 'upset the plot of Mr. V.C. [Mulock] and the native party, who counted on my quarrel with the government.'[231] The battle was continued in private correspondence with George Ross and Oliver Mowat. Ross seemed unable to withstand the force of Wilson's arguments (at least while he was present), and his assurances were recorded by Wilson in his journal with such phrases as 'very satisfactory interview with Minister of Education.'[232]

Unfortunately, these assurances were subject to the prevailing political wind, and Ross kept trimming his sails. Even while he was soothing the president, the minister prepared for any eventuality by making tentative enquiries about the feasibility of coeducation in the college. Wilson painstakingly detailed the minimal requirements needed to make it accessible to women students; they included several rooms and the hiring of a matron, 'on whom the care of the female department will devolve.'[233] He also outlined three possible degrees of coeducation, from setting aside part of the day for lectures for women to full coeducational classes. And he cautioned the minister, alluding to his past profession, 'Persons who insist on appealing to the experience of School-life for the conduct of a College can have little idea how totally different the two are. It is not in the lecture room that trouble is to be apprehended, or danger incurred.'[234]

Meanwhile, William Houston continued his strident arguments in favour of coeducation. In the *Varsity* he contended that 'there is not the slightest chance of a separate institution like University College being at any future time established and endowed for the advantage of women,' and he stated flatly that 'to talk of the present over-worked staff of the College repeating their lectures during the session is absurd.'[235] In the

Toronto press he advocated strong measures, including an 'appeal for relief to the Courts, the Legislature, and the public,' and concluded with a veiled threat: 'If there is to be discussion it will probably be thorough, and will embrace in its scope the whole management, work and discipline of the institution.'[236] It is no wonder that Wilson took offence at such statements from a junior member of the Senate. Of Houston, who on a good day in the deliberations of that body was '*comparatively quiet*,'[237] he wrote, 'Never surely was a mortal more utterly devoid of the elements that go to the making of a gentleman. Charges that would make most men blush pass over him as zephyrs over a pine forest.'[238] This view was widely shared; the mild-mannered Hutton described him as 'even in the language of compliment, an apple of discord.'[239]

The decision came down in the only way it could; the government did not have the political will to provide for female students facilities comparable to those enjoyed by the men. In the fall of 1884 it passed an order-in-council that forced University College to admit women students that very term. Wilson wrote bitterly in his journal, 'On the 9th of last month the Minister of Education for the third time gave me official, though unfortunately only verbal assurance, that things were to go on in the College without change for another year. No lady students.' He complained that the local press had been 'abusing me with all their virulence, and calling on the Minister to "show some backbone," which he accordingly does by changing his mind once more ... and so we shall have to admit young women without even the rudest preparations for needful accommodation.'[240]

But Wilson was not finished. On commencement day, 17 October 1884, he delivered a speech on coeducation, speaking of it as a limited and interim system of education for women and expressing hope that a proper college for them would be built on the university grounds when government funds became available. Afterwards he noted in his journal, 'Minister of Education present, to my satisfaction, as I had a word to say specially for his ear and that of his colleagues.'[241] Both Wilson's correspondence and his journal show that he still hoped that the 'experiment' would be only a temporary measure. To Dawson the following year he wrote, 'Experience has in no way altered my opinion as to co-education. But thus far my arrangements for our lady students have worked satisfactorily and I have had no trouble with them.'[242] He also noted, with some satisfaction, that 'the ladies are moving with a view to petitions for a Ladies' College. If they manage it well good may come out of it.'[243]

Nevertheless, coeducation at University College had become a fact, and Wilson, true to his word, undertook to make it work. Five years later a journal entry records his inviting to his residence 'lady undergraduates, 63 in number, besides Professors, Minister of Education, &c., with their wives.' The fourth-year men had been there the previous week (Wilson still preserving a separation of the sexes in his private entertaining at least), and he remarked, 'Amused to note the essential difference of the two. The young ladies are much more at their ease, don't care for portfolios, albums, &c., prefer talking to one another, and are much more easy to entertain.'[244]

University Federation

The next battle the president faced was university federation. He had no enthusiasm for it, nor, initially, was there much elsewhere in the university except in the mind of William Mulock. Many years later, when 'setting the record straight,' Mulock would claim that, when he stood for vice-chancellor in 1881, he 'was unwilling to accept the office ... unless the Senate sympathized with those views and was disposed to give effect, if possible to the policy,' and that by electing him, it 'practically committed itself' to it.[245] Certainly, the issue was being both discussed at the university – even the students wrote about it in their first newspaper, the *White and Blue*, using the term 'university consolidation'[246] – and acted upon immediately after Mulock became vice-chancellor. Early in 1881 the Senate passed a statute for the affiliation of St Michael's College, and later in the year Mulock led negotiations with Western University of London, Ontario (now the University of Western Ontario). When this scheme proved abortive, however,[247] the Senate lost interest.

Wilson's great fear was that Mulock would sacrifice the interests of University College to his political ambitions. The Methodist vote was crucial to the vice-chancellor's success at the polls, which, in educational terms, meant satisfying the ambitions of Victoria College. By the 1880s it and the other church colleges were finding themselves increasingly hampered by their limited resources, 'so that if they failed to gather support for scientific education they might find themselves eventually teaching only theological subjects, as Goldwin Smith and others [such as Edward Blake] wished, or at best offering a truncated program in the liberal arts.'[248] President Nelles of Victoria thought that 'the Methodist people are strong enough to sustain an independent University,' but his college was $40,000 in debt and ill-equipped to handle an increasing numbers of students. He concluded, 'on the whole I think Federation better for the general interest of Higher Education.'[249] He was determined that Victoria would be the senior partner over its arch-foe, University College, in any new arrangement with the University of Toronto.

Mulock forced the federation issue in his commencement address of 1883 by speaking of the need for an increase in public funding for the university. This remark raised the ire of the financially strapped sectarian colleges and alarmed Wilson, who wrote in his journal, 'it has always seemed to me the most short-sighted folly to dream of a legislative grant.'[250] And Mulock, having raised the flag, then immediately lowered it over the affiliation application of the Woman's Medical College, as his own interests were not being served.[251] The wary president thought that he could see his way 'to confederation on a just and sound basis, if the politicians – including our own Chancellor and Vice-Chancellor – don't sell us for their own party purposes.' But he feared that University College would be dragged down to the level of its rivals. 'I would fain place it on a substantial foundation for the future, and that must be done by the students all ranking as undergraduates of a common university, none of them specially as ours. We must become the University Teachers for all that will avail themselves of our instruction.' That would, he noted in his journal, 'give them a common interest to sustain us, instead of being banded together by a common jealousy against a favoured rival.'[252]

Mulock and his allies, fearing the damage that Wilson could inflict, kept him in the dark for several months after the first meeting about federation in July 1884. Thus he did not see a special report prepared by representatives of the denominational colleges for that meeting until early in November (and then only by accident)[253] and did not participate in several other meetings in the autumn. Nor was he privy to the private correspondence between the vice-chancellor and Nelles over unresolved issues arising from the July meeting – principally whether University College would be maintained and the relationship between the various professoriates (it had already been generally agreed that the teaching staff would be divided into college faculties and a university professoriate). Mulock and Nelles concluded that University College should be moved out of its building and its faculty allocated by the government 'in a fair and proper way, so as to secure the best efficiency both of the College and the University.'[254]

When Mulock told Loudon that it 'might be necessary to transfer the University College faculty to the old Parliament Buildings on Front St'[255] (effectively returning the college to its homeless state of thirty years before), Loudon was so shocked that he subsequently hardened his stand on federation. For this he was applauded by Wilson, who had by then found Mulock out.[256] Loudon's position prompted a worried letter from Nelles, unsure about his own supporters. 'I think you and your friends will now make a mistake if you insist too much on your checks and guarantees for U.C.'[257]

The federation proposal, devised by representatives of the colleges and George Ross himself, was submitted to the College Council and the Senate on 5 January 1885.[258] While Wilson saw 'little appearance of statesmanship in the patchwork thus far,' the enemy had, for the moment, retreated on the matter of the college building.[259] Though still worried that the college might be sacrificed to political expediency, he maintained a low profile until the Methodist Conference in June, when he stirred up matters in the press.[260] University federation was not forgotten, for during the summer and early fall three theological colleges – Wycliffe, the Toronto Baptist College, and Knox – applied for and were granted affiliation. Wilson was particularly supportive of Wycliffe, which he had helped to found.[261]

When the Conference rejected the federation proposal, Wilson chose his platform to speak publicly on the matter, University College's commencement in October. He reiterated his support for 'secular education, pure and simple as the better, the more excellent way' and 'thoroughly in accordance with the whole spirit and tendencies of the age.' He criticized many aspects of the proposed federation scheme, including the dual professoriate, which was 'classified on no logical system, but confusedly arranged on a basis suggested by the still more inadequate equipment of certain confederating colleges.' However, he conceded that 'if the compromise, as agreed to, is carried out as a whole, in good faith, I am prepared to give it a fair trial.'[262] Wilson soon discovered that, though willing to compromise, he was not being treated fairly. In April the following year Mowat seemed to backtrack on the college building and the university professoriate. Wilson immediately offered his resignation to 'clear the way for some better arrangement on the basis of a new President suitable to the Methodists.'[263] Mowat would not hear of it and backed down.

Wilson's most enduring contribution to university federation occurred in the spring of 1887. On 15 March he was approached by Ross for assistance in the writing of the federation bill. He described the draft that he received as 'a piece of wretched confusion in which University and College functions are jumbled together like the conflicting atoms of primaeval chaos.' So he 'sat over it till midnight' and 'fashioned a University Council out of the proposed new professoriate, the College Council, and the School of Science combined; transferring to it all the old powers of the College Council.' The next day he had a long interview with the minister, 'who jumps at my proposal, as a means of clearing up what he had found to [be] an inextricable confusion. He favours nearly all my suggestions.'[264]

From then on Wilson worked closely with the minister on further revisions of the bill. To protect University College, he tied it even more closely to the university through a University Council that would be independent of the Senate. He even proposed to abolish the College Council, but had to abandon the idea. To outmanoeuvre the Methodists, he moved most of the college professors over to the university professoriate and again threatened to resign if Victoria was given a veto, as Mulock wished, over the deliberations of the Senate.[265]

Wilson was satisfied with his work and had one hope for the passage of the bill: 'if my "University Council" escapes unscathed I shall be content. But that all depends on the Victoria men failing to discover my aim.' A few days later he noted, 'It will be a triumph if I can succeed in nominally giving up the powers of the College Council and preserving them amply with a mere change of name!'[266] After witnessing the debate in the legislature, he wrote, 'it is now safe, I hope ... The Minister of Education drove me home and I had the pleasure of saying to him in all sincerity that I had appreciated the frank straightforward manner he had deal with me throughout. He very graciously acknowledged my services to the matter; and so we parted on the best of terms.'[267] When the bill passed in June, Wilson, though with reservations still, had hopes for the future. 'This new Federation Bill restores to the University its teaching powers, and when fairly and fully in force, with its University Faculty and University Council, will more nearly approach my idea – though by no means my ideal – of what it should be.'[268]

It was almost two years (April 1889) before the act was proclaimed. Some sections, relating primarily to the restoration of the faculties of medicine and law, took effect immediately. University College, which was not permitted to expand beyond the core of subjects that had been taught in 1887, was left with even fewer subjects. With Wilson's support, history and the natural sciences were transferred to the new university professoriate, to which was added medicine and law. The college retained only one chair, that of classics.[269] In May 1887 Wilson had warned Ross that any delay in implementing the bill would create 'trouble and confusion, if we have, for the first time University professors, without the University Council,' and he was anxious to get the system up and running before Victoria joined, 'so they will enter under the new order of things without realizing any change; and so avoid needless friction.'[270] The two-year hiatus fatally undermined the opportunity for a University Council as Wilson envisaged it, and as the College Council was without 'a legal quorum, ... the whole government of the University and College in relation to Professors, Lecturers and students is beset with uncertainty.'[271] Furthermore, his own authority was weakened by the failure of the government to appoint him president of the university until 23 June 1890.[272]

When the University Council was finally created immediately after the act was proclaimed,[273] Wilson fully intended to treat the two councils as one. 'The only reason for any further recognition of the myth of University College consequently disappears.'[274] But he found that he could not do so, and he also faced complaints from modern languages about not being represented on either council. The president was forced to change tactics. Late in 1890 he drafted, for the government's consideration, two orders-in-council creating boards of management in law and arts, with the president to chair both. The Board of Management in arts was designed to 'restore that unified action among the professors in all the Departments of Arts and Science, which the separation into two distinct Councils of University and College, has seriously infected.' Wilson would have like to add a third board, for medicine, which he felt to be developing 'interests apart from those of the University as a whole.' But he dared not challenge Mulock directly on this matter.[275] Had this scheme been adopted, the office of the president would have been greatly strengthened.

For two years after 1887, Wilson's authority was eroded from two directions. In the Senate the vice-chancellor chose to regard him as president of University College only and refused him any say in the Faculty of Medicine. This proved a blessing in disguise since the problems soon to beset the faculty were Mulock's creation. They led to his fall from grace, and Wilson, truthfully and happily, was able to claim ignorance.[276] The president also lost his chairmanship of the School of Practical Science in 1889 when it was reorganized. Its board was replaced with a council headed by a principal, John Galbraith, who acted under the direct authority of the Department of Education. Galbraith was one of Wilson's animals – 'the Donkey' – and long an ally of Mulock and Loudon. He now occupied 'the delicate position of go-between vis-a-vis the Ministry of Education and the President of the University.'[277]

Fortunately for Wilson, Mulock's preoccupation with the Faculty of Medicine and his political activities left him less time to devote to the Board of Trustees. Wilson's influence there gradually increased; he rarely missed a meeting and developed new allies in men such as John Hoskin and engineer and businessman Sir Casimir Gzowski. The fire that gutted University College in February 1890 further diluted the vice-chancellor's authority, for it brought Edward Blake back into university affairs in a direct way for the first time in a decade.

That 'very miscellaneous, and somewhat uncertain body,' the Senate, continued to test Wilson's ingenuity and patience, with 'the Education Office, with the Minister at its head ... sometimes pulling one way; the Senate another, and some few of us trying to find a *via media*, less objectionable than either.'[278] The president learned that, rather than trying to direct debate, it was sometimes better if he 'let them talk, wearied them out, and then asked for them to swallow the whole at one gulp.'[279] When Edward Blake expressed impatience with some regulations that the Senate had passed, Wilson responded, 'you cannot more strongly object to the entire range of utopian and impracticable propositions than I do ... But I have learned by experience that it is not always wise for me to protest against such proposals. If gentlemen will propose that the University undertake to build a railway to the moon; and a majority of the Senate sustain them; I find it prudent to let the resolution carry unopposed.'[280]

Wilson and the Students

In the 1880s the students 'tended mainly to be graduates of private schools or of the handful of better high schools in the larger centres of the province.'[281] The student body at University College in 1880 was small and intimate – there were only 349 registrants[282] – but over the next twelve years, with the addition of new faculties, it doubled in size. At the beginning of the period, the college residence still provided the focus of student life, as there were few other outlets. But as it could accommodate at most about 40 students, the majority lived at home or boarded off campus. It was inevitable that the significance of the residence in college life would gradually decline unless its facilities could be extended.

The student of the 1880s has been described as 'often hard drinking but generally docile,' but in the following decade a new type began to appear, 'less amenable to discipline, more inclined to indulge in violent "hustles" and pranks, and more independent, puritanical and self-righteous.'[283] For most of his presidency it was the earlier kind that Wilson had to deal with, and it was one with which he was clearly comfortable. His attitude to the students of his college had always been marked by a degree of goodwill and understanding matched in only a few of his colleagues. He possessed a deep understanding of and genuinely liked them. 'His private kindness towards his students and all who came to him for advice or help was inexhaustible.'[284]

He regarded most student pranks with amused tolerance and detested the self-appointed guardians of public morals who saw in the enthusiasms of youth a means of attacking the college. On one memorable occasion, responding to this type of negative comment in the press, Wilson speculated on 'what would they say at home about a correspondence with the Attorney-General about a students' fracas over a song, in itself sufficiently innocent, and proceedings at worst amounting to no more than some rough pranks such as no English schoolboy would ever dream of complaining of outside the circle of his school mates.'[285]

Such frothings Wilson ignored whenever possible. When the criticisms moved from being plain silly to injurious, he stoutly defended the students. During the call-up for the Riel Rebellion in 1885 there was 'much wrath among the students owing to an ill-timed attack on them in the *Globe* for some effervescence of youthful excitement in a march of the whole band of undergraduates to the Union Station to see their classmates off.' So Wilson 'wrote to the Editor ... Sent him a sort of ultimatum, in shape of an article on "Our student soldiers."'[286] For the students who fought in the northwest, he did even more. He introduced a resolution in the Senate, which was quickly passed, that they 'shall be allowed their examinations in their respective years, and in the case of men who have been pursuing the Honor Course they shall be allowed their options in their several Departments.'[287]

When student behaviour went beyond the 'effervescence of youthful excitement,' however, the president was quick to act. In 1884 an unusual escalation in student pranks at Hallowe'en sparked trouble with the city police. Wilson, having learned that the students were to plot some retaliatory action the following night in Moss Hall, which housed the gymnasium and the offices of the *Varsity*, outmanoeuvred them. 'The President being there before them ... gave them a word or two on common-sense, on the great wisdom of fighting the police whom everybody but thieves and housebreakers thought their friends ... They gave him three cheers and marched off to join the Meds.'[288]

The more serious trouble of student hazing he treated similarly, though he seldom used terms harsher than 'foolish.' 'Some foolish "hazing" carried on among the students was made the subject of unfriendly comment and gross exaggeration by the press. Then came a letter from a country Methodist minister telling me his son carried a revolver, and had his permission to use it under certain circumstances, in self-defence.' Wilson spent a week in careful investigation, ferreted out two of the culprits, and hauled them before the College Council. 'Hope that the scare they have had, and the resolution adopted by the Council, will have some good effect. But I could not induce the Council to adopt the strong measures I thought advisable.'[289] He may have been thinking of measures similar to those adopted four years earlier. In 1885, when an incident of hazing threatened to get out of hand, he had called a special meeting of the College Council and got 'full power to deal with the students ... and to withhold from them the use of Convocation Hall for their public debates.'[290]

The occasional use of 'strong measures' indicated that the president would not tolerate gross misbehaviour, for he was always concerned about incidents that might undermine discipline. His stand on this issue was made clear when he threatened to resign over a clause proposed for the university federation act that would have allowed students to appeal decisions of the College Council to the university Senate: 'Discipline would, or at least might, be made nearly impossible with such divided authority.'[291] Nor would he tolerate cheating, and disruptions during examinations. In 1882 a special meeting of the Senate, called just before convocation, assessed the penalties against three students. Two, who had physically attacked their examiner and did not satisfactorily explain their conduct, were suspended, while another, who had been caught cheating, was not allowed to present himself for any examination before 1884.[292]

While Wilson supported students' right of expression, he was a canny judge of when to listen and when to ignore them. The pitfalls for college presidents became apparent in an incident at Victoria College, in which two students were expelled. It had arisen because 'the Victoria University authorities have, it seems, been foolish enough to notice a criticism in their students' College paper'[293] (of the same incompetent professor whom Wilson had stopped Ross from dumping on the university in 1887). Principal Nathanael Burwash wanted to know 'how we discipline such flagrant delinquents! I fear he will be shocked to learn that we should never dream of taking the slightest notice of their criticisms.'[294] While Wilson was privately sympathetic to their cause, he would not agree to break rank and admit them to University College. His self-assurance and appreciation of the students' natural expressions of enthusiasm in themselves was demonstrated at an undergraduate dinner. The professors had been seated at a side table and some were offended. Wilson's sage observation put the whole matter in perspective. 'But the young gentlemen found last year that, in giving place to the Dons, the latter did all the speechifying – in which case, what was the use of having a dinner at all?'[295]

The president was also adept at directing student energies away from mischief at official functions such as the annual college convocation. Noting the 'growing tendency to disorder on such occasions' – the students *would* 'intrude College songs at inopportune times' – Wilson decided to put their talents to good use. He 'made music part of the programme, handed over the gallery to the Glee Club, ... holding them responsible for any disorder there,' and was afterwards pleased that 'the legitimatizing of the singing enlisted the best men on the side of order.'[296] The *Mail* declared whoever thought of this innovation 'a genius. The novelty ... did much to sooth the ruffled feelings of a fun-loving undergraduate, and as a consequence the visitors were not as much annoyed as on former occasions by "chestnutty" ejaculations.' The paper was pleased to report that 'the boys behaved with marvellous circumspection, and although they applauded vociferously at "hence accordingly" [Wilson's trade-mark phrase] and several other notable utterances ... [the bedel, McKim] was less singled out for witty remarks than formerly.'[297]

Wilson's ability to appeal to 'the best men' was related in an incident, more amusing than anything else, in which the arts and medical students, even then traditional enemies, clashed in a college lecture hall in November 1890. The occasion was a class in elementary physics, part of the new curriculum for first-year students from the two faculties. What comes through clearly in his account is his amusement and satisfaction at his small victory for industry over riot. As the students assembled for the lecture, Wilson, passing by in the corridor, found himself 'in the midst of a grand scuffle' (one wonders where the lecturer was). 'Arts and Medicos it seems had been in wrathful contest as to who should have the front seats. With some difficulty I got a hearing and asked them, as an act of respect to me, to retire quietly.' This was agreed to and also that the arts men would leave first. 'The Medicos ranged themselves on either side of the narrow corridor – a legacy of the fire – and the main source of the trouble. As they were walking out, a Medico with solemn gravity addresses an Arts man who was passing out with his hat on: "Take off our hat out of respect to the President!" And as he said this he banged it over his eyes, and of course all was renewed turmoil. An appeal however to the good faith of the Medicos brought the better men to my side: and matters were quieted.'[298]

This was not the end of the affair, for the spirit of interfaculty rivalry, as Wilson well knew, was not so easily quelled. The next morning he 'got an inkling that the whole band of medical students' would muster in the corridor after the 9 a.m. lecture and aid their co-conspirators inside in overpowering the arts men. Wilson postponed the lecture an hour, 'locked the doors, and met the grand rally outside,' where he had 'a quiet talk' with the students. The presence of some policemen, whom he had telephoned for as a precaution, 'created a little fresh ire, but by and by they settled down to a football match, and we resumed work at 11 o'clock in good order.'[299]

In 1887, with the coming of university federation, a concerted effort was made by the minister of education to abolish the college residence as a part of his proposed reorganization of the School of Practical Science. According to Alfred Baker, the dean, 'his plan was to convert it [the residence] into Chemical and Biological Laboratories and move Wright, Pike, and Ellis over here, leaving Galbraith alone in the School.'[300] Wilson, whose support for the residence never wavered, counter-attacked immediately. In his opinion, the building was 'totally unsuited to any such purpose,' and he demanded and got interviews with both Mowat and Ross.[301] He wrote bluntly to Ross that the move would cause serious injury to the college. 'The influence of the resident students on the *esprit de corps* and the general conduct and feeling in relation to College questions ... very far exceeds that of all the other students combined.' He pointed out that their influence spread throughout the student body, 'in the College Societies, the Gymnasium, the Games, in Convocation, and in all general action of the graduates in the interest of the University.' With the coming of federation, their impact would be more crucial than ever. Moreover, such a decision would put him 'in a novel position as President, if summarily called upon to carry on the work, deprived of what experience assures me is a valuable element of success, and this without even opportunity to advise with my colleagues.'[302]

The president, however, received 'such poor backing' from the college professors 'that I question how far it worth while spending my strength for naught. There is such a narrow selfishness. Each man thinks of his own Department and that only.'[303] He also faced other challenges. Opponents of the residence eagerly seized upon charges of 'lax discipline and misconduct,' but Wilson was not for a moment deceived: 'it is the old trick. It suits the cheap scheme of the University reform to confiscate the Residence for needed lecture-room accommodation; so the game now is: "Give the dog an ill name and hang him!"'[304] He criticized the rising tide of 'teetotalism' for making 'no distinction between beer and whiskey' being consumed by the residents. 'According to the ideas of my own younger days, they lead a wonderfully orderly life. A glass of ale seems to be their strongest potation, and that in their own rooms when they have a

friend to dinner.' Wilson concluded that 'there has been no intemper-
ance in any true sense of the term.'[305]

The residence could accommodate only a fraction of the student body,
and because it was expensive, only those from wealthier families could
afford to live there. It was thus an easy target for the charges of 'elitism'
levelled by its opponents, especially William Houston, who was then a
confident of the minister and whose 'vulgar nature rebels against even
the aristocracy of intellect and high culture.'[306] While Wilson rejected
this argument, he admitted that the prejudice 'against anything approaching a caste or class renders my arguments in favour of a select class
of more refined students, under strict College discipline, an offence
instead of any reason for maintaining the system ... Why, who wants tone?
Everybody is as good as his neighbour.'[307]

Refusing to give up, he marshalled his forces from outside the college,
with gratifying results. Since he knew the influence that its 'old boys'
wielded in the province, he wrote to twenty-three graduates who had lived
in the residence[308] and to parents. He also went further afield, soliciting
letters from William Dawson at McGill and from as far away as the University of Edinburgh. On 4 November he 'left the whole correspondence'
with the premier 'for his perusal.'[309]

This battle was won, but the war continued. After the fire in 1890,
Houston would raise the cry for abolition again. But he had lost his influence with Ross, and a relieved president reported that 'the Minister ... has
stood very fairly and handsomely by me; which, seeing that he does not
favour the Residence, deserves all grateful recognition.'[310] Wilson could
not resist, in his convocation address that year, putting in a plug for the
extension of the residence. He stated that he had already received for the
cause a gift of £100 sterling from a gentleman in Edinburgh, who
observed in his accompanying letter, 'The want of College Residence is
one of the great weaknesses of the Scottish system.'[311] In 1891 the Senate
passed a resolution preventing the diversion of residence rooms to other
use without its approval. This move anticipated another request from
Loudon for the space that he had been denied in 1888; this time Wilson
made certain he chaired the committee that resolved the issue.[312]

He had his final round with Ross on the matter of the residence at Hallowe'en in 1891. Students destroyed the ancient fence, of which the minister had been very protective, around the Toronto Normal School, and
Ross brought his wrath down upon University College. Wilson, after
ascertaining that none of the residence students had been involved,
wrote to him, 'It cannot be supposed that I am to patrol the streets till

midnight looking after our non-residence students.' He could not resist adding 'an expression of regret at his persistent opposition to the extension of the College residence.'[313]

In his fostering of student spirit in the college and, through the Literary and Scientific Society and the residence, the development of a more refined type of student, Wilson was amply rewarded. An example of his legacy was recorded in minutes of the society in 1890: 'Resolved that this Society is in favor of keeping up the time-honored custom, that students in the class-room should rise to their feet on the entrance of the professor or lecturer and that the members of this Society encourage the continuance of this custom.'[314] The students had become the guardians of tradition.

Only Canadians Need Apply

Many of the challenges that Wilson faced as president came from the Senate's Convocation members and their allies among the graduates, who 'will have no body but our own men appointed to any Chair.'[315] These 'sectionalists,' the larger and more influential of the nativist factions at the university during the decade, for most appointments included Mulock, Loudon, Galbraith, and Blake. They and the broader nationalists (usually imperial federationists) shared the belief that any appointee had to be an Anglo-Saxon Canadian or a British subject (Americans came last), the difference being the emphasis on Toronto graduates.[316] Of this group, none proved more irritating to Wilson than William Houston.

Houston was a social reformer rather than an academic, widely read – Blake commented wryly that 'if he knew how to keep a Library, [he] would know everything'[317] – and tenacious. Darting about 'like a bird getting insects,'[318] he constantly introduced motions in the Senate on issues such as the curriculum, the college residence, and the opening up of Senate meetings. A few were innovative measures that Wilson supported, but most were merely irritants that took up time. No sooner was a motion defeated than Houston would attempt another way of introducing it. On one memorable day were 'navigated, withdrawn, or otherwise disposed of eleven statutes, motions, etc. of the irrepressible W.H., including one that "phonetic spelling be accepted at University examinations"! I had to preside; so could not escape.'[319] This last proposal was doubly ironic since Houston, recently the judge of a student essay contest, had complained about the poor spelling.

William Houston epitomized the unseemly scramble for appointments in the wake of university federation 'as the promotion of self-interest reached frenzied heights under the guise of sacrifice.'[320] By the late 1880s he had so ingratiated himself with the minister of education that he was in a position to push his claim and applied for three chairs in succession. When Ross seriously considered him for a lectureship in law, Wilson was appalled. He deplored the 'mischievous system growing up, of men setting their minds on some post at the University; bringing all sorts of influence & pressure to bear on the Government, so that, before those who are responsible for the conduct of the institution are consulted, there is really no free choice.' He bluntly told Ross to 'seriously reconsider this. I know few men, among all the hundreds of good honour men who have been pupils, so peculiarly deficient in the qualities for a professor. It is with extreme reluctance that I offer any objection to an appointment to which you seem to have given countenance. But I should consider that one so very objectionable that I would rather abandon all idea of organizing a Faculty of Law.'[321]

The demands for a political science program created other pressures, for Wilson feared that the students might become involved in more than the discussion of political theory and that the consequences might be unpredictable. When Houston founded a Political Science Club in 1886, the president refused it space on campus. The following year Wilson pressed for a full professorship in which the appointee would remain aloof from party politics. To this individual, in addition to his teaching duties, would be entrusted the control of the club, 'which requires careful handling to keep us out of trouble.'[322] Wilson's concerns were taken seriously. The appointment to the chair of political economy in 1889 was left to the premier and the chancellor, who thoroughly briefed the candidates as to what was expected of them. In William Ashley, an English appointee, Wilson hoped 'for excellent results in all ways,'[323] though he had personally preferred an American.

Any candidate for the chair of English, Wilson insisted, should be a good German scholar, have a knowledge of Anglo-Saxon and some of Icelandic and a whole group of Scandinavian languages, and have 'made some reputation in English Literature.'[324] The government, under intense pressure from the nativists, adopted an old ruse of keeping the advertising 'so limited as necessarily to confine it to Canadian candidates.'[325] Among these, of course, was Houston, 'a wretched creature, who employed all the unscrupulous tactics of a skilled ward politician in the detraction of his opponents – especially for Keys – and in enlisting a phalanx of political allies on his behalf.'[326] As the government had 'a right to definite advice from me, and I have no desire to evade the responsibility,'[327] Wilson narrowed the candidates to two, 'with tolerable certainty of getting the best man that has offered.'[328]

William John Alexander proved an inspired choice, but having attended University College for only one year, he was not acceptable to Houston's supporters, who demonstrated how petty the disappointed nativists were becoming over appointments. In venting their spleen by attacking Wilson in the press, they unwisely used the example of Paxton Young's appointment (which they claimed Wilson had opposed), whereupon the revered professor came to the president's defence. His letter, along with one from Wilson, reiterated his principle of 'selection of the very best man, wherever he may have been born or educated,' and pointed out that the majority of appointments since 1880 had been Varsity graduates, effectively blunting the nativists' attack.[329]

Two other appointments, a successor to Paxton Young, who died suddenly in February 1889, and one in the Department of Oriental Languages, gave Wilson more trouble than most, and for different reasons. The choice of Young's successor had the usual native Canadian element, but with a new twist. The sectionalists argued that only a Varsity graduate could be hired to continue in his philosophical footsteps. Their candidate was John Watson Hume, a brilliant, but untried graduate. But the discipline was changing, and though Wilson saw in Hume a man of promise, he was determined to have in the chair a proven administrator with sterling academic qualifications.[330] His choice was James Mark Baldwin, an American; but as a result of Executive Council interference, he also had to settle for Hume, who was appointed to a junior position provided that he spent two years in Germany broadening his education.[331] The fight over the appointment was spread all over the press. It concluded with 'the comical feature' of the premier requesting Wilson to write to the *Globe* and the *Mail* in order to put the best possible spin on the controversy: 'this result won from them in spite of endless intrigue and chicanery.' Wilson concluded, charitably, 'In the whole matter, however, the attorney-general has honestly striven to do his best,' and he noted that the letters 'put me once more on a friendly footing with the politic and political patrons of university chairs.'[332]

The Department of Oriental Languages was headed by Wilson's old comrade Jacob Hirschfelder, who had been in harness since 1845. He no longer met the academic standards demanded by, among others, the principals of Knox and Wycliffe. Wilson was, with difficulty, able to deflect Ross from hiring yet another unqualified local candidate and to appoint John McCurdy, formerly of Princeton, who had both a doctorate and an international reputation.[333] The old and the new did not get along, and the students faced the unique spectacle of both Hirschfelder and McCurdy lecturing on the entire curriculum and acting quite independently of each other. The charade continued for months as Wilson tried to find a solution that would salve Hirschfelder's feelings, while ensuring that McCurdy would be professor and head of the department, along with a promise of a future raise.[334] He was ultimately successful, and Hirschfelder retired in November 1888.[335] Then Ross, without any consideration of the real needs of the university or the impact of a bad appointment on it, again demanded a post for his local candidate. Wilson stood firm,[336] but it was a close call. The Executive Council had even agreed to the appointment and sent Paxton Young to wear down Wilson's resistance.[337]

With these academic appointments all announced, Wilson wrote in his journal, 'And now I hope my colleagues will be considerate enough to live forever, or at least until I have shuffled off the mortal coil of presidency or of life.'[338] These and other administrative pressures, added to those of teaching and marking examinations, were wearying, and Wilson was no longer robust. They made imperative his escape each summer to the cool air of the White Mountains in New Hampshire. The gruelling session of 1886–7 had left him prostrated with a severe bilious attack, and the difficulties over the successor to Paxton Young brought on another breakdown in 1889.[339] To compound matters, Wilson developed cataracts. By the spring of 1889 he had, beyond a sense of light, no sight remaining in his right eye, and that of his left was blurred.[340] But he remained surprisingly sanguine. Adversity had unfailingly brought out hidden reserves of strength and resourcefulness, and Wilson had always enjoyed small pleasures. He was delighted in 1886 when biscuit manufacturer William Christie donated $2,000 to found the Daniel Wilson Scholarship in the natural sciences.[341] He also got much satisfaction from tracking down and retrieving the original charter of King's College, about which he had made enquiries from time to time.[342]

The University in Flames

Sir Daniel (he was knighted in 1888) would need all his inner resources, for on the night of 14 February 1890 most of University College was destroyed by fire. Summoned from his residence two blocks away, he watched the work of so many years go up in flames. Lost in the conflagration were 'thirty-three thousand carefully selected volumes' in the library, the ethnological museum that he had so painstakingly created, 'my whole 37 years of accumulated lecture notes' (the famous 'yellow lectures' to a generation and more of students), 'boxes of precious correspondence, the holographs and exquisite drawings which he had brought with him in 1853.'[343]

The circumstances the university faced were very different from thirty-five years earlier. Then there had been one building committee controlled by a single man, one building to worry about, and a supportive governor. Now there were three competing groups within the university – the Board of Trustees, the Senate, and the faculty – which had to be cajoled into working together, and a notoriously tight-fisted government. There was a gutted main building (only the lower floor to the west of the main tower and the residence survived), a library that had to be restocked, and new buildings to be erected as well. Finally, Wilson's reserves of strength were limited.

The president rose to the challenge. He could see clearly what had to be done and knew that something better could arise, like the phoenix, from the ashes: 'if we can only get money enough, we shall restore the fine building in all its old beauty; and much better fitted internally for the work we have to do.' His strong sense of faith helped to ensure that he 'never gave way to despondence. My spirits rise with the necessity of the occasion; and, in spite of very hard work, I never was better.'[344] Assistance came first from an unexpected source: Edward Blake, now free of political commitments in Ottawa. The chancellor's appearance, at the behest of the university registrar, H.H. Langton,[345] immediately re-established him – such was his prestige – as the power-broker at the university. Wilson welcomed his formidable intellect, his capacity for hard work, and his mastery of detail. 'I am glad to find myself at work with an honest, straightforward ally. I do detest having to deal with tricksters. The V.C. is alternately insolent and oily-gammonish, and the unctuous phase is by far the worst of the two.'[346]

The alliances within the nativist group immediately began to shift with Blake's appearance. The vice-chancellor realized the danger to his authority, for Blake's tacit support in the past had masked his disapproval of many of Mulock's actions, such as stripping the Senate of its financial authority and his direct appeal for government funds in 1883. Blake also believed that denominational colleges federating with the university should shed their arts programs and teach theology only.[347] Mulock thought that Loudon had summoned Blake, and a major row resulted.[348] Loudon, who saw himself as the heir to Wilson's 'old shoes,' began calculatedly to distance himself from Mulock, and by 1892, with his old friend embroiled in the controversy over the Park Hospital (a proposal to build a hospital on the university grounds near the School of Practical Science) and the building of an addition to the biological building, the break was complete. Wilson was disgusted. 'The way in which J.L. has deserted his old ally and bosom friend, as his fortune declined, and turned to worship the rising sun – the Chancellor – is scandalous.' When the Senate called for a vote of censure of Mulock in June 1892, Wilson felt sorry for him, and 'though he had small claim on me for my courtesy – I took his side and voted his acquittal.'[349]

As Mulock was absent from most of the crucial board meetings in the three months following the fire, Wilson chaired them. The chancellor, with whom he worked easily, attended most Senate meetings throughout 1890 and thereafter took the chair. From mid-October, Blake also regularly attended the board meetings. A year later he supported an order-in-council that permitted the board to elect its own chairman. This change signalled the end of Mulock's power base in the board, and thereafter it is Blake's sprawling handwriting that can be seen most often in the minutes as approving or directing activities.

Wilson was thus given considerable freedom to use his talents in the restoration of his beloved college. Though he offered support in all quarters, he concentrated on those areas where he would have the most effect, the centre of activity being the Board of Trustees. It met with the university architect, David B. Dick, the day after the fire and within forty-eight hours had a preliminary plan of action ready for the government to consider. The proposal recommended the restoration of the building with a view to making it, as Wilson had said, 'much better fitted internally for the work we have to do.'[350] The board assumed the lead in establishing committees to deal with a myriad of activities. Wilson chaired the most crucial of these, the building committee, which took 'all requisite steps for the construction of the [college] building' and the library. He also initially chaired the library restoration committee, charged with restocking the library; was a member of delegations to the city and the province; and with Mulock and one other, canvassed locally for funds to build a convocation hall.[351]

One of Wilson's proud claims, for which he was widely praised, was that lectures resumed on Monday morning after the fire 'without the loss of an hour.'[352] Space was offered by his colleagues in the university and the denominational colleges, except Dean Galbraith of the School of Practical Science, whom Wilson 'had not thought to or had time to ask.' Sensitive about his newly bestowed prerogative, Galbraith demanded written permission from the minister of education to use the spare rooms in the new wing of his building and taped the doors.[353] These rooms, suitable for the processing of incoming books for the library, were not provided until August, causing considerable inconvenience.[354]

Another problem was that Cumberland's partner, W.G. Storm, who survived him, owned the original drawings for the college. The board, hoping to save valuable time, offered to buy them. Storm, however, would not accept its price and lost any hope he had of being appointed architect for the reconstruction. Thus when Dick got the job on 27 March, he had to make new drawings.[355] The only consensus on the interior layout of the college building was that there would be no room for the library or convocation hall, both of which had, in any case, become too small. The plans had first to be approved by the building committee, no simple task in itself. 'Here I am negotiating with a committee of a dozen, and behind them Professors, Lecturers, Fellows, and members of senate fully persuaded that they live not in Canada, but Utopia.'[356]

The plans were then sent to the faculty and the Senate, meeting separately. Many of the former wanted individual sets to take away for 'study,' each well aware that his immutable requirements could be met only at the expense of his fellows. The 'study' faction was defeated by a single vote; only Wilson's deftness in persuading one professor to reverse his decision saved the day. In the Senate the process was almost derailed by Loudon, who supported the plans, but 'who has no idea of ever pursuing a conciliatory course, got up and irritated the opponents in every conceivable way; denounced our beautiful old Convocation Hall as a big barn, made a coarse personal attack on A.B. [Alfred Baker], and did his best to defeat his own aims.'[357]

Following approval in principle, subcommittees went over the details, and their recommendations were submitted to the Board of Trustees, which dealt with the contractors. The building committee then met with the architect to approve each stage; so there was always further friction. Wilson, describing one incident over heating and ventilation plans, excoriated Loudon, who, as a member of the subcommittee, had approved a course of action, but then baulked. 'Mr. Mole ... must needs play the mole as usual, decline responsibility and flourish red tape, and make himself as discourteous and cranky as the opportunity allowed. Happily the Cad was absent – for they hunt in couples. Got the matter passed after an hour's wrangle.'[358]

Funding remained a constant worry, since the money voted by the provincial government was barely sufficient to restore the fabric of University College. Nothing was left for the library and convocation hall or for rebuilding the ethnological museum. Wilson was gratified with the responses from his many contacts in the museum and archaeological fields[359] and hoped for similar support in the one area where funds could be sought widely: books and periodicals for the library. As chair of the library restoration committee, he delegated a great deal of the legwork to the very able Walter Barwick, but faced endless correspondence from this and other activities, which left him 'wearied beyond measure.' Still, he much preferred writing to politicians, university officials, and benefactors such as industrialist Andrew Carnegie and titled people in Britain and Europe – 'I can beg best in this form' – to personal solicitations. He noted wryly that the reception he and Mulock received from Goldwin Smith, when they went round to solicit funds for the new convocation hall, 'was enough to freeze us into icicles. We were literally shown the door as if we had been a pair of tramps.'[360]

An unexpected benefit from the enormous labour involved in restocking the library was the departure of the librarian, Van der Smissen, who could not handle the pressure. He was replaced by Hugh Hornby Langton, registrar of the university and University College since 1887. That he had also been assistant librarian, though in name only, enabled Wilson to groom him for the position. The appointment must have been doubly sweet for the president. Hugh was the son of his old friend John Langton, and Wilson successfully fought off, by raising the spectre of political interference, the candidate of his foe Mulock.[361] He was satisfied in other ways. The 33,000 volumes lost in the fire had, a year later, largely been replaced with more appropriate ones. By April 1891, 29,121 volumes had been catalogued; of these 740 had escaped the fire, and 26,622 were gifts.[362]

The building of a new library itself had been put on hold until the reconstruction of University College was under way. In June 1890 Dick was instructed to begin preparing plans and estimates for the library building, 'whether isolated or in connection with the main building.'[363] Again Wilson was very much involved. His discerning eye and knowledge of the architectural heritage of Europe enabled him to suggest design changes that improved the look of the building and, by simplifying the elevation, kept costs down. The arched doorway at the base of the tower was 'an almost exact copy of the doorway in the north transept of the 12th-century Kelso Abbey,' which Sir Daniel 'had praised in his *Prehistoric Annals of Scotland*.'[364]

The work of rewriting his lectures, though, was 'very hard on me. Started afresh; and each day is a scramble, in spite of a tolerably well-stored memory ... the old spirit is wanting with which I used to sketch out a new lecture, and look to polishing and giving it new poignancy in future years. I cannot hope for such now.'[365] But in moments snatched between endless correspondence, meetings, and his lectures, he could be found in the makeshift library, peering through a large magnifying glass at books spread out before him. In just over a year he had 'rewritten notes for 72 lectures to replace what perished in the fire.'[366]

Wilson's other duties still weighed heavily on him. The principal problem after 1890 was to hang on to the new professors, for opportunities abounded in the United States and in the new universities in Canada and Australia. He was especially worried about James Mark Baldwin, with whom he quickly developed personal ties and professional respect, partly because of their mutual interest in 'handedness.'[367] The fire destroyed the site of Baldwin's proposed psychological laboratory, and he had to make do by borrowing apparatus from the biological and physical laboratories. It was only in the summer of 1891 that he was finally able to set up his laboratory, the first on British soil and the only one in North America specifically designed for psychological research.[368]

The continuing tight finances meant that 'his laboratory remained equipped and manned far less than expected,' even though the number of students was increasing. Baldwin desperately needed a demonstrator, but his request was not given top priority by the newly created committee on university requirements.[369] Wilson continued to offer encouragement and to send warnings to Blake and Ross,[370] but nothing happened until March 1992, after Baldwin had received a generous offer from Princeton. Even though Blake found funds for both a fellowship and a demonstratorship,[371] Baldwin was eventually hired away.

There were also incessant demands from others colleagues, particularly relating to wages. Where these were tied to the cost of living or retaining a valued colleague, Wilson was a doughty champion of requests for pay increases. But when other factors, particularly the enhancement of status, figured largely, he was far less sympathetic, as the lecturers in modern languages quickly discovered. There had been no chair in this field for thirty years, in spite of a Senate resolution in 1883. So the lecturers in French, German, and Italian had no direct representation on the College Council. When Wilson supported the representation of lecturers on the University Council, he soon discovered that what those in modern languages really wanted was upgrading to full professors. This he would not

countenance since, financial considerations aside, he had worked hard to
ensure that appointees to professorships had a proven academic record
and some claim to international recognition. He wrote frankly to Blake
that neither Van der Smissen in German or W.H. Fraser in Italian and
Spanish should be appointed above the rank of lecturer.[372]

The lecturers' response was to petition the Senate, which, not surprisingly, supported their upgrading. This report was at variance with one
from the Board of Arts Studies, chaired by Wilson, which considered the
broader picture. It emphasized the necessity of making the best use of
appointments with the funds available and urged that 'the Senate recommend no new appointment in Arts till they are in possession of information showing the present requirements of all departments.'[373] To resolve
these conflicting recommendations the Senate and the Board of Trustees
in January 1891 created a joint committee on the revenues and requirements of the University of Toronto and University College. Its members
were Wilson, Edward Blake, and William Mulock, but much of the work
was done by the chancellor. He spent three months receiving evidence
from the teaching departments, canvassing other institutions for information, and writing the report, at a personal cost of some $6,000, before pre-
senting it on 13 April. The document, which became the university's
guide for the next decade, 'laid out in magisterial form the assets of the
university, the annual revenues to be expected, and the order in which its
projected requirements should be met.' For the teaching staff, there was
to be 'a set graduation of ranks, Professor, Associate Professor, Lecturer,
Demonstrator, and Fellow.'[374]

The implementation of any of the recommendations depended on the
availability of funds and required much negotiation over the ensuing
months. In the Senate, Wilson 'in the strongest terms ... protested against
the idea that, in introducing the proposal of "*Associate Professors*" the Committee had in view any individual case now under appeal, but that their
aim was solely directed to the permanent interests of the University in its
future developments; but in vain.'[375] The issue was still not resolved a year
later and had to await his successor.

In February 1892, as a result of showing a visiting dignitary around the
library in inclement weather, Wilson caught a chill that turned into pneu-
monia. He had to hire a replacement to give his history lectures, and he
never fully recovered. Even after he returned to the Senate in April, his
participation was noticeably diminished.[376] A brief respite was the annual
commencement on 11 June. The press referred to him as the 'venerable
Sir Daniel,' and for the first time, his frailty kept him from making a

speech. Afterwards he showed his visitors through the new buildings, including the ladies' rooms, 'and said proudly that not the smallest irregularity had occurred during the seven years that had elapsed since the admission of women.'[377]

Five days later he learned that Blake had been offered an Irish seat in the British House of Commons. Wilson feared that he would accept it and 'leave us in the lurch in University matters, for he has carried us half way in a grand borrowing scheme and inaugurated a system of financial intermeddling by the Senate which demands his strong hand to keep it within bounds.' Wilson added, in the most plaintive entry of his entire journal, 'I wish he would stay where he is.'[378] The rumoured departures of Ashley and Baldwin also continued to cause him great anxiety, and on 26 June Ashley's departure was confirmed. If both he and Baldwin went in one year, Wilson lamented, 'it would be worse than the fire.'[379]

The day before, Sir Daniel, his health 'very unsatisfactory' and his eyesight failing badly, concluded it might be wise – 'my plans are provisional' – to resign the presidency if he could make reasonable terms for retiring. Two days later Mulock resigned as chair of the Board of Trustees, and on 30 June Blake replaced him, with John Hoskin as vice-chairman (and chairman-in-waiting). It was also Wilson's last board meeting. The day before, having seen Dr Reeve about his eyes, he had handed his resignation of the presidency to John Hoskin to negotiate with the premier.[380]

Wilson's Legacy

The death of Sir Daniel Wilson in August 1892 marked the end of an era for the University of Toronto. By then the social and academic values which he epitomized were being replaced by others that were less genteel, more democratic, and more parochial. The broad academic disciplines were being supplanted by narrower, subject-oriented ones, and the increased administrative demands of the office of university president meant that the idea that its occupant should also teach was rapidly passing into history.

Wilson's achievements as a administrator were many. McCaul's status in University College had owed much more to his standing as a classicist than to his holding the office of president. When Wilson came to the job, his chair did not have the status of McCaul's, but he already possessed a proven record as an administrator, to which he added the great advantage of his reputation as an educationalist. By the time he died, the office of president, now of both the university and the college, could stand on its own, though it would be another fifteen years before a president would be appointed as an administrator only. Through sheer ability, hard work, and personality, standing on principle where it really mattered but knowing how to bend, and always mindful of his political masters, Wilson had won through. He was, the *Globe* stated in its tribute to him, 'largely gifted with the infectious enthusiasm that makes light of difficulties and brings success out of the most unpromising conditions.'[381]

His temperament was ideally suited to the difficulties of maintaining and enhancing the status of an office that had little legal authority, in an era of competing jurisdictions where others had more authority than he. His successor, James Loudon, 'a reserved, unconciliatory man, who lacked the gifts of personal or moral leadership,'[382] was unable to mediate among factions and demonstrated to all the glaring weaknesses of the acts of 1853 and 1887. When Loudon was forced to retire in 1906 and a royal commission reported on the governance of the university, it made recommendations that Wilson might have written and, if in place in the 1880s, would have made his duties as president much less onerous. The report accepted 'the policy of maintaining a complete system of higher education by the State with one purse and one governing board ... as definitely settled.' It deplored the 'exceptional and unsatisfactory method by which the powers of the Crown in relation to the University have been exercised' and the 'lack of clearly defined division of authority in matters of academic policy.'[383]

The University of Toronto Act of 1906 greatly enhanced the status of the president by eliminating conflicting jurisdictions; the legacy of the strife between Wilson and Mulock and between Mulock and Loudon was the abolition of the vice-chancellorship. By removing the minister of education from any responsibility for the day-to-day running of the university, including authority over appointments, the act also largely eliminated the pernicious political interference that had been so much of a trial to Wilson. As well, the president was relieved of all teaching duties and presided at meetings of the Senate.

The 1906 act continued the college system so as to 'maintain the importance of a liberal culture in the face of commercial and industrial development, and the growth of scientific activity.' Sir Daniel's staunchly held view of the value of residences was reaffirmed, for the act provided for their re-establishment in University College and their maintenance elsewhere as 'places wherein students may be profoundly influenced by contact with one another and with their instructors. The value of the residential system has been abundantly demonstrated both in the Old World and the New.'[384]

A century later Wilson's legacy has become clearer. In the 1920s H.H. Langton deplored the fact that University College had not been able to attain its rightful place in the university. Today Wilson seems more visionary than he was then given credit for. University College is now on the same footing in the Faculty of Arts program as the federated colleges, since all the courses for the past twenty years have been university (not college) ones. The uniqueness of those colleges is now based, as Wilson believed it should be, on their theological programs and the sense of community that comes from maintaining residences and keeping the number of students relatively small. University College has retained its own traditions as a non-denominational institution and its sense of place in the university, and it continues to attract members of an increasingly diverse student body. It has been assisted by the construction of a women's residence and the restoration of the men's residence, which Wilson so doughtily defended, in the form of a new and much larger building that bears his name.

NOTES

The fire in University College in 1890 destroyed the great bulk of the administrative records of the university, as well as much of Sir Daniel Wilson's correspondence, the drawings that he had brought with him in 1853, and his holograph notes. The Senate minute books survived, except for the volume, begun in 1887, that had been left out for use. The minutes of the College Council were destroyed and also those of the University Council, if any were kept. Fortunately, the minutes of the Board of Management/Trustees survived, for, with the Senate minutes and other sources, it is possible to reconstruct a great deal of what went on. For most of the entries from the Senate minutes prior to 1877, we have used Hodgins's *Documentary History of Education in Upper Canada*, but for a few entries we have referred to the original minute books.

1 Macallum, 'Huxley and Tyndall and the University of Toronto,' 70. The chairs were history and English literature, modern languages, natural philosophy, natural history, geology and mineralogy, and civil engineering. The last was never filled.
2 UTA, B84-0033/001(01), Extract of letter from Dr Simpson (undated); Valentine collection, J. Scott Porter, Belfast, to Wilson, 12 July 1853.
3 Valentine collection, George E. Day, St Andrews, to Wilson, 1 November 1851.
4 McKillop, *Matters of Mind*, 19.

5 Schull, *Edward Blake*, 1: 22.
6 Walllace, *A History of the University of Toronto*, 62–3.
7 Province of Canada, Statutes, 13 & 14 Vic., cap. 49, sec. 1 (10 August 1850).
8 Wilson, 'The University of Toronto and University College' (1887), 23.
9 Province of Canada, An Act to Amend the Laws relating to the University of Toronto ... (22 April 1853), 16 Vic., cap. 89.
10 Wilson, 'The University of Toronto and University College' (1887), 23.
11 Ibid., 22.
12 *Calendar of University College, Toronto for 1857–1858*, 15, 37.
13 *The University of Toronto and Its Colleges*, 113, 123.
14 UTA, B84-0033/001(01), Wilson to Lord Elgin, 14 November 1851, and Wilson to John Strachan, 29 January 1852, enclosing letter from Nathaniel Gould dated 23 January 1851 [*sic*].
15 UTA, B84-033/001(02), 'Testimonials in Favour of Mr. Daniel Wilson,' letters from Edward Forbes, C. Innes, Alexander C. Fraser, 9–11.
16 Hodgins, 15: 220–1.
17 UTA, B65-0014/004(01), 39–40 (4 May 1877).
18 Ibid., 10 (letter, 5 November 1853).
19 W.S. Reid, *The Scottish Tradition in Canada*, 248–9, 253, 260–1; *The University of Toronto and Its Colleges*, 80–1.
20 UTA, B65-0014/004(01), 10 (letter, 5 November 1853).
21 Ibid.
22 UTA, B93-0022/001(08), Wilson to David Laing, 8 September 1855.
23 Wilson, *Address at the Convocation of University College* (1885), 2.
24 Province of Canada, University of Toronto Act, 16 Vic., cap. 89 (1853).
25 For respective examples, see orders-in-council for 5 July 1856, 7 May 1855, 19 August 1858 (UTA, A70-0024/053(02), /054(01) and (03)).
26 W.A. Langton, *Early Days in Upper Canada*, 279.
27 UTA, B65-0014/004(01), 8 (letter, 21 September 1853).
28 Fairclough, 'Sir Daniel Wilson,' 121.
29 UTA, B65-0014/004(01), 47 (28 October 1879).
30 Ibid., 8 (letter, 21 September 1853).
31 W.A. Langton, *Early Days in Upper Canada*, 284–6.
32 UTA, B65-0014/004(01), 9 (letter, 15 October 1853).
33 Ibid., 9 (letters, 1 and 15 October 1853).
34 UTA, B76-0020/004(05), Typescript of 'Sir William Mulock: A Short Biography,' 39.
35 UTA, B72-0031/016(11), 'Memoirs of James Loudon,' 8.
36 King, *McCaul: Croft: Forneri*, 82.
37 Biggar, 'The Reverend William Hincks, MA.'

38 Macallum, 'Huxley and Tyndall and the University of Toronto,' 71, 75.

39 UTA, B65-0014/004(01), 19 (21 February 1854).

40 Ibid.

41 Ibid., 18 (3 February 1854).

42 Fairclough, 'Sir Daniel Wilson,' 120.

43 UTA, A69-0011/001, University College Literary and Scientific Society minutes, 2 November 1860.

44 *White and Blue*, 7 October 1879, 3.

45 UTA, B65-0014/004(02), 111 (8 February 1887).

46 Bowker, 'Truly Useful Men,' 4.

47 W.A. Langton, *Early Days in Upper Canada*, 286, 284.

48 Ibid., 280–2.

49 Ibid., 287.

50 W.S. Reid, *The Scottish Tradition in Canada*, 250.

51 *The University of Toronto and Its Colleges*, 83.

52 Hodgins, 15: 215.

53 W.S. Reid, *The Scottish Tradition in Canada*, 251.

54 Hodgins, 12: 259–60, 263.

55 W.A. Langton, *Early Days in Upper Canada*, 296, 289.

56 Hodgins, 13: 103–11.

57 UTA, B65-0014/004(01), 6 (letter, 21 September 1853).

58 Hodgins, 11: 147.

59 Wilson, *Address at the Convocation of Faculties of the University of Toronto* (1891), 3.

60 H.H. Langton, 'Sir Daniel Wilson,' 3–4; H.H. Langton, *Sir Daniel Wilson*, 76–7; Blackburn, *Evolution of the Heart*, 26.

61 W.A. Langton, *Early Days in Upper Canada*, 293.

62 *Globe*, 5 October 1858, p. 2, col. 7; Hodgins, 14: 34.

63 Wallace, *A History of the University of Toronto*, 72.

64 Hodgins, 15: 213.

65 UTA, A70-0024/053(02), John Langton to David Buchan, 17 October 1856.

66 W.A. Langton, *Early Days in Upper Canada*, 288–9.

67 UTA, B65-0014/004(02), 109 (15 January 1887); Hodgins, 15: 231.

68 Hodgins, 16: 198–9, 201, 203.

69 UTA, B93-0022/001(01), Wilson to R. Bell, Smithsonian Institution, 20 October 1876; Wilson to William H. Dall, Smithsonian Institution, 1 November 1889.

70 The years when he was not a member were 1866 and 1874–6.

71 UTA, B65-0014/004(01), 12–13 (letter, 12 November 1853); Blackburn, *Evolution of the Heart*, 11, 36.

72 Hodgins, 11: 147.

73 Hodgins, 11: 257; UTA, A70-0024/053(03), John Langton to David Buchan, 17 October 1856; Blackburn, *Evolution of the Heart*, 319.

74 Hodgins, 17: 143; UTA, B93-0022/001(01), Wilson to R. Bell, Smithsonian Institution, 20 October 1876.

75 H. H. Langton, *James Loudon and the University of Toronto*, 2.

76 UTA, A70-0024/055(02), Statute of University College Council, passed by the Senate on 23 January and approved by the governor general on 17 April 1866.

77 UTA, A70-0024/055(02), Report of the Senate committee on the financial position of the university; undated but 1863. The committee was appointed on 4 March (see Hodgins, 17: 309).

78 The shield incorporated the elements that we know today, and the motto was *Velut arbor aveo*, but the crest was a maple tree, rather than the oak that the College of Heraldry substituted later. See Hodgins, 13: 103, 116.

79 Letter to the *Globe*; quoted in Hodgins, 14: 209, and Wallace, *A History of the University of Toronto*, 79.

80 H.H. Langton, *Sir Daniel Wilson*, 78.

81 Ibid., 8.

82 Hodgins, 15: 209, 211, 214–15.

83 Ibid., 80.

84 Hodgins, 18: 20.

85 These are bound in UTA, B88-0002/005, /012, and /015.

86 Wallace, *A History of the University of Toronto*, 84–5.

87 Schull, *Edward Blake*, 1: 23.

88 UTA, B72-0031/016(11), 'Memoirs of James Loudon,' 15.

89 Hodgins, 18: 152.

90 Wilson, 'The University of Toronto and University College' (1887), 26–7.

91 UTA, B84-0033/001(03), Wilson to William Dawson, 10 May 1861.

92 Wilson, 'The University of Toronto and University College' (1887), 29.

93 *Globe*, 11 February 1871.

94 Robert M. Stamp, 'Crooks, Adam,' in *DCB*, 11: 221.

95 McKillop, *Contours of Canadian Thought*, 82.

96 Hodgins, 15: 256–7.

97 J.G. Snell, 'Moss, Thomas,' in *DCB*, 11: 622.

98 UTA, B72-0031/016(11), 'Memoirs of James Loudon,' 9–10; Wallace, *A History of the University of Toronto*, 101.

99 R.D. Gidney, 'Young, George Paxton,' in *DCB*, 11: 942–3.

100 Paxton Young to the editor, Toronto *Mail*, 9 February, 1889, published 11 February, p. 5.

101 'That he taught us philosophical truths of the last importance, was still a

slighter thing than teaching us to think and teaching us to live' (MacMechan, *Reminiscences of Toronto University*, 13).

102 UTA, B84-0033/001(03), Wilson to William Dawson, 28 October 1871.

103 Ontario, An Act respecting the University of Toronto, 36 Vic., chap. 29 (29 March 1873); Wallace, *A History of the University of Toronto*, 95–6.

104 UTA, B72-0031/016(11), 'Memoirs of James Loudon,' 29; McKillop, 'The Research Ideal and the University of Toronto,' in *Contours of Canadian Thought*, 85–6. See also Suzanne Zeller's essay in this volume.

105 McKillop, 'The Research Ideal and the University of Toronto,' in *Contours of Canadian Thought*, 79, 85.

106 UTA, B72-0031/016(11), 'Memoirs of James Loudon,' 29.

107 Ibid., 24–8; 'Proceedings of the Senate of the University of Toronto, 1874' [17 June], in Hodgins, 27: 184. The degree of BSc was not introduced until 1960.

108 UTA, B65-0014/004(01), 33 (21 April 1874).

109 UTA, B92-0030/009(04), J.B. Cherriman to Wilson, 28 July 1875.

110 UTA, B72-0031/016(11), 'Memoirs of James Loudon,' 32.

111 UTA, B92-0030/009(04), J.M. Mason, Hamilton, to James Loudon, 24 September 1875.

112 Ibid., Wilson to James Loudon, 27 July 1875.

113 Ibid., J.A. McLellan to James Loudon, 8 July 1875 (emphasis in original).

114 Ibid., J.M. Mason, Hamilton, to James Loudon, 24 September 1875.

115 Ibid., J.L. McDougall to Edward Blake, 14 July 1875; Edward Blake to Oliver Mowat, 19 July 1875.

116 Ibid., James Bethune to Neil McNish, 10 September 1875; UTA, B72-0031/016(11), 'Memoirs of James Loudon,' 33–4.

117 UTA, B92-0030/009(04), Paxton Young to James Loudon, 26 July 1875; John McCaul to James Loudon, 28 July 1875.

118 UTA, B72-0013/001(01), Oliver Mowat to Edward Blake, 30 July 1875.

119 UTA, B92-0030/009(04), Wilson to James Loudon, 27 July 1875.

120 Moss was, like Wilson, a convert to Anglicanism, supporting the low church. Larratt W. Smith, who had replaced Adam Crooks as vice-chancellor the year before, did not seek re-election.

121 UTA, B65-0014/004(01), 53 (8 January 1881).

122 'Proceedings of the Senate of the University of Toronto, 1875,' in Hodgins, 27: 193–8.

123 Wallace, *A History of the University of Toronto*, 97.

124 UTA, B72-0013/001(01), James Loudon to Edward Blake, 27 December 1875; Thomas Moss to Edward Blake, 21 March and 29 December 1876; A70-0024/056(03), Adam Crooks to Thomas Moss, 17 June 1878.

125 C.R. Young, *Early Engineering Education at Toronto*, 60–1.

126 The total university budget for 1878–9 was $55,000, most of which went for salaries. The library committee received $1,500 for books, while Wilson got $50 for his ethnological museum. A separate appropriation of $8,000 was made from capital accounts for equipment for the school. See UTA, A70-0024/008(01), Board of Management minute book no. 1, 6 (24 June 1878).

127 B92-0030/009(03), Unsigned letter (last page missing), but Ramsay Wright to James Loudon, 7 July 1878.

128 B72-0031/016(11), 'Memoirs of James Loudon,' 37–37a; C.R. Young, *Early Engineering Education at Toronto*, 62–3.

129 The chancellor was added in 1880, and the Senate received two additional seats the following year. In 1884 the elected members were increased to seven: five from the Senate and two from the Council. See UTA, B72-0031/017(10), Copy of an Order-in-Council approved by ... the Lieutenant-Governor, 31 May 1884.

130 UTA, A70-0024/008(01), Board of Management minute book no. 1, 7, 17 (24 June and 11 July 1878).

131 UTA, B65-0014/004(01), 30 (22 July 1873).

132 Ibid., 33 (21 June 1875).

133 Ibid., 46 (7 July 1879).

134 Ibid., 46 (1 October 1879).

135 University of Toronto, *Return of an Address to His Honour the Lieutenant Governor*, 4, 8.

136 UTA, B65-0014/004(01), 47 (28 October 1879).

137 Toronto *Mail*, 13 August 1879.

138 UTA, B84-0033/001(03), Wilson to William Dawson, 2 December 1880.

139 UTA, B65-0014/004(01), 49 (17 January 1880).

140 UTA, B84-0033/001(03), Wilson to William Dawson, 2 December 1880.

141 Ibid., 10 March 1880.

142 UTA, B92-0030/009(10), W.D. Pearman to James Loudon, 6 March 1881; Robert M. Stamp, 'Crooks, Adam,' *DCB*, 11: 223.

143 UTA, B72-0031/016(11), 'Memoirs of James Loudon,' 45.

144 UTA, B65-0014/004(01), 48 (17 November 1879).

145 Ibid., 50–1 (20 May 1880).

146 Ibid., 52–3 (1 January 1881).

147 *Canada Educational Monthly* 2 (October 1880): 478.

148 Crooks had got rid of the incumbent dean, W.D. Pearman, in the manoeuvring over the retirement of McCaul. Pearman blamed Wilson, without any evidence to support his case. See UTA, B92-0030/009 (09), W.D. Pearman to James Loudon, 23 August, 3 October 1880.

149 UTA, B84-0033/001(03), Wilson to William Dawson, 16 August 1880.

150 Hoff, 'The Controversial Appointment of James Mark Baldwin,' 59.

151 *Canada Educational Monthly* 2 (September 1880): 425; 2 (October 1880): 478.

152 UTA, B65-0014/004(01), 51 (October 1880).

153 UTA, B84-0033/001(03), Wilson to William Dawson, 16 August 1880.

154 UTA, B65-0014/004(01), 51–2 (16 October 1880).

155 Ibid., 52 (16 October 1880); letter of 28 September 1880, printed in the *Globe*, 30 September, p. 4.

156 UTA, B72-0031/016(11), 'Memoirs of James Loudon,' 45–6. Hutton was rewarded several years later with a preferential rate on a housing lot. The salary of a professorial chair at this time was $3,600.

157 UTA, B65-0014/004(01), 54 (29 January 1881); A70-0005/003, Senate minute book no. 3, 393, 21 January 1881.

158 Blackburn, *Evolution of the Heart*, 50; UTA, A70-0005/003, Senate minute book no. 3, 400 (3 February 1881). This date does not coincide with that in Wilson's journal, so there must be an error in the typescript.

159 UTA, B72-0013/001(12), Notes by Edward Blake for convocation (?) address, undated but 1881.

160 Schull, *Edward Blake*, 2: 179.

161 UTA, B72-0031/016(11), 'Memoirs of James Loudon,' 47–8.

162 UTA, B65-0014/004(01), 54 (15 January 1881).

163 UTA, B92-0030/009(22), William Mulock to Alfred Baker, 20 February 1890.

164 UTA, B65-0014/004(01), 76 (28 January 1884).

165 He received eleven votes to Wilson's four (UTA, A70-0005/003, Senate minute book no. 3, 393, 21 January 1881). Loudon and the representatives of the College Council on the Senate, Edward Chapman and George Buckland, did not vote.

166 UTA, B65-0014/004(01), 55 (27 May 1881); see also B92-0030/009(16), James Loudon to William Mulock, 9 December 1886.

167 UTA, B65-0014/004(01), 76 (28 January 1884); see also B72-0031/016(11), 'Memoirs of James Loudon,' 62.

168 UTA, B72-0031/016(11), 'Memoirs of James Loudon,' 48–9.

169 C.R. Young, *Early Engineering Education at Toronto*, 76–9; UTA, B65-0014/004(01), 55 (27 May 1881).

170 B65-0014/004(01), 73 (13 October 1883).

171 Ibid., 57 (15 November 1881); Wilson, *On the Practical Uses of Science in the Daily Business of Life* (1881); C.R. Young, *Early Engineering Education at Toronto*, 75–6.

172 The first annual report of the University College Council during his tenure was printed in the Ontario *Sessional Papers* was for 1881–2. The school reports

were much more comprehensive because of the interest of the minister of education.

173 The issue arose with frequency, increasing as the city grew to surround the university. There had been major discussions, for example, in 1874 and 1876–7. See 'Proceedings of the Senate of the University of Toronto, 1874,' in Hodgins, 27: 181 (4 May 1874); UTA, A70-0005/003, Senate minute book no. 3, 136, 1 February 1877.

174 UTA, B65-0014/004(01), 141 (18 September 1888).

175 UTA, A70-0024/008(02), Board of Management minute book no. 2, 55 (27 January 1881), 141–2 (23 September 1881), 184 (8 December 1881), 239–40 (23 March 1882), 281–2 (28 June 1882), 289–90 (13 July 1882), 412 (27 September 1883), 463–4 (5 January 1884).

176 UTA, B65-0014/004(02), 140 (1, 18 September 1888); A70-0024/008(03), Board of Management minute book no. 3, 506, 514, 559, 567 (16, 25 April, 31 August, 30 September 1888); Wilson, *Address at the Convocation of the University of Toronto* (1888), 7.

177 Ontario, An Act Validating a Certain Agreement between the University of Toronto and the Corporation of the City of Toronto, 52 Vic., chap. 53; Wilson, *Address at the Convocation of the University of Toronto* (1888), 7.

178 UTA, A70-0005/003, Senate minute book no. 3, 391 (13 December 1880).

179 UTA, A70-0024/008(02), Board of Management minute book no. 2, 445, 340, 351, 426 (1 May 1884, 23 November 1882, 18 January, 6 November 1883); B72-0031/016(11), 'Memoirs of James Loudon,' 62, 66.

180 See, for example, UTA, A70-0024/008(02), Board of Management minute book no. 2, 496 (2 October 1884), and /008(03), no. 3, 5 (30 October 1884), 91 (23 April 1884), 131 (15 October 1885).

181 UTA, B72-0031/016(11), 'Memoirs of James Loudon,' 62.

182 For example, see UTA, A70-0024/008(03), Board of Management minute book no. 3, 115 (2 July 1885) and 191 (25 February 1886).

183 UTA, A70-0005/003, Senate minute book no. 3, 487 (13 January 1882); Ontario, *Sessional Papers*, 1884, no. 97, 3. The recommended subjects were Greek, Latin, French and Italian, German, English, Hebrew, history, political economy, constitutional law and jurisprudence, mathematics, natural philosophy, mental science, chemistry, physiology, geology and mineralogy, zoology, and botany.

184 UTA, B65-0014/004(01), 59 (19 May 1882).

185 UTA, A70-0005/003, Senate Minute Book no. 3, 524–6 (15, 19 May 1882); B72-0013/001(01), Wilson to Edward Blake, 24 April 1882. Wilson's teaching load, on top of his greatly increased administrative duties, had become intolerable. He had always had some of the largest classes in the college.

186 UTA, B65-0014/004(01), 59 (19 May 1882). Loudon, who had promised
     Wilson loyal support when he became president, harboured a litany of griev-
     ances against him (UTA, B72-0031/016(11), 'Memoirs of James Loudon,' 30,
     32, 41, 44), and so his support could be relied upon only when his own inter-
     ests were being served.
187 UTA, B65-0014/004(01), 60–2 (20, 30 May 1882); A70-0024/008(02), Board
     of Management minute book no. 2, 277–8 (18 May 1882); B72-0031/
     016(11), 'Memoirs of James Loudon,' 51.
188 UTA, B65-0014/004(01), 60 (27 May 1882).
189 UTA, B72-0013/001(01), Wilson to Edward Blake, 30 October, 2 November
     1882; B65-0014/004(01), 61 (26 October 1882); B84-0033/001(03), Wilson
     to William Dawson, 20 April 1882.
190 UTA, A70-0024/008(02), Board of Management minute book no. 2, 319
     (2 October 1882), 323–4 (26 October 1882); B65-0014/004(01), 61
     (28 October 1882).
191 UTA, B72-0013/001(01), Wilson to Edward Blake, 2 November 1882.
192 UTA, B92-0030/009(17), Alfred Baker to James Loudon, 5 May 1887, and /
     009(19) D.R. Keys to James Loudon, 3 May 1887.
193 UTA, B65-0014/004(01), 62 (16 February 1883).
194 Ibid., 80 (17 May 1884). Other examples are the entries for 15 October and
     1 November 1883.
195 The first reference to this development in Wilson's journal was on 30 Octo-
     ber 1883; see also UTA, A70-0024/008(02), Board of Management minute
     book no. 2, 417–18 (10 April 1883).
196 Fairclough, 'Sir Daniel Wilson,' 120.
197 UTA, B92-0030/009(13), Wilson to Loudon, 19 May 1883.
198 UTA, B92-0030/009(11), Wilson to Loudon, 4 December 1882, the second of
     three letters written on the subject the same day in an attempt to calm him; for
     other examples, see /009(13), Wilson to Loudon, 2 February, 15 May 1883.
199 UTA, B65-0014/004(01), 86, 88 (8 November, 6 December 1884).
200 UTA, B92-0030/009(29), Alfred Baker to James Loudon, 20 and 23 May
     1887.
201 Ibid., Alfred Baker to James Loudon, 22 July 1888; UTA, B65-0014/004(02),
     120 (14 June 1887).
202 AO, RG 2-29-1-1, no. 14, 250, Wilson to George Ross, 19 November 1891.
203 Ibid., 249, Wilson to George Ross, 10 March 1889; UTA, A70-0024/009(01),
     Board of Trustees minute book no. 4, 92 (19 March 1889).
204 UTA, B65-0014/004(02), 201 (22 December 1891).
205 UTA, B72-0013/001(05), Wilson to Edward Blake, 18 December 1891. The
     issue was not finally settled until after Wilson's death.

206 UTA, A70-0024/008(02), Board of Management minute book no. 2, 177–8 (24 November 1881), /009(01) Board of Trustees minute book no. 4, 32 (6 December 1888); AO, RG 2-29-1, no. 14, 249, Wilson to George Ross, 15 June, 25 October 1888.

207 Fairclough, 'Sir Daniel Wilson,' 120.

208 UTA, B65-0014/004(01), 47 (28 October 1879), 98 (9 December 1885), 103 (5 April 1886); AO, RG 2–29–1, no. 14, 247, Wilson to George Ross, 9 December 1885.

209 McKillop, *Matters of Mind*, 128, 124.

210 *Globe*, 18 October 1884.

211 Ontario, *Sessional Papers*, 1882, no. 20, letter to Miss Goodwillie, 5 January 1882.

212 UTA, B84-0033/001(03), Wilson to William Dawson, 2 November 1885.

213 *Globe*, 18 October 1884.

214 *Varsity*, 11 December 1880, 84.

215 UTA, A70-0005/003, Senate minute book no. 3, 135, 139, 163, 181 (25 January, 8 March, 18 May, 5 June 1877).

216 UTA, B84-0033/001(03), Wilson to William Dawson, 22 December 1885.

217 Ibid., Wilson to William Dawson, 20 December 1885.

218 Ontario, *Sessional Papers*, 1882, no. 20, letter from Henrietta Charles, 31 December 1881.

219 Published as 'A Return Shewing What Applications Have Been Made by Females for Admission to Any of the Lectures of University College for the Session of 1881–82' in Ontario, *Sessional Papers*, 1882, no. 20.

220 UTA, B65-0014/004(01), 58 (3 February 1882).

221 Ontario, *Sessional Papers*, 1882, no. 20, letter to L.S. Fitzgerald, 7 January 1882.

222 UTA, B83-1285, Wilson to Teresa Vanderburgh, St Catharines, 25 September 1883.

223 UTA, A70-0005/003, Senate minute book no. 3, 365 (29 July 1880).

224 Ibid., 487 (13 January 1882).

225 Ibid., 637 (16 October 1883), 644 (9 November 1883), 656 (4 January 1884), 666 (9 May 1884).

226 UTA, B65-0014/004(01), 66 (28 February 1883).

227 Ibid., 74–5 (23 November 1883).

228 Ibid., 77 (4 March 1884).

229 Ibid., 77–8 (9 March 1884).

230 Wilson, *Coeducation* (1884).

231 UTA, B65-0014/004(01), 78 (18 March 1884).

232 Ibid., 79 (2 April 1884).

233 AO, RG 2-29-1-247, Wilson to George Ross, 16 March 1884.

234 Ontario, *Sessional Papers*, 1885, no. 58, Wilson to George Ross, 16 March, 20 June 1884.

235 *Varsity*, 5 April 1884, p. 286.

236 *Globe*, 19 October 1883.

237 UTA, B92-0030/009(16), Alfred Baker to James Loudon, 16 November 1886 (emphasis in the original).

238 UTA, B65-0014/004(01), 96 (7 November 1885).

239 UTA, B72-0013/001(03), Hutton to Edward Blake, undated but 1892.

240 UTA, B65-0014/004(01), 84 (1 October 1884).

241 Ibid., 84 (17 October 1884).

242 UTA, B84-0033/001(02), Wilson to William Dawson, 2 November 1885.

243 UTA, B84-0033/001(03), Wilson to Dawson, 5 May 1885.

244 UTA, B65-0014/004(02), 186 (13 December 1890).

245 Mulock, '*The University Act*,' 8.

246 *White and Blue*, 31 January 1880, 1; 14 February 1880, 4.

247 UTA, A70-0005/003, Senate minute book no. 3: 412–13 (11, 14 March 1881), 454–5 (15 September 1881), 467 (17 November 1881), 478 (25 November 1881).

248 McKillop, *Matters of Mind*, 27; UTA, B72-0013/001(11), Edward Blake to George Ross, 13 June 1892.

249 UTA, B92-0030/009(15), Samuel Nelles to James Loudon, 7 February 1885.

250 UTA, B65-0014/004(01), 74–5 (17 October 1883).

251 UTA, B72-0031/016(11), 'Memoirs of James Loudon,' 66.

252 UTA, B65-0014/004(01), 76 (22 February 1884).

253 Wallace, *A History of the University of Toronto*, 122; UTA, B65-0014/004(01), 118 (16 April 1887). The July report is produced in full in *The University of Toronto and Its Colleges*, 45–6.

254 UTA, B92-0030/009(14), William Mulock to Samuel Nelles, 24 November 1884, and Nelles to Mulock, two letters of 29 November 1884. The second, more detailed one Nelles marked 'private,' but he permitted Mulock to show it to 'any individuals or members of the Committee with whom you may wish to advise.' Wilson never saw it.

255 UTA, B83-1234, H.H. Langton, 'The Student Strike of 1895' (MS), 8.

256 UTA, B65-0014/004(01), 88 (12 December 1884), 93 (11 April 1885); / 004(02), 118 (16 April 1887).

257 UTA, B92-0030/009(15), Nelles to Loudon, 7 February 1885.

258 Wilson's journal gives the date as 9 January, which is incorrect.

259 UTA, B65-0014/004(01), 90 (9 January 1885); A70-0005/003, Senate minute book no. 3, 731–3 (5 January 1885).

260 UTA, B65-0014/004(01), 89, 91–3, 95 (9 January, 14 March, 11 April, 18 June 1885).

261 UTA, A70-0005/003, Senate minute book no. 4, 20 (8 May 1885), 31 (30 May 1885), 52–3 (10 June 1885), 59 (3 July 1885), 71–2 (23 October 1885), 81 (30 October 1885). On Wilson's links with Wycliffe, see also Elizabeth Hulse's essay in this volume.

262 UTA, B65-0014/004(01), 96 (8 and 16 October 1885); Wilson, *Address at the Convocation of University College* (1885), 6–7.

263 UTA, B65-0014/004(01), 100–3 (2–4 April 1886).

264 UTA, B65-0014/004(02), 113 (16 March 1887).

265 Ibid., 113–17 (16, 18, 23, 26, 29 March, 5, 6 April 1887).

266 Ibid., 114–15 (23, 26 March 1887).

267 Ibid., 117 (16 April 1887).

268 Ibid., 121 (15 June 1887).

269 Only Maurice Hutton was not a member of the University Council. With Wilson's support, he lobbied hard for an appointment to the university professoriate and in March 1888 became professor of comparative philology. This designation assured him of a seat on the University Council when it was created, while he retain his position on the College Council. See UTA, B65-0014/004(02), 131 (30 March 1888).

270 AO, RG 2-29-1, no. 14, 248, Wilson to George Ross, 31 May 1887.

271 'Annual Report of the Council of University College ... for the year 1887–8,' in Ontario, *Sessional Papers*, 1889, no. 6, 212; UTA, B65-0014/004(02), 144 (16 November 1888). The College Council consisted of the president, four college professors who also lectured there, and the dean of residence.

272 Ontario, An Act respecting the Federation of the University of Toronto and University College with Other Universities and Colleges, 50 Vic., cap. 43,; AO, RG 2-29-1, no. 14, 250, Assistant secretary, Province of Ontario, to minister of education, 18 June 1890.

273 AO, RG 2-29-1, no. 14, 249, Wilson to George Ross, 22 April 1889.

274 UTA, B65-0014/004(02), 131 (30 March 1888).

275 AO, RG 2-29-1, no. 14, 250, Wilson to George Ross, 26 November 1890.

276 UTA, B65-0014/004(02), 119 (23 April 1887).

277 Ibid., 180 (21 February 1890); Moriarty, *John Galbraith*, 45.

278 UTA, B84-0033/001(03), Wilson to William Dawson, 21 September 1888.

279 In this case, four statutes, including one affiliating the Toronto Baptist College and another setting the arts curriculum for the next four years; see UTA, B65-0014/004(01), 95 (4 July 1885). Wilson, due to sail on a much-awaited trip to Scotland the following week, was determined to leave on time.

280 UTA, B72-0013/001(01), Wilson to Edward Blake, 12 June 1891.

281 Bowker, 'Truly Useful Men,' 19.

282 The attendance figures from 1843 to 1906 are given in *The University of Toronto and Its Colleges*, 361.

283 Bowker, 'Truly Useful Men,' 19.

284 H.H. Langton, *Sir Daniel Wilson*, 13.

285 UTA, B65-0014/004(01), 58 (26 November 1881).

286 Ibid., 93 (2 April 1885).

287 UTA, A70-0005/004, Senate minute book no. 4, 40 (4 June) and 52–3 (10 June 1885).

288 UTA, B65-0014/004(01), 85 (2 November 1884). See also Walden, 'Male Toronto College Students Celebrate Hallowe'en, 1884–1910.'

289 UTA, B65-0014/004(02), 144–5 (18 January 1889).

290 UTA, B65-0014/004(01), 98 (12 December 1885).

291 UTA, B65-0014/004(02), 113 (18 March 1887).

292 UTA, A70-0005/004, Senate minute book no. 3, 532–4 (5 June 1882).

293 UTA, B65-0014/004(02), 129 (1 April 1888).

294 Ibid., 131 (9 April 1888).

295 UTA, B65-0014/004(01), 107 (10 December 1886).

296 UTA, B65-0014/004(02), 142 (20 October 1888).

297 Toronto *Mail*, 20 October 1888.

298 UTA, B65-0014/004(02), 184–5 (25 November 1890).

299 Ibid., 185 (25 November 1890).

300 UTA, B92-0030/009(17), Alfred Baker, Toronto, to James Loudon, London, England, 6 June 1887.

301 UTA, B65-0014/004(02), 121 (14 June 1887).

302 AO, RG 2-29-1, no. 14, 248, Wilson to George Ross, 12 June 1887.

303 UTA, B65-0014/004(02), 122 (20 June 1887).

304 Ibid.

305 Ibid., 123 (22 June 1887).

306 Ibid., 181 (16 March 1890), 120–1 (14 June 1887).

307 Ibid., 121 (14 June 1887).

308 Ibid., 124 (16 July 1887).

309 Ibid., 126 (4 November 1887).

310 Ibid., 181 (16 March 1890).

311 Wilson, *Address at the Convocation of the University of Toronto* (1890), 10.

312 UTA, A70-0005/005, Senate minute book no. 5, 246–9 (23 June), 257 (10 October), and 287 (11 November 1891).

313 UTA, B65-0014/004(02), 199–200 (2 November 1891).

314 UTA, A69-0011/003, University College Literary and Scientific Society minutes, 10 October 1890.

315 UTA, B84-0033/001(03), Wilson to William Dawson, 17 February 1882.
316 Hoff, 'The Controversial Appointment of James Mark Baldwin,' 66.
317 UTA, B72-0013/001(11), Blake to Oliver Mowat, 11 June 1892.
318 W.J. Loudon's research notes for his *Sir William Mulock*, in UTA, B76-0020/004(01).
319 UTA, B65-0014/004(01), 99 (13 March 1886); A70-0005/004, Senate Minute Book no. 4, 102–3, 113, 118 (22 February, 13 March, 8 April 1886).
320 McKillop, *Contours of Canadian Thought*, 83.
321 AO, RG 2-29-1, no. 14, 249, Wilson to Ross, 20 April 1888; UTA, B65-0014/004(02), 131 (19 April 1888).
322 AO, RG 2-29-1, no. 14, 248, Wilson to George Ross, 21 April 1887.
323 UTA, B65-0014/004(01), 103 (21 April, 20 May 1886), /004(02) 137 (30 June 1888); McKillop, *Matters of Mind*, 194–5.
324 AO, RG 2-29-1, no. 14, 248, Wilson to George Ross, 28 April 1887.
325 UTA, B65-0014/004(02), 145 (21 January 1889). The single exception had earlier sent in his testimonials.
326 Ibid., 146 (30 January 1889).
327 Letter from Wilson, 9 February 1889, published in the Toronto *Mail*, 11 February 1889, 5.
328 UTA, B65-0014/004(02), 145 (21 January 1889).
329 Letters from Paxton Young, 9 February 1889, and Wilson, 9 February 1889, published in the Toronto *Mail*, 11 February 1889, 5; Hoff, 'The Controversial Appointment of James Mark Baldwin,' 62–3.
330 UTA, B65-0014/004(02), 171 (19 October 1889).
331 For an excellent analysis of this appointment, see Hoff, 'The Controversial Appointment of James Mark Baldwin.'
332 UTA, B65-0014/004(02), 172–3 (19, 21 October 1889).
333 UTA, B65-0014/004(01), 97 (1 December 1885); AO, RG 2-29-1, no. 14, 249, Wilson to Ross, 20 April 1888.
334 UTA, B92-0030/009(16), Alfred Baker to James Loudon, 16 November 1886; /009(17), Baker to Loudon, 15 January 1887; AO, RG 2-29-1, no. 14, 248, McCurdy to Wilson, 26 October 1886, Wilson to Ross, 23, 28 October 1886, 31 May, 9 July 1887.
335 UTA, A70-0024/057(01), Assistant clerk to the Executive Council of Ontario to the provincial secretary, 5 November 1888.
336 AO, RG 2-29-1, no. 14, 249, Wilson to Ross, 20, 23 April 1888.
337 UTA, B65-0014/004(02), 130–3 (19, 21, 24, 26 April, 17 May 1888).
338 Ibid., 173 (21 October 1889).
339 UTA, B93-0022/001(04), Wilson, Campton, NH, to Frederick W. Putnam, New York City, 12 August 1887; UTA, B65-0014/004 (02), 168 (26 September 1889).

340 UTA, B65-0014/004(02), 141–2 (15 October, 3 November 1888), 151 (13 April 1889).
341 Ibid., 107 (22 October 1886).
342 Ibid., 185–8 (10 December 1890, 14 March 1891).
343 Ibid., 178–9 (15 February 1890), 187 (9 March 1891); Dall, 'Sir Daniel Wilson,' xxvii.
344 UTA, B84-0033/001(03), Wilson to William Dawson, 22 February 1890.
345 Schull, *Edward Blake*, 2: 180.
346 UTA, B65-0014/004(02), 199 (10 October 1891).
347 Schull, *Edward Blake*, 2: 181; UTA, B72-0013/001(11), Edward Blake to George Ross, 13 June 1892.
348 UTA, B92-0030/009(02), Mulock to Alfred Baker, 20 February 1890, James Loudon to Mulock, 23 February 1890, and Mulock to Loudon, 24 February 1890.
349 UTA, B65-0014/004(02), 209 (4 June 1892).
350 UTA, B84-0033/001(03), Wilson to William Dawson, 22 February 1890.
351 UTA, A70-0024/009(01), Board of Trustees minute book no. 4, 266, 274 (20, 24 February 1890); B72-0031/001(02), Wilson to J.E. Berkeley Smith, 14 June 1890.
352 UTA, B84-0033/001(03), Wilson to William Dawson, 22 February 1890.
353 UTA, B65-0014/004(02), 179 (21 February 1890).
354 UTA, A70-0005/005, Senate minute book no. 5, 68 (7 August 1890).
355 UTA, A70-0024/009(01), Board of Trustees minute book no. 4, 260, 270–3, 284, 298–9, 302–3 (17, 21, 27 February, 13, 27 March 1890).
356 UTA, B65-0014/004(02), 182 (28 March 1890).
357 UTA, A70-0024/009(01), Board of Trustees minute book no. 4, 326 (24 April 1890); B65-0014/004(02), 182–3 (25 April 1890).
358 UTA, B65-0014/004(02), 189 (21 March 1891).
359 Ibid., 180, 181 (26, 28 April 1890); UTA, B93-0022/001(01), Wilson to William H. Dall, U.S. National Museum, 4 April 1890, and /001(04), Wilson to Frederick W. Putnam, curator of the Peabody Museum, 19, 24 February, 1890; B72-0031/001(02), Wilson to J.E. Berkeley Smith, 14 June 1890.
360 UTA, B65-0014/004(02), 180–1 (26, 28 February 1891).
361 Ibid., 199 (23 October 1891).
362 Blackburn, *Evolution of the Heart*, 74–7, 82–4; UTA, A70-0005/005, Senate minute book no. 5, 182, 240 (10 April, 19 June 1891); B65-0014/004(02), 199 (23 October 1891). Wilson, who had been on the Senate's library committee for over thirty years, would have been the natural person to move a motion of appreciation for Van der Smissen. Instead, it was done by Principal William Caven of Knox College and seconded by James Loudon.

363 UTA, A70-0024/009(01), Board of Trustees minute book no. 4, 351 (19 June 1890).
364 Blackburn, *Evolution of the Heart*, 89–90.
365 UTA, B65-0014/004(02), 187 (9 March 1891).
366 Ibid., 191 (16 May 1891).
367 Hoff, 'The Controversial Appointment of James Mark Baldwin,' 177–8.
368 Ibid., 170–3, 191; UTA, A70-0024/009(01), Board of Trustees minute book no. 5, 72, 84, 136, 162–3, (13, 28 November 1890, 8, 29 January 1891).
369 Hoff, 'The Controversial Appointment of James Mark Baldwin,' 191–3.
370 B72-0013/001(07), Wilson to Edward Blake, 9 March 1892.
371 UTA, B65-0014/004(02), 204 (14 April 1892); B72-0013/001(07), Blake to Wilson, 21, 26, 28 March 1892, Blake to George Ross, 19 April 1892; A70-0005/005, Senate Minute book no. 5, 351–9, 389 (8, 28 April 1892).
372 UTA, B72-0013/001(11), Wilson to Edward Blake, 15 May 1892.
373 UTA, A70-0005/005, Senate minute book no. 5, 101–2 (31 October 1890).
374 Schull, *Edward Blake*, 2: 184–5.
375 UTA, B72-0013/001(04), Wilson to Edward Blake, 12 June 1891.
376 UTA, A70-0005/005, Senate minute book no. 5, 302–422 passim; B65-0014/004(02), 204 (14 April 1892).
377 *Globe*, 11 June 1892; Dall, 'Sir Daniel Wilson,' xxviii.
378 UTA, B65-0014/004(02), 209 (16 June 1892).
379 Ibid., 210 (26 June 1892).
380 UTA, B65-0014/004(02), 210 (26 June 1892); A70-0024/009(02), Board of Trustees minute book no. 5, 340–2 (27 and 30 June 1890).
381 *Globe*, 8 August 1892.
382 Bowker, 'Truly Useful Men,' 24.
383 Ontario, Royal Commission on the University of Toronto, *Report*, xxix; *The University of Toronto and Its Colleges*, 273.
384 Ontario, Royal Commission on the University of Toronto, *Report*, xlviii–xl.

Daniel Wilson as Littérateur:
English Professor, Critic, and Poet

HEATHER MURRAY

The term 'littérateur' is somewhat outmoded now, but in denoting a 'literary man' and connoting varied and sometimes non-professional literary interests, it is suited to the career – or, more accurately, one of the careers – of Daniel Wilson. From youth an enthusiastic reader, writer, and debater, Wilson supported his early activity as an engraver, and then a fledgling family, with freelance reviewing and literary work. The latter transmuted into a lifelong amateur compositional interest, with the production of poetry (largely on natural and scientific subjects) and miscellaneous writings (including essays and children's stories). Appointed to the chair of history and English literature at Toronto in 1853, he was the first dedicated professor of English in British North America and one of the first in the world. He continued to teach the subject until this aspect of his job was phased out in the 1880s, and he was in many respects responsible for defining this amorphous area as a field, by developing it as an elective and then as part of an honours specialty at Toronto and by generating and directing new appointments, compiling textbooks, and working with the organizations through which Canadian modern language study was made. Active also as a critic, Wilson produced book-length treatments of Chatterton and Shakespeare, while among the literary reviews penned for the *Canadian Journal* is perhaps the first scholarly assessment of an emergent English-Canadian literature.

However, he remains known in Canada largely as a university administrator and in Scotland primarily as an antiquarian, as Carl Berger has noted, while his activities as a pedagogue, poet, and critic have received less or no attention.[1] Certainly, it is difficult to reconstruct some aspects of his literary career: of Wilson's work as an English professor, for example, little direct evidence remains, since his lecture notes were destroyed in the University College fire of 1890 and his journal was edited to retain primarily those entries relating to his administrative work. (In any case, the journal was fragmentary for those periods when Wilson worked mostly as a literary instructor, according to Langton.)[2] Wilson's poetry may remain ignored because it appears formulaic in both idea and expression; and while the criticism offers more to interest the modern reader, it has been overshadowed by the greater bulk of the ethnological writings.

Further, it is in some cases difficult to separate the 'literary' from the 'scientific' streams of work. Wilson's own definition of 'literary' work would have included his antiquarian and historical writings: these are studded with literary references and benefit – sometimes suffer – from his highly elaborated prose style. The reverse is also true: his archaeological and anthropological interests permeate what we would now more narrowly define as his 'literary' endeavours (the scientific viewpoint of the sonnets, for example, or the antiquarian and anthropological approaches to Chatterton and Shakespeare respectively), while his characteristic argument by induction often underpins both poetry and critical prose. Some difficulties in delineating Wilson's literary career are caused by his own ambivalences: he would deplore the 'potboiler' quality of his earlier writings (the term is his), gradually drop his teaching duties in English altogether, and produce very little criticism after 1873; and he was dogged in opposition to a literature section for the nascent Royal Society of Canada.[3]

However, while Wilson may have underestimated the importance of his literary career, he was a bridge between the earliest evolution of the discipline of English studies and its more or less modern manifestation; and his combination of literary and national-historical interests would provide a direction to English studies at Toronto, and by extension throughout the country, that persists to this day. Examination of Wilson's critical writings and career therefore allows a way of tracking the earliest (and continuing) relations of English studies with nationalist and racialist theories and with the new science of anthropology in particular (although, as I hope to show, his career demands that we assess these connections with somewhat more care than is currently the case). A more specific benefit is to be obtained from the way that analysis of his critical and creative writing may further illuminate those aspects of his thought which have already received attention, for while A.B. McKillop has examined the scientific and Baconian aspects of Wilson's outlook in relation to his poetic

sympathies, less notice has been paid to his aesthetic formation in theories of the picturesque and the sublime and the ways in which they may
have influenced his more general notions of perspective and the relationship between observer and observed.[4]

It is indexical rather than ironic that the first professor of English literature in British North America would be Scottish born and trained, for
Scotland, and the University of Edinburgh in particular, initiated English
literary studies (and, some would argue, 'English literature' itself) and
developed this subject methodologically almost a century before the
English themselves would do so. And it is again symptomatic that Wilson
would combine these interests with a lifelong career in anthropological
and ethnological research, for the two young disciplines emerged in tan-
dem under the same intellectual and political pressures (although Wilson
himself is perhaps unique in the double-jointedness of his intellectual
work). Following the Act of Union in 1707, eighteenth-century Scottish
academicians were preoccupied with two related concerns, according to
Robert Crawford: the comparison of societies at different stages of development and the question of how they 'improve.'[5] While this was a general
topic of the Enlightenment, it gained a special intensity in Scottish literature and academic speculation; and the pursuits were closely interlinked,
as Daniel Wilson himself noted in the preface to *Prehistoric Annals of Scotland*, with the new antiquarian work finding a first form in the endeavours of the Roxburgh, Bannatyne, and Abbotsford literary clubs, and
receiving a further spur from the writings of Walter Scott.[6]

A more specific result was the development in the Scottish universities
of the study of rhetoric, driven by the demand for improvement (a
demand which also ensured that it was English and not Scottish literature
which would provide examples and models for the classroom). The
degree to which the quests for economic and cultural improvement were
interlocked is dramatically illustrated by the fact that the first formal university lectures on English literature were delivered at Edinburgh by
Adam Smith between 1748 and 1751.[7] The line of succession from Smith
would include Hugh Blair and William Spalding, each of whom produced
textbooks popular in Canada for both college and self-instruction; and
Daniel Wilson himself would apply for the Edinburgh chair in rhetoric
left vacant in 1865 by the death of William Edmonstoune Aytoun,
although he was defeated by David Masson.[8]

Wilson's limited academic training was typical of the first generations
of English instructors: it would be near the end of the century before
English studies was sufficiently institutionalized for professors to have a

first, let alone a second, degree in that specialty. But his parallel literary education was also characteristic of those early proponents of the discipline. He was born into a family of literary inclinations: his mother and brother George wrote verse, as did a close cousin, James Russell, and the topical, scientific, and religious poetry of the latter two was published posthumously as *Memorials of Cousins*.[9] George Wilson was also an essayist and scientific biographer, while sister Jessie became the family chronicler and her husband, James Sime, would produce lives of Goethe and Lessing.[10] (Their daughter, Jessie Georgina Sime, also worked as an editor and reviewer before moving to Montreal to begin an independent literary career, and she is currently being rediscovered as one of Canada's 'new woman' novelists. The prolific novelist 'Mrs Oliphant,' a second cousin, was another, albeit more remote, literary connection.)[11]

Daniel Wilson's own literary education began early: the family library held an imposing inherited 'collection of ponderous folios, and little dumpty vellum-bound quartos of sound divinity,' he recalled, but also folk and fairy tales, the Arabian Nights and *Pilgrim's Progress*. Their mother read aloud to them, often from *Paradise Lost* or the romantic poets – affected by the anti-slavery sentiments of Cowper's *Task*, the children renounced sugar in their tea, to hasten the end of the triangle trade – and she encouraged their juvenile writing activities.[12] (A more detailed account of the family's reading and writing activities is given in Marinell Ash's sketch of Wilson's early life at the beginning of this volume.) When their father joined the Edinburgh Select Subscription Library, 'we were turned loose, like colts in a rich field of clover, to revel as we pleased in the wide range of English literature,'[13] and the brothers and cousins organized a debating and paper-reading group, grandly called the 'Edinburgh Zetalethic Society.' Wilson, like his friends and family, tried his hand at a number of literary forms; kind, but critical assessment by a respected professorial mentor of his verse drama 'Evelyne' (now, it appears, lost) discouraged him from a career as a playwright and pushed his interests in an antiquarian direction.[14]

While Wilson himself described his inclinations in those days as 'more artistic than literary,'[15] it is this artistic inclination that would have formed, more than anything else, his literary tastes: for the 'picturesque' and the 'sublime' were aesthetic ideologies not confined to the visual arts alone.[16] The search of Wilson and his schoolmates for the vanishing 'picturesque' aspects of Edinburgh found a perfect verbal counterpoint in the novels of Walter Scott, which Wilson like other young people of the day devoured.[17] (The 'objectified' stance of the spectator on which the theory of the picturesque is grounded would prove to be enduringly compatible with Wilson's scientific views, as was the picturesque's predilection for the antique and ancient.)[18] Later his work with the artist J.M.W. Turner would have allowed him to think in some detail about theories of the 'sublime,' traces of which are found (in a somewhat inflected form) throughout Wilson's own critical and poetic work. He is drawn, for example, to the excessive and curious and the grotesque, as well as to the mysterious: the challenge to the senses and sense posed by large or mysterious natural phenomena is translated into a concluding meditative moment in his essays and verse.

It was to literary pursuits that Wilson turned as an early means of support. After training as an engraver, he produced a variety of short pieces and reviews for a number of popular journals, and he would continue this work on returning from London to Edinburgh. A list in his journal includes contributions to *Chambers's Journal, Tait's Edinburgh Journal,* the *Gentleman's Magazine,* the *Athenæum,* and the *Scotsman* for this period, although anonymous or pseudonymous publication means that few pieces have been traced.[19] A steadier source of income soon appeared, for a long-standing friendship with William Nelson, the death of whose father, bookseller Thomas Nelson, had made head of the family firm, allowed Wilson to undertake book publications for money. Nelson's had early seen the opportunity for large print runs of attractive and accessible material, aimed at the new 'common reader' of the nineteenth century. As we have seen, Wilson produced a variety of works for different Nelson's series, including popular histories of Oliver Cromwell and the Pilgrims, as well as short pieces in the 'British Library' series, which purchasers would collect in instalments.

The sentimental tale of *The Curate's Daughter* (1847?) has an impoverished young woman of good family wrongly imprisoned for theft when she tries to pawn a locket to save her dying widowed mother and starving sibling, but wealthy relatives are discovered just in time.[20] The poetry, while still moral and didactic, gives a greater indication of Wilson's later works: *The Sabbath Bell* combines a topographic poem with the hymn of praise and moves in a fashion characteristic of the picturesque from detailed near views to the further sky and sea; while a ballad, *Henry Hudson,* is Coleridgean in its spooky evocation of the 'demon crew.' Again anonymity and pen-names make it difficult to calculate the exact extent of Wilson's contribution to Thomas Nelson's. Meditating in later years on the inauspicious start of Carlyle's career, he was able to write with some feeling of 'that dreadful battle of a literary man for bread, while all the

promptings of his genius impel him to the productions of priceless creations, that cannot be coined into the needful market currency.'[21]

While Wilson's literary output was substantial, it is interesting to note
that he did not offer either the creative writing or the reviews as evidence
of qualification in his 1851 application for the position in English and history at Toronto, and he presented in support the same *Testimonials* that
he had collected for an earlier application in Scotland as an antiquarian.
In fact, Wilson's referees have little to say that pertains to English studies:
these professors of botany, logic and metaphysics, anatomy, medicine,
Latin, and the like make only brief reference to his 'use ... of our language and all its resources' or the mastery of 'that not very common
acquisition, a plain and elegant English narrative,' manifested in the
recently published *Prehistoric Annals*. Nor have they much to say of his
considerable oratorical skill, although they are fulsome on his zeal, moral
character, and antiquarian expertise.[22] But Wilson's eclecticism fitted
him as well for the position as anyone else of that day, especially given a
prevailing uncertainty as to exactly what a professor of English was supposed to do.[23] It appears that this uncertainty was shared even by University College, and Wilson was surprised to find on his arrival that President
John McCaul – himself appointed in 1842 to the chairs of classical literature and belles-lettres and logic – considered shifting the terms of the
appointment to ancient history.

It is therefore not quite correct to say that Wilson had his work as an
English professor cut out for him when he commenced the position in
1853 – he had to do the cutting from whole cloth. He would continue to
occupy this area for thirty years until the appointment of lecturer David
Reid Keys to a variety of modern language subjects (including English)
allowed Wilson to focus whatever hours remained from administrative
duties on historical and ethnological topics. The early years of his
appointment coincided with a time of intense curricular and institutional
reorganization at University College, in which he became a major player.
A four-year series of courses was designed, as well as five levels of examinations (including matriculation), and English was established as a subject
in both the pass and honours courses.

A watershed in the discipline's development is marked by the much-
reported debate between Wilson, speaking for University College, and
Victoria College's principal, Egerton Ryerson, at legislative hearings in
1860 on the question of student options. Both were keen proponents of
vernacular literary education; both were attentive to the educational
needs of colonial students; but they differed markedly in their ap-

proaches, with Ryerson favouring a more pragmatic rhetorical one. Wilson, however, was bent on introducing a more expressly literary study, with an emphasis on reading rather than writing or oratory, in which literary texts were deployed, not as stylistic models, but as evidence of the expressions of a culture; and he proved himself a most able defender of the purposes and practices of the new modern languages study.[24] Under Wilson, 'English' at Toronto commenced its characteristic blending of literary and historical studies, which identifies the work of the department to this day; in broader terms, as Henry Hubert has argued, the debate of 1860 marks the moment at which rhetorical and composition studies became displaced, then replaced, in the college and university curriculum.[25]

While there were modifications over the years – culminating in the establishment of English, along with the other modern languages, as an honours specialty in 1877 – the English curriculum under Wilson's direction maintained its shape for almost thirty years. Students in the pass program used a variety of survey histories of the English language and of English literature, answering examination questions on etymology, terminology, and literary facts and figures; there was little or no direct study of works of literature. (This limitation would become a bitter complaint of student journalists in the *Varsity* by the mid-1880s, who moaned about Craik and Spalding, and Ryerson had taunted Wilson for using texts that were, in his opinion, more suited for young ladies' seminaries. But Wilson would stick to his principles in providing what he felt to be necessary background for students drawn from an uneven provincial educational system.) While the honours students also covered etymology and prosody at a more advanced level, their course was distinguished by the first-hand study of literary texts, with Milton and Shakespeare featuring prominently and Chaucer, Spenser, Pope, Cowper, and Wordsworth added in the 1860s. (Philology and Anglo-Saxon would not be offered until the arrival of D.R. Keys.) Examination questions for the honours students were more likely to involve textual comparisons, critical analysis, and interpretation of difficult lines. These students also studied composition from the second year and were expected to hand in written assignments on a weekly basis, while composition study was reserved until the final year for the pass students.[26]

The classroom notes taken down by student William Nesbitt Ponton for the first-year honours English course in 1873 give a more intimate glimpse of Wilson's teaching. The section on prosody, if Ponton's notes are a fair guide, commenced with a standard taxonomy of literary genres in which three types of poetry – lyric, epic, and dramatic – are further subdivided (epic is classical, romantic, didactic, idyllic, and so forth), with epic appearing to get the lion's share of attention, perhaps because of Wilson's own classical training and its suitability to his historical interests. The sections on metrics could have been cribbed from any textbook of the period; only the statement that 'among primitive peoples poetry always precedes prose' gives a sense of the way that Wilson might have been able to infuse this dry material with his own anthropological interests.[27] In addition, perhaps remembering the Edinburgh Zetalethic Society, he was instrumental in launching the University College Literary and Scientific Society; a slightly modified version of the 'Lit' is active to this day. Another organization with which he was involved – albeit more problematically – was the Ladies' Educational Association, to which he lectured on literary topics from its inception in 1877.

While Wilson was willing to welcome women to the campus and classroom in these restricted ways, and while he would advocate the establishment of a women's college, his opposition to coeducation was fierce. The battle between supporters of coeducation and Wilson (by then college president) on this matter has received considerable analysis (see, for example, the preceding essay by Averill and Keith); less attention has been paid to the specifically literary manifestations of the struggle. But the quest for entry of women to the provincial university was in many respects a struggle for entry to the modern languages and to English, courses for which women were likely to have the necessary background and which could equip them for teaching careers. And it was a women's literary and political group – the Toronto Women's Literary Club, headed by suffragist-physician Emily Stowe – which lobbied the provincial legislature to override the university's ban. Wilson was thus doubly affected – in his capacities as administrator and as holder of the English chair – and the controversy would continue even after women's admission, focused on the issue of a bowdlerized curriculum for them. This contretemps would pit Wilson once more against the indefatigable reformer and university Senate member William Houston (who had been active in the fight for women's admission and who was concurrently and quite independent of Wilson designing a new English curriculum for Toronto, to be placed before the Senate).[28]

The question of Shakespeare's morality had engaged Wilson's attention some twelve years earlier: in 'Anne Hatheway: A Dialogue' (1872) the anagrammatic *porte-parole* 'Delina' had rebutted the view that Shakespeare had a loveless or merely expedient marriage to this older, perhaps plain, but financially comfortable woman, and had provided ingenious explanations for the vexing fact that Shakespeare had addressed his famous love sonnets to a man. Letters written in December 1885 to his friend and fellow president William Dawson of McGill outline a dilemma that could not be so easily solved.[29] The difficulty was the sexual frankness of Shakespeare, which would in a mixed classroom provide 'a painful ordeal to some; and a source of mischievous jest to others.' While Wilson would distinguish between a play such as *Measure for Measure*, 'where the entire plot turns on adultery,' and *Hamlet*, for example, where the theme of adultery is subordinated to 'profound metaphysical speculations admirably suited for critical reading,' this was only to emphasize the desirability of avoiding such plays as *Measure* and *Othello* altogether and of proceeding even more warily where women were concerned.

Thus even as he began to shed the position in English to pursue his ethnological interests and administrative duties, Wilson continued to drive the development of English at Toronto and indeed throughout the province. He was active in choosing his provisional replacement, D.R. Keys, and as university president attempted to control the process through which W.J. Alexander was eventually selected to fill the new chair in English in 1889 (although he himself had tried to attract Oxford- and Cambridge-trained candidates).[30] He was the first honorary president of the Modern Language Association of Ontario and the second president of the Ontario Educational Association. (His multiple interests were an advantage during his OEA tenure, for he spanned the pedagogic and intellectual interests of scientists and humanists, and addressed the association in frequent talks ranging from literary forgeries to 'The Place of Science in Modern Education,' maintaining in the latter lecture a favoured theory that the scientific study of language could bridge the two academic realms.)[31] He was frequently in the press and in the public eye on literary matters: even as he was resigning his duties in English, for example, Wilson would air controversial opinions to the Modern Language Association on the subject of grammatical standards in Canada, which attracted a heated correspondence when the newspapers published his remarks; and then, contrariwise, he would go on to blame slipping standards in the English matriculation examinations on the examiners' inept and cryptic questioning.[32] He would extend his tastes and principles by advising on lower-school textbook selections both in Canada (the Fourth and Fifth Chinook Readers) and for Nelson's (the Royal Readers); some of Wilson's own poetry was excerpted, a de facto acknowledgment of him as a Canadian poet which stands in an interesting tension with opinions on Canadian letters that he expressed in the course of his work for two other organizations.

The Canadian Institute was originally founded, in the fashion of the times, as a 'mutual instruction' society, in this case designed to further the state of scientific and practical knowledge with special reference to the professions of engineering, surveying, and architecture (see also the essay by Suzanne Zeller in this volume). Inclusion of literary and cultural topics appears to have followed from the institute's absorption of another society, the Toronto Athenaeum, in 1855; building on this development, when Wilson assumed the editorship of the institute's *Canadian Journal* in 1856, he introduced literary notes – news of literati and publishers, largely lifted from the English press – and original reviews commissioned for the journal.[33] He himself wrote a number of reviews for the *Canadian Journal,* and these remain of interest as examples of some of the first 'academic' literary criticism produced in Canada.

Wilson had several critical modes, which sometimes overlapped and sometimes occasioned contradictions. He could be unabashedly adulatory of writers such as Scott and Burns, especially when addressing public gatherings, as, for example, the centenary celebration of Burns's birth.[34] But he was also analytical, textually oriented, and drawn to interpretational puzzles: authorial hoaxes, textual cruxes, and complexly structured or symbolized works. (This interest allowed Wilson to take on the formidable Goldwin Smith on the question of Browning's philosophically inclined poetry, for Smith, like many other late-nineteenth-century readers, felt that good poetry should not require explanation.)[35] Wilson devotes considerable attention to unlocking a particularly complex diagonal anacrostic in a verse of Poe's, although he is more conditional about the poet's sensibilities.[36] His respect for the literary tour de force is also at war with his moral sense in the review of Whitman's *Leaves of Grass*: the poems are full of 'egotism, extravagance and spasmodic eccentricities of all sorts' (the telling phrase 'spasmodic eccentricities' may euphemize the homoeroticism that concerned Wilson in Shakespeare's sonnets). But he appears far more drawn to the raw 'ore' of Whitman than to the 'polish' of Aytoun's decorous poem on Mary Queen of Scots, to which *Leaves* is compared.[37]

The reviews also provide further examples of Wilson's characteristic overlap of interests, as he defends the much-criticized archaisms and much-parodied metrics of Longfellow's *Hiawatha* for their fidelity to the alliterations and rhythms of early verse forms.[38] Of particular interest is a review essay on Canadian poetry, in which his theories of the rise of nations and cultures are applied to Canada itself: contemporary Canadian poetry is situated in the unfortunate interregnum between 'the poetic birth-time which pertains to the vigorous infancy of races' and 'the era of refinement from which a high civilization educes new phazes [*sic*].' Removed from the vigour of the founding years, it is straining for a sophistication which can only be derivative; a return to 'native' sources of inspiration may produce real, if modest gains, as illustrated by McLachlan's poem of canoeing on Lake Couchiching.[39]

The complexity of Wilson's view of Canadian literature is more fully manifested some thirty years later in his actions on the occasion of the formation of section 2 of the Royal Society of Canada in 1882. Asked by the governor general, the Marquis of Lorne, to head the proposed section, Wilson expressed his reservations frankly to Dawson, the society's first president. Not only did he doubt the wisdom of combining history and ethnology with literature (as he would later object to the division of French from English scholars in those areas), but he was sceptical – in fact, scornful – of the need for a literature section in the first place: 'I do not see why I should march through the country at the head of a troop, not one of whom would, in England, be thought of otherwise than mediocre in such a body!' he wrote (excepting Goldwin Smith from the criticism). 'Shall we write school-boy essays, or criticisms on the Literature of the day; or theses on the want of Literature?'[40] But Lord Lorne's plans prevailed (perhaps because Wilson expressed these reservations more tactfully to the society's patron), and Wilson co-chaired, with Goldwin Smith, the initial section 2, 'English Literature, History, and Allied Subjects' (among which were anthropology and psychology).

Characteristically, he devoted considerable energy to both the section and the society, and was able to steer section 2 into what (he would have considered) more-profitable directions than the boosting of a substandard Canadian literature. At the inaugural meeting, he recommended that the literature section should most fruitfully concentrate on comparative philological study undertaken with the historians and ethnologists.[41] In addition, Wilson appears to have been able to exercise some control over the development of section 2 through influencing membership selection: of the initial twenty members only two – William Kirby and Charles Sangster – are known today primarily for their literary achievements, and they were outnumbered by the four professors of philosophy, for example. While a majority of the members, like Wilson himself, also engaged in some belles-lettristic activity, producing occasional verse, essays, criticism, or all three, of the twenty almost all were also amateur explorers of linguistic or philological topics.[42]

But Wilson did in some important respects use his position (and his later presidency of the society) to advance the interests of Canadian authors. He was noted in his day for encouragement to authors, both scientific and literary, and was partly responsible for the appearance of such books as Paul Kane's *Wanderings of an Artist*.[43] And always mindful of his years as a penurious freelancer – and more recently surprised to discover a pirated United States edition of his own ethnological writings – Wilson made an important intervention in the question of 'Canadian Copyright' in a piece that received wide circulation in England and the United States as well as in Canada.[44] While his own scholarly work for section 2 remained anthropological, reflecting the consolidated interest of his later years, he still was able to draw upon his wide range of literary interests, judiciously weighing the references to the 'Lost Atlantis' in myth and poetry, for example, in his consideration of the evidence for its existence, or contemplating, in 'The Artistic Faculty in Aboriginal Races,' the ideographic or writing function of early rock paintings.[45] One distinction between the literary and more strictly scientific writings should be mentioned, however; while, as A.B. McKillop has noted for the scientific writings, Wilson characteristically avoided undue extrapolation, the typical turn of the poetry is to a concluding meditative or conjectural moment following a series of observations.[46] And his more sustained critical efforts were mildly speculative in the book on Chatterton and wildly so for his study of *The Tempest*; contemporary reviewers of *Caliban* would make a point of remarking on Wilson's speculative tendency.

At first glance, Chatterton seems an odd choice of topic for this staid and analytical Scot. A writer of wickedly satirical verses and pseudo-medieval literary hoaxes, Chatterton was dead by his own hand – of arsenic or opium – at the age of seventeen. Widely reputed to be dissolute (and venereally diseased), in the hundred years since his death, he had been taken up by successive generations of Romantics and post-Romantics as the prototype of the tragically misunderstood artist. Coleridge and Wordsworth lamented him; Keats copied him; de Vigny's stage play was held responsible for a rash of suicides among the Paris bohemians. The pre-Raphaelite attitude is best represented in Henry Wallis's well-known depiction (for which the writer George Meredith apparently modelled) of the corpse of the poet draped attractively over a divan.[47] But Chatterton's life and work held several points of interest for Wilson, to be explored in his (rather less tendentious) *Encyclopaedia Britannica* entry and in the lengthy scholarly study of 1869.

First, Wilson maintained an interest in literary forgeries and impersonations: in the same year he would examine the forged historical writings of 'Ricardus Coriensis,' which had misled historians of Roman Britain for almost a century, and observe with interest the systematizing of North American literary antiquarianism in reaction to the much-publicized 'discovery' of runic and Hebrew inscriptions throughout the United States.[48] In addition, he admired the antiquarian spirit of Chatterton, perhaps detecting in the fantasies of the young poet some of the enthusiasms that had animated his own youthful researches into the vanishing stories and streetscapes of old Edinburgh. (Like Chatterton, Wilson himself had written pseudonymously, and he would go on to compose *jeux d'esprit* in a comic mock-medieval mode.)[49] His particular interest, however, is in Chatterton's achievement and in the unity of the imaginative world that he had constructed, something to which even the boy poet's Romantic defenders had paid little explicit attention. Although they at times studied or modelled his metrics, their primary interest was in his exemplary or emblematic life, while scholars, on the other hand, were concerned more with the authenticity or ethics of the forgeries. Wilson's attempt is to assess Chatterton's work as a literary production and to elucidate this lesser-known writer for an audience baffled by Chatterton's archaisms, neologisms, and stylistic fancies. (A more regularized edition of Chatterton's work, prepared by the eminent philologist W.W. Skeat, was still a few years away.)

Wilson's is a detailed and lengthy study, and a letter to Bristol resident D. Beddoes shows the pains that he was taking in the interests of accuracy, as he wrote to his fellow antiquarian for help in obtaining scarce materials and to verify some topographical details.[50] For Wilson, the principal point of interest is Chatterton's 'Rowley' manuscripts: in a manner flatteringly similar to Wilson's admired Scott, Chatterton had from the age of ten conjured an imaginary world set in fifteenth-century Bristol, based in part on his reading of documents from the muniments room at the parish church where his family had for generations been sextons.[51] He created a fanciful circle of heroes and artisans to be celebrated by the equally fictitious poet-priest Thomas Rowley (a pseudonymous alter ego, as Wilson demonstrates), the entire construct buttressed with invented memoirs, letters, and other 'documentation.' Wilson used his own considerable skills as an antiquarian to assess not only the veracities of Chatterton's work, but also his success in creating the spirit of a lost time and language. He considers the poetry as an allegory of Chatterton's life, aspirations, and relationships and the degree to which this idealized circle (in which the pre-Raphaelite brothers sensed a model) functioned as a criticism of the narrow materialism and mercantilism of late-eighteenth-century Bristol.

Wilson was always the friend of youth, and he displays towards Chatterton some of his well-known tolerance for the antics of boisterous undergraduates; his Chatterton is more sinned against than sinning, led astray by the ignorance and veniality of his patrons, and refused assistance by wiser figures who could have moulded his talents. Other elements of Wilson's project of moral reclamation are less convincing, for he draws a Chatterton excessive only in his love of tea, hard work, and pranks, whose freethinking tendency is balanced by the becoming piety of the 'Rowley' verses.[52] However, it is a moral, but not a moralistic assessment, for internal evidence indicates that Wilson was thoroughly familiar, if only at second hand, with the scurrilous, blasphemous, and even pornographic writings that closed Chatterton's career. The *London Quarterly Review* would give *Chatterton* a belated assessment along with the Skeat edition, euphemistically recommending this 'earnest and honest' study as a basis for future biographies.[53]

Wilson's *Caliban: The Missing Link* (1873) is perhaps, as the title indicates, the work that most closely binds his ethnological and literary interests. This extended character study of Caliban shares the Romantic sympathy with the 'salvage and deformed slave' of Shakespeare's *Tempest* and stands in a line of post-Romantic reclamations of the play.[54] (Until the original was staged in 1838, audiences were familiar only with Dryden and Davenant's extensively rewritten version – of which Wilson is repeatedly scornful – where Caliban's part is reduced in importance and the character rendered grotesque.)[55] *Caliban* is in many respects a typical example of nineteenth-century bardolatry, full of praise for Shakespeare's genius as manifested by his blending of fact and fancy, the range of his sympathies, and the infinite variety and shadings of his characters, but it is unusual in resting the case on this secondary figure. For Wilson, the character of Caliban not only exceeds the imaginative possibilities of Shakespeare's day, but 'anticipates and satisfies the most startling problem of the nineteenth century': 'only now, two centuries and a half after its production on the English stage, has it entered into the mind of the scientific naturalist to conceive of such a being as possible.'[56] For the nineteenth-century reader, Caliban provides not only an imaginary prototype of the 'missing link' between brute creation and man, as postulated by Darwin, but also raises the metaphysical and theological problem of where in humanity's descent (Wilson prefers 'ascent') did the capacity for conception of a higher being evolve. In this work, as A.B. McKillop notes, Wilson had left the more certain domain of his scientific expertise to consider the philosophical and psychological implications made necessary by *The Descent of Man*.[57] It is this aspect of *Caliban* that has proven to be of primary interest to later commentators; McKillop, for example, provides a lengthy analysis of the book as illustrative of Wilson's realist-idealist dualism.

But *Caliban* also deserves a place as a work of literary criticism, despite the lengthy and formulaic encomiums. It is up to date (if not innovative, except for the novel notion of Shakespeare's previsioning); according to Andrew F. Hunter, Wilson maintained a correspondence with North American Shakespeare scholars such as E.P. Whipple.[58] His knowledge of the texts is thorough and close, the product of a lifelong interest and many classroom hours: the preface mentions his purchase of a 1632 folio from an Edinburgh bookstall and his experiences teaching Shakespeare to Toronto undergraduates. This close textual knowledge is apparent in four final, almost appended, chapters standing apart from the book's main argument, which consider textual questions and cruxes in *The Tempest* and, to a lesser degree, *A Midsummer Night's Dream*. After attacking the careless amendments of eighteenth-century editors, Wilson deploys a combination of common sense and etymological learning to restore or resolve the wording of a number of disputed passages.[59]

For the *London Quarterly Review*, however, these textual emendations were sometimes 'infelicitous' or unconvincing; clearly, Wilson was a 'disciple of the boldest school of conjectural emendators.' Other reviewers were more positive about the book's critical contribution, while remaining wary of the anthropological argument. The *Spectator* found the title enticing but misleading, and judged the character study more convincing than Wilson's thesis, while the *Fortnightly Review* considered his theory 'suggestive' only of Shakespeare's magical touch. Only the *Canadian Monthly* was uniformly positive, praising the welding of the two forms of research into a 'homogenous whole' and finding the work a success 'both as a poem and a valuable contribution to knowledge.'[60] The lukewarm reviews of Wilson's work may have dissuaded him from further efforts; certainly, he produced little critical writing after 1873 and confined his output to ethnological topics. However, the primary influence of his study was not literary-critical but theatrical; according to Stephen Orgel, F.R. Benson's famous Stratford production of the 1890s was based on Wilson's approach.[61] Benson studied for his part by observing the apes in the London Zoo, and in his surprisingly athletic performance he entered the stage with a fish between his teeth and delivered lines hanging upside down from a tree branch.[62]

While Wilson's critical and literary works are contiguous with his antiquarian, archaeological, and anthropological study, the reverse is also true: the scientific writings make frequent reference to literature and mythology (sometimes deeding the latter a quasi-evidentiary value, either as a residuum of the knowledge of past cultures or as the literary illustration of scientific truths). Further, the works themselves may also be considered as 'literary,' placed in the context of Wilson's larger literary output, both broadly and narrowly defined. They are literary in the generous nineteenth-century definition of the term; not yet shrunk to our current restriction to non-fictional genres, 'literature' denoted essays, historical and philosophical writings, and frequently the scientific – the 'prose of thought,' to use a useful term still retained by some at Wilson's own department.[63] Certainly, when he himself spoke of this literary work – or the lack of time for such – he would have been including the production of written records of his ethnological explorations, for example. But his scientific and social-scientific writings need to be placed in relation to the 'literary' as it is defined even in our now-narrower sense. 'The aesthetic bent of Wilson's mind,' A.B. McKillop succinctly argues, 'must constantly be recalled when considering his scientific, as well as his literary work; so should the function of rhetoric, thus defined, when assessing the scientific writings of Wilson (and others) in the nineteenth century.'[64] Wilson's 'poetic sensibility' infused the subject matter of his scientific writing, just as his rhetorical concerns ruled their style and structure; as much as any other prose texts of any time, they can be read 'rhetorically' as a series of ideological arrangements which grammar is bent to serve.

Wilson's literary style deserves some concluding attention, if only because he was noted for it (both positively and negatively) in his own time. His early *Testimonials* praised him for his rhetorical power; a more enduring testimonial took the form of the words 'Windbag Dan' carved on a desktop by a desperate student, according to college apocrypha. For Andrew F. Hunter (who parallels him to both Cicero and Gladstone in his verbosity), Wilson took Scott as his model: 'The ponderous & well-rounded sentences of the master became even more ponderous and well-rounded in the disciple ... The "hence, accordingly" that used to ring in so many of his colossal sentences is a fair sample of the duplication of words, that tinctured his whole diction. Most men are content to use one of these conjunctions ... but he never failed to let off both barrels, however small the game.' For Hunter, this could be credited to the characteristic style of the Edinburgh literary circle (or, he hints, it is an occupational hazard for writers who have at one time been paid by the inch);[65] or it might be a side effect of the public oratory which Wilson was frequently called upon to perform. It can be further read as a display of both the heuristic and the material pressures of his complex situation; given his multidisciplinary orientation, in any one piece Wilson could argue deductively, inductively, and through moral suasion, deploying the accompanying structures and styles appropriate to each – piling on secondary evidence in an inverse proportion to the degree to which his heavy labours prohibited first-hand research, and maintaining, through elaborate example, his intent to clarify, preserve, transmit, and make relevant the imaginative repertoire of a culture.

So distinctive was Wilson's prose idiolect that it was still being lovingly mimicked by his one-time student Stephen Leacock in platform performances and radio broadcasts of the late 1930s. 'Sir Daniel had adopted the old-fashioned way of always putting in proper connecting words, so that every sentence would begin with "however" and then "nevertheless" and then, as the chief one of all, "hence, accordingly" ... Sir Daniel lectured on that up and down system of voice, like a pump, working hard ... and you'd hear his voice getting up and up and up and then it would start all over again – "hence, accordingly."' In Leacock's telling of this piece of campus folklore, it was 'Hence, Accordingly' that the desperate student carved.[66]

By contrast, Wilson's verse and fictional writing seems direct, lighter-handed, and sometimes lighter-hearted (to use evaluative terms common to his day, if not to ours). 'Bachelor's Buttons,' for example, is a piece of doggerel verse on the domestic ineptitudes of the unmarried man, while 'Good Mother Cara and Her Glass Slippers' is a moral children's tale in couplets, where the Christmas fairy helps a little girl to be virtuous for a day. (It was originally written for a Christmas celebration at St James' Cathedral.) A series of 'varsity' lyrics penned by Wilson was intended to channel into song the famously disruptive spirits of the male undergraduates when they gathered in the convocation hall. *Spring Wild Flowers*, first published under 'Wil. D'Leina' in 1845 and later reprinted under his own name, incorporated some of his early writings for Nelson's and was in turn later excerpted in several readers and the *Canadian Monthly*. It provides an overview of the variety of his verse production: sentimental scenes of family life, an ode to Burns, and a sequence of twenty-six sonnets with a *tempus fugit* theme (followed by closely related parodies, offering meditations on mortality occasioned by the death of bugs). The core of the book is a pseudo-historical narrative, 'Edward. A Tale of the Reformation,' composed in a series of loosely rhymed and half-rhymed triplets in an abc/abc pattern, which was a verse experiment on Wilson's part.

'To a casual reader,' he wrote, 'the peculiarity may escape observation, as the rhymes are purposely arranged at such intervals as to secure to it the general character of blank verse, while still he may be conscious of a sense of musical harmony.'[67]

For the most part, however, Wilson worked within well-travelled forms, often adeptly executed, and the production of *jeux d'esprit* and comic and occasional verse – frequently mailed to the *Scotsman* – continued to the end of his life. It seems to have provided a necessary counterbalance to his heavy work and burdensome responsibilities, as illustrated by his completion of the ballad of 'Mary Stuart' for his 'Old-Edinburgh ballads' series on the day after the devastating fire that had reduced his beloved college to a shell.[68]

It is difficult to determine, in Wilson's comic body-and-soul verse debate between 'The Critic Dragon and the Author Moth' from *Spring Wild Flowers*, on which side the author's own sympathies lie. But certainly, from our later perspective, his continuing importance to the discipline of English studies and to Canadian intellectual history is to be found in his critical and pedagogic contributions and in their complexity. Wilson's writings and career open a window onto a period of English studies that has received almost no attention to date: that is, to the decades between the first founding of 'rhetorical' instruction in the early settler academies and the modernization of the discipline that occurred with the hiring of dedicated professors of English literature in the 1880s. His work illustrates, however, that there was a distinctly 'literary' mode of analysis in operation – both in criticism and in the classroom – in this transitional period, and that its admixture of rhetorical, etymological, aesthetic, biographical, historical, and ethical analysis makes it more highly inflected than we have previously supposed.

At the same time as Daniel Wilson's work and career provide a point of entry to the earlier years of English study in this country, they also demand that we develop a more serious and contextual examination of two forms of critical activity characteristic of those early years. In the first place, we are ill-equipped to react in other than dismissive ways to a sustainedly 'moral' criticism. In the second place, current examinations of English studies generated in the context of post-colonial theory have emphasized the conservative and imperializing consequences of the intrication of 'English' with 'nationalist' discourses and mandates, without considering the potentially more progressive dimensions. Determinedly 'racialist' and fascinated with the 'primitive,' Wilson was only ambivalently 'nationalist' in his thinking, and he undertook cultural-anthropological studies designed to show the concurrences of cultures and the commonalities of peoples. A critic operating in a colonial and then newly (and conditionally) post-colonial situation, a pedagogue with one eye on the greats and another on the grass roots, an uneasily immigrant author advocating a literature of unique national experience, he lived and left as a legacy many of the cultural contradictions of our own situation today.

NOTES

1 Berger, 'Wilson,' 1109.

2 H.H. Langton, *Sir Daniel Wilson*, 72.

3 Langton says that Wilson would have preferred to keep the English teaching rather than the history, and he offers the superiority of the literary publications as evidence of Wilson's inclinations (*Sir Daniel Wilson*, 156). However, Wilson produced almost no literary criticism after 1873 – perhaps deterred by the lukewarm reviews of *Caliban* – and the sale catalogue of his personal library indicates that he continued to keep up to date with ethnological publications, but not the new literature or criticism (Britnell, *Catalogue*).

4 See, especially, McKillop's chapter on 'Evolution, Ethnology, and Poetic Fancy' in *Contours of Canadian Thought*.

5 Crawford, *Devolving English Literature*, 16. I have relied on Crawford for his examination of the intrication of early anthropological and literary developments.

6 Wilson, *The Archæology and Prehistoric Annals of Scotland* (1851), preface. Fellow archaeologist Andrew F. Hunter would credit the work of Scott – and *The Antiquarian* in particular – for providing Wilson with sound antiquarian principles (AO, F 1084, Draft of 'Sir Daniel Wilson and His Books,' 10). For a detailed account of the influence of Scott on Wilson, see Ash, 'A Past "Filled with Living Men,"' and her essay on *Prehistoric Annals* in this volume.

7 Court provides a detailed overview of Smith's lectures in *Institutionalizing English Literature*, 17–30.

8 On the use of Spalding's book in Canada, see Tilson, 'Who Now Reads *Spalding?*'

9 This work is of some interest in showing how Wilson's early cohorts attempted to reconcile their religious faith with scientific speculation. However, the text offers no support for Langton's listing of it as a publication of Wilson's. He – or Jessie Aitken Wilson – may have undertaken the editing, however.

10 H.H. Langton, *Sir Daniel Wilson*, 14–15. Hunter in his draft (69) credits George Wilson with the composition of 'Old King Cole' – incorrectly, since

eighteenth-century variants of this rhyme approximate the version that children know today.

11 See, for example, Sandra Campbell's introduction to the reissue of Sime's
Sister Woman and K. Jane Watt, 'Passing Out of Memory.' Sime was born after
Wilson moved to Canada, and she herself settled there after his death; so the
influence of this literary uncle would have been at the best intermittent.
According to Jane Watt, who has discovered Sime's papers, there is only one
brief mention of Wilson in Sime's unpublished material and correspondence.
Oliphant biographer Elisabeth Jay notes that Daniel and George Wilson
helped their cousin to form important early literary connections; it appears
that an active relationship was not maintained into later life, however (see Jay,
Mrs Oliphant, 13–14).

12 J.A. Wilson, *George Wilson*, 13–14.

13 Daniel Wilson, cited in J.A. Wilson, *George Wilson*, 25.

14 H.H. Langton, *Sir Daniel Wilson*, 22.

15 Ibid., 22.

16 The 'sublime' and the 'picturesque' are often considered, not entirely accurately, as the rival aesthetic theories of the eighteenth and early nineteenth
centuries. Edmund Burke contrasted beauty and sublimity and linked the sublime with the infinite: faced with great or powerful phenomena, the mind
must halt or confront its normal modes of cogitation. The 'picturesque' (for-
mulated by William Gilpin, among others) is often defined as an attempt to
find a middle ground between the sublime and the beautiful and to develop
artistic principles from this, for sketching and painting especially.

17 Fellow explorers George Brown and George Paxton Young would both also
move to Toronto, the first to become famous as a politician and publisher of
the *Globe,* the latter as the university's revered metaphysician.

18 A very interesting analysis of Canadian adaptations of the picturesque, and a
defence of the theory's much-underestimated complexities, is provided by
Michasiw, 'Nine Revisionist Theories on the Picturesque.'

19 UTA, B65-0014/004(01), 19–29 (1865).

20 I am grateful to Dr Margaret Mackay for obtaining a copy of this story for me.

21 UTA, B65-0014/004(02), 128 (13 January 1888).

22 Wilson, *Testimonials* (1851), 7, 10.

23 This would not be surprising: English studies would not be established at Cambridge or Oxford for some decades, and even at the pioneering University of
London there was a constantly shifting sense of what a professor of English
ought to do (see Court, *Institutionalizing English Literature*, 39–84).

24 The debate before a select committee of the Legislative Assembly is reported
verbatim in Hodgins 15: 98–315.

25 On the debate and its consequences, see Hubert, 'The Vernacular in Nineteenth-Century Anglophone Colleges.'

26 On the curriculum under Wilson, see Harris, *English Studies at Toronto*, 14–24, and Hubert, *Harmonious Perfection*, 94–6.

27 UTA, B65-0034/001, William Nesbitt Ponton, Honours English notebook, 1873.

28 Houston had included a broad and uncensored range of materials in his proposed curriculum. When there was criticism in the letters columns of the press, he had defended himself by citing Dawson (without the latter's knowledge).

29 UTA, B84-0033, Wilson to William Dawson, 22 December 1885.

30 On Wilson's role in the search for a professor of English, see Murray, 'The Appointment of W.J. Alexander.'

31 Guillet, *In the Course of Education*, 48, 70. Wilson also presided over a controversial motion to provide equal grammar school education for girls and a unanimous resolution against racial segregation in the schools (Guillet, 31).

32 Wilson, 'English at Junior Matriculation' (1889).

33 The institute founded a short-lived philological section in 1887 to study Native languages and to report on the utility of a proposed international language, Volpükt. However, Wilson does not appear to have been involved with this section.

34 Wilson's address on Burns was reported in the *Journal of Education for Upper Canada* under the headline 'Burns – His Short Career – His Songs and the Universality of Their Diffusion' (1859). His encomiastic mode could displace critical analysis. Gender stereotyping, in addition, may be behind a review of Elizabeth Barrett Browning which says nothing of her poetry and much of her invalidism and 'pathos' (Wilson, Review of *Last Poems* [1862], 210). But it could also occasion interesting contradictions, where in his Scott centenary address this poet of the 'old Homeric school' is offered as an antidote to an age which 'rejoices in the genius of Browning and Tennyson' (Wilson, 'The Genius of Scott' [1871], 342, 346) – the same Browning whom Wilson would in other contexts admire and defend; the same Tennyson whose acquaintance, developed in the last years of their respective lives, was to be one of his most cherished memories.

35 On attitudes to Browning, see H.H. Langton, *Sir Daniel Wilson*, 202.

36 Wilson, Review of *Tales of Mystery, and Poems* (1857).

37 Wilson, Review of *Bothwell ... and Leaves of Grass* (1856), 546.

38 Wilson, Review of *The Song of Hiawatha* (1856).

39 Wilson, Review of *The St. Lawrence and the Saguenay* [and other Canadian poetry] (1858), 17.

40 UTA, B84-0033, Wilson to William Dawson, 6, 12 January 1882. Wilson's devel-
   opmental views meant, however, that he supported the creation of a French
   literature section, on the grounds of its more venerable history and surer connections to the *francophonie*.

41 *PTRSC* 4 (1886): xv. The patron and president appear to have been prepared
   for these criticisms: the Marquis of Lorne was optimistic that the society could
   encourage younger authors, while Dawson reminded his audience 'that in a
   country situated such as this nearly everything is in some sense premature'
   and that this was 'a time of breaking-up ground and sowing and planting'
   (*PTRSC* 4 [1886]: v, vi).

42 These figures are based on Bourinot's *Bibliography* of Royal Society members.

43 AO, F 1084, Hunter, 'Sir Daniel Wilson and His Books,' 92. Wilson also maintained connections to literary circles in England and Scotland, partly through
   the Nelson firm, as well as long-standing friendships with poets James Ballan-
   tine and J.S. Blackie and the pre-Raphaelite William Bell Scott.

44 On the pirating of Wilson's work, see UTA, B65-0014/004(02), 132–3
   (29 April 1888).

45 Wilson, 'The Lost Atlantis' (1886), and 'The Artistic Faculty in Aboriginal
   Races' (1885).

46 McKillop, *Contours of Canadian Thought*, 97.

47 Kelly's *The Marvellous Boy* is a good overview of the impact of Chatterton
   throughout the nineteenth century.

48 Wilson, 'Ricardus Coriensis' (1869), and 'American Literary Forgeries'
   (1869).

49 Wilson's *Ane Auld Prophecie* (1849), a mock-medieval comic poem on the
   destruction of Edinburgh's Trinity College Church in 1848 to make way for
   the railway, has been quoted in the article by Ash, Cruft, and Hulse in this
   volume. He may have had a further point of enjoyment in the Chatterton
   study, for it allowed him to criticize as 'slight' (Wilson, *Chatterton* [1869], xii)
   an earlier study of Chatterton, *A Story of the Year 1770*, by David Masson, who
   had only recently defeated Wilson for the Edinburgh chair in rhetoric.

50 UTA, B84–1079, Wilson to D. Beddoes, 10 August 1868. In this letter Wilson
   wrote, 'I have abandoned more than one literary project from the impossibility of getting hold of the needful books of reference.'

51 Wilson draws the comparison to Scott directly (*Caliban* [1873], 64). In his
   Scott centenary address, he would describe how 'The dreams of his boyhood
   already bodied forth the forms of things unseen; and imagination busied itself
   with the fantasies of a world of its own creating' ('The Genius of Scott' [1871],
   342).

52 Hunter felt that Wilson's treatment ignored the symptoms of mental disease

in Chatterton, for 'He shared in the prevalent inability of that day to know the subtle symptoms of mental disease' (AO, F 1084, Hunter, 'Sir Daniel Wilson and His Books,' 87). A more recent psychoanalytic treatment, however, praises Wilson's portrait as well balanced and finds the argument 'logical and sympathetic' (Kaplan, *The Family Romance*, 196–7).

53 *London Quarterly Review* 41 [no. 81] (1873): 424.

54 The phrase 'salvage and deformed slave' is from the cast list of the Folio edition. Whether or not it is Shakespeare's, it has achieved a certain fame.

55 On the varying attitudes to Caliban over time, see Vaughan and Vaughan, *Shakespeare's Caliban*.

56 Wilson, *Caliban* (1873), 192, 66.

57 McKillop, *A Disciplined Intelligence*, 130.

58 AO, F 1084, Hunter, 'Sir Daniel Wilson and His Books,' 90.

59 This etymological untangling occurs also in Wilson's lengthy review essay of *The Romantic Scottish Ballads* (1859), where he rebuts Robert Chambers's contention that most of the 'early' Scottish ballads were eighteenth-century forgeries.

60 *London Quarterly Review* 40 [no. 81] (1873): 484–6; *Spectator* 41 [no. 2380] (7 February 1874): 180–2; *Fortnightly Review*, n.s. 13 [no. 75] (1 March 1873): 484; *Canadian Monthly* 2 (December 1872): 573–5.

61 Orgel, 'Introduction,' 73.

62 Vaughan and Vaughan, *Shakespeare's Caliban*, 185–6.

63 Which does not mean that he would have held this definition without distinction. Wilson might well have been annoyed – or at the least puzzled – by the disinterring of *The Curate's Daughter* by this member of his department.

64 McKillop, *Contours of Canadian Thought*, 105.

65 The comments on Wilson's style are from Hunter's notes to chapter 14 in A0, F 1084, series V [unpaginated].

66 Leacock, *Professors*. I am grateful to Bruce Trigger for bringing this tape to my attention and to the Stephen Leacock Museum for giving me a copy.

67 Wilson, *Spring Wild Flowers*, preface to the 1853 edition, viii–ix. This poem is called 'The Orphan of Lowden: A Tale of the Reformation' in the later edition.

68 H.H. Langton, *Sir Daniel Wilson*, 180.

'In Some Form, My Life-Pursuit': Daniel Wilson, Artist

ROBERT STACEY

The hats we don on first entering the theatre of work are rarely those we doff when we acknowledge the plaudits that greet – if we are lucky – our retirement from the stage. In considering the multifarious achievements of Sir Daniel Wilson, therefore, we do well to remember that it was officially as 'artist,' rather than as ethnologist, comparative anthropologist, man of letters, or even as 'student or collector of antiquities,' that this ambidextrous polymath was elected a fellow of the Society of Antiquaries of Scotland on 23 February 1846. Yet in the seventy-four years between that *annus mirabilis* and 1920, when a small exhibition and sale of Wilson's watercolours was mounted at the Art Gallery of Toronto, the fact that the subject of this modest show had made his start as an apprentice to a prominent engraver and worked for a spell as a print dealer and art critic had been largely, if not completely, forgotten – this despite the fact that, some eighteen years earlier, a rather partisan memorialist had pronounced Wilson 'probably the most skilful amateur in Canada. The same readiness and decision in taking a full view of affairs which distinguished him in public matters made him a bold and effective sketcher, with a grasp of the composition of a scene that raised him head and shoulders above the ordinary amateur, and indeed above many artists.'[1]

Certainly, the dour, Darwinesquely bearded sexagenarian of Hamilton Plantagenet MacCarthy's 1890 plaster bust does not betray the fact that the subject had a private creative life, much less a pawky sense of humour and a wide sentimental streak.[2] Neither does Sir George Reid's searching tripartite portrait of Wilson, originally painted for the Scottish National Portrait Gallery in 1891 and copied by the artist for the University of Toronto in 1909, even though it presents a wider range of facets. Still, the teachers-in-training who watched the bust grow a mantle of dust in the stuffy gloom of the Educational Museum of the Toronto Normal School and the students and faculty who avoided the late principal's flinty glare as they hurried through the corridors of University College must instinctively have known that they were in the presence of a complex personality. Just how complex and varied, however, they were hardly in a position to appreciate.

Both the MacCarthy bust and the Reid portrait show Wilson in an entirely serious light, as befits such official effigies. We must refer to the autobiographical excerpts transcribed by H.H. Langton for confirmation that the 'Venerable Shade' affectionately mocked by Stephen Leacock in a 1916 poem subtitled 'A Song in Praise of the University of Toronto'[3] was in fact outgoing as well as introspective, light-hearted as well as grave. And only those familiar with the more obscure titles in Wilson's extensive bibliography can attest that the brain of the scientist sheltered the soul of a poet who penned lyrical as well as satirical rhymes, published a study of Caliban as 'The Missing Link,' and painted a vision of *Puck in the Forest*, perhaps for the amusement of a child or the delight of a fellow Shakespearean.[4] Nonetheless, the multifaceted quality of this formidable character is admirably suggested by Reid's composition, which recalls Sir Anthony Van Dyck's famous portrait, *Charles the First in Three Positions*, painted in 1635–6 to assist the Rome-based Bernini in the carving of a marble bust of the English king. The message is clear – there was more than one Wilson – and Reid surely would have known that his sitter was a lifelong corresponding, if not full-time, member in the universal brotherhood of artists.

The first public display of the results of Wilson's private hobby came about through his niece, the Montreal-based writer Jessie Georgina Sime, who had inherited a number of his watercolours.[5] But it was at the suggestion of a professional painter, a 'Miss Des Clayes' (most probably Berthe Des Clayes, of the painterly triumvirate of Des Clayes sisters), that she had approached Edward R. Greig, secretary and curator of the Art Gallery of Toronto, with a request for assistance in disposing of them. That the show attracted scant notice and realized – despite prices as low as five dollars – only moderate sales is hardly surprising, in view of the fact that the Canadian art event of 1920 was the holding there in March of the first collective showing of the newly formed Group of Seven, which was destined to become the dominion's first internationally acclaimed art movement. The Group's bold assault on the granitic fastnesses of northern Ontario was, on first viewing at least, entirely at odds with the expatriate Scotsman's gentle and restrained evocations of the byways of picturesque Edinburgh and of Canadian and American vacationland scenery in water-colours (that politest of media). Yet a perusal of the titles listed, in no dis-cernible order, on the two-page typed inventory of the AGT exhibition[6] suggests less of a complete breakaway from Victorian pictorial nicety than a continuation of a venerable practice that the Group, in claiming it as their own, would elevate to heroic, not to say mythic, stature.

While such titles as *Wolfe's Cove, Chaudière Falls,* and *Among the Thousand Islands* could have been found in any number of such catalogues in the early days of the Art Association of Montreal, the Ontario Society of Art-ists, or the Royal Canadian Academy of Arts (established respectively in 1860, 1872, and 1880) or in the sketchbooks of non-professional artists during the colonial and pre-Confederation eras, *Pictured Rocks – Lake Superior, Camp Fire, Trading Lake,* and *Camping Ground, Rocky Portage* have a more contemporary ring. Their echoes sounded throughout the cata-logue of the first exhibition of the Group of Seven and likewise through that of the memorial exhibition of paintings by Tom Thomson, also held at the AGT in 1920: *Northern River, The Log Chute, The Wild River, Beaver Dam, March Storm, Georgian Bay,* and so forth.

Even if expunged from the later titles, the key word that connects the Daniel Wilson watercolours with the Group canvases by which they were overshadowed is 'camping,' that non-ironic transference to the great out-doors of one's urban or suburban domestic arrangements, the better to observe in would-be arcadian wilderness discomfort the so-called satisfac-tions of the simple life. This insistence on the spiritual and physical bene-fits of fresh-air recreation, this determined wooing of the muses of the lake and the forest, was just beginning to become one of the touchstones of the culture that this self-proclaimed 'fervent lover of Edinburgh' at first grudgingly and then more receptively accepted after making his reluctant decision to commit himself to Canada and its mixed blessings. The factious intellectual community of the University of Toronto may have been united only in its determination to disagree about virtually everything, but on this topic it was unanimous: an annual northward flight from the city was essential both as a restorative and as a stimulus.

'Camping' is a somewhat generic term for the various arrangements available to vacationers, from tents to cabins to summer houses to luxury hotels. As commonly understood, the aestival rite entailed a change of accommodation, a change of clothes, and above all a change of scene. Spring term concluded and exam time over, Daniel Wilson gladly swapped mortarboard for Scotch bonnet, the sombre habit of the dedicated campus man for the rustic outfit of the camper. Thus it was that his countryman E.R. Greig characterized the 'considerable collection of water colour sketches' on view: 'They were done on various camping trips, between the years 1850 and 1884, and apart from their artistic value, are very interesting mementos of the early days and of one whom we all remember with deep gratitude and pleasure.'[7]

In fact, the earliest dated picture in the list is from 1843 – *Allison's Close, Cowgate, Edinburgh* – and the latest watercolours are souvenirs from one of Wilson's last visits, in 1886, to a favourite summer destination, the bucolic state of New Hampshire. It was a long enough journey between Arthur's Seat and Thunder Cape, the High Street and Yonge Street, but at least the latter places were in Canada, a British colony-turned-dominion. But Wilson's horizons were wider, and wiser. Despite his commitment to the imperial vision of a Greater Britain that Alfred Lord Tennyson laid before him during his visit with the poet laureate in 1891, Wilson, once acclimatized to North America, turned into a firm continentalist. It is entirely to his credit that we can state that, unlike so many of his fellow émigrés, he was as much at home in Quebec's Citadel as in Edinburgh Castle and on the ancient serpent mounds of Ohio as on their namesake in his home town.

To embrace such opposites, to leap with aplomb such yawning geographical gaps, was, after all, part of the life kit of Wilson's intellectually restless generation, a generation of immigrants, explorers, and pioneers. Subject to abrupt changes of fortune and violent displacements, the enterprising Scot could blithely trade a feather (or, for that matter, a heather) bed for a mattress of fresh-cut cedar boughs, the burr of the burn for the roar of the rapid. Did not the same boreal stars wheel overhead, the same northern lights flash in the subarctic sky? To embrace, with a poet's or painter's reflexive equanimity, diametrically opposite cultural realities, to span yawning geographical distances, to cross an ocean or a continent to find a kindred spirit, to make the most of one's surroundings, is the mark of a true adventurer; accepting one's lot as the best of all possible choices is the sign of a genuine citizen of the world.

How Daniel Wilson in 1831 'was entered as a pupil in the studio of William Miller ... with the idea that art was to be, in some form, my life-pursuit,'[8] and how in 1837 he successfully sought out a commission to engrave Turner's virtually unrenderable *Regulus* is outlined earlier in this volume, though a fuller treatment of this illustrative and amusing episode is called for elsewhere. Also deserving of more expansive discussion are the interrelated worlds of antiquarians and artists in which Wilson moved after his return to Edinburgh in 1842, as well as his links with the Scottish school of landscape painting.[9] Aptitude in draughtsmanship was a key tenet of the generation of artists with whom he was associated. Pencil drawing formed a link between the writers and the artists, the scientists and the historians, the naturalists and the philosophers of the Scottish Enlightenment, as it did for those autodidacts and amateurs who, like Wilson, negotiated among their friendly camps. In his rather unusual case, the implement with which he visually communicated his archaeological and architectural findings to a wider audience than the Society of Antiquaries of Scotland was not the pencil or the brush, but the graver. After all, a graphic language remains a private, hence silent, one until it can be published. Wilson himself defended the 'engraver's art' as more than 'mere copying. The painter has all the advantages of colour, and aims at reproducing Nature in her own garb and atmosphere. But the engraver's work is equivalent to that of the translator of a poem into another language. His is a translation in which the equivalents of colour have to be rendered by texture, and light and shade.'[10]

That Wilson did not, so far as we know, paint 'pure' landscapes while in Scotland suggests that his choice of media – graphite, sepia wash, watercolour, and ink – was chiefly utilitarian. Further, he was firmly fixed in his native city and either saw no need to look to broader horizons or had no opportunity to do so. His abiding objective was to find an appropriate medium for the minutely accurate, yet atmospherically suggestive, rendering of Edinburgh streetscapes, buildings, carvings, sculptures, ancient implements, and ornaments. Nor does it appear that these illustrations were regarded by either their maker or their audience as artworks in themselves, however much pleasure and instruction they may have conferred. Rather, they served as references to guide the eye and hand of that crucial middleman, the engraver.

W.A. Langton, a Toronto architect and amateur artist who had sketched alongside Wilson, characterized his manner of rendering in this pre-emigration period as 'that of the old-fashioned "water-colour drawing."' He describes this modus operandi as follows: 'After the outline was made the shades and shadows were laid in rather dark with a neutral tint composed of French blue and brown madder, inclining to the warm side, and the local colour laid over this in pure washes. A reed pen put in the markings on this with a "crumbling" touch and the thing was done. It is a good rapid mode of execution, affecting general truths rather than particular, and well suited to the broad masses of buildings.'[11] In other words, the medium served the message, which was less artistic self-expression than the conveying of vital information about subject matter overlooked by the general populace in its rush to industrialized modernity. If Edinburgh was hell-bent on destroying its built environment and physical heritage, Wilson and his fellow antiquarians would fight to preserve what remained with all the political, documentary, and reprographic weapons available. Hence his ability to resolve the seeming contradiction of abandoning his nascent career as a producer of engravings 'after' contemporary artists in Edinburgh and London, and yet subsequently returning to the copper and steel plate and the boxwood block in order to pay tribute to the forgotten achievements of the anonymous artisans and builders of his own country's ancient and more recent past.

Wilson's lifelong habit of drawing bespeaks a preference for observed fact and a faith in objective truth over abstract theory, received precepts, and second-hand gossip. We can appreciate this work ethic, not only in the innumerable vignettes, figures, and plates in *Memorials of Edinburgh in the Olden Time* (1848), but also in William Douglas's remarkably clear engravings after Wilson's meticulous drawings for the plates, textual figures, and vignettes of *The Archæology and Prehistoric Annals of Scotland* (1851). In these illustrations we have a classic example of why white-line woodcut engravings of artefacts are considered by archaeologists to be preferable in certain ways to photographs, bringing into sharp linear relief as they do the intricate details and differing textures of a highly wrought stone celt or bone knife, iron staple or bronze ring-fibula, silver bodkin or gold funicular torc, ivory comb or jet necklace, bejewelled cup or triple-knot-decorated powder horn, runic inscription or lintel monogram, silver-gold crozier[12] or Lewis chess piece, ogee window tracery or carved corbel. But in representing these various objects with the requisite degree of accuracy, the wood engraver was dependent on the information supplied by the draughtsman, for here there could be no admitting the creative fudging or interpretive gap-filling of the kind that the reproductive engraver was called upon to perform in the 'translation' of a lightning sketch by Turner into a fully realized study in lights and shadows wrought on a thin sheet of smoke-blackened steel.

In a further sign of Wilson's independence from conventional norms and notions, he approvingly reviewed the first and second volumes of Ruskin's *Modern Painters* in 1847, concurring at the outset with its then-controversial assessment of Turner as 'the greatest landscape painter in this or any other age.' This position did not prevent him, however, from taking issue with the as-yet-unidentified 'graduate of Oxford' on the sore

topic of the value of engravings after Turner's paintings (particularly the
much-reworked later ones). Nor did Wilson see any point in addressing
himself to the vexed task of 'grappling with the recondite themes of the
second volume – the Theoretic Faculty, the Impressions of Sense, and the
old questions of Beauty and the Sublime, wherein Burke and Allison [*sic*]
laboured to so little purpose' – as, by implication, did Ruskin himself.
'What is beautiful,' Wilson pragmatically argued, 'we can all determine,
with more or less sense, as well as what is not; and most of us can render
some reason for the opinion we maintain. But, what is beauty? is another,
and a more difficult question ... Beauty is truth, or fitness, or association,
or some other thing to which the name is applied ... Truth and fitness,
and pleasing associations, are beautiful in different degrees; but they are
not beauty, any more than the rose is, or the rose-like blush of the
maiden's cheek, or any other object wherein it is developed.'[13]

If Daniel Wilson confined his artistry in Scotland to interpretive
draughtsmanship and engraving, sticking to civic and historic themes and
steering clear of landscape, in Canada his practice more closely tallied
with that of the topographical view sketchers who had introduced North
American vistas to Britain and Europe. Scottish engravers and lithogra-
phers may have played a disproportionately large role in translating the
watercolour impressions of military travellers (the first aesthetic tourists
in the New World), but the officer class that took down the primary visual
data was almost to a man English, and its pictorial ethos followed pretty
strictly the dictates of the eighteenth-century arbiters of the anglicized
'beautiful' and 'picturesque.' As later commentators would observe, neither of these aesthetic doctrines was applicable, except with drastic qualifications, to Scotland or to its offspring, Canada.

Furthermore, while 'Edinburgh Wilson' drew and engraved for a public many of whose members he knew by name, 'Toronto Wilson' painted
more for himself and his family circle than in accordance with an educa-
tive and conservational mission. It was as if, deprived of his original audience and unsure of the loyalty or interest of an unfamiliar new one, he
determined to pour his creative energies into the keeping of complementary (though not always congruent) written and pictorial diaries in which
he documented his vacations and excursions. This shift was accompanied
by a change not only in technique but in choice of subject matter.

It seems only reasonable that, having settled in Toronto, Wilson should
have turned his attention to his immediate surroundings. These he was
prepared to find alien and primitive, but, as he confessed in a letter of
1853, 'I am surprised how well I can adapt myself to this new place – new

in every sense – plank roads, venerable stumps of the primeval forest still
lingering in by-roads and streets, frame houses, shanties, &c. &c.'[14] However, despite sharing Charles Dickens's favourable reaction to the 'life
and motion, bustle, business, and improvement' noted by the novelist on
his flying visit to the town in 1842,[15] Wilson painted few Toronto images.
Furthermore, the sites that he did choose to depict tended to have historical associations: for instance, the squared-timber blockhouse on Sherbourne Street in suburban Yorkville (demolished in 1865). Not that there
was any lack of sketchworthy material, in the city itself and its outlying 'vil-
lages,' in the thickly wooded ravines of the Rosedale district just to the
north, or in Don Vale to the south. Nonetheless, only one rendering of
this urban wilderness is recorded: *Yorkville Creek*, dated 22 August 1865.
However, there was the pleasure of conversation and conviviality with the
'pleasant circle of educated, intelligent Society' that was quick to welcome this impressive newcomer.

Among the first to extend an invitation was George William Allan
(1822–1901), the laird of Moss Park, a severely neoclassical mansion on
the west side of Sherbourne Street erected in 1828 by his father, William
Allan. Wilson described him as 'a wealthy citizen here who possesses a
fine collection of colotypes [*sic*], drawings, etc., a man of taste who has
travelled much.'[16] Allan, a prominent lawyer and politician, became
mayor of Toronto in 1855 and served as speaker of the Senate of Canada
from 1888 to 1891. A public-minded citizen, he also put in terms as president of the Canadian Institute, the Ontario Society of Artists, and the
Upper Canada Bible Society, and chaired the Art Union of Canada. Wilson's interest in photography is also reflected in his comment of 1853
that a Trinity College professor, the Reverend G.C. Irving, 'is a Cambridge man, and an amateur calotypist, so we were friends at once in spite
of our rival colleges.'[17] His expression of pleasure suggests that he shared
Irving's hobby, but if he practised photography in Canada, examples of
his craft definitely attributable to him cannot be located.[18] Like many collectors, he may have preferred reference photographs purchased from
commercial suppliers and fellow amateurs over his own efforts.

Other Toronto acquaintances with whom Wilson shared artistic interests were John Langton, vice-chancellor of the University of Toronto,
whose sister, Anne Langton (c. 1804–93), was a proficient painter of
miniatures and landscapes in graphite and watercolours and whose sons
were Hugh Hornby, Wilson's first biographer, and William Alexander,
the artist and architect who wrote an early sketch of our subject 'as an
artist.' Also through the collegial connection, Wilson found an ally in the

prominent engineer, architect, and later legislator and historian Frederic W. Cumberland (1821–81), who together with his partner, W.G. Storm, won the competition to design the University College building in 1856. At Cumberland's residence in February 1854, Wilson had met another kindred spirit, Francis Cayley, a wealthy eccentric with a pronounced artistic, architectural, and literary bent. An 'amateur artist with a Victorian taste for whimsy and drama,'[19] he adorned the wide central hall and adjacent drawing room of his Regency-style villa, Drumsnab, with scenes from Faust and other equally fanciful, if less-sinister decorations.

But of the small cadre of professional artists working in Toronto in the early 1850s – George Theodore Berthon, Hoppner Meyer, Paul Kane, Edwin Whitefield, W.G.R. Hind, William Armstrong, and the young Lucius O'Brien – whom might Wilson have had occasion to meet? There is no direct evidence that he was personally acquainted with any of these figures except Paul Kane, but the painter most nearly allied to Wilson on the social plane was Lucius O'Brien (1832–99). Dennis Reid lists Wilson as being 'Among other artists close to the vital issues of the day in the city'[20] who would have certainly have been known to O'Brien. A foundation member of the Ontario Society of Artists, O'Brien would work closely with the governor general, the Marquis of Lorne, to establish the Royal Canadian Academy, of which he was the first president from 1880 to 1890. Through his sweeping interpretations of the Atlantic and Pacific coasts and the Rocky Mountains (the latter at the behest of the newly completed Canadian Pacific Railway), he helped to endow Canadian art with a truly national vision.

Wilson's rapid acclimatization to his new environs was another side of that innate responsiveness which opened him to the creative possibilities of a daunting range of unfamiliar phenomena and radically altered premises. Not all his fellow expatriates could be credited with reacting so affirmatively to the challenges that confronted them on their disembarkation on Canadian shores. This adaptability extended to Wilson's artistic practice. Contrasting his previous manner with the approach that he adopted in Canada, W.A. Langton relates that

> when Sir Daniel Wilson came to this country of diffused light and squandered masses, that are so trying to artists, he found it necessary to acquire a new method. After a season or so of muzzy trees, with neutral tint 'grinning through' the green, he gave up his old-fashioned work and adopted a new style to suit a new country. Here he showed power as an artist even more than in the beautiful drawings of Edinburgh; for he had to invent a method

for himself. The delicate old water-colour school furnished no model for application to the garish lighting and uncomposed landscapes that have broken the spirit of so many artists in this country. But Sir Daniel Wilson contrived to get hold of what there is in the landscape. There was always composition in his sketches, and the veritable character of the country; yet what they were chiefly remarkable for was what he did not have in them. The original paper, with a toning wash over it, would do duty for a whole sunlighted hillside. It was not flat; it was not bare; but, when one came to look into it, a few twists of the brush to mark the shady side of a boulder or so, a touch of white where the sun caught them, a delicate variation in the tone, hardly discernible at close quarters, were all that went to make a modelled hillside. Beyond – a mass of trees in shadow of an undaunted depth, a distant valley, a cloud, and the sketch was done; a full account of the scene; the points all in, the twaddle all out. His methods were vigorous – tinted paper, Chinese white, washing, scraping, a dry brush, a quill pen, the granulated appearance given to colour by the impression of the human thumb, were all recognized aids. He had no preciosity, but it must not be supposed that his work was therefore coarse. His scale was large and his handling broad; but being broad it could not be coarse, for the essence of breadth is delicacy.[21]

What Langton does not say here is that Wilson was in fact remaining true to the gospel of Turner, as adapted and extended by him from the teachings of John Robert Cozens, Paul and Thomas Sandby, Francis Towne, Thomas Girtin, Peter De Wint, John Varley, David Cox, and John Sell Cotman. This sacred doctrine declared that watercolours should be built up in thin washes of translucent colour on sheets of white paper, the colour of which was used to illuminate the lighter areas of the composition. Not for this traditional method's hard-core adherents the trickery and trumpery licensed by the Victorian practitioners, who in the 1830s and 1840s began to adopt the use of Chinese white squeezed from lead tubes, of opaque body colour as a pigment, and of gum arabic as a medium, in order to give watercolours something of the richer chromatic range, the flexibility, and (not least) the consumer cachet of oils and the textured detail-quotient allowable with gouache.

Wilson's concessions to the new, additive mode extended only to the occasional use of Chinese white and of tinted papers. For dazzling highlights – sunbeams sparkling on choppy water, for instance – he preferred the trusty razor blade that had served Constable, Turner, Cox, and Cotman so well. (The 'granulating' thumbprint effect mentioned by Langton is, by the way, a definitive Turnerian touch, now focused on by art detectives literally to confirm the hand of the master in disputed works.)

Wilson's rejection (or perhaps ignorance) of the post-purist school again testifies to his regard of watercolour as a medium for the communication of private pleasure rather than as a vehicle for public utterance. As Langton comments, Wilson's artistic horizons were widened, on his settling in Toronto, by an access to an annual block of leisure time and the unprecedented freedom to travel that is one of the rewards of academic tenure: his 'sketches were made almost entirely during the excursions of his summer vacation. Belonging to that enviable class of men who find refreshment in change of occupation, he always came back with a large collection. On his very last vacation, if I am not mistaken, he came back with eighty sketches; and when his family came down to breakfast on the first morning after the return they found the whole set mounted and put away in a portfolio.'[22] This typical display of industry is a proof of Wilson's contention that 'one does more in the spare moments of the busiest times than in all the leisure of a long vacation. For in truth the proper work of holiday time is to be idle.'[23] The production of a large haul of watercolours over the course of a summer was play, not work, to this tireless overachiever.

One of the consequences of the survival of Wilson's journals only as transcribed excerpts made by H.H. Langton is that his painting activities must be reconstructed from other sources, leaving numerous lacunae. Would that we possessed something from the writer-artist's own hand about his sensations on first venturing northward from Toronto to the dense forests and sparkling lakes of the Precambrian Shield. All we can surmise is that Wilson's introduction to what would later become known as 'cottage country' occurred shortly after his arrival. As he assured David Laing, 'even while cherishing all my old affections for Edinburgh and its unrivalled attractions without abatement, I have repeatedly met with Mr. and Mrs. Sanson of Orillia, which is a favourite summer excursion, and have indeed pressing invitations to partake of their hospitality.'[24] If Wilson did accept this couple's entreaties to stay with them at their holiday place on Lake Simcoe, no watercolours from this early resort destination appear to have survived.

As we have seen in earlier essays in this volume, the first of Wilson's more extended expeditions – a jaunt up Lake Huron to the Straits of Michilimackinac (Mackinac) and Sault Ste Marie, and so on across the length of Lake Superior to Fond du Lac – took place in July of 1855. The presence in his now-disbound scrapbooks of a clipping from the Detroit

Weekly Advertiser for 7 August 1855 recounting the 'Excursion on the steamer Illinois to Lake Superior' strongly suggests that Wilson was one of the 350 passengers on this landmark voyage. Although he failed to name the ship or the port of embarkation, he did report to Laing the occasion for the journey and the route followed. 'This season the opening of a Canal, constructed round the Sault Ste. Marie, a rappid [*sic*] of about a mile long on the River St. Mary, which joins Lake Superior to Lake Huron, has for the first time admitted of vessels passing from the Lower to the Upper Lake. Taking advantage of this, I have gone the range of the great fresh water Lake, penetrating to the River St. Louis at the very head of Lake Superior. The result was highly gratifying in many ways.'[25]

It is in this letter that Wilson announced his pleasure on discovering that the shores of Lake Superior – 'excepting at a few points, where mining operations have commenced' – were 'in their wild natural state.' Even more exciting was the fact that along this rugged coast were still to be viewed specimens of 'the red Indian savage, painted, and adorned in his genuine native costume.'[26] Wilson's non-pejorative reference to undomiciled Indians living more or less as they had done for untold centuries contrasts sharply with the anonymous Detroit memorialist's recounting of a shipboard sermon delivered by Dr Tappan, of the University of Michigan, in which he 'contrasted our condition' with that of 'the degraded Indian, and, in an eloquent extemporaneous address, thanked God who had made us to differ from them, and had made "our paths in pleasant places."'[27]

On the return voyage down the lake near Marquette, Michigan, an archaeological thrill lay in store for excursionists in the form of the far-famed Pictured Rocks, first speculated upon as to origin and purport by Henry Rowe Schoolcraft, the Indian agent at Sault Ste Marie, Michigan, in 1820.[28] The enigmatic pictographs on these rocks left the writer of the report in the Detroit *Western Advertiser* groping for words: 'Sublimity, grandeur, beauty and grandeur are comprehensive terms, but feeble when used in connection with the "Pictured Rocks"; to be appreciated, they must be seen.' So too the scenery, which also defied description while demanding it: 'The gems of islands in the vicinity afford good retreating lees for vessels or steamers. Leaving them in the distance, a "mirage" of great beauty restored them to our vision when more than 40 miles off.' Earlier, the correspondent had enthusiastically commended the sunsets of Lake Superior, which 'cannot be surpassed in beauty in any clime; the pure, serene atmosphere is no interruption to vision, while the still water reflects the hues of departing glory. Then the Aurora Borealis flashes with great brilliancy during the night.'[29]

Such effects would be noted by the successive waves of painters and writers, American, Canadian, British, and European, who flocked to the upper lakes to take advantage of the new accessibility conferred by the completion of the Sault Ste Marie canal and the introduction of steam navigation on Lake Superior, and subsequently by the construction of the Canadian Pacific Railway along the rugged north shore. Much as he may have disliked that designation, Wilson was participating in an early exercise in mass tourism. Less than ten years before, in much more primitive circumstances, the Irish-born painter Paul Kane on his way to the Pacific had traversed the lake by the Hudson's Bay Company fur-trade route, hugging the same majestic coastline that would go on to attract Frances Anne Hopkins, T. Mower Martin, Frederick Arthur Verner, William Armstrong, and, in our own century, F.H. Brigden, the Group of Seven, Charles Comfort, Yvonne McKague Housser, and a host of other painters.

Some eight watercolours from Daniel Wilson's first exposure to the wild heart of North America are recorded, two of them of the Pictured Rocks, another of the Arched Rock, Mackinac Island, and yet another of Saultaux bark wigwams at Sault Ste Marie. So unlike anything that Wilson had seen before were these vast prairies of water dotted with rocky, pine-plumed islands and wave-carved shorelines that he was forced to adopt that fresher, freer mode of rendering attributed by Langton to a literal change of air and scene: a salubrious shift from the closed-in murks of Auld Reekie to the 'garish lighting and uncomposed landscapes' of the great North American outback.

Throughout his first Canadian decade, Wilson utilized his vacations and academic travels to get to know his adoptive continent as far south as Virginia and Kentucky, as far east as Prout's Neck, Maine, as far west as the St Louis River, and as far north as Lake Nipigon.[30] August of 1858 found him putting in at various ports of call on the St Lawrence River between the Thousand Islands and Île d'Orléans (latterly the domain of the Barbizon-influenced Canadian painter Horatio Walker) and then making the obligatory ascent of the mighty Saguenay to Ha Ha Bay. Here again Wilson was sketching terrain and features – the Falls of Shawinigan on the Saint-Maurice river, the deep, dark, granite-palisaded canyon of the Saguenay – that later would become the signature landmarks of the generation of painters who founded the Royal Canadian Academy in order to put Canadian art on an officially sanctioned professional footing: Lucius O'Brien, Otto R. Jacobi, John A. Fraser, Henry Sandham,

Allan Edson, Robert S. Duncanson, F.M. Bell-Smith, et al. In the swirling atmospherics of *Fog on the St Lawrence* the lingering influence of Turner may be seen. Twenty-two years hence, in 1880, O'Brien's luminous *Sunrise on the Saguenay* would be given pride of place at the inaugural exhibition of the Royal Canadian Academy in Ottawa.

In 1858 Wilson sketched on the Otonabee River and at Sturgeon Lake, in the Kawarthas of what is now eastern Ontario, possibly at the suggestion of his friend John Langton, who had homesteaded in this region in the 1830s. Though still several decades away from becoming a Mecca for adepts of the new cult of the campfire and the canoe, these mixed-forested highlands, which had only recently been made accessible through the construction of the government-funded colonization roads and the Trent-Severn waterway, had already been timbered over several times and were now attracting a rush of prospectors and miners. Anne Langton had been one of the first artists to depict this terrain.

An adverse reaction to the rigours of roughing it on the southern hem of Canada's lake district may well have persuaded Wilson to seek out an altogether different sort of holiday experience the following year. Lake George, in the Adirondacks of northeastern New York, and Lake Champlain, in the Green Mountains of Vermont, had long been domesticated for seekers after picturesque but unthreatening vistas. For Wilson they offered the further amenity of historic remains in the form of Fort Ticonderoga and interesting geological features such as the Shelving Rock and St Anthony's Nose on Lake George. Far more pastoral, yet rich with ethnological associations, was the Grand River of southwestern Ontario, which drew Wilson in September of the same year, presumably to conduct research into the Six Nations Iroquois, who had settled along the shores of this broad waterway after the American Revolution, but also to dip his squirrel-hair brush, passim, in unfamiliar waters.

A creature of habit as well as a footloose wanderer in search of new evidence to support his theories about the asynchronous but parallel development of so-called primitive societies, Wilson enjoyed paying return visits to favourite recreational destinations; thus he was back on the St Lawrence in July of 1865, holidaying in the Murray Bay (La Malbaie) region, again heading up the Saguenay, and painting pines and sunsets at Pointe-au-Pic. And a recovery of that memorable first exposure to the glories of Lake Superior country – albeit only of the American south shore – could no longer be deferred.

Travel on the upper Canadian lakes had been greatly facilitated when, in 1855, the Northern Railway from Toronto reached Collingwood, at the

southern tip of Lake Huron's Georgian Bay. Soon paddle-wheel steamers
bound for Mackinac, Green Bay, Chicago, the 'Soo,' and Lake Superior
were regularly departing from this shipbuilding port. In 1864 the *Algoma*
came to berth at Collingwood and entered the Lake Superior trade, calling at HBC posts and small settlements along the Superior north shore
en route to Fort William. It was probably on board this ship that Daniel
Wilson made his way to the lakehead in July of 1866. Seven years earlier
his friend F.W. Cumberland had been appointed general manager of the
Northern Railway. Another source of tantalizing first-hand information
about the great northwest was artist Paul Kane (1810–71). G.W. Allan's
daughter, Maude Allan Cassels, in an unpublished reminiscence about
Kane, states that, after Wilson's arrival in Toronto in 1853, he 'made Paul
Kane's acquaintance fairly soon. Drawn together by mutual interests, they
must have seen a great deal of each other, Sir Daniel keen to learn everything in his own line that Kane could tell him about the Indians. Both to
Sir Daniel and my Father, sure of their sympathy and understanding,
Kane, though a very reserved man, would talk freely, at all events about
his travels.'[31]

Wilson could have met Kane at one of Allan's Moss Park soirées, but
they became professionally associated through the Canadian Institute,
where, as Wilson pointed out a decade after its founding in 1849, 'The
pages of our own Journal have been repeatedly enriched from his notes
of travel.'[32] Near the conclusion of his *Canadian Journal* review of this stirring narrative in book form, Wilson remarks that Kane had received a
commission for 'an extensive series of oil paintings executed by him for
his liberal friend and patron, Mr. Allan. These amount to upwards of a
hundred, including many highly characteristic life-size portraits, pictures
of Indian games, dances, hunts, and combats, and of their lodges, cere-
monies, canoes, &c., as well as of studies of the remarkable scenery of the
great rivers of the North-West. In addition to these, Mr. Allan also possesses a valuable collection of Indian dresses, weapons, implements, carvings, medicine rattles, pipes, &c., obtained by the author during his
travels.'[33]

Kane would have been particularly fascinating to Wilson because, like
himself an outsider-amateur, he mixed art with ethnology, utilizing the
former in the service of the latter, while his desire to match the achievements of George Catlin in turn provided the motive for his painterly travels. As Maude Cassels recorded, when Wilson in 1862 'brought out his big
book, with its memorable title, "Prehistoric Man," he returned thanks
again, and very handsomely at length "To Mr Paul Kane, the author of

the 'Wanderings of an Artist Among the Indians of North America,' for sketches made during his travels, as well as for information derived from recollections of the incidents, and observations, among the Indian tribes of the Hudson's Bay Company.'" The book reproduced two of the Moss Park pictures.[34]

An enquiring mind such as Wilson's could hardly have resisted an opportunity to see for himself (albeit as a tourist rather than as an explorer or surveyor) some of the scenes that these trailblazers passed through on their way to the 'Far West.' In addition to the growing body of exploration literature and the publication of studies of the natural history, geology, and ethnology of the upper Great Lakes, there was the burgeoning illustrated press, which fuelled the popular imagination with breathless accounts of the central North American hinterland. For instance, two years before Wilson made his second Lake Superior pilgrimage, the readership of the *Canadian Illustrated News* was treated to an article on the beauties and wonders of the 'freshwater sea.' At its head appeared an engraving of the 'Ancient Water Margins on the Shore of Lake Superior,' after a sketch by Major George Seton, completed during this British army topographer's trip to the region in 1862. As the anonymous author (possibly Seton himself) proudly exclaimed, 'The scenery of the lakes and the rivers flowing into and out of them will never be exhausted in these pages ... There will always be natural scenery, varieties of changing industry, and incidents of past and current history to yield in rich profusion, pictures of beauty and narratives of instructive interest.'[35]

This rhapsody merits quotation at some length because its tone and content evince an attitude, more and more common in this era of transcontinental Canadianism, that had clearly been informed by scientific and ethnographical investigations and publications of the kind the Canadian Institute both conducted and endorsed.

Few portions of America can vie in scenic attractions with this interior sea. Its size alone gives it all the elements of grandeur; but these have been heightened by the mountain masses which nature has piled upon its shores ...

When the visitor to these remote and boundless waters comes to see this wide and varied scene of complicated geological disturbance and scenic magnificence, he is absorbed in wonder and astonishment. The eye, once introduced to this panorama of waters, is never done looking and admiring. Scene after scene, cliff after cliff, island after island, and vista after vista are presented. One day's scenes of the traveller are but the prelude to another; and when weeks and even months, have been spent in picturesque rambles

along its shores, he has only to ascend some of its streams, and go inland a
few miles, to find falls, and cascades, and cataracts of the most beautiful or
magnificent character. Go where he will, there is something to attract him.
Beneath his feet are pebbles of agates; the water is of the most crystaline [*sic*]
purity. The sky is filled at sunset with the most gorgeous piles of clouds. The
air itself is of the purest and most inspiring kind. To visit such a scene is to
draw health from its purest sources, and while the eye revels in intellectual
delights, the soul is filled with the loveliest symbols of God, and the most
striking evidences of his creative power.[36]

How could so receptive a sensibility as Wilson's have resisted such an
enticing summons? While there is no evidence that he read these words,
they express a point of view then increasingly common, attesting to an
unaccustomed national confidence and a desire to embrace rather than
shun a wilderness that offered renewal as well as material rewards.

Whatever factors motivated Wilson to undertake a second ascent of the
upper lakes, he exploited the experience thoroughly, trading steamship
for canoe in order to make the soon-obligatory side trip up the Nipigon
River. Wilson's practice of dating his watercolours allows us to sketch out
the itinerary: by 6 July his party had reached Station Island, St Ignace; two
days later they were paddling up the Amethyst River to the first falls; and
the next day they were camping at the mouth of the Current River   in
Thunder Bay. The dominant topographical feature of the bay, the
beetling, red-granite Thunder Cape (complete with its complementary
Sleeping Giant), elicited from the sketcher's brush over a half-dozen ren-
derings. Was he perhaps reminded by this brooding headland of the leo-
nine southwestern brow of Arthur's Seat? On 13 July Wilson recorded
landing on a misty evening at 'Neepigon Gut'; over the rest of the week
the canoeists proceeded up this majestic stream, struck their last camp on
25 July, and then made the reverse journey down the river and back to
Thunder Cape.

Midway on this expedition, Wilson committed to paper three views that
show him fully in harmony with what I have elsewhere called the 'canoe-
eye-view,' that water-level perspective of the artist ensconced amidships
(or beneath the arching ribs), between the thwarts of this most supple
and limber of vessels.[37] In *Katsagegan Lake, Nipigon*, we see an unfolding
of cliff and forest, with a paddler advancing into the composition on the
extreme lower right. In *West Cliff, Nipigon*, we are perched in the elevated
bow in the HBC-issue bark itself, looking towards the stern-enthroned

steersman wielding his blade to warp around a cliff-corrugated shore, while mosquito-netted lady sketchers – wife or daughters? – placidly work away at their tablets in the foreground. (Where now, by the way, are their witnessings of this interesting scene?) Wilson extolled the adaptiveness of the native craft as a makeshift temporary shelter in *Under the Canoe in a Shower, Head of the Long Portage, Nipigon*. On 30 July the artist sketched bark wigwams on the Kaministiquia River, and on 4 August he marked the hulking silhouette of Mount Mackay from Fort William. The lack of any watercolours of that title suggests that he did not venture up the Kam as far as Kakabeka Falls – the 'Niagara of the North' – whose lower rapids Frances Anne Hopkins would put into the foreground of a contemporary Canadian history painting when she depicted the arrival of the Red River Expedition at the foot of the portage in 1877, and whose full primeval force Lucius O'Brien would suggestively capture five years later.

On his descent of Lake Superior, Wilson paused to record George and Magpie falls on the Michipicoton River, the subjects, some four decades later, of Edmund Morris's brush when in 1905 this Toronto-based painter canoe-trekked through northern Ontario in company with the poet and Indian Affairs bureaucrat Duncan Campbell Scott on assignment to negotiate Treaty no. 9. Four years hence, another Toronto artist, Frederick H. Brigden, would be persuaded to seek out the north Superior shore by the son of F.W. Cumberland, Frederic Barlow Cumberland, who, after service with the Great Western Railway, worked as freight and passenger agent of the Northern Railway and traffic manager of the Lake Superior line of steamships. Among the first to lend an ear to Bridgen's excited reports of the grandeur of this unspoiled 'new' landscape were Lawren Harris, J.E.H. MacDonald, and Frank Johnston, who in September 1918 headed north on the Algoma Central to investigate the terrain for themselves. This first boxcar trip is generally cited as the true beginning of the Group of Seven as a painting and exhibiting collective.

Barlow Cumberland was instrumental in launching the nascent Ontario tourism industry, which he touted continentally through the publication of his *Northern Lakes of Canada* in 1886. Daniel Wilson was again well ahead of this promotional barrage, having anticipated the rush by at least a decade when in 1870 he, Judge Thomas Galt, and William Nelson, his Edinburgh school chum and publisher, made a canoe circuit of the Muskoka River, Sparrow Lake, and the Severn River. Once more, there was an abundant harvest of watercolours, registering such typical subjects as campfires, logjams, deadheads, stormy mornings, portages, and rapids. On this occasion the immigrant played host and cicerone to the Old World visitor, introducing his former countryman to the novel scenes that, once foreign to himself, had become an integral part of his imaginative and aesthetic make-up.

More even than in his Lake Superior watercolours, with these on-site impressions Wilson was leaving behind the gentle pastoralism of his rural views, still very much in evidence in his northeastern United States landscapes, to embrace a new approach to northern subject matter. This change was necessitated by the nature of the terrain itself, as well as by the mode of transportation through it. Here the horizon-seeking eye found its way barred by a densely overgrown interior landscape, a maze of complicated foregrounds offering little room for stepping back to take in the larger picture, except on those occasions when one emerged from the forest path onto trail's end to gaze across open water to the mirrored ramparts of the far shore. The trees were coniferous rather than deciduous, the wind-blown boughs of the white pine replacing the billowing rondures and feathery silhouettes of elm and oak. It would no longer do to haul out the Claude glass or invoke Gaspard Poussin or 'Grecian' Williams. Instead, we see Wilson unwittingly anticipate the strategies employed by Tom Thomson in painting sketch-panels *in situ*.

Always on the lookout for the unusual angle or unexpected point of view, Wilson on this trip played with the theme of inside versus outside, as expressed by the device of the tent-opening view: the domestic sanctuary of the canvas home-away-from-home gives onto a triangular fireside nocturne, with silhouetted campers gathered around the night-dispelling blaze. This unusual composition echoes one of some years earlier, *Chapelle Hervieux, Pointe-au-Père*, only here the vista-framing aperture is the mouth of a lacustrine cave which takes the form of a primitive gothic arch – light succeeding dark, claustrophobic confinement opening out into the sweet relief of recessive space.

The single largest cluster of extant watercolours by Wilson is the set of New Hampshire landscapes dating from between August 1881 and September 1887. A vacation in 1883 also took Wilson and family to the Atlantic coast of Maine, while the escape of August 1884 from Toronto's torrid climate found the artist wandering the Adirondacks around Lake Placid in upstate New York. Wilson's summer jaunts of 1886 and 1887 were again to New Hampshire – Black Mountain, Cascade Brook, Mount Osceola, Mount Tecumseth, the Mad River, and Scar Ridge – indelibly North American names in which he clearly revelled. Savage names, yet doubtlessly delightful to the ear and eye of the venturesome scholar who rejoiced at his opportunities to study 'the Red Indian in his Native state' and to explore 'the traces of his primitive Arts.'[38]

Throughout his Canadian years, Wilson worked quietly but assiduously to achieve for Toronto what he had sought to secure for Edinburgh: a lively regard for the past and a vigorous appreciation of the present, as it was expressed by all the allied arts and sciences. This devotion came home with him when he departed the campus and the rostra of the societies to which he committed so much dedicated energy. As W.A. Langton comments, 'Though he cleared away the art of the vacation before beginning university work, he did not absolutely deny art in term time. For several winters after he became President of the University, and was busiest with its affairs, a sketching club met at his house once a week during the winter. He was himself the shining light of the club, and any member of it will, in thinking of the club, remember chiefly the dexterous drawings he used to make with his left hand, and the stump of a pencil, upon tinted paper touched up with Chinese white.'[39]

An exactly contemporaneous development was another sketching club, the Toronto Art Students' League, founded in 1886 on the model of its New York precursor, as an after-hours life class for students, teachers, amateurs, and professionals. In its turn, the Toronto Art League (as it became) evolved, after disbanding in 1904, into the Graphic Arts Club, renamed the Canadian Society of Graphic Arts in 1925; through its outdoor sketching regimen and promotion of Canadian subject matter, the league laid the groundwork for the national campaign of the Group of Seven. During its first years of existence, the TASL was observed with interest by the Scottish-born William Cruikshank (1848–1922), the teacher of (among many others) George Agnew Reid, J.W. Beatty, C.W. Jefferys, J.E.H. MacDonald, and Tom Thomson.

G.A. Reid's biographer informs us that it was while he and Langton were studying art in Toronto in the winter of 1879 that he 'began to do pen-and-ink drawings. He learned much about the technique of pen-drawing from Langton and, applying himself seriously to it as he did everything he attempted, made marked progress.'[40] Langton, as we have seen, probably picked up this method from Daniel Wilson, whose fluency with the quill and steel nib verged on the masterful. Reid would then pass on this skill to his many pupils, including, among the first and second generations, C.W. Jefferys, W.W. Alexander, F.H. Brigden, F.S. Challener, J.E.H. MacDonald, and Franklin Carmichael, most of whom would go on to instruct further generations at the Ontario College of Art. Knowing this link, we can now draw an unbroken line from such Scottish master draughtsmen-engravers as William Geikie, David Wilkie, Andrew Geddes, Daniel Maclise, and James Drummond to the Group of Seven, several of whom were the sons of Scottish immigrants.

Daniel Wilson played a modest, but by no means insignificant, role in the cultural coming of age of Toronto, assisting in the creation of the city's institutional infrastructure. Against this contribution, we must weigh the limitation inherent in his colonialist intellectual program, as inadvertently disclosed in the continuation of the last sentence of his September 1855 letter to David Laing. First-hand Native studies, he states, 'appear to me of great value as throwing light on the Ancient arts of Prehistoric Britain.'[41] But what of Canada? Did its scenes and stories, artefacts and prospects, peoples and peopling, only deserve study because of the illumination they might shed on the dawn of Scottish civilization? Does one detect a note of despair in Wilson's declaration 'The history of America cannot repeat that of Europe'? He saw this divide as being geographically determined, for in his view the continent's 'great river valleys and vast prairies present a totally different condition of things from that in which the distinctive arts, languages and nationalities of Europe have been matured.'[42] But might not new arts, new languages, new nationalities eventually be 'matured' in North America? Surely the gist of Wilson's *Prehistoric Man: Researches into the Origin of Civilisation in the Old and the New World,* first published in 1862, is that, given sufficient time and nurturing, they will.

What then of the fruits of the early avocation which, right up to the end, was also, in some ways, a 'life-pursuit'? From the vantage point of our own distance from Daniel Wilson's era, we can apply to this long-hidden visual legacy the words that the Scottish art historian Stanley Cursiter used to describe the landscapes of Daniel's precursor, Andrew Wilson: they are 'simple, honest, and unpretentious, informed by a quiet regard for truth.'[43] Equally fitting is Samuel Redgrave's earlier assessment of the elder Wilson's watercolours: 'simply painted, without the use of body colour. They are carefully finished; his distance tender, and the whole work marked by much refinement.'[44] Not, perhaps, the most ringing of endorsements, but meet commendation nonetheless, especially in an era when such modest, undeclamatory virtues, in art as in society and the professions, are increasingly rare.

Daniel Wilson's right to recognition as an artist was conceded twelve years after the posthumous Art Gallery of Toronto exhibition by the author of the first monograph devoted exclusively to landscape painting in this country. 'Throughout his distinguished Canadian career he was an enthusiastic amateur painter,' wrote A.H. Robson, 'and produced a great number of pictures of Canadian scenery which are valuable pictorial records of the Canada of his time.'[45] This commentator was the former art director of Tom Thomson and several members of the future Group of Seven during their days as commercial illustrators and designers, and he did much to promote the reputations of the so-called Algonquin School through publications and his activities as president of the Art Gallery of Toronto. But despite his vested interest in contemporary Canadian painting in general and in the movement he helped to foster, Robson was aware of the need to pay homage to the contributions of the largely forgotten or overshadowed nineteenth-century artists whom he gathered together under the title 'The Pioneer Group.'

Daniel Wilson would surely have taken pride in being so categorized, for to range from antiquary to pioneer in one eventful lifetime was no mean achievement. We now can see him as a pioneer in another sense, permitting us through his pictures not only to measure the distance between his generation and that of the Group of Seven, but also to appreciate how many of the themes, motifs, and subjects which the younger artists were to claim as their own had been enthusiastically adopted as early as sixty years before Harris, MacDonald, Jackson, and company took the Canadian art world by storm. Without ever pretending that his heart did not belong to Scotland in general and Edinburgh in particular, and perhaps without conscious intention of carrying out such a program, the newly arrived Wilson had set out in the 1850s to make the first tentative steps towards the goal announced in Lawren Harris's much-quoted foreword to the catalogue of the first Group of Seven exhibition: 'an Art must grow and flower in the land before the country will be a real home for its people.'[46]

NOTES

The author wishes to express his indebtedness to a number of colleagues who have offered information and suggestions in the writing of this essay, most notably Elizabeth Hulse, whose patience in acceding to the numerous delays in its delivery is gratefully acknowledged, as are her indispensable preliminary researches into Daniel Wilson's life, career, publications, and production of artworks. Her encouragement and sage editorial guidance are similarly hailed. Thanks are also due to Jim Burant and Kate O'Rourke, of the National Archives of Canada and the Archives of Ontario; Margaret Mackay, of the School of Scottish Studies at the University of Edinburgh; Jane Ryder, representing the Marinell Ash estate; Antoinette Watkins, of the National Museums of Scotland; the Toronto architectural historian Stephen Otto; Ken Lister, of the Royal Ontario Museum, Toronto; and Ian S. MacLaren, of the University of Alberta in Edmonton. I am grateful as well for the assistance received from the staffs of the E.P. Taylor Reference Library of the Art Gallery of Ontario (in particular, Randall Speller); the Baldwin Room, Toronto Reference Library; the University of Toronto Archives; and the libraries of the National Gallery of Canada, the National Museums of Scotland, and the University of Edinburgh. A grant from the Marinell Ash estate enabled me to travel to Edinburgh in May 1995 to examine the Valentine collection of Wilson watercolours before their transferral to the National Archives of Canada. As ever, Maggie Keith.

1 W.A. Langton, 'Sir Daniel Wilson as an Artist,' 180–1.
2 Sculpted from life in 1890, the year of the devastating University College fire, the bust was a commission for Egerton Ryerson's Educational Museum (one of the forerunners of the Royal Ontario Museum and the Art Museum of Toronto); it is now on view at the Ontario Legislative Buildings, Toronto, as part of the Government of Ontario Art Collection (acc. no. MGS 619734).
3 Leacock, 'Laus Varsitatis,' 115: 'Read me that lecture on the Third Crusade,' Leacock entreated. 'Noble Wilson – dare we call him Dan? – ... Let thy grave voice its even tenor keep, / Read it again. This time I will not sleep.'
4 A large watercolour of this title, inscribed 'those merry wanderers of the night a Midsummer Night's Dream' on the support, was sold at the D. and J. Ritchie Inc. Canadian art auction on 2 June 1992 (lot 429, illus.). It came from the estate of Canon Richard W.E. Greene, who had received it from the artist.
5 The pictures remained available for viewing and purchase until 1924. The watercolours now in the AGO and the NGC were bought from the Sime sale, and a number of others, which were returned unsold to Sime in 1924, have been tentatively identified with paintings acquired from the Montreal art dealer Sidney Carter by W.H. Coverdale for the Canada Steamship Lines collection (now in the NA) and by the University of Toronto (now in the UTA), which had earlier bought a number of watercolours from Sime herself. The EUL Wilsons were donated to that institution by Sybil Wilson in 1913. The extensive Valentine family collection, highlights of which were exhibited at the RMS from November 1992 to March 1993 under the title *A Brush with Nature: Watercolours of North America*, was acquired by the NA through a grant from the Eaton Foundation in 1995.
6 AGO Archives, A3.9.2, Correspondence.

7 Ibid., E.R. Greig, form letter on Art Gallery of Toronto stationary, n.d. (c. December 1920).

8 UTA, B65-0014/004(02), 153–4 (25 May 1889).

9 Wilson's artistic output and his relationship to his Scottish contemporaries and antecedents deserve more extensive treatment than it is possible to give them here, ideally in the form of a full-scale exhibition and catalogue.

10 UTA, B65-0014/004(02), 164 (25 May 1889).

11 W.A. Langton, 'Sir Daniel Wilson as an Artist,' 181.

12 In *Prehistoric Annals of Scotland* (1851), 664–5, the wood-engraved illustration of the Crozier of St Fillan is taken from James Drummond's *Archaeologica Scotica*. However, by 1859 Wilson had seen the precious relic, then in Canada. He wrote to David Laing, 'From the nature of the object, it does not admit so readily of copying by means of photography as some other articles would; but the views [photographs to be handed over to the SAS] will at any rate give you some tolerable means of judging the original ... I have made a careful drawing, and purpose to have it lithographed for the Canadian Journal' (Wilson to Laing, 7 March 1859; published in *PSAS* 3 [1859]: 233). A lithograph by Fuller and Bencke of Toronto after Wilson's drawing appears in the *CJ* and a pamphlet privately published in 1859. However, it was from photographs that W. and A.K. Johnston made the lithograph that was reproduced in the *PSAS* that year.

13 Wilson, Review of *Modern Painters*, vols. 1 and 2 (1847), 483. The Alison alluded to was the Reverend Archibald Alison, whose hugely influential *Essays on Taste* were first published in book form in 1790.

14 UTA, B65-0014/004(01), 10 (5 November 1853).

15 Dickens, *American Notes for General Circulation*, 248.

16 UTA, B650014/004(01), 18 (17 February 1854).

17 Ibid., 14 (25 November 1853).

18 Wilson assembled several collections of photographs: an album of family and friends, now part of the Valentine collection; one entitled 'My Poor Relations,' now in the Department of Ethnography, ROM; and a number of stereo views, now in the possession of a Toronto photographer and collector. Several of these views were sent to Wilson by British topographical artist Westcott Witchurch Lyttleton and other acquaintances. See also the following essay by Elizabeth Hulse in this volume.

19 Dendy and Kilbourne, *Toronto Observed*, 31.

20 D. Reid, *Lucius O'Brien*, 16.

21 W.A. Langton, 'Sir Daniel Wilson as an Artist,' 182.

22 Ibid.

23 UTA, B65-0014/004(02), 191 (16 May 1891).

24 EUL, Special Collections, La.IV.17, no. 6, Wilson to David Laing, 8 September 1855.

25 Ibid.

26 Ibid.

27 'The Excursion,' Detroit *Weekly Advertiser,* 7 August 1855; clipping in TRL, S65.

28 See Schoolcraft, *Narrative Journal.* The Pictured Rocks were next noted by Thomas L. McKenney in his *Sketches of a Tour of the Lakes,* published in 1827.

29 'The Excursion,' Detroit *Weekly Advertiser,* 7 August 1855.

30 Just how early were Wilson's trip to the Nipigon area in 1866 and his Muskoka excursion in 1870 is confirmed by Patricia Jasen's study of tourism in Ontario between 1790 and 1914 in *Wild Things,* but unfortunately, she does not discuss landscape painting.

31 ROM, Dept of Ethnology, Cassels, 'Paul Kane,' 22. I am grateful to Elizabeth Hulse for alerting me to the existence of this document.

32 Wilson, *CJ,* n.s., no. 4 (May 1859): 186. Note the passive voice. One might infer from this that Kane was a regular contributor to this organ, but in fact, as his manuscript journal of his travels indicates, he verged on illiteracy, being at best a phonetic speller, and a veritable committee of interested parties helped to put his field research into order while seeking a means of ensuring its publication in readable form. (See in this context MacLaren, 'The Metamorphosis of Travellers into Authors: The Case of Paul Kane,' in which he discusses the possible roles played by Wilson, H.Y. Hind, J.H. Lefroy, and others in preparing the manuscript for publication.) Similarly, as the minutes of the Canadian Institute reveal, the 'Notes on Travel among the Walla-Walla Indians, by Paul Kane, Toronto,' published in the *CJ* in September 1856, were indeed 'Read before the Canadian Institute, 5th April, 1856,' but by G.W. Allan, not by the ostensible author. (I am indebted to Conrad Heidenreich and I.S. MacLaren for this information.)

33 Wilson, Review of *Wanderings of an Artist* (1859), 194.

34 ROM, Dept of Ethnology, Cassels, 'Paul Kane,' 19. The 'Moss Park pictures' commissioned by G.W. Allan are now in the ROM. By Cassels's account (20), Wilson's admiring obituary of Kane, which appeared in the *CJ* in 1871, was substantially based on information supplied by her father. 'Sir Daniel wrote to him in Ottawa in the spring of 1871 asking for some material for his sketch of Paul Kane. Of the substance to be found in the few hastily written, disjointed pages, which were found crumpled up and forgotten at the back of a drawer, much was incorporated in Sir Daniel's articles [*sic*], and there is little that is new to be drawn from them.'

35 'Shores of Lake Superior. Ancient and Modern,' *Canadian Illustrated News* (Hamilton) 2 (13 June 1863): 52.

36 Ibid.

37 See Stacey, 'Frances Anne Hopkins and the Canoe-Eye-View.'

38 EUL, Special Collections, La.IV.17, no. 6, Wilson to David Laing, 8 September 1855.

39 W.A. Langton, 'Sir Daniel Wilson as an Artist,' 183.

40 Miner, *G.A. Reid: Canadian Artist*, 19. Miner continues: 'A portrait sketch of Reid done by Langton that winter shows him bent over his task, and, although at this time Reid was nearly twenty, he looked much younger than that. Langton playfully ascribed to it the title: "A chiel amang us takkin' notes."' This study, Miner's footnote informs us, 'was reproduced with an article on art schools in a Montreal magazine' (i.e., the *Canadian Illustrated News*). Langton kept it until, forty years later, with mock ceremony he presented it to Reid upon the latter's retirement from the Ontario College of Art in 1929.'

41 EUL, Special Collections, La. IV. 17, no. 6, Wilson to Laing, 8 September 1855.

42 Wilson, 'Pre-Aryan American Man' (1883), 39.

43 Cursiter, *Scottish Art*, 91.

44 Redgrave, *A Dictionary of the English School*, 476.

45 Robson, *Canadian Landscape Painters*, 40.

46 L. Harris, foreword, in *Catalogue: Group of Seven Exhibition of Paintings*.

'A Long and Happy Life':
Daniel Wilson with Family and Friends

ELIZABETH HULSE

When Daniel Wilson set out for Toronto in August 1853, he left behind in Edinburgh his wife, Margaret, and two young daughters, Jessie Eleanor, born in 1843, and Janie Sybil, three years younger.[1] Together with his mother, bachelor uncle Peter Wilson, and unmarried brother and sister, George and Jessie, they had recently moved to Elm Cottage. This pair of attached houses in Gothic-revival style had been built by Uncle Peter on part of the former Whitehouse estate in the area now known as the Grange. Daniel had chosen the name 'on account of the elm trees beside it,'[2] and he may also have helped to design the houses.[3] Throughout his life, he would 'continue to lament the cosy and picturesque Elm Cottage and to long for some change of fortune which might enable him again to occupy his half of the joint establishment.'[4]

For the family in Elm Cottage, Wilson kept a journal about his adventures in the New World that he forwarded home.[5] After arriving at Philadelphia, where he stayed for several days, he travelled to Albany, New York, and then on to Rochester. On route he narrowly escaped serious injury when his train was hit by another while it was standing in the station at Oneida. He had just returned to his seat after taking a cup of coffee when

> crash! the whole carriage was a heap of ruins. I was jammed in between two seats, both my legs wedged in, while shrieks, groans, and cries for help resounded amid the most frightful confusion ... My legs were caught below the knee and fixed between the seats which were driven together ... I saw at once that both my legs must be broken in another second, and seizing hold of a brass rail which runs along the inside of the carriage for light luggage, I

took advantage of the recoil of the carriage before it returned with a second crash, and swinging myself up I held on there by my hands clear of the danger; while the poor fellow who sat next me, and who appeared to have lost all presence of mind, had both his legs broken.[6]

Arriving at Rochester, Wilson discovered that the boat for Toronto had already left. Reluctantly, he took the train via Niagara Falls and earned the admiration of Canadian colleagues by successfully demanding compensation from the railway company.

Toronto, when Wilson arrived there in 1853, was

a busy, bustling, active town of nearly 40,000 inhabitants, and bearing such evident marks of rapid increase that I should not wonder if ten years hence it be found to number nearer an hundred thousand. Its public buildings are creditable and really handsome. Some of them would be regarded as great ornaments to the city, if erected in Edinburgh instead of this new-born city ... Everything indicates wealth and prosperity. As to the shops, many of them are equal to the best in Edinburgh, and if a person has only money, he need want for nothing here that he desires ... Along with this, however, there are many indications of the new growth of the place: streets half-formed and unpaved, foot-paving of wood, plank roads, – i.e., the middle of the road laid with wooden planks, instead of stone or macadamization, &c, &c.[7]

Some New World habits amused him. 'It is quite the settled custom here for the gentlemen to do the marketing. It excites no surprise to see a clergyman with a basket on his arm, pricing the butter and eggs for breakfast! ... This is the continent for ladies, they have it all their own way.'[8]

By early 1854 Wilson's wife and daughters were looking forward to joining him. In March, Jessie wrote to George about the two girls, 'It was touching to see how they both cling to the thought of going to papa.'[9] Daniel travelled to New York in May to meet them, and after an anxious wait of several days when the ship failed to arrive on schedule, he was reunited with his family. He was able to report that he had returned to Toronto 'with Wife and Bairns all hale and sound.'[10] Two boxes of household effects were on their way from Leith by way of Montreal.

Having spent his first months in lodgings, Wilson had found a house on Bloor Street at the northern limits of the city, 'about as far from the City of Toronto as Elm Cottage is from Princes Street.'[11] His was the most easterly of eight cottages, collectively called Abbotsford Place, which had been built a few years earlier on the south side of Bloor just east of St

Paul's (Anglican) Church, Yorkville, then a small wooden structure. Two of the other cottages were occupied by professors at University College, Edward Chapman and Henry Croft, both Wilson's good friends, and the most westerly one by the Reverend J.G.D. Mackenzie, the incumbent of St Paul's. Other neighbours in the 1850s included Jacob Hirschfelder, professor of Oriental languages at the college, James Beaven, who taught metaphysics and ethics, and William Agar Adamson, chaplain and librarian to the Legislative Council. Later, John Langton, vice-chancellor of the University of Toronto and father of Wilson's future biographer H.H. Langton, lived nearby.[12] 'In those days there were but a few scattered cottages on the north side of the street, and from his house Wilson looked into the ravine and over it to the woods beyond. At the top of Sherbourne Street on the edge of the ravine there stood then an old blockhouse, built originally for defence against hostile Indians who might be approaching Toronto from the Don Valley by way of the subsidiary ravine.'[13] In this congenial setting the Wilsons would live until the early 1880s.

Some twenty-three years after Daniel Wilson had arrived in the city, the *Weekly Globe* could report: 'Few forms are more familiar to the people of Toronto than that of Prof. Wilson, owing partly to his activity in social life and movements, and partly to his frequent appearances in one capacity or another on public platforms during a residence of nearly quarter of a century in our midst. During that time he has helped to educate many generations of students who are now engaged in one part of the Province or another in professional pursuits. The kindly recollections ... cherished by those who were once members of his class, his frequent visits to different localities in search of scientific facts or for the purpose of delivering lectures, and his unwearied assiduity with pen and pencil have conspired to make his name a household word.'[14]

In 1865 Wilson had become president of the Toronto branch of the Young Men's Christian Association, a position he held for five years. After its establishment in 1853, the Toronto YMCA had had an uneven existence in its first decade. It was then reorganized and by 1867 had a total membership of 337.[15] With its evangelical emphasis in the early years and its focus on young people, this association would have had a strong appeal for Wilson. In 1873, with his encouragement, a branch of the YMCA was established at University College, and by 1886 it had its own building on a site provided by the university. Wilson regularly addressed meetings of this group, and it supplied a student teacher for another of his philanthropic interests, the Newsboys' Lodging, and members organized games, read stories, and sang songs to the boys.[16]

Wilson had not lost the impulse to private charity that he had learned as a child in Edinburgh. Langton observes, 'Many entries in his journal testify to his generosity even when he suspected, or more than suspected, that the applicant was undeserving.'[17] Other than those that Langton himself quotes, these entries have not survived, but one from 1884 ends with a revealing comment. 'N—— sends me pawn-ticket. He has pawned his watch and dress-coat and wishes me to retrieve them. The last of many demands was to borrow $6. He does not even hint at the word "borrow" having any such significance as "repay" attached to it. A shiftless Bohemian ... Eheu! for here too is Mr. —— to whom I have promised the "loan" of a hundred dollars. He tells me he will repay it in two years. I was once poor myself.'[18]

Since the 1850s Wilson had been active in the affairs of the Church of England in Toronto, serving as a delegate to the diocesan synod, first from St Paul's, Yorkville, and then from St James' Cathedral. At the synod of 1860 he had presented a report on the lack of religious instruction in prisons and reformatories. Evidently this was an ongoing concern of his. Nearly twenty years later, he lectured to some three hundred convicts at the central prison. The governor, Captain Prince, had restricted him to a 'purely secular lecture.' Wilson 'took him and them by guile.' He talked to the inmates about the Danish sculptor Bertel Thorvaldsen, 'a humbly born boy, the son of a poor carpenter, who by ability and diligence won his way to honour, rank and admiration.' Wilson had seen Thorvaldsen's work in the Frue Kirke at Copenhagen the year before and 'was able to make its magnificent colossal figure of Christ in benediction, its twelve Apostles, St. Paul, St. Peter, the doubting Thomas, etc., pegs on which to hang naturally words with a deeper meaning, that might possibly, with God's blessing, reach some poor darkened soul, and give them a motive to try for higher – nay, for highest, things.'[19]

But as the profile in the *Weekly Globe* noted, of all the charities to which Daniel Wilson gave time and money, 'the institution in which he takes probably the deepest interest, and of which he may be justly proud,' was the Newsboys' Lodging and Industrial Home. This shelter had been established in 1869 to provide for 'a class of vagrant boys frequenting the streets of Toronto, earning a precarious subsistence by means which neither tend to develop industrious habits, nor lead to any useful training for after life.'[20] It had grown out of discussion about street children at the diocesan synod the year before. When representation to the Toronto Board of School Trustees by a committee of synod was rejected, a public meeting was held in December 1868. 'Professor Wilson proposed to procure a House, in which vagrant children could be taken care of by a women [*sic*] employed for the purpose.'[21]

For the sum of ten cents, the boys received three tickets, which entitled them to supper, bed, and breakfast. A small additional fee covered laundry. They were encouraged to deposit their surplus earnings in a savings bank, and at their own suggestion a 'mutual aid fund' was set up to lend money to destitute boys. The home also provided 'instruction and innocent occupation for their leisure hours.' Ultimately, it was hoped that permanent employment would be found for them. Wilson served as deputy chairman of the managing committee and for the rest of his life contributed in other ways to keep the home going. 'Whenever funds ran low or some special emergency arose he was ready to give a public lecture or to organize some other form of entertainment in aid of it.'[22] In 1887, for example, he lectured on 'America before Columbus' and brought in $196.75 for the cause. Four years later, at the age of seventy-five, he was still labouring to raise money. He recorded in his journal, 'A weary day. Started out collecting for the Newsboys. From morning to 3 p.m. toiled at uncongenial work. Got $60, and after a cup of coffee at a restaurant spent another two hours at the Board of Trustees.'[23]

While Wilson's interests in Toronto widened, his family circle had narrowed. Although his brother George's health had been precarious for many years, his death in 1859 at the age of forty-one must have devastated Daniel. Since early childhood, George had been his dearly loved friend and companion. After Daniel moved to Toronto, his brother had written every week about his scientific interests and his advancing career, as well as about family affairs. Following George's death, Daniel gathered his brother's letters and other family documents into a large volume titled 'Leaves from the Vanished Years,' and on the title-page, under a photograph of George, he wrote lines from Cowper's poem *The Task*:

> I had a brother once –
> Peace to the memory of a man of worth,
> A man of letters, and of manners too!
> Of manners sweet as Virtue always wears
> When gay Good-nature dressed her in smiles.
> He graced a College, in which order yet
> Was sacred; and was honour'd, loved, and wept,
> By more than one, themselves conspicuous there.[24]

And to a memoir of George written by their sister Jessie, Daniel contributed his recollections of their childhood together.

Four years after George's death, accompanied by his daughter Sybil, Daniel Wilson made an extended trip to Britain and Europe, his first visit home since he had settled in Toronto. It would be the last time he saw his mother. The following year, Jessie had the painful responsibility of reporting the deaths, first in January, of Uncle Peter and then, in August, of Janet Aitken Wilson, the remarkable woman who had been such a formative influence on her children. Among those who had admired Mrs Wilson was Daniel's second cousin, the novelist Margaret Oliphant. The link between Cousin Maggie, as George had called her, and the Wilsons had been reinforced in 1852 when her older brother, Francis (Frank) Wilson, had married Daniel's youngest sister, Jeanie. In an article titled 'Recollections of Mrs. Oliphant,' published in the 1950s, Jessie's daughter, Georgina Sime, gave an account of the disaster that eventually overtook this marriage. Already living beyond his means, Frank faced a financial crisis when a note that he had signed for a friend as guarantee for a substantial sum of money was about to come due. He 'borrowed' the amount from the bank where he had worked for a quarter-century, intending to repay it out of his salary. But he was found out before he could do so, and he fled to his sister at Windsor. She hid him from the police, helped him to get out of the country, and then settled the account.

Recent biographies of Margaret Oliphant tell a somewhat different story. According to Merryn Williams, Frank Wilson had for several years suffered from 'a nervous illness which made his hands shake badly.' This condition, his sister believed, also affected his mind, and as a result he lost his job. She 'agreed to pay his bills and over the next few months tried to find another job for him.'[25] Whatever the explanation, he and Jeanie and their two younger children went to live in France. He subsequently obtained a position with a company building a railway in Hungary. In 1870, while they were resident there, Jeanie died suddenly of a fever. Frank, a 'broken man,' returned to England to live with his sister, and according to Sime, he 'never attempted to pull himself together again.'[26]

Responsibility for their four children, Francis (Frank) and Jeanie Helen (Nelly), who had been living with Margaret Oliphant, and the younger daughters, Margaret (Madge) and Janet (Denny), fell principally on her. Daniel Wilson provided money for Frank's education and eventually adopted Nelly, who came to live in Toronto in 1880.[27] Oliphant brought up the two younger girls. They were only the last of a long line of relatives whom she was forced to support by her writing. In 1873, in reply to a letter from Wilson, she acknowledged: 'I do, as you remark, write a great deal too much; and it is impossible that I can do myself justice. But the circumstances in which I am placed leave me no alternative. I have made a sacrifice of my hopes of literary reputation; and while I try to do the best I can, I am obliged to consider the necessities of living, and keeping up under the great burdens thrown upon me rather than anything more solid.' And Wilson comments, 'Very hard, and very sad; but if all that she has done for husband, brothers, sisters, sons, and orphan nephews and nieces were blazoned forth, there would be no lack of an enviable reputation.'[28]

In March 1869 the congregation of St James' Cathedral, Toronto, had voted its special thanks to Wilson 'for the stand taken by him in defence of the Evangelical Principles of the Church of England at the last Provincial Synod.'[29] For many years the Anglican diocese of Toronto had been caught up in the reverberations of the Oxford Movement. Soon after his arrival in 1853, Wilson had met Henry James Grasett, the rector of St James'. Unlike many of the clergy in the diocese, but like most of the laity, Grasett had a low-church orientation. 'He is very pleasant,' Wilson told his family, 'and I fully believe a pious Christian minister. He is a liberal man, too, in matters of Bible and Missionary Societies, from which the High Churchmen here as elsewhere stand aloof.'[30] Wilson had evidently attended St Paul's, Yorkville, in the 1850s, but he later became a member of St James', perhaps attracted by Grasett's outlook on church matters, which was much akin to his own.

At meetings of the diocesan and provincial synods, the issues of ritualism, habitual confession, and the real presence of Christ in the Eucharist, as well as the growing aspirations of the laity against the authority of the bishop and the clergy, were fought out. For Wilson, as for others in the diocese, any movement towards doctrines and practices associated with the Roman Catholic Church was a betrayal of the Reformation. The controversies over lay rights concerned 'university education, patronage, the oversight of diocesan officials, the stewardship of mission funds, and the training of the clergy.'[31] A particular target of the low-church party was Trinity College, the institution founded in 1851 by Bishop John Strachan after the secularization of the University of Toronto. Evangelical Anglicans accused the college and its provost and sole professor of theology, George Whitaker, of teaching students to disown the Reformation.

In 1873, after the high-church party had prevented the election of any evangelicals to the provincial synod or the executive committee of the diocese, a number of prominent evangelicals founded the Church Association of the Diocese of Toronto to promote their position. William Henry Draper, chief justice of the Court of Error and Appeal for Ontario, was chosen president, and Grasett, Samuel Hume Blake, a lawyer and the vice-chancellor of the province, and Wilson were vice-presidents. On 15 August Wilson wrote to an unidentified correspondent, 'We completed matters, after a late sederunt last night, by the above four waiting on the Bishop [Strachan's successor, Alexander Neil Bethune] this morning as a deputation to ask him to become patron of the Association! Poor old gentleman, he was in a terrible fix. He did not wish to say yes; yet he did not dare to say no; so it gave me an opportunity of telling him in very respectful form some very wholesome truths about Church matters. We left our Constitution in his hands, and he will have to write us his reasons, if he declines, as I presume he will.'[32] Grasett and ten other clergymen were later charged with depraving the government and discipline of the church for their involvement in this organization. The charges against the ten were dropped, and Grasett was eventually exonerated when it was determined that he had transgressed no canon law. A cartoon in the comic paper *Grip* in February 1875 shows Wilson lecturing on 'The Martyrs of the "Reformation."' He has just completed a sketch of Grasett tied to the stake by 'church discipline.' The Anglican and Catholic bishops of Toronto confer in the background.

The Church Association founded its own paper, the *Evangelical Churchman*, in 1876. The following year it succeeded in establishing an alternative to Trinity College for the training of the clergy. The Protestant Episcopal Divinity School opened on 1 October in the schoolhouse of St James' Cathedral with ten students under the direction of James Paterson Sheraton. Bishop Bethune announced that he would not ordain any graduates from the school nor would he license Sheraton. However, with the support of a number of prominent citizens, the school, eventually called Wycliffe College, prospered. A building was erected in 1882, and three years later Wycliffe became affiliated with the University of Toronto, enabling students from University College to take its courses. It became a federated college of the university in 1889 and two years later moved to its present location on Hoskin Avenue. Wilson served on the college's Board of Management or Council from 1879 until his death. A resolution in the Council's minutes records that 'throughout his life he contributed generously to [the college's] support and manifested an unflagging interest in its welfare.'[33]

The evangelical party achieved perhaps its greatest success with the election of Arthur Sweatman as bishop of Toronto in 1879, following the death of Bethune. Wilson was a lay delegate to the special meeting of synod that wrestled for five days without producing a candidate with the required number of clerical and lay votes. Finally, after some negotiations between the leaders on each side, a compromise candidate was put forward. On 5 March Wilson recorded in his journal, 'This evening the election of the Ven. Archdeacon Sweatman as Bishop of Toronto, after a prolonged contest, in which I took an intense interest. From Thursday 27th February, when the Synod met on to Monday 19th [i.e., 20 March] ballots were taken, in the attempt to force Provost Whitaker, the representative of High Church clerical absolutism, on the laity. But the lay delegates stuck manfully together, the spirit manifested by them was excellent throughout. We could not carry Dr. Sullivan; but our hope is that in Mr. Sweatman God has given us in answer to many prayers the man of His choice.'[34] Though the new bishop identified himself with the evangelical position on ritualism, confession, and the Eucharist, he was tolerant of differing opinion. Peace descended on the diocese, and as part of the compromise the Church Association was disbanded.

The same year that Wycliffe College had been founded, the low-church bishop of Huron, Isaac Hellmuth, offered Daniel Wilson the headship of a new university with an Anglican theological faculty (the future University of Western Ontario) at London. Wilson would be provost and vice-chancellor at a salary of $3,000, with a residence. Out of courtesy to the bishop, Wilson agreed to consider the offer, but he already knew his position: 'I do not believe in Denominational Colleges other than theological. Orthodox science is generally another name for shallow bigotry.'[35] The next day he wrote to Hellmuth: 'I highly appreciate the great importance of the movement you have in view for the establishment of a university including a theological faculty of our own Church, thoroughly evangelical in its teaching and exercising a high-toned Christian influence over the whole training of the College ... But ... I have no doubt on this point, that I am not the man under whose guidance success is to be looked for.'[36] As Averill and Keith have noted in their article on Wilson and the University of Toronto earlier in this volume, the letter is an eloquent statement of his strongly held belief in non-sectarian education.

The year 1877 had been an eventful one in other ways for Wilson. In March he learned that his elder daughter, Eleanor, had died in Jersey. Some six years earlier she had married Lieutenant John Charles Bell of Edinburgh, who had served in Canada with the 53rd Regiment of Foot.[37] Although her father had been concerned about the unsettled life that she would lead as the wife of an army officer, the match at first seemed propitious. His sister Jessie told him, 'You will become richer instead of poorer, when you find yourself the father of such a son.'[38] Something seems to have occurred, however, to turn Wilson against his son-in-law; possibly Bell mistreated Eleanor. On 28 July 1874 she gave birth to a son, Oswald George Wilson Bell, in Toronto.[39] But some eighteen months later she and her small son left the city for Britain. She lived first at Aldershot, where she was occasionally able to see her aunt Jessie, now resident in London. In 1876 her husband's regiment was transferred to Jersey; Eleanor soon after suffered a miscarriage. Then early the next year she developed pleurisy. Jessie was summoned to her bedside, but arrived too late to see her niece alive.

In the second of two long letters to her brother, Jessie wrote, 'I can imagine you ready now to vent on [Bell] all the indignation, which years of anguish caused by him has roused. I pray God you may be enabled to resist such a temptation. It cannot help her *now*, & I really believe he is not quite accountable for his actions. His eyes have a strange expression from which you involuntarily turn away.'[40] H.H. Langton notes that on 17 March, when Wilson received the news of his daughter's death, he merely recorded the fact in his journal and inserted her last letter to him. 'There are no further entries for a month, until he notes the arrival from Scotland of proofs of his *Reminiscences of Old Edinburgh*, and adds "how weary, stale and unprofitable it seems to me now," by contrast with the pleasure with which he had read it in manuscript, chapter by chapter as it was written, to the fireside audience which included the daughter he had lost.'[41]

Of all Wilson's inner circle it is his wife, Margaret (Maggie), who remains indistinct to us. Almost no letters between them survive, and very few from her to anyone else. Evidently she shared his interest in philanthropy: for many years she headed the ladies' committee of the newsboys' home. Langton says that she 'supplied just that element of caution and carefulness in the management of this world's goods which her husband lacked, and her calm, equable temperament balanced and corrected his enthusiasm and impetuosity.'[42] That she was the 'lodestar'[43] of his life is evident from occasional references in his journal and letters, but his reserve, or that of his biographer, has left her in the shadows. A month after she died suddenly in 1885, Wilson wrote to his niece Denny, 'She was indeed most loving and loveable; and the home she made so bright and happy for me is left very desolate.'[44] For the tombstone that he would eventually share with his wife he chose the Latin epigram *Dulcissimae margaritae margaritae uxorum*, together with a bunch of marguerites carved in stone and the lines 'Erected by Daniel Wilson in loving memory of Margaret, the wife of his youth and the sunshine of a long and happy life.'[45]

We do not know what he recorded in his diary at her death, but on 19 November 1887 he commented, 'Just two years ago on this day I laid my loved one in her last earthly resting-place, and the Saturday thereafter completed the three lectures on Browning for the same object [the news-boys' home]. The previous Saturday she was there among my auditors.'[46] Langton observes, 'Those who were present at the third lecture thus alluded to, which was faithfully delivered on the Saturday after Mrs. Wilson's death, will remember the changed appearance of the lecturer, his haggard face, weak voice and hesitating movements, all testifying to the severity of the blow that had fallen on him.'[47] The historian George M. Wrong, too, remembered Wilson's courage in delivering this lecture. 'He would do his duty, even though his cherished world was falling to pieces.'[48]

What Margaret had meant to her husband is perhaps best revealed in his comments on the home life of others. After his schoolfellow George Brown, now a prominent newspaper publisher and politician in Toronto, had been shot in March 1880, Wilson observed, 'My poor friend Mrs. Brown looks the picture of calm despair, very self-possessed, but all the deeper in her sorrow. How inexpressibly sad to see a happy wedded union thus abruptly broken by such a cause.'[49] A biography of Darwin suggested a comparison in Wilson's mind with Carlyle 'in all his domestic and social relations.' Darwin was 'gentle, kindly, considerate, and lovingly self-sacrificing in all his relations with wife, children, servants, and friends ... Darwin had children – sons and daughters – who grew up to cheer his hearth, sympathize with his work and engage the true womanly sympathies of their mother in healthful home-life – a terrible want in the Chelsea home.'[50]

After Margaret's death, Wilson's surviving daughter, Sybil, became his principal companion. She too shared his interest in the newsboys' home and other charities. When she was seriously ill in December 1878, he recorded that friends and admirers had been 'unbounded in their kindness.' 'They would literally lay all at our feet. The dear pet is so loved and does she not deserve it? Her shop-girls, her Sunday School pupils, the hospital patients, and some of the poor little news-boys – it is so touching at times. For the sympathy is so unmistakeably genuine, and the desire to be allowed to do something so manifest.'[51] After Wilson's death, Sybil would become head deaconess for the Anglican church in Canada and turn over the family home to this work. When he became president of University College in 1880, Wilson had been provided with a residence, rented by the university, on the east side of St George Street backing on the college grounds. But by 1888 he and his daughter and niece had moved to a house on the west side of the street at the corner of Russell, to which he gave the playful name 'Bencosie.'[52] It was to be his home for the remaining years of his life.

Daniel Wilson had first visited the White Mountains of New Hampshire in the summer of 1881. How he came to vacation in this area is not known, but its attraction for him is very evident. Except for the years 1885 and 1891, when he visited Britain, and 1884, when he holidayed in the Adirondacks, he would return to New Hampshire every summer for the rest of his life.[53] The discovery of the region seems to have revived his love of painting, which had apparently been dormant since the holiday he took in Muskoka in 1870. 'His chief occupation during the summer vacation was sketching. He used to walk and sketch indefatigably ... As a rule he produced two [watercolour sketches] a day during those holiday excursions, one on his morning walk, the other in the late afternoon. But often, from the testimony of his daughter, his constant companion on these walks and herself an artist, he would have completed his sketch before hers was half done, and then turning to another point of view would dash off a second before she had finished her first.'[54]

In a letter to one of his nieces, Wilson describes the first of these holidays. 'Sybil & I had a famous time of it, last August, among the White Mountains of New Hampshire; where we sketched almost daily, and walked about from morning till night. Sybil is a famous walker, she walked one day twenty one miles. We got astray in search of a road home by another track; but she was not a bit the worse for it. Nelly walks very well to [sic]; and joined us in some of our long rambles, though she does not sketch. American ladies do not walk. Some of them thought we were crazed to go walking about as we did, when we might hire a carriage, but others who sat in their rocking chairs and physiced themselves all evening, had sense enough to feel a little envy when they saw Sybil and Nelly come home in best of spirits ready to enjoy a hearty tea, or abundance of warm milk and corn-cake.'[55]

Returning from a holiday in New Hampshire in 1887, Wilson learned of the death of his friend William Nelson. 'Sudden, I imagine, but the harsh abruptness of telegraphic communication comes with cruel brevity. I was just about to reply to a long letter which reached me while in the New Hampshire highlands and which I could not answer till I got back to my books. He was my oldest and dearest surviving friend, and such a friend! No brother could be truer.'[56] After he had settled in Canada in 1853, Wilson had maintained links with many colleagues whom he had known in Scotland, among them the antiquarian David Laing, the artist

George Harvey, to whom he dedicated his biography of Chatterton, and
Alexander Macmillan, who published most of his major works from 1862
on. The ethnologist Horatio Hale recorded after Wilson's death, 'He
shone as a correspondent. Few idle men kept up so large a correspondence as this extremely busy one. His letters, frank, cordial, sympathetic,
full of lively touches, apt suggestions, and pleasant reminiscences, were
highly prized by all who were favored with them ... The fortunes of his
friends were always in his mind. Nothing of joy or sorrow could happen
to one of them without eliciting from him a letter of sympathy, which
exactly fitted the need.'[57] A lifelong collector of photographs, Wilson
requested portraits from his correspondents. As he told his niece Denny
in 1883, 'A photo is a capital missive at all times. It tells better than a score
of letters, how you are looking.'[58]

Among the many friends Wilson made in Canada was the American
writer on women's issues Caroline Healey Dall, whom he got to know when
her husband was the Unitarian minister in Toronto in the 1850s. Entries in
her journals provide a wonderful picture of Wilson reading aloud to family
and friends – Scott's *Antiquary*, the poetry of William Dunbar, and William
Edmonstoune Aytoun's newly published *Firmilian: A Spasmodic Tragedy*.[59]
After Dall left Toronto in 1854, she and Wilson carried on a regular correspondence until the end of his life.[60] He and his wife stayed with her at her
home at Medford near Boston when he delivered a series of lectures at the
Lowell Institute in December 1863, and she evidently returned to Toronto
from time to time. Wilson's letters to this intelligent woman reveal the
frank, lively quality that Hale says characterized his correspondence. After
his death, Caroline Dall wrote a fine tribute to this 'lovely man' in the journal of the American Social Science Association.[61]

But of all his friends, none was as close as the Edinburgh-born publisher William Nelson, whom he had known since early boyhood. Among
the interests they shared was the history of their native city (for Nelson's
involvement in the conservation of its buildings, see also the essay by Ash,
Cruft, and Hulse in this volume). The links between the two had been
reinforced in 1862, when Nelson's sister Anne married George Brown.[62]
William Nelson and his wife visited Toronto in 1870 in the course of an
extended trip across North America. 'At Toronto attractions of a different, but not less acceptable, kind awaited him. He started for the backwoods, and fished in Lake Muskoka with his old school-mate for his
guide.'[63] On their return to the city, 'a party of the fellow-students of early
years met at dinner' under Wilson's roof: Sir Andrew Ramsay of the British Geographical Survey, in Canada on a visit, Alexander Sprunt, who had

come from North Carolina to place his son in the University of Toronto, George Brown, David Christie, speaker of the Canadian Senate, and Professor George Paxton Young. After an interval of more than forty years, they recalled memories of school and college together. Nelson wrote to his sister, 'You may imagine with what delight I met so many of my old school-fellows, and how we did talk over the days of auld lang syne!'[64]

Eight years later, in the summer of 1878, Nelson accompanied Wilson on a trip to Scandinavia, 'starting at a few hours' notice with that indifference to elaborate preparation so characteristic of him as a traveller.'[65] In the summer of 1880 the two friends spent some weeks at Philiphaugh, in the valley of the Yarrow, famous as the scene of Montrose's final battle. Their last holiday together was in 1885. Nelson wrote to say that he had taken Glen Feochan, six miles from Oban. 'How delightful it would be if you and Mrs. W. and Janie would come over and pay us a visit at this Highland home.'[66] Wilson commented in his journal, 'Would it not! I feel strongly tempted. But this weary University confederation plot, I much fear, bars the way.'[67] He and his wife and daughter did, however, spend part of the summer at Glen Feochan. From this house in the West Highlands, the friends made expeditions to places of historic interest, including Iona, Glencoe, Loch Etive, and Eilean Naoimh.

Three months after Nelson's death, his widow asked Wilson to write a memoir of her husband; this, he said, 'I shall willingly do if I can recover incidents to give life to it. But a mere piece of eulogy, however sincere, if expanded into a memoir is a poor tribute to the memory of a good man, as dear William most assuredly was. It is only for private circulation. But shall I be able to satisfy the ideal of my dear friend Mrs. N. as a memorial of her husband?'[68] The memoir, which appeared in 1889, is a tribute to their friendship. From his own memories, as well as those of acquaintances, Wilson recreated their boyhood and schooldays together. The accounts of Nelson's travels and summer vacations also draw largely on experiences that the two men had enjoyed together. The small volume was, as Wilson put it, 'the laurel and the cypress laid together on the grave of a generous and loved old friend.'[69]

Writing to his niece Denny in 1885, Wilson invented a characteristic *jeu d'esprit* for her and her sister Madge, who was studying wood engraving. He imagined a publication to which they would all contribute. 'In the press, and shortly to be published Reminiscences of a Returned Exile, by Dan. Wilson, A.B.C: X.Y.Z. &c. Illustrated by the celebrated artists Margaret Oliphant & Denny Wilson, members of the Royal Academies of Art of Florence, Bologna, Parma, Venice; A.R.A; R.S.A., X.Y.Z. &c. &c. &c. With an appendix & supplementary illustrations by the distinguished Canadian Artist J. Sybil Wilson. Wilsons for Ever!!!'[70]

Though he would visit Scotland that year and again in 1891, Wilson never became a 'returned exile.' But he continued to keep up his Scottish antiquarian interests, as the record of his published work demonstrates. One of the most precious artefacts of medieval Scotland, the coigrich, or crozier, of St Fillan, said to have been in the tent of Robert the Bruce on the eve of Bannockburn, had been brought to Canada early in the nineteenth century by its hereditary keeper, John Dewar. Wilson had been aware of its whereabouts before he arrived in Toronto. Its migration to Canada is mentioned in *Prehistoric Annals of Scotland*, and in 1852 the Canadian politician Malcolm Cameron had written to the Society of Antiquaries of Scotland proposing to sell the relic for £420 sterling. It had already been offered to Lord Elgin, then governor of the Province of Canada, but 'the parties could not agree.'[71] In 1858 Wilson told David Laing, 'Since I came to Canada I have made repeated attempts to get sight of the "*Quigrich*" of St. Fillan, of which you know; and now at length have it lying before me ... It is a most beautiful and massive relic, and one which it is lamentable to think should be any where, out of Scotland. You have nothing in the Museum, – not even *the Maiden*,[72] – to compare with it in historic interest; and its beauty as a work of art will compare with anything in the R.I. Academy at Dublin.'[73]

Wilson tried to raise money among Scots in Canada to purchase the crozier, without success. In fact, it would be nearly twenty years before he achieved his dream of returning it to Scotland. In December 1876 he received a draft for £100 from John Stuart, one of the secretaries of the Society of Antiquaries. As he noted in his journal, 'I have had the fine old Bannockburn relic in view for years. £500. sterling was the least sum named for it at starting. Now I hope to secure it for $500 ... I have been in dread lest Barnum should hear of it. If he only knew its history the relic would have been secured by him long ago. If once I had it I shall be anxious till it is safe in Scotland.'[74] On 8 January Wilson recorded that he had drawn a cheque for $500 in favour of Archibald Dewar and now had 'the choice national relic in my custody, preparatory to its restoration to Scotland after an interval of 59 years.'[75] The crozier was dispatched on 24 January 1877 ('May Atlantic gales be propitious'), and on 22 February Wilson received confirmation that it was 'once more safe in Scotland, which relieves me of an anxiety I could not repress ... Well, it is something to have accomplished this, if no more, for dear Auld Scotland.'[76]

Wilson holidayed in New Hampshire in the summer of 1888, but there are no known paintings from that year and only a few from 1887. The probable reason is suggested by an entry in his journal in October 1888. 'After having consulted both Dr. Reeve and Dr. Ryerson about my failing vision, saw Dr. Burnham to-day and learned from him what I have suspected for some time; that cataract is forming on my eyes, and that inevitable blindness awaits me before long, unless the happy release comes before to dismiss me to that land where there is no more night.'[77] The following month he again saw Dr Reeve. 'It is beyond question that the sight of my right eye is gone. If I close my left eye I "see men as trees walking," that is really all, and the left eye, I fear, is going the same way, at what rate the doctor will be able to say somewhere about Christmas. He talks with pleasant composure about gouging out my eyes, by an operation that in a certain number of cases succeeds.'[78]

At that point Wilson 'abandoned hope of further literary work. Beyond the sense of light, the sight of my right eye is totally gone. I cannot, with the help of the strongest magnifying glass, distinguish a letter in large print. The other eye is impeded, with motes and opaque streaks.'[79] But by the following April he realized that he could much more easily write than read. The 'old temptation of authorship besets me, in spite of seemingly hopeless impediments, and to-day I set my pen to the first lines of an oft-imagined project: "America before Columbus." What of history had this so-called New World? Is there an Old World in the New? Perhaps my old eyes – or rather the half of an eye that is left, will allow me to work out this problem in some very impartial way at least. At any rate I note here that on this Saturday morning I have made a beginning.'[80]

Indeed, in May 1891 he was able to record in his journal that, despite many demands on his time, he had that winter, in addition to rewriting notes for lectures lost in the fire that had destroyed University College in February 1890, 'prepared for the press and read all the proofs of my "Right Hand: Lefthandedness"; prepared also for the press my "Ethnographic Studies," or by whatever other name I shall call my collected "Glimpses of an Old World in the New."'[81] That summer he and Sybil set off for Britain. They stayed with Margaret Oliphant and the nieces at Windsor, and while in the south of England, Wilson had the great pleasure of paying several visits to Tennyson, whose work he had long admired, at the poet's summer home at Aldworth. He and Sybil then travelled to Edinburgh, where on 20 August he received the honour that he undoubtedly valued the most, 'the freedom of my dear old native city.'[82] He also sat for the triple portrait by George Reid, a fitting image, as Wrong later remarked, for a 'many-sided' individual.[83]

Another distinction had been accepted only reluctantly after a long struggle. In June 1888 he had received a telegram from the prime minister, Sir John A. Macdonald, informing him that he was to receive a knighthood. He immediately replied 'declining the rank of Knight Bachelor, as a slight upon letters and science when men who have attained to eminence in political life are admitted to one or other of the Orders of Knighthood.'[84] The honour had already been announced, however, and his attempts to refuse it became more and more embarrassing, particularly when he learned that he had been proposed by the outgoing governor general, Lord Lansdowne. Wilson 'thought for a moment of accepting, rather than wound his feelings; but I cannot overcome my repugnance to such a sham knighthood as the mere Bachelor title amounts to, and so I shall adhere to my first resolution. And in truth knighthood in any form could only be a trouble to me. Were it worth having at all, it comes too late, but truly the title of President is more honour by far.'[85]

Lansdowne appealed to Wilson personally, urging him not to decline an honour that he had exerted himself to obtain, and Wilson repeated to him his view that the rank was insulting to Canadian letters and science. The matter was still unresolved when he returned from New Hampshire at the beginning of September. But an option to refuse the knighthood was soon taken out of his hands. The new governor general, Lord Stanley, visited the University of Toronto on 11 September, and in his reply to the 'loyal address from the Faculty and graduates,' he congratulated Wilson and the university 'on the dignity conferred by Her Majesty. To persist in any further refusal would be liable to misinterpretation in a way very displeasing to me; so I give in, and here I am knighted after all.'[86] A week later Wilson told a friend, 'To a jolly old bumble-bee the process of feeding on honey and being smothered in rose leaves is probably the ideal of happiness; but to a wingless biped like myself a little goes a long way. And what are most covetable honors, now that my Maggie is gone?'[87]

After his return from Britain in 1891, Daniel Wilson had one last year before him, but it would be a difficult struggle. A 'wretched day of chill rain' spent inspecting the new library building 'was the origin of what ended in congestion of the lungs, and nearly made an end of me. A fortnight is oblivion to me. Then came a time when I realized my condition, on the verge of the dark river ... It was with a sense of regret that I realized some faint return of strength and thought that I had all the hard journey to retrace.'[88] In June that year, after a talk with 'my good friend Dr. Hoskin,' he began to think that he should resign 'if I can make reasonable terms for retiring. Eyesight fails me sadly. Health at present is very

unsatisfactory, but that, I hope, my holiday in the mountains may set right
... My plans are provisional. When I get back from the mountains in September I shall be able to come to a determinate conclusion.'[89]

But four days later Wilson wrote out his resignation from the presidency. Then it was as if, having let go of the reins, he had nothing more
to live for. 'He seems to have taken to his bed within a day or two, because
Miss Wilson notes that on July 4, on waking, she hurried to find out how
he was ... On July 27, after an unconsciousness of many days, he recovered
possession of his faculties, spoke to his daughter, asked if he was dying,
and specified the men he wanted to be his pall-bearers. He also gave
directions about the as yet uncorrected proofs of the new edition of his
"Atlantis," and added "Tell Mr. Douglas to be sure to make an index" ...
He gave directions also as to the inscription on the monument in his family plot. On August 5 he was up in his chair for an hour, but weak and
wandering. His last conscious words that evening were to the nurse: "He
will never leave me nor forsake me."'[90] Wilson died the following afternoon; he was seventy-six.

Daniel Wilson's temperament – impetuous, quick to anger, full of enthusiasm for whatever interested him – can be read between the lines of his
journal and the few personal letters that survive. H.H. Langton, who
knew him well, says that he had 'an irascible disposition.' One of Wilson's
sisters 'has related that her brother in his younger days was given to gusts
of temper, and that she remembers him in one of these passionate out-
breaks slashing and destroying an engraving plate on which he was at
work. But on the first visit he paid to Scotland from Canada ... the family
were struck by the complete self-control to which he had schooled himself. This absolute mastery of his temper henceforward never failed him.
When a sentiment or argument offended or displeased him he could
manifest a certain lofty and dignified disapproval, but he rarely condescended to angry words. His expression of scorn on these occasions is
suggested in the middle head of Sir George Reid's triple portrait ... But
although in public and in conversation he restrained his natural irascibil-
ity he seems to have indulged himself to some extent in vehement language when writing his journal.'[91]

But in 'private circles,' Langton relates, Wilson 'was noted for his enjoyment of fun of all kinds and his readiness to joke and laugh with the
youngest of his friends. He could find opportunity also for witticisms in
the most formal gatherings; the writer remembers more than one occasion on which the dignity of a Senate meeting was upset by his irrepress-

ible sallies. Even in his journal he cannot resist some humorous comment or allusion.'[92] 'Those who had the privilege of knowing him in his private life remember chiefly his warmth of heart, his overflowing humour and gaiety, and his old-fashioned gallantry and politeness.'[93]

NOTES

1 When Wilson's daughters were children, they were known by their first names, Jessie and Jane (Janie). Later they used their more distinctive second names, Eleanor and Sybil, respectively, although they were sometimes still called Jessie or Janie by family members and close friends.

2 J.A. Wilson, *George Wilson*, 398.

3 The Wilsons are first listed as living at Elm Cottage in the Edinburgh city directory for 1853–4. I am grateful to the present owners of Elm Cottage West, Sheena and Alasdair MacDonald, for their kindness in showing the house to Margaret Mackay and myself in November 1992.

4 H.H. Langton, *Sir Daniel Wilson*, 49. After Peter Wilson's death in 1864, Daniel inherited the property, and although he transferred the title to Jessie the following year, he always hoped to retire there. Information about the ownership of the house was provided by the Edinburgh solicitors Scott Moncrieff & Dove Lockhart, WS, in a letter to Marinell Ash dated 27 January 1987.

5 The early part of Wilson's journal, which survives as typed extracts made by H.H. Langton, consists of two passages from a journal dated September 1853 interspersed and followed by letters from 1853–4 (see UTA, B65-0014/004(01), 1–19). In correspondence from his family now in the Valentine collection in Scotland, there are references as late as 1856 to a journal written for the family at home. George in September 1855 informs his brother, 'Your letters to me & Uncle & the latter half of the Journal came together, jumbling us a little concerning the relative Geographical Positions of Simcoe & the Saults' (Valentine collection, Letterbook, George Wilson to Daniel Wilson, 28 September 1855). The following May, Jessie asks, 'Has the Journal No 2 ever been acknowledged? If not, I may report the general approval of the household, from Uncle downwards, of its contents' (Jessie Wilson to Daniel Wilson, 22 May 1856).

6 UTA, B65-0014/004(01), 4 (19 September 1853).

7 Ibid., 6–7 (21 September 1853).

8 Ibid., 12 (12 November 1853).

9 Valentine collection, Letterbook, Jessie Wilson to George Wilson, 31 March 1854.

10 Ibid., Peter Wilson to Daniel Wilson, 26 May 1854.

11 UTA, B65-0014/004(01), 13 (25 November 1853).

12 For a description of this community at about the time the Wilsons settled there, see Henderson, 'Bloor Street, Toronto, and the Village of Yorkville in 1849.' Information about its residents comes from this article and the Toronto directory for 1856.

13 H.H. Langton, *Sir Daniel Wilson*, 68. Wilson's house was still standing in the 1920s when Langton wrote his memoir.

14 *Weekly Globe*, 3 March 1876; copy in AO, F 1084, series VIII.

15 A history of the organization is provided in Ross, *The Y.M.C.A. in Canada*.

16 University College YMCA, *Annual Report ... 1888–89*; Ross, *The Y.M.C.A. in Canada*, 115, 118.

17 H.H. Langton, *Sir Daniel Wilson*, 188.

18 Ibid., 188–9.

19 UTA, B65-0014/004(01), 48 (10 November 1879).

20 Newsboys' Lodging and Industrial Home, *First Report* (1870), 7.

21 Hodgins, 20: 274; reprinted from the *Globe*.

22 H.H. Langton, *Sir Daniel Wilson*, 189–90.

23 Ibid., 190.

24 This volume is now in the Valentine collection. It has been cited as 'Valentine collection, Letterbook,' in the notes to this article. A number of the letters are reproduced in Jessie's memoir of George.

25 M. Williams, *Margaret Oliphant*, 91. Williams had access to family papers, but she does not appear to have seen the article by Sime. See also Jay, *Mrs Oliphant*.

26 Sime, 'Recollections of Mrs. Oliphant,' 42.

27 M. Williams, in *Margaret Oliphant*, 99, states that Jessie Sime, Daniel's sister, 'did the absolute minimum. She had reluctantly taken the eldest girl, Nelly, but made it clear that she expected her to get a job as soon as possible.' As a result, relations between the Wilsons and Margaret Oliphant were cool. Sime, in 'Recollections of Mrs. Oliphant,' 26, agrees that her mother and Oliphant did not get on, but ascribes the friction to a difference in temperament. Letters between Daniel Wilson and Margaret Oliphant quoted in his journal and the fact that he visited with her during trips to Britain in 1880 and 1891 suggest a more cordial relationship. According to Williams, Nelly 'had grown up to be very eccentric and failed to find work as a governess' (115). Possibly the household in Toronto was more congenial. Wilson writing to her sister Denny in 1885 says that Nelly 'is most kind and anxious to do all she can' for Sybil after the death of her mother (NLS, MS 23203, f107, Wilson to Denny Wilson, 21 December 1885). Nelly would later assist Sybil with her work as an Anglican deaconess.

28 UTA, B65-0014/004(01), 30 (31 March 1873).

29 Valentine collection, Extract from minute book, St James' Cathedral, 29 March 1869.

30 UTA, B65-0014/004(01), 14 (25 November 1853).

31 Hayes, 'The Struggle for the Rights of the Laity,' 14.

32 UTA, B65-0014/004(01), 31 (15 August 1873).

33 Wycliffe College Archives, Wycliffe College Council, Minutes, 17 November 1892.

34 UTA, B65-0014/004(01), 45 (5 March 1879).

35 Ibid., 38 (4 May 1877).

36 Ibid.

37 Bell, who was a nephew of Wilson's old friend and fellow antiquarian the novelist David Macbeth Moir, had been born in 1839. He joined the regiment as an ensign in 1857 and served in the Indian Mutiny of 1858–9, for which he was mentioned in dispatches and received a medal. Between 1866 and 1869 his regiment was stationed in Canada, first in Ontario and then at Quebec City. In October of the latter year it was transferred to the West Indies. When or where Eleanor met Bell is not known, but they were married on 1 December 1870, probably in Toronto. From June that year he had been on half pay. In 1875 he joined the 47th Foot, but he returned to half pay three years later. I am grateful to Stuart Sutherland for tracing Bell's military career in *Hart's Army List* and other sources. See also MHS, Caroline Healey Dall Papers, Wilson to Dall, 12 November 1870.

38 Valentine collection, Jessie Wilson Sime to Daniel Wilson, 29 January 1870.

39 Soon after their marriage, the couple had taken a house on Church Street; but Bell is not listed in the Toronto directories after 1872, and Eleanor may have been living at her parents' home when her son was born. See also the reference below to her being in the 'fireside audience' for Wilson's reading of his manuscript for *Reminiscences of Old Edinburgh*.

40 Valentine collection, Jessie Wilson Sime to Daniel Wilson, 6 March 1877.

41 H.H. Langton, *Sir Daniel Wilson*, 192–3; these entries do not appear in the typed transcript that Langton made from the journal. In 1953 he told Stewart Wallace, 'Much of the diary was taken up with the domestic troubles of his daughter Jessie, and these of course I omitted' (UTA, B65–0014/003(01), Langton to Wallace, 13 June 1953).

Wilson seems to have had very little contact with his only grandchild after his daughter's death, possibly because of the antagonism that had developed between him and the child's father. In 1883 he told his niece Denny, 'I got recently from Edinburgh one [photograph] of my little grandson, which shows his dear mother's face in her little orphan boy; and is precious to us all beyond measure' (NLS, MS 23203, f56, Wilson to Denny Wilson, 10 March 1883). When, in 1891, Wilson and his daughter Sybil were planning a visit to Britain, she told Lady Margaret Dawson, 'As to dear Oswald, it would be a terrible disappointment again to be prevented seeing him, he is 16 now, we have scarcely heard a word about him, since last in England, when we were not allowed to see him. I wish you would ask if it is God's will, we might see him this time. I never speak of him to anyone, so this is only for you' (MUA, Acc. 976, Sybil Wilson to Lady Dawson, 24 March [1891]). Whether they saw young Oswald during this, Wilson's last, visit to Britain is unknown, but he dedicated his study *The Right Hand: Left-Handedness*, published that year, to his grandson, who was also left-handed (see MHS, Caroline Healey Dall Papers, Journals, entry for 13 June 1892).

Oswald died unmarried on 5 December 1902 in the sanatorium at Kingussie, Scotland. He is buried with his parents in the Dean cemetery, Edinburgh. His father survived him by seven years, dying in 1909 at the age of seventy (information from the gravestone and from Oswald's death record at the New Register House, Edinburgh).

42 H.H. Langton, *Sir Daniel Wilson*, 36–7.

43 UTA, B65-0014/004(02), 156 (25 May 1889).

44 NLS, MS 23203, f107, Wilson to Denny Wilson, 21 December 1885.

45 Wrong, 'Sir Daniel Wilson,' 152. The lines in English are also preserved with a letter that Wilson wrote to Caroline Healey Dall on 27 November 1885 (MHS, Caroline Healey Dall Papers). Margaret and Daniel Wilson are buried in St James' Cemetery, Toronto, but the inscription on her side of the tall Celtic cross is all but illegible, and his is partly so.

46 H.H. Langton, *Sir Daniel Wilson*, 195.

47 Ibid.

48 Wrong, 'Daniel Wilson,' 153.

49 UTA, B65-0014/004(01), 50 (23 May 1880).

50 UTA, B65-0014(02), 127 (13 January 1888).

51 UTA, B65-0014(01), 44 (28 December 1878).

52 This word, with its echoes of both a Highland place name (from the Gaelic *beinn*, mountain) and a cosy wee 'but and ben' in Lowland parlance, was probably one of Wilson's characteristic puns.

53 H.H. Langton, *Sir Daniel Wilson*, 108. This statement is partly confirmed by surviving watercolours and by entries in his journal. However, there are no paintings or any references in the journal to visits in 1882 or 1890.

54 H.H. Langton, *Sir Daniel Wilson*, 108.

55 NLS, MS 23203, f51, Wilson to Denny Wilson, 23 January 1882.

56 H.H. Langton, *Sir Daniel Wilson*, 205.

57 Hale, 'Sketch of Sir Daniel Wilson,' 265.

58 NLS, MS 23203, f56, Wilson to Denny Wilson, 10 March 1883. Wilson's interest in photography may first have been stimulated by his friendship with the Edinburgh artist and photographer David Octavius Hill in the 1840s. See also the preceding essay by Robert Stacey in this volume.

59 MHS, Caroline Healey Dall Papers, Journals; see especially the entries for 29 August, 19 September, and 7 October 1854.

60 Wilson's letters to Caroline Healey Dall are preserved in her papers at the Massachusetts Historical Society. I am grateful to librarian Peter Drummey and reference librarian Jennifer Tolpa for making copies of the letters and journal entries available to me and to director William M. Fowler Jr for allowing me to refer to the material; also to Professor Helen R. Deese of Tennessee Technological University, Cookeville, for providing me with a list of Wilson letters and references in the journals.

61 Dall, 'Sir Daniel Wilson.'

62 As well as attending the Royal High School of Edinburgh together, Brown and Wilson shared an interest in the anti-slavery movement, and the two young men had served as stewards for a soirée in honour of abolitionist George Thompson when he returned to Edinburgh from the United States in 1836 (see Stouffer, *The Light of Nature and the Law of God*, 30). In Toronto they were again drawn together by mutual interests (see the essay by Averill and Keith in this volume).

63 Wilson, *William Nelson* (1889), 142.

64 Ibid., 143.

65 Ibid., 157. It was during this trip that Wilson observed the work of the sculptor Thorvaldsen in the Frue Kirke at Copenhagen, which inspired his talk to prison inmates in 1879.

66 UTA, B65-0014/004(01), 94 (1 June 1885). In the transcript of Wilson's journal, the place is given as 'Glen Groshan,' but this is probably a misreading of his handwriting. It is clear from the account of this holiday in *William Nelson* (1889) that the reference is to Glen Feochan.

67 UTA, B65-0014/004(01), 94 (1 June 1885).

68 H.H. Langton, *Sir Daniel Wilson*, 206.

69 UTA, B65-0014/004(02), 177 (2 January 1890).

70 NLS, MS 23203, f95, Wilson to Denny Wilson, 22 January 1885.

71 Valentine collection, Malcolm Cameron to the president or secretary of the Society of Antiquaries of Scotland, 31 August 1852.

72 The Maiden is a guillotine dating from the sixteenth century that was used for executions.

73 EUL, Special Collections, La.IV.17, no. 7, Wilson to David Laing, 21 June 1858.

74 UTA, B65-0014/004(01), 36 (5 December 1876).

75 Ibid., 36 (8 January 1877).

76 Ibid., 37 (22 February 1877).

77 UTA, B65-0014/004(02), 141–2 (15 October 1888).

78 Ibid., 142 (3 November 1888).

79 Ibid., 151 (13 April 1889).

80 Ibid.

81 Ibid., 191 (16 May 1891). Langton says that it was Wilson's lifelong habit to have a book or article 'on the stocks' at all times and to break off in mid-sentence in order to pick up the train of thought when he resumed writing. 'Another principle of his was to abandon writing when ideas or words did not come quickly, and take a walk in the fresh air' (H.H. Langton, *Sir Daniel Wilson*, 230).

82 UTA, B65-0014/004(01), 198 (17 August 1891).

83 Wrong, 'Sir Daniel Wilson,' 159.

84 UTA, B65-0014/004(02), 133 (2 June 1888).

85 Ibid., 135 (5 June 1888).

86 Ibid., 140 (11 September 1888).

87 Hale, 'Sketch of Sir Daniel Wilson,' 262. The recipient of the letter is not identified but may have been Hale himself.

88 H.H. Langton, *Sir Daniel Wilson*, 221.

89 UTA, B65-0014/004(02), 210 (25 June 1892).

90 Ibid., 211. Part of a lengthy note added at the end of Wilson's journal, presumably by H.H. Langton.

91 H.H. Langton, *Sir Daniel Wilson*, 121.

92 Ibid., 190.

93 Ibid., 234.

Appendix:
A Chronology of Daniel Wilson's Life

1816 – (3 January) born in Edinburgh
1820 – begins school; later attends the Royal High School of Edinburgh
1831 – becomes a pupil of engraver William Miller
1837 – (autumn) goes to London to work as an engraver
1840 – (28 October) marries Margaret Mackay in Glasgow
1841 – (9 October) birth of daughter Anne Eliza (d. August 1842)
1842 – returns to Edinburgh; sets up in business as an artists' colour-man and print-seller; works as a miscellaneous writer
1843 – (2 June) birth of daughter Jessie Eleanor
1846 – (23 February) elected fellow of the Society of Antiquaries of Scotland
     – (18 March) birth of daughter Jane Sybil
1846–7 – *Memorials of Edinburgh in the Olden Time* published in parts
1847 – (30 November) elected one of the secretaries of the SAS
1848 – sells his shop; an unsuccessful candidate for the position of keeper of the Faculty of Advocates library
1849 – *Synopsis of the Museum of the Society of Antiquaries of Scotland* published
1851 – *The Archaeology and Prehistoric Annals of Scotland* published; a candidate for the chair in history and English literature at University College, Toronto
     – (8 November) receives an LLD from the University of St Andrews
1853 – appointed to the chair at Toronto; (late August) leaves for Canada via Philadelphia
1854 – offered the principalship of McGill College in Montreal

- (May) wife, Margaret, and children arrive in Toronto
1855 – (July) trip to Lake Superior and Mackinaw
1856 – (summer) visits the Ohio valley to view the prehistoric earth-works
1857 – establishes the first regular course of instruction in an anthropological discipline in English
1859 – (22 November) death of brother George
1860 – appears before the select committee of the Legislative Assembly inquiring into the management of the University of Toronto
1861 – (July or August) hopes to obtain the chair in history at St Andrews
1862 – *Prehistoric Man* published
    – (December) visits Washington and Civil War battle sites in Virginia
1863 – an unsuccessful candidate for the chair in English literature at Edinburgh
    – (summer) in Britain and Europe with daughter Sybil
1864 – (6 August) death of his mother, Janet Aitken Wilson
1865 – (August) an applicant for the chair in rhetoric and belles-lettres at Edinburgh
1866 – (July–August) trip to Thunder Bay and the Nipigon and Kaministiquia rivers
1869 – *Chatterton: A Biographical Study* published; helps to found the Newsboys' Lodging and Industrial Home
1870 – (23 April) death of his sister Jeanie in Hungary
    – (August) trip on the Muskoka and Severn rivers with Thomas Galt and William Nelson
1873 – *Caliban: The Missing Link* published
    – (August) helps to found the Church Association of the Diocese of Toronto
1874 – (summer) visits Native sites in Ohio and Kentucky
    – (28 July) birth of grandson, Oswald George Wilson Bell, in Toronto
1875 – (June) declines the post of minister of public instruction for Ontario
1877 – (1 March) death of daughter Eleanor in Saint Helier, Jersey
    – (3 May) declines the headship of the proposed Church of England college at London, Ontario (later the University of Western Ontario)

1878   – *Reminiscences of Old Edinburgh* published
       – (summer) in Scotland, Denmark, Sweden, and Norway with William Nelson

1879   – (February–March) a delegate to the diocesan synod at which the evangelical party forces the election of a compromise candidate to succeed Bishop Alexander Neil Bethune

1880   – (5 June) leaves for Britain not expecting to return; (29 July) receives a cable announcing his appointment as president of University College effective 1 October
       – (August) holidays with William Nelson and family at Philiphaugh in the Scottish borders

1881   – (August) holidays in the White Mountains, New Hampshire, for the first time
       – (October) an unsuccessful candidate for the post of historiographer royal of Scotland

1885   – becomes president of the Royal Society of Canada
       – (summer) holidays with William Nelson and family in the Scottish highlands
       – (16 November) death of wife, Margaret

1888   – (11 September) forced to accept a knighthood when he is publicly congratulated by Lord Stanley
       – (October) cataracts diagnosed

1889   – (26 April) receives commission as president of the University of Toronto

1890   – (14 February) University College gutted by fire; oversees the rebuilding of the college and the restoration of the library
       – (23 June) appointed president of the University of Toronto

1891   – (20 August) receives the freedom of the city of Edinburgh

1892   – (29 June) resigns from the university presidency
       – (6 August) dies in Toronto

Bibliography

Manuscript and Archival Sources

Note: Not included in this list are locations for Daniel Wilson's watercolours; the public institutions with major collections are the Art Gallery of Ontario, the Edinburgh University Library, the National Archives of Canada, the National Gallery of Canada, and the University of Toronto Archives.

CANADA

Archives of Ontario, Toronto
F 2, series B-12, Edward Blake Papers
    Letters to Blake
F 3, series 2, Oliver Mowat Family Papers
    Letter to Jane Ewart Mowat, 5 June 1888
F 775, Miscellaneous Collection
    Letter to George Kennedy, 7 November 1887
F 980, series B-1, Henry John Cody Papers
    Student diary, 1885–9
F 1084, Sir Daniel Wilson Papers
    Notes, draft, and other material for a planned biography of Wilson by Andrew Frederick Hunter
RG 2-29-1, Education Department
    Letters to George W. Ross, minister of education, 1882–92
RG 22, Court Records, series 155, no. 9242
    Estate file for Wilson

Art Gallery of Ontario Archives, Toronto
A3.9.2, Correspondence
   Correspondence with Jessie Georgina Sime and others regarding the exhibition and sale of watercolours by Wilson in 1920–4; list of watercolours, with purchasers' names

McGill University Archives, Montreal
Acc. 927, John William Dawson Papers
   Letters to Dawson, 1858–92
Acc. 976, Dawson Family Papers
   Letters from Margaret Mackay Wilson and Jane Sybil Wilson to Lady Dawson
   [undated]
(Photocopies in UTA, B84-0033)

National Archives of Canada, Ottawa
MG 24, B40, George Brown Papers
   Letters to George and Anne Nelson Brown, 1860–80
MG 24, D16, Buchanan Papers, Correspondence
   Letter to W. Mackay (possibly Wilson's wife's brother), Messrs Buchanan,
   Harris & Co., 1863
MG 26, A, Sir John A. Macdonald Papers
   Correspondence regarding Wilson's knighthood, 1888; donations after the
   University College fire, 24 March 1890
MG 27, I B4, Marquis of Lorne Papers, Correspondence
   Letter to Lorne, 14 April 1890
MG 29, B1, Sir Sandford Fleming Papers
   Letters to Fleming, 1873–92
MG 29, B18, Henry Scadding
   Letters to Scadding, 1877 and 1879, regarding papers to be published or
   delivered to the Canadian Institute
MG 29, D48, Gustave Delapierre, Belgian diplomat, London
   Letter to Delapierre, 21 October 1875
MG 29, D72, James Macpherson Lemoine Papers
   Letter, 1 March 1882, inviting Lemoine to become member of the English
   literature section of the RSC
MG 29, D98, Charles Belford Correspondence
   Letter to Belford, 19 July 1860
RG 5, C1, vol. 375, Canada West, Provincial Secretariat, Correspondence Register,
   1853, University of Toronto

Letters and printed testimonials in support of Wilson's application for the chair of history and English literature at the University of Toronto, 1851–2

Private Collection, Fort Langley, BC
Jessie Georgina Sime, Untitled memoir

Private Collection, Toronto
William Houston, Letter books, 1884–92
    Copies of letters from Houston to Wilson regarding the admission of women to the University of Toronto

Royal Ontario Museum, Toronto
'My Poor Relations' [c. 1881]
    Photograph album presented to the Ethnological Museum, University College, October 1892, by Sybil Wilson; now in the Dept of Ethnology, ROM
Maude Allan Cassels, 'Paul Kane,' unpublished typescript in the Dept of Ethnology

Thomas Fisher Rare Book Library, University of Toronto, Toronto
General MSS
    Letter to Rev. M. MacDougal, 30 May 1884
MS Collection 1, Sir Byron Edmund Walker Papers
    Walker to Wilson, 2 April 1890 (copy)
MS Collection 36, George Mackinnon Wrong Papers
    Letter to J.K. Kerr, 1 March 1876; to editor of *Varsity*, undated; outline of lectures in medieval history
MS Collection 47, Henry Sproatt Collection
    Letters from Francis Assikinack, 11 May 1858; W.M. Wilson, 21 July 1860; Oronhyatekha, 20 February 1864; W. Proudfoot, 24 December 1890
MS Collection 61, Charles Mason Papers
    Letter from Charles Mason, 19 June 1891; with manuscript copy of Le Roman de Rou, by Robert Wace, transcribed by Mason
MS Collection 193, Royal Canadian Institute Papers
    Early records, 1849–93; council minutes, 1852, 1861, 1887–1908; regular meetings, minutes, 1849–94
Daniel Wilson, *An Auld Prophecie bot Doubte be Merlyne* (1849)
    Letter to Lord Napier and Ettrick, 4 February 1892, tipped in

Toronto Reference Library, Toronto
S65, Sir Daniel Wilson Collection
    Scrapbooks, 1847–91: 1, Archaeological, 1847–53; 2, Ethnological; 3–4,

Memorials of Edinburgh (1848), interleaved copy; 5, *Memorials of Edinburgh* (1848), page proofs with notes and sketches; 6, Engravings and drawings of Edinburgh scenes. Robert Chambers, *Traditions of Edinburgh* (1825; Wilson's interleaved copy with manuscript notes and sketches). Society of Antiquaries of Scotland, *Synopsis of the Museum of the Society of Antiquaries of Scotland* (1849; Wilson's interleaved copy with holograph notes)

University College Archives, University of Toronto, Toronto
Tea service presented to Wilson by the Society of Antiquaries of Scotland, 1852; patent of knighthood, 1888; casket and burgess ticket presented to Wilson on the occasion of his being given the freedom of the city of Edinburgh, 20 August 1891; name plate from 73 St George Street, his former residence

University of Guelph Library, Guelph
XS1MSA100, Sir Daniel Wilson Collection
  Letters to Professor Thomson, Aberdeen, regarding a new edition of Stuart's *Caledonia Romana*, 1842, 1852

University of Toronto Archives, Toronto
A68-0004, University of Toronto, Senate, Library Committee, Minute book, 1890–1920
A69-0011, University College, Literary and Scientific Society, Minute books, 1860–82
A69-0016, University College, Council, Minutes
A70-0005, University of Toronto, Senate, Minutes, 1850–87, 1890–2
A70-0024, University of Toronto, Board of Governors
  /008–009, Board of Management/Trustees, Minute books, no. 1–6, 1878–92
  /053–058, Orders-in-Council and Government Letters, 1850–90
A73-0026/517(99), University of Toronto, Department of Graduate Records
  Clippings relating to Wilson, photographs, convocation address, etc.
A78-1217, Office of the President, 1893, Sir Daniel Wilson Memorial
  Printed circular
B65–0014, John Langton Family
  H.H. Langton, 'Some reminiscences'; 'Letters and journals of Sir Daniel Wilson' [excepts]; Notes by John Langton, 9 March 1956, omitted from *Early Days in Upper Canada*
  The typed transcript of excerpts from Wilson's letters and journal (B65-0014/004) was deposited in the University of Toronto Library by H.H. Langton on 5 October 1927. From the original journal, to which he had access, he omitted nearly all references to Wilson's personal life, and there are no entries between

1854 and 1873. However, he had used the journal for his *Sir Daniel Wilson: A Memoir* (1929), which includes entries not in the transcript. As well, any references critical of Sir William Mulock, who was chancellor at the time, were omitted from the memoir. After Langton had used the journal, he returned it to a niece of Wilson's, according to a note that he wrote to Stewart Wallace in 1953; unfortunately, he does not say which niece, and the present whereabouts of the journal, if it still exists, is unknown. According to Langton, Wilson had directed his daughter to destroy his papers. However, a small collection of personal papers is now in the possession of the Valentine family in Scotland (see below).

B65-0034/001, William Nesbitt Ponton
Lecture notes, 1873

B72-0013/001, Edward Blake

B72-0031, James Loudon
Letters to G.W. Ross regarding the university residence; 'Memoirs of James Loudon'

B73-1124, William E. Lingelback
'Reminiscences and autobiographical notes (Feb. 24, 1948)' (manuscript prepared for the American Philosophical Society)

B76-0020, William James Loudon
Notes for and manuscript of a biography of William Mulock

B80-0033/001, Bessie M. Scott Lewis
Student diary, 1889–91

B83-1234, Hugh Hornby Langton
'The Student Strike of 1895' (manuscript)

B83-1253, Hugh Hornby Langton
Letter from George Reid to Langton, 24 April 1909, regarding his portrait of Wilson

B83-1256, Daniel Wilson
Letter from Julius Rossin to Wilson, 20 November 1889, regarding a scholarship in German

B83-1285, Daniel Wilson
Letters to William Oldright, 24 April 1871; Teresa Vanderburgh, 25 September 1883, Walter Berwick, 20 November 1891; miscellaneous manuscript items

B84-0033, Marinell Ash
Photocopies of letters from Wilson in other institutions

B84-1079, Daniel Wilson
Letter to D. Beddoe, Clifton, 1868, regarding Wilson's projected work on Chatterton

B87-0056, Robert Bell
Letters to Bell, 1889

B88-0002, John George Hodgins
  'The University Question' (17 vols.)
B88-0009, W. Glenholme Falconbridge
  Notices and press clippings concerning activities of the Senate
B92-0030/009, Henry John Cunningham Ireton
  Correspondence from Wilson and others with James Loudon, 1875–90
B93-0022, Marinell Ash
  Photocopies of letters from Wilson in American institutions

Wycliffe College, University of Toronto, Toronto
Wycliffe College, Trustees and Board of Management, Minutes, 1879–92
Wycliffe College, Council, Minutes, 1883–92
Church Association scrapbook

UNITED STATES

American Antiquarian Society, Worcester, Mass.
American Antiquarian Society, Correspondence
  Letters to Ebenezer Torrey, S.F. Haven, and E.M. Burton, 1861–90
  Letters relating to Wilson's election as member of the society, contributions to
  its transactions(?), and Canadian publications for its library
(Photocopies in UTA, B93-0022)

American Philosophical Society Library, Philadelphia
American Philosophical Society Archives
  Nomination of Wilson as member, 1862; letters from Wilson to the society,
  1863–90
  Letters to J.C. Dent, R.W. Douglas, Professor Henry, and Henry Phillips, 1877–90
Franz Boas Papers
  Letters to Boas regarding his fieldwork on the northwest coast of Canada, spon-
  sored by the British Association for the Advancement of Science, 1889–91;
  drafts of replies from Boas
(Photocopies in UTA, B93–0022)

Harvard University Archives, Cambridge, Mass.
HUG 1717.2.1, Frederic Ward Putnam Papers
  Letters to Putnam, 1879–92
UAV 677.38, Peabody Museum, Director's Correspondence, 1879–92
  Letters to F.W. Putnam, 1875–92
(Photocopies in UTA, B93–0022)

Massachusetts Historical Society, Boston
Caroline Healey Dall Papers
    Caroline Healey Dall journals; letters from Wilson to Dall

Smithsonian Institution Archives, Washington, DC
RU 26, Office of the Secretary (Joseph Henry, Spencer F. Baird), 1863–79,
    Incoming Correspondence
    Letters to Henry, 1862–75
RU 31, Office of the Secretary (Samuel P. Langley), 1891–1906, Incoming
    Correspondence
    Copies of letters from Langley to Wilson [1892]
RU 33, Office of the Secretary (Henry, Baird, Langley), 1865–91, Outgoing
    Correspondence
    Copies of letters from Henry and Baird to Wilson, 1869–84
RU 52, Assistant Secretary (Spencer F. Baird), 1850–77, Incoming Correspon-
    dence
    Letter to R. Bell, 20 October 1876
RU 53, Assistance Secretary, 1850–77, Outgoing Correspondence
    Copies of letters from Baird to Wilson, 1858–64
RU 189, Assistant Secretary in Charge of the United States National Museum,
    1860–1908, Incoming Correspondence
    Letters to W.H. Dall, S.P. Langley, and A.T. Langley, April–May 1892, asking for
    help in replacing crania in the ethnological collection destroyed in the Univer-
    sity College fire
RU 7073, William H. Dall Papers, c. 1839–58, 1862–1927
    Letters to Dall, 1870–89
(Photocopies in UTA, B93–0022)

University of Rochester Library, Rochester, NY
Lewis Henry Morgan Papers
    Letters to Morgan, 1859–76
Henry Augustus Ward Papers
    Letter to Ward, 8 June 1886, asking about skulls
(Photocopies in UTA, B93–0022)

BRITAIN

British Library, London
Add. MS, 55124, Macmillan Papers, ff. 1–119b,
    Letters to Alexander Macmillan

Edinburgh University Library (Special Collections), Edinburgh
Dk.6.23/1, Francis Jeffrey MSS
  Letters from Jeffrey to George Wilson
La.IV.17, David Laing MSS
  Letters to Laing, 1845–77; draft of a letter from Laing to Wilson
1/6080–3, Sir Charles Lyell MSS
  Letters to Lyell

National Library of Scotland, Edinburgh
Acc. 7314, Daniel Wilson to Geo. Seton [c. 1850]
Acc. 9213, W. and R. Chambers Papers
  Dep. 341/20, 341/315, 341/98, Letters to Robert Chambers; 341/30, Robert
  Chambers, diary; 341/291, 341/316–8, Authors' ledgers
MS 584, Watson Collection
  Letter to unknown, [185–]
MSS 1734–8, Edinburgh Castle
  Letters to Hippolyte Blanc and William Nelson, 1885–91, about the restoration
  of St Margaret's Chapel; drafts of letters from Blanc to Wilson
MS 1956, John Knox's House
  Papers collected by Wilson as secretary to the John Knox's House preservation
  committee, 1845–50
MSS 2623–9, Blackie Papers, Correspondence
  Letters to John Stuart Blackie, 1852–70
MS 3446, Lee Papers
  Letter from the Society of Antiquaries of Scotland to John Lee, 1848, regarding
  the reinterment of Mary of Gueldres
MS 5509, Liston Papers
  Letter to unknown, 1849
MS 8887, Small collections and single letters
  Letters to Albert Way, 1852–3
MSS 9393–401, John Hill Burton, Correspondence and Papers
  Letters to J. Hill Burton, 1848–78
MS 14303, Charles Rodgers, Letters
  Letter to Rodgers, 1852
MSS 23193–210, Margaret Oliphant Papers
  Letters from Wilson to his nieces, 'Madge' and 'Denny' Oliphant, 1882–5
  (MS 23203); other Wilson family letters

National Library of Wales, Aberystwyth
MS 5118D, Charles Roach Smith Papers
  List of Roman finds from Castlecary compiled by Wilson, 1840

National Museums of Scotland Library, Edinburgh
Society of Antiquaries of Scotland, Communications, 1842–52;
   Correspondence, 1844–55; Minute books, 1840–68; Visitors' books
   Includes letters to and from Wilson in his capacity as secretary of the SAS
The Daniel Wilson Scrapbooks
   Drawings, engravings, maps, and broadsheets relating to Edinburgh and Leith,
   presented to the SAS by Wilson in 1869

St Andrews University Library, St Andrews
University Muniments
   Letter to George Buist, rector, 11 November 1851, regarding the degree of LLD
   conferred on Wilson

Sheffield City Museum and Mappin Art Gallery, Sheffield
Bateman Papers
   Letter to Charles Roach Smith

Valentine Collection, Scotland
   Letterbook, 1859 (containing letters mostly from George and Jessie Wilson to
   Daniel Wilson, 1830–42, 1853–9, and miscellaneous family documents; some
   published in J.A. Wilson, *George Wilson*); letters to Wilson from other correspondents, 1851–90; diplomas and certificates from universities and learned societies, etc. [183–?-1890?]; photograph album of family and friends assembled by
   Wilson; portrait photograph of Wilson; clippings and miscellaneous ephemera

EUROPE

Nationalmuseet Archives, Copenhagen
Kongelige Nordiske Oldskriftselskab
   Record of the proposal of Wilson for membership, 11 November 1878
J.J.A. Worsaae Archiv
   Letters to Worsaae, 1849–66

Universitetet i Oslo, Oslo
P.A. Munch Papers
   Letters to Munch (published in Munch, *Lærde Brev fraa og til P.A. Munch*)

Published Works by Daniel Wilson

Notes: Entry is by publication date, except for lectures and papers in the transactions of societies, which are listed under the year in which the paper was deliv-

ered. Some presentations to the Society of Antiquaries of Scotland and the
Canadian Institute were published only as abstracts or third-person summaries in
those organizations' proceedings. They have been included in this bibliography
to provide a record of Wilson's activities. Offprints of journal articles have generally not been listed, but separate publication in pamphlet form has been noted
under the citation for the article.

Authorship for early anonymous work and for articles published anonymously
in the Toronto *Globe* in the 1870s is based on lists in Wilson's journal recorded in
1865 and 1872 (see UTA, B65–0014/004(01), 19–29). According to the first of
these entries, his earliest 'pen-work' included articles and poems published in
Tait's Edinburgh Magazine, Chambers's Journal, the *Scotsman,* and other serial publications. Only a few of these works have been identified. 'The Provost and the Coal
Bunker,' possibly clipped from the *Scotsman,* where it originally appeared, sur-vives
in Wilson's copy of *An Auld Prophecie* (1849), now in the TRL (it was reprinted in
Reminiscences of Old Edinburgh [1878], 2: 136–8). In his journal Wilson also lists
'The Bailies' Raid,' which was published in the *Scotsman* at about the same time.
This poem has not been located.

Halkett and Laing's *Dictionary of Anonymous and Pseudonymous English Literature*
gives Wilson as the author for *Saint Catherine of the Hopes; or, Marie of Roslyne: A Ballad, Historical, Romantic, and Traditionary,* by a Modern Minstrel (Haddington,
1847), but a presentation copy, now in the NLS, to D.O. Hill 'with the Minstrel's
Regards' from 'Batchelor's Hall,' 18 May 1867, makes such an attribution
unlikely.

* Items marked with an asterisk have not been seen.

[n.d.]
'Three pairs of slippers.' A mock-up, now in the TRL, possibly for publication as a
    pamphlet; apparently clipped from a newspaper or magazine.

1845
Review of *The First Reading of the Bible in Old St. Paul's* [engraving by R. Graves after
    Harvey]. In *British Quarterly Review* 2: 592. In his journal, Wilson lists 'George
    Harvey' as one of his contributions to the *British Quarterly Review.* This brief
    notice in November 1845 of the engraving after Harvey was followed in August
    1846 by a longer review, also unsigned, of *The Covenanter's Communion* and *The
    First Reading of the Bible in the Crypt of Old St Paul's;* see *British Quarterly Review* 4:
    251–9.

[1845?]
*Spring Wild Flowers. By Wil. D'Leina, Esq., of the Outer Temple. Edinburgh:
    P. Wilson. No known copies; reviewed in the *British Quarterly Review* 3 (February

1846): 264; described in the preface to the 2d ed. of 1875 and in Wilson's journal; see also under 1853.

1846

*Memorials of Edinburgh in the Olden Time. 2 vols. Edinburgh: H. Paton; sold by
G. Gallie, Glasgow. Issued in parts in 1846–7.

Reason and Instinct. Nelson's British Library, no. 2. London and Edinburgh: Thomas Nelson. This work and the others in the series are undated, but numbers 1
to 4 were reviewed in the British Quarterly Review in November 1846.

[1846?]

Tahiti and Its Missionaries. Nelson's British Library, no. 9. London and Edinburgh:
Thomas Nelson.

[1847?]

The Curate's Daughter. Nelson's British Library, no. 32. London and Edinburgh:
Thomas Nelson. Issued with The Sabbath Bell, a poem.

Henry Hudson: A Ballad. Nelson's British Library, no. 41, pp. 30–2. London and
Edinburgh: Thomas Nelson. Issued with The Only Son by an unidentified
author.

1847

Review of Modern Painters, vols. 1 and 2, by a graduate of Oxford [John Ruskin];
A Glossary of Terms Used in Grecian, Roman, Italian and Gothic Architecture, 4th ed.;
and A Companion to the Glossary of Architecture. In British Quarterly Review 5: 469–91.

1848

Memorials of Edinburgh in the Olden Time. 2 vols. Edinburgh: Hugh Paton; London:
Simpkin, Marshall & Co. Also published in a large paper edition; see The English
Catalogue of Books for 1835–63.

Oliver Cromwell and the Protectorate. [Nelson's British Library, New Series.] London
and Edinburgh: Thomas Nelson. Reprinted in 1849 and *1852 with minor revisions.

Testimonials in Favour of Mr. Daniel Wilson, One of the Secretaries of the Society of Antiquaries of Scotland ... [Edinburgh]. Candidate for the position of keeper at the
library of the Faculty of Advocates.

1849

'Ancient Implements of Popular Sports.' Chambers's Edinburgh Journal, n.s., 11:
139–40.

Ane Auld Prophecie, bot Doubte be Merlyne or Thomas of Erceldoune, Fundin under yᵉ
Altar-stane of yᵉ Quenyis College ... [Edinburgh] Imprented be Andrew Jack ...
Niddryes Wynd. Wilson's copy of this work (now in the TRL) is bound with The

Queen's Choir (1853), 'The Provost and the Coal Bunker' (presumably clipped from the *Scotsman,* where it first appeared), and views of Trinity College Church, portraits, and other illustrations. The manuscript title-page to the volume reads, 'Memorial of the Collegiate Church of the Holy Trinity fovnded at Edinbvrgh by Queen Mary de Gveldres A.D. MCCCCLXII. Demolished A.D. MDCCCXLVIII.'

'The Pilgrim Fathers.' In *History of the Puritans in England, and The Pilgrim Fathers,* by the Rev. W.H. Stowell and D. Wilson, 337–508. London: T. Nelson; New York: R. Carter and Brothers. Reprinted *1850, *1852, and *1888.

Synopsis of the Museum of the Society of Antiquaries of Scotland. Edinburgh: Printed for the Society. Wilson's interleaved, annotated copy is in the TRL.

'A Visit to the Scottish Antiquarian Museum: First Article' and 'Second Visit to the Antiquarian Museum.' *Chambers's Edinburgh Journal,* n.s., 11: 278–81, 328–31.

1850

'Inquiry into the Evidence of the Existence of Primitive Races in Scotland prior to the Celtae.' In *Report of the Twentieth Meeting of the British Association for the Advancement of Science, Held at Edinburgh in July and August 1850,* pt 2: 142–6. London, 1851.

'The Scottish Gael.' In *Authenticated Tartans of the Clans and Families of Scotland, Painted by Machinery,* 1–21. Mauchline: W. and A. Smith.

1851

'Anniversary Address.' *PSAS* 1: 2–7.

The Archæology and Prehistoric Annals of Scotland. Edinburgh: Sutherland and Knox; London: Simpkin, Marshall, and Co. and J.H. Parker.

'Arthur's Seat – An Apology.' *Tait's Edinburgh Magazine* 18: 667–8. Poem.

'The Dunvegan Cup.' *PSAS* 1: 8–9.

Guide through Edinburgh, with Pleasure Excursions in the Environs. Edinburgh: Black. Attributed to Wilson in Mitchell and Cash, *A Contribution to the Bibliography of Scottish Typography,* 1: 146.

'Iron Dagger, East Langton.' *PSAS* 1: 73–4. Quotes Wilson's account of the dagger's discovery from *The Archæaeology and Prehistoric Annals of Scotland,* 433.

'Primitive Scottish Bells.' *PSAS* 1: 18–22. Abstract.

Review of *The Roman Wall,* by J.C. Bruce. In *Chambers's Edinburgh Journal,* n.s., 15: 362–4.

Testimonials in Favour of Mr. Daniel Wilson ... [Edinburgh]. Candidate for the chair of history and English literature at the University of Toronto.

1852

'Bronze Matrix with Hebrew Inscription.' *PSAS* 1: 39–41.

'Notices of the History and Architectural Features of the Ancient Church of St Cuthbert at Coldingham.' *PSAS* 1: 84–5.

'On the Class of Stone Vessels Known in Scotland as Druidical Pateræ.' *PSAS* 1: 115–18.

'Roman Antiquities, Fifeshire.' *PSAS* 1: 60–6. Abstract.

'Roman Camp at Harburn.' *PSAS* 1: 58–9. Excavation report.

'St Margaret's Chapel, Edinburgh Castle.' *PSAS* 1: 70.

[1853?]

Modern Edinburgh. Monthly Volume, [no. 97]. London: The Religious Tract Society. This and the following title are listed under the series in *The English Catalogue of Books* for 1835–63, but without authorship. Wilson states in his journal that they were written in 1851. Approximate publication date is that given in *BLC.*

Old Edinburgh: A Historical Sketch of the Ancient Metropolis of Scotland. Monthly Volume, [no. 86]. London: The Religious Tract Society.

1853

'Archaeology.' In *Encyclopædia Britannica*, 8th ed. Edinburgh: A. and C. Black, 1853–60.

'Notice of Discoveries of "Celtic Pipes" in the Vicinity of Edinburgh; with Some Remarks on the Period to Which They Belong.' *PSAS* 1: 182. Abstract.

'Notice of the Recent Discovery of Several Fine Bronze Swords, and Other Bronze Relics, in Forfarshire.' *PSAS* 1: 181.

'On Some Suggestive Examples of Abortive Discovery in Ancient Art.' *PSAS* 1: 175–80. Abstract.

The Queen's Choir: A Revery in the Roslin Woods. [Edinburgh]. 'Thirty copies printed at the press of Thomas Nelson and Sons, Hope Park, July 1853.'

Spring Wild Flowers. By Wil. D'Leina, Esq. of the Outer Temple. London and Edinburgh: T. Nelson and Sons. Preface dated 29 January 1845; presumably a reprinting of the first edition (see under 1845?).

1854

'Remarks on Some Coincidences between the Primitive Antiquities of the Old and the New World.' *CJ* 2: 213–5.

'Remarks on the Intrusion of the Germanic Races on the Area of the Older Keltic Races of Europe.' *CJ* 2: 246–50. Reprinted in *ENPJ* in 1855.

1855

'Displacement and Extinction among the Primeval Races of Man.' *CJ*, n.s., 1: 4–12. Reprinted in *ENPJ* in 1856.

'Hints for the Formation of a Canadian Collection of Ancient Crania.' *CJ* 3: 345–7.

'Observations Suggested by Specimens of a Class of Conchological Relics of the Red Indian Tribes of Canada West.' *CJ* 3: 155–9.

'On the Intrusion of the Germanic Races into Europe.' *ENPJ*, n.s., 1: 33–47.

'Some Associations of the Canadian and English Maple.' *CJ* 3: 380–3.

'The Unity of the Human Race.' *CJ* 3: 229–31. Signed DW.

1856

'The Ancient Miners of Lake Superior.' *CJ*, n.s., 1: 225–37.

'Antiquities of the Copper Region of the North American Lakes.' *PSAS* 2: 203–12.

'Discovery of Indian Remains, County Norfolk, Canada West.' *CJ*, n.s., 1: 511–19.

'Displacement and Extinction among the Primeval Races of Man.' *ENPJ*, n.s., 4: 39–49.

'Ethnology and Archæology.' *CJ*, n.s., 1: 76–9.

'Ethnology and Archæology: Artificially Compressed Crania; America Peopled from Asia; Working of African Native Iron; Value of Natural History to the Archæologist.' *CJ*, n.s., 1: 189–92.

'Ethnology and Archæology: Crania of the Native Britons.' *CJ*, n.s., 1: 484–6.

'Ethnology and Archæology: Indian Remains; Sandwich Islanders.' *CJ*, n.s., 1: 554–7.

'Ethnology and Archæology: Peruvian Golden Shroud; Greek Slave of the Fifteenth Century; Indians of Guatemala.' *CJ*, n.s., 1: 391–2.

'Preliminary Address.' *CJ*, n.s., 1: 1–4. Introduction to the new series of the *CJ*.

Review of *Bothwell: A Poem in Six Parts*, by W. Edmonstoune Aytoun, and *Leaves of Grass* [by Walt Whitman]. In *CJ*, n.s., 1: 541–51.

Review of *Junius Discovered*, by Frederick Griffin. In *CJ*, n.s., 1: 58–63.

Review of *Letters from the United States, Cuba, and Canada*, by the Hon. Amelia M. Murray. In *CJ*, n.s., 1: 160–4.

Review of *Modern Geography, for the Use of Schools*, by Robert Anderson. In *CJ*, n.s., 1: 464–6.

Review of *Narrative of the Expedition of an American Squadron to the Chinese Seas and Japan ... under ... Commodore M.C. Perry*, by Francis L. Hawks. In *CJ*, n.s., 1: 523–8.

Review of *Notes on Central America ...*, by E.G. Squier. In *CJ*, n.s., 1: 359–77.

Review of *On the Course of Collegiate Education*, by J.W. Dawson; *The Progress of Educational Development*, by Henry P. Tappan; and *On the Advancement of Learning in Scotland*, by John Stuart Blackie. In *CJ*, n.s., 1: 168–86.

Review of *The Pilgrimage and Other Poems*, by the Earl of Ellesmere. In *CJ*, n.s., 1: 302–6.

Review of *The Song of Hiawatha*, by H.W. Longfellow. In *CJ*, n.s., 1: 48–53.

'The Southern Shores of Lake Superior.' *CJ*, n.s., 1: 344–56.

1857

*Class Book of Poetry Chronologically Arranged. Edinburgh and London: Nelson. Listed under Wilson's name in The English Catalogue of Books for 1835–63. The BLC lists 1852 and 1857 editions of a work entitled The Class Book of Poetry, published without authorship by the National Society.

'Narcotic Usages and Superstitions of the Old and New World.' CJ, n.s., 2: 233–64, 324–44.

'Notice of Some Indian Antiquities, as Compared with British in a Letter from Dr Daniel Wilson, Toronto, Upper Canada, to David Laing.' PSAS 2: 423–4.

Pipes and Tobacco: An Ethnographic Sketch. Toronto: Lovell and Gibson. 'Fifty copies printed.'

Review of The Canada Educational Directory and Calendar, for 1857–8 ..., edited by Thomas Hodgins. In CJ, n.s., 2: 207–8.

Review of Catalogue of Human Crania in the Collection of the Academy of Natural Sciences of Philadelphia ..., by J. Aitken Meigs. In CJ, n.s., 2: 364–6.

Review of Crania Britannica ..., by Joseph Bernard Davis and John Thurnam. In CJ, n.s., 2: 443–8.

Review of Indigenous Races of the Earth ..., by J.C. Nott and Geo. R. Gliddon. In CJ, n.s., 2: 208–16.

Review of Journal de l'instruction publique (Montreal) ... and Journal of Education (Montreal). In CJ, n.s., 2: 282–5.

Review of Tales of Mystery, and Poems, by Edgar Allan Poe. In CJ, n.s., 2: 103–9.

'Supposed Prevalence of One Cranial Type throughout the American Aborigines.' CJ, n.s., 2: 406–35. Reprinted as 'On the Supposed Uniformity of Cranial Type, throughout All Varieties of the American Race,' in PAAAS 11, pt 2: 109–27; also in ENPJ in 1858.

1858

'Ceremony at the University of Toronto and University College Building.' Journal of Education for Upper Canada 11: 165–6. Contains the toast proposed by Wilson at the ceremony of placing the coping stone on the turret of University College. Reprinted in 'Ceremony of Placing the Coping Stone on the New Buildings of the University of Toronto and University College [4 October 1858].' In Hodgins, 14: 33–4.

'On the Supposed Prevalence of One Cranial Type throughout the American Aborigines.' ENPJ, n.s., 7: 1–32.

Review of American editions of the Edinburgh Review, the London Quarterly Review, the Westminster Review, and the North British Review. In CJ, n.s., 3: 137–53.

Review of The Canada Directory, for 1857–58. In CJ, n.s., 3: 34–41.

Review of *The Canadian Almanac, and Repository of Useful Knowledge, for the Year 1859*. In *CJ*, n.s., 3: 509–14.

Review of *The Englishwoman in America*, by Isabella L. Bird. In *CJ*, n.s., 3: 129–34.

Review of *The Geography and History of British America* ..., by J. George Hodgins. In *CJ*, n.s., 3: 47–50.

Review of *The Hand-book of Toronto*, [by George P. Ure]. In *CJ*, n.s., 3: 502–9.

Review of *History of Ancient Pottery*, by Samuel Birch. In *CJ*, n.s., 3: 254–60.

Review of *The St. Lawrence and the Saguenay, and Other Poems*, by Charles Sangster; *Poems*, by Alexander McLauchlan [*sic*]; *Oscar and Other Poems*, by Carroll Ryan; and *A Song of Charity*, [by E.J. Chapman]. In *CJ*, n.s., 3: 17–27.

Review of *The Sandwich Islands Monthly Magazine* ... (Honolulu), *The New Era, and Argus* (Honolulu), and *The Victoria Gazette* (Vancouver's Island). In *CJ*, n.s., 3: 451–8.

Review of *The Temple of Serapis at Pozzuoli*, by Sir Edmund Walker Head. In *CJ*, n.s., 3: 336–42.

'Some Ethnographic Phases of Conchology.' *CJ*, n.s., 3: 377–409. Reprinted in *ENPJ* in 1859.

1859

'Burns – His Short Career – His Songs and the Universality of Their Diffusion.' *Journal of Education for Upper Canada* 12: 35–6. Speech at the Toronto Burns celebrations; reprinted from the *Globe*.

'Early Notices of the Beaver, in Europe and America.' *CJ*, n.s., 4: 359–87.

'Ethnology.' *CJ*, n.s., 4: 225–32. Extract from a letter by Lewis H. Morgan on kinship terminology.

'Notice of the "Quigrich," or Crozier of Saint Fillan.' *PSAS* 3: 233–4.

'The Quigrich.' *CJ*, n.s., 4: 429–41.

The Quigrich; or, Crozier of Saint Fillan. Toronto: Lovell and Gibson. 'Fifty copies printed.' Wilson's copy (now in the TRL) is bound with an article on the crozier by Lord Talbot de Malahide, originally published in the *Archaeological Journal*, and various documents relating the artefact's return to Scotland in 1877.

Review of *Annaler for Nordisk Oldkyndighed og Historie*. In *CJ*, n.s., 4: 51–3.

Review of *The Ballads of Scotland*, edited by William Edmonstoune Aytoun. In *CJ*, n.s., 4: 295–316.

Review of *The Bookseller, a Hand-book of British and Foreign Literature*. In *CJ*, n.s., 4: 194–203.

Review of *Crania Britannica* ..., decade III, by Joseph Bernard Davis and John Thurnam. In *CJ*, n.s., 4: 142–5.

Review of *Description of a Deformed Fragmentary Skull* ..., by J. Aitken Meigs. In *CJ*, n.s., 4: 487–90.

Review of *Holbein's Dance of Death ...*, by Francis Douce, and *Holbein's Bible Cuts ...*, by Thomas Frognall Dibdin. In *CJ*, n.s., 4: 211–21.

Review of *The Romantic Scottish Ballads; Their Epoch and Authorship*, by Robert Chambers. In *CJ*, n.s., 4: 468–87.

Review of *Wanderings of an Artist among the Indians of North America ...*, by Paul Kane. In *CJ*, n.s., 4: 186–94.

'Some Ethnographic Phases of Conchology.' *ENPJ*, n.s., 9: 65–82, 191–206.

1860

Address before the Select Committee of the Legislative Assembly, Appointed to Inquire into the Management of the University of Toronto, in Opening the Defence on Behalf of University College. Reported by J.K. Edwards. Toronto. Also published in John Langton, *University Question: The Statements of John Langton ... and Professor Daniel Wilson ...* (Toronto: Rowsell & Ellis), 51–90; and in Hodgins, 15: 207–37. Wilson's examination by the committee appears in Hodgins, 15: 250–1, 256–60.

'Canadian Institute ... Address Presented to the Prince of Wales, by the Canadian Institute, on the Occasion of the Recent Visit of His Royal Highness to Toronto.' *CJ*, n.s., 5: 475.

'Notice of a Skull Brought from Kertch, in the Crimea.' *CJ*, n.s., 5: 321–31. Reprinted in *ENPJ* in 1861.

'Notice of the Old Calton Burial Ground and the Historical Reminiscences Associated with It.' Appendix B in *Memoir of George Wilson*, by Jessie Aitken Wilson, 523–4. Edinburgh: Edmonston and Douglas.

'The President's Address ... Read before the Canadian Institute, January 7th, 1860.' *CJ*, n.s., 5: 109–27.

'Professor George Wilson, M.D., F.R.S.E.' *CJ*, n.s., 5: 62–3. Published anonymously, but probably by Wilson.

'Remarks by Dr Daniel Wilson on a Deformed Fragmentary Skull Found in an Ancient Quarry Cave at Jerusalem. Described by Aitken Meigs.' *ENPJ*, n.s., 11: 164–6.

'Report of the Editing Commitee.' *CJ*, n.s., 5: 229–31.

Review of *The Family Herald ...* (Montreal). In *CJ*, n.s., 5: 57–8.

Review of *Historical Pictures Retouched ...*, by Mrs Dall. In *CJ*, n.s., 5: 532–7.

Review of *Journal de l'instruction publique ...* and *The Journal of Education for Lower Canada ...* (1859). In *CJ*, n.s., 5: 365–7.

Review of *A New History of the Conquest of Mexico ...*, by Robert Alexander Wilson. In *CJ*, n.s., 5: 442–51.

Review of *North West Territory. Reports of Progress ...* by Henry Youle Hind. In *CJ*, n.s., 5: 187–95.

Review of *A Summary of Canadian History, from the Time of Cartier's Discovery to the Present Day*, by J.A. Boyd. In *CJ*, n.s., 5: 537–8.

1861

'Illustrative Examples of Some Modifying Elements Affecting the Ethnic Signifi-
cance of Peculiar Forms of the Human Skull.' *CJ*, n.s., 6: 414–25. Reprinted as
'On Some Modifying Elements Affecting the Ethnic Significance of Peculiar
Forms of the Human Skull' in *ENPJ*, n.s., 14: 269–81.

'Notice of Skulls Found at Kertch, in the Crimea.' *ENPJ*, n.s., 13: 279–91.

'The President's Address ... Read before the Canadian Institute, January 13th,
1861.' *CJ*, n.s., 6: 101–20.

Review of *Coins, Medals, and Seals, Ancient and Modern ...*, edited by W.C. Prime. In
CJ, n.s., 6: 192–3.

Review of *Narrative of the Canadian Red River Exploring Expedition of 1857 ...*, by
Henry Youle Hind. In *CJ*, n.s., 6: 175–83.

1862

'Ethnical Forms and Undesigned Artificial Distortions of the Human Cranium.'
CJ, n.s., 7: 399–446. *Also issued separately by Lovell and Gibson, Toronto.

'Notes of the Search for the Tomb of the Royal Foundress of the Collegiate
Church of the Holy Trinity at Edinburgh.' *PSAS* 4: 554–65.

Prehistoric Man: Researches into the Origin of Civilisation in the Old and the New World.
2 vols. Cambridge and London: Macmillan and Co.

Review of *Last Poems*, by Elizabeth Barrett Browning. In *CJ*, n.s., 7: 210–13.

Review of *Seven Years' Residence in the Great Deserts of North America*, by the Abbé Em.
Domenech. In *CJ*, n.s., 7: 47–71.

'Science in Rupert's Land.' *CJ*, n.s., 7: 336–47.

1863

'Ethnology and Archæology: Artificial Occipital Flattening of Ancient Crania.' *CJ*,
n.s., 8: 76–85.

'Illustrations of the Significance of Certain Ancient British Skull Forms.' *CJ*, n.s.,
8: 127–57. Reprinted in *ENPJ*, n.s., 18: 51–83.

'Indications of Ancient Customs, Suggested by Certain Cranial Forms.' *PAAS*,
meeting of 29 April 1863, 40–63. Reprinted in *British American Magazine* 1:
449–60.

'Physical Ethnology.' In *Annual Report of the Board of Regents of the Smithsonian Institution ... for the Year 1862*, 240–302. Washington: Government Printing Office.

Prehistoric Annals of Scotland. 2d ed. 2 vols. London and Cambridge: Macmillan
and Co.

Review of *Nelson's Atlas of the World ...*, *Nelson's Wall Maps*, and *Nelson's Family Maps*.
In *CJ*, n.s., 8: 54–7.

'A Washington Picture.' *Globe*, 25 February. Abstract of a lecture delivered under
the auspices of the YMCAs of Cooke's and Knox churches.

1864

'Historical Footprints in America.' *CJ*, n.s., 9: 289–316.

'Inquiry into the Physical Characteristics of the Ancient and Modern Celt of Gaul and Britain.' *CJ*, n.s., 9: 369–405. Reprinted in the *Anthropological Review* in 1865.

1865

'Inquiry into the Physical Characteristics of the Ancient and Modern Celt of Gaul and Britain.' *Anthropological Review* 3: 52–84.

Prehistoric Man: Researches into the Origin of Civilisation in the Old and the New World. 2d ed. London: Macmillan and Co.

Review of *An Account of the Smithsonian Institution* ..., by William J. Rhees, and *Annual Reports of the Board of Regents ... of the Smithsonian Institution ... for the Years 1857–1862.* In *CJ*, n.s., 10: 119–34.

'The Teachers' Educational Association of Upper Canada, 1865.' In Hodgins, 19: 52–8. Wilson delivered the opening address.

1866

'Mary Bradley, the Deaf and Blind Mute.' *CJ*, n.s., 11: 184–6. Anonymous; possibly not by Wilson.

'Notice of a Collection of Primitive Implements of the Ancient Swiss Lake-dwellers, from Concise, on Lake Neufchatel.' *PSAS* 6: 376–86.

'On the Vocal Language of Laura Bridgeman.' *CJ*, n.s., 11: 113–23.

1868

'Doctor Wilson on the Best Way of Dealing with the Street Arabs.' In Hodgins, 20: 268–9.

'Higher Education for Woman.' *CJ*, n.s., 12: 308–20. Address given at the Music Hall, Toronto, 22 October 1868.

'Notice of Bishop Strachan.' *PAAS*, no. 49: 21–3.

1869

'American Literary Forgeries.' *CJ*, n.s., 12: 134–48.

Chatterton: A Biographical Study. London: Macmillan and Co.

'Extract of a Letter to the Foreign Secretary from Dr Daniel Wilson, Toronto ... respecting a Volume Containing Views of Old Buildings in Edinburgh, Sent for Presentation to the Society.' *PSAS* 8, pt 1: 223–4.

'Higher Education for Ladies.' *Journal of Education for Ontario* 22: 181–3. Extract from a lecture.

'Race Head-Forms and Their Expression by Measurements.' *CJ*, n.s., 12: 269–303.

'Ricardus Corinensis: A Literary Masking of the Eighteenth Century.' *CJ*, n.s., 12: 177–206.

1870

'The Law of Copyright: Pike vs. Nicholas.' *CJ*, n.s., 12: 415–29.

Review of *Alaska and Its Resources*, by William H. Dall. In *CJ*, n.s., 12: 480–9.

1871

'The Genius of Scott: An Address ... at Toronto Celebration of the Scott Centenary, 1871.' *CJ*, n.s., 13: 341–7.

'The Huron Race and Its Head-Form.' *CJ*, n.s., 13: 113–34.

'Paul Kane, the Canadian Artist.' *CJ*, n.s., 13: 66–72.

'Righthandedness.' *CJ*, n.s., 13: 193–231. *Also issued separately in 1872 by Copp,
Clark, Toronto.

1872

'American Hoaxes.' *Globe*, 5 June.

'Anne Hatheway: A Dialogue.' *CMNR* 1: 19–26.

'The Day after Death.' Review of a book with the same title by M. Fignier. *Globe*,
5 June.

'Dr. Ryerson's Other Book, "My Second Little Book."' *Globe*, 20 February.

'Educational Hot-beds.' *Globe*, 5 April.

'Female Education in Edinburgh.' *Globe*, 12 April. In his journal Wilson lists
'Higher Education for Ladies,' possibly a reference to this article.

'The Fly on the Wheel.' *Globe*, 2 April.

'Handwriting in Evidence.' *Globe*, 10 April.

'A Historical Relic of 1783.' *Globe*, 14 June.

'A Man's Thoughts.' Review of a book with the same title by the author of *The
Gentle Life*. *Globe*, 10 June.

Memorials of Edinburgh in the Olden Time. New ed. Edinburgh: A. Elliot; London:
Simpkin, Marshall & Co. Unauthorized edition.

'Modern Scepticism.' Review of *Christian Theology and Modern Scepticism*, by the
Duke of Somerset. *Globe*, 29 March.

'A New Canadian Author [Henry Alleyne Nicholson].' *Globe*, 15 April.

'On a Dead Fly Found Crushed in My Scrap-Book.' *CMNR* 2: 73. Poem.

'Our Evening Pastimes.' *Globe*, 8 April.

'Our Great Social Vice.' *Globe*, 11 April.

'Our Indian Reserves.' *Globe*, 5, 9 March.

'Our Indians and Their Reserves.' *Globe*, 1 April.

'Our Native Indian Population.' *Globe*, 28 February.

'Our Shade Trees.' *Globe*, 12 April.

'The Romans in Chicago.' *Globe*, 11 March.

'Valuable Gift to the University of Edinburgh.' *Globe*, 1 April.

'Where Our Toys Come From.' *Globe*, 1 April.

1873

'An Account of Alexander Gordon, A.M., Author of the *Itinerarium septentrionale*, 1726 ... with Additional Notes concerning Gordon and His Works, by David Laing.' *PSAS* 10: 363–82.

'Alexander Gordon, the Antiquarian.' *CJ*, n.s., 14: 9–37. *Also issued separately in 1873 by Copp, Clark, Toronto.

Caliban: The Missing Link. London: Macmillan and Co.

'Canada.' *CMNR* 4: 471–3. Poem.

'Toronto of Old.' *CMNR* 4: 89–96.

'Unsectarian Union.' *Globe*, 14 March.

1874

'Bachelors' Buttons.' *CMNR* 5: 55–6. Poem.

'The Long Peruvian Skull.' *Nature* 10: 46–8, 355.

'The Present State and Future Prospects of the Indians of British North America.' *Proceedings of the Royal Colonial Institute* 5: 222–45. Submitted to, but not read at, the meeting of 30 June 1874. *Also published separately by Unwin Bros., London.

1875

'Archæology,' 'Canada,' 'Chatterton, Thomas,' 'Edinburgh,' 'Federal Government,' 'Fergusson, Robert,' 'Montreal,' 'Ontario,' and 'Toronto.' In *Encyclopædia Britannica*, 9th ed. Edinburgh: A. & C. Black, 1875–89.

'Doubt. From "Spring Wild Flowers," a Volume of Poems.' *CMNR* 8: 315–6.

'Hybridity and Absorption in Relation to the Red Indian Race.' *CJ*, n.s., 14: 432–66.

Memorials of Edinburgh in the Olden Time. 3d ed. Edinburgh: Printed at the Ballantyne Press for Thomas C. Jack; London: Simpkin Marshall & Co. Unauthorized edition.

'Notices of Sculptured Rocks and Boulders Recently Observed in Ohio and Kentucky, United States of America, and of the Probable Origin of the Cupmarkings Which Occur on Stones There and in Other Countries.' *PSAS* 11: 266–72.

'Sonnet. From "Spring Wild Flowers."' *CMNR* 8: 8. ('I stood upon the world's thronged thoroughfare').

'Sonnet. From "Spring Wild Flowers."' *CMNR* 8: 114. ('True love is lowly as the way-side flower').

Spring Wild Flowers. London: T. Nelson and Sons.

'Wolfe and Old Quebec.' *CMNR* 7: 105–13.

1876

'Alexander Gordon, the Antiquary: A Supplementary Notice.' *CJ*, n.s., 15: 122–44.

'Brain-Weight and Size in Relation to Relative Capacity of Races.' *CJ*, n.s., 15: 177–230. *Also issued separately by Copp, Clark, Toronto.

'Lefthandedness.' *CJ*, n.s., 15: 465–85.

Prehistoric Man: Researches into the Origin of Civilisation in the Old and the New World. 3rd ed., rev. and enl. 2 vols. London: Macmillan and Co.

*'Tecumseh's Remains.' *Weekly Globe*, 6 October. Extract.

'Three Generations.' *CMNR* 9: 397–401.

1877

'Address of Professor Daniel Wilson, Chairman of the Subsection of Anthropology.' *PAAAS* 26: 319–34. Reprinted as *Legitimate Lines of Anthropological Research* in 1878.

'Notices of the Quigrich or Crozier of St Fillan and of Its Hereditary Keepers in a Letter to John Stuart ...' *PSAS* 12: 122–31.

'Supposed Evidence of the Existence of Inter-glacial American Man.' *CJ*, n.s., 15: 557–73.

1878

Legitimate Lines of Anthropological Research: An Address before the American Association for the Advancement of Science ... at Nashville, Tenn., August, 1877. Salem: Printed at the Salem Press.

Reminiscences of Old Edinburgh. 2 vols. Edinburgh: David Douglas.

1879

'An Ancient Haunt of the Cervus Megaceros: or, Great Irish Deer.' *PCI*, 3rd ser., 1: 207–24.

'Canadian Institute: Interesting Papers by Prof. Wright and Dr. Wilson.' *Globe*, 3 November. Abstract of an address on the 'earlier Indian tribes of Ontario.' Also reported in 'Canadian Institute: Professor Wilson on the Early Indian Tribes of Ontario,' *Mail*, 3 November.

'The Canadian Institute: Lecture by Dr. Daniel Wilson.' *Globe*, 20 October. Abstract of an address on 'A Comparison of the Succession of Archaeological Periods in America with Those of Europe.'

'Some American Illustrations of the Evolution of New Varieties of Man.' *JAI* 8: 338–59.

[1880?]

Twenty Views of Old Edinburgh. 2d ser. Edinburgh: Andrew Elliot. From Wilson's *Memorials of Edinburgh in the Olden Time.* The plates are numbered 21 to 40 and are accompanied by brief descriptive text. The publication date is that suggested in *BLC.* The first series has not been located.

1880

'Cosmopolitan Time and a Prime Meridian Common to All Nations: Memorandum.' In *Papers on Time-Reckoning and the Selection of a Prime Meridian to Be Common to All Nations* ... [Toronto]. The five-page memorandum by Wilson, dated
5 April 1880, appears with some copies of the *Papers*, which was issued by the
Canadian Institute.

'University College Convocation.' *CEM* 2: 478. Includes a brief description of Wilson's address on assuming the presidency of University College.

1881

Good Mother Cara and Her Glass Slippers: A Christmas Fairy Tale. [Toronto: Privately
printed]. Originally written for the Sunday school Christmas festival at St
James' Cathedral in 1877 (see H.H. Langton, *Sir Daniel Wilson*, 186–7); printed
by Wilson as a Christmas greeting in 1881 (see NLS, MS 23203, f49, Wilson to
Madge Wilson, 23 January 1882).

'Notice of a Remarkable Memorial Horn, the Pledge of a Treaty with the Creek
Nation in 1765.' *PCI*, 3rd ser., 1: 255–60.

*On the Practical Uses of Science in the Daily Business of Life: The Inaugural Lecture to the
Evening Courses of Lectures for Working Men.* Toronto: Printed by C. Blackett Robinson. At head of title: 'School of Practical Science, Province of Ontario, fourth
session, 1881–1882.'

'Religious Instruction in the Public Schools.' *CEM* 3: 321–7.

'Report of the Council for 1880–81.' *PCI*, 3rd ser., 1: 236.

1882

*'Address by Daniel Wilson ... Vice President, Section II: Some Physical Character-
istics of Native Tribes of Canada.' *PAAAS* 31: 531–58. Also issued separately as *Some
Physical Characteristics of Native Tribes of Canada* ... (Salem Press, Salem, Mass.).

'General Wolfe and Old Quebec.' In *Advanced Reader,* Royal Canadian Series,
3–12. Toronto: Canada Publishing Co.

'Holy Island, and the Runic Inscriptions of St Molio's Cave, County of Bute.' *PSAS*
17: 45–56.

'Hymns from Chatterton (1752–1770).' In *Fifth Book of Reading Lessons,* Royal
Readers, Special Canadian Series, 208–9. Excerpt from Wilson's article on
Chatterton in the *Encyclopaedia Britannica* and two poems with brief introduc-
tions from his *Chatterton* (1869).

'Inaugural Address. Read May 25, 1882.' *PTRSC* 1, section 2: 1–12. Reprinted as
'New-World Beginnings' in *CEM* 4: 365–76.

'Lecture on Ethnology.' *Toronto Mail*, 19 January. Abstract.

'University College, Toronto: President Wilson's Address at the Annual Convocation.' *CEM* 4: 409–12.

1883

'In Memoriam: Henry Holmes Croft ...' *Varsity*, 10 March. Signed Δ; for authorship see UTA, B65-0014/004(01), 67.

'Pre-Aryan American Man.' *PTRSC* 1, section 2: 35–70. Reprinted in *The Lost
Atlantis* (1892), 130–84.

'Prehistoric Man.' In *Third Book of Reading Lessons*, Royal Readers, Special Canadian Series, 217–18. Toronto: Thomas Nelson and Sons, and James Campbell
and Son. Excerpt from *Prehistoric Man*, chap. 1.

'St Ninian's Suburb and the Collegiate Church of the Holy Trinity, Founded at
Edinburgh by Queen Mary of Gueldres, the Widow of James II., in 1462.' *PSAS*
18: 128–70.

'The Scot Abroad (from "Spring Wild Flowers").' In *Fourth Book of Reading Lessons*,
Royal Readers, Special Canadian Series, 29–30. Toronto: Thomas Nelson and
Sons, and James Campbell and Son.

'University College, Toronto. President Wilson's Address at the Annual Convocation.' *CEM* 5: 455–9. 'From the Toronto *Mail* report, revised and corrected by
the author for The Monthly.'

1884

'Address at the Convocation of University College, 1884.' *CEM* 6: 417–24.
*Also issued separately by the Canada Educational Monthly Publishing Co.,
Toronto.

Coeducation: A Letter to the Hon. G.W. Ross, M.P.P., Minister of Education. Toronto:
Hunter, Rose & Co., printers.

'Free Public Libraries.' *CEM* 6: 145–50.

'The Huron-Iroquois of Canada, a Typical Race of American Aborigines.' *PTRSC*
2, section 2: 55–106. Reprinted as 'The Huron-Iroquois: A Typical Race' in *The
Lost Atlantis* (1892), 246–306.

'The Kilmichael-Glassrie Bell-shrine.' *PSAS* 18: 79–93.

'The Professor's Romance.' *Toronto World*, 31 October.

1885

Address. In 'Addresses by the President, Vice-President and Dr. Chauveau.'
PTRSC 3: xii–xiii. Abstract.

Address at the Convocation of University College, Toronto, October 16th, 1885. Toronto:
Rowsell & Hutchison, printers. Also published as 'University College: President
Wilson's Address. Specially revised for The Monthly' in *CEM* 7: 337–46; as
'University College. Annual Convocation and Presentation of Prizes. President
Wilson's Address ...' in *Globe*, 17 October.

'Address at the Opening of the Annual Exhibition of the Royal Canadian Academy.' *Educational Weekly*, 21 May, 323. Abstract.

'Archaeology.' In *Anthropology and Archæeology*, by Daniel Wilson and E.B. Tylor, The Humboldt Library of Science, no. 71 (Sept. 1885): 34–55. New York: Humboldt Publishing Co. Reprinted, without permission and with minor textual alterations, from the *Encyclopædia Britannica*; the authors' names have been transposed, with 'Anthropology' assigned to Wilson and 'Archaeology' to Tylor.

'The Artistic Faculty in Aboriginal Races.' *PTRSC* 3, section 2: 67–111. Reprinted as 'The Æsthetic Faculty in Aboriginal Races' in *The Lost Atlantis* (1892), 185–245.

'Palæolithic Dexterity.' *PTRSC* 3, section 2: 119–33.

'Primæval Dexterity.' *PCI*, 3rd ser., 3: 125–43.

'The So-called Roman Heads of the Nether Bow.' *PSAS* 19: 203–9.

1886

Address. In 'Addresses of the President and Vice-President.' *PTRSC* 4: xiv–xx. Reprinted as 'Our Native Languages' in *CEM* in 1887.

'The Lost Atlantis.' *PTRSC* 4, section 2: 105–26. Reprinted in *The Lost Atlantis* (1892), 1–36.

Memorials of Edinburgh in the Olden Time. New ed. Edinburgh: Thomas C. Jack; London. Unauthorized edition.

'The President's Address at Convocation.' In *The Year Book of the University of Toronto ... 1886–87*, ed. J.O. Miller and F.B. Hodgins, 39–51. Toronto: Rowsell & Hutchison, 1887.

'The Right Hand and Left-Handedness.' *PTRSC* 4, section 2: 1–41.

'Some Illustrations of Early Celtic Christian Art.' *PSAS* 20: 222–39.

1887

Address at the Convocation of University College, Toronto, October 14th, 1887. Toronto: Rowsell & Hutchison, printers. Also published as 'Annual Convocation University College, Toronto: President Wilson's Address (Revised specially for The Monthly)' in *CEM* 9: 337–45.

'Conferring of Degrees at the University of Toronto: The President's Address.' *CEM* 9: 256–60.

'Left-Handedness – A Hint for Educators.' *Educational Weekly*, 3 March, 933. Abstract of a paper delivered to the RSC. Reprinted from *Science* 9, no. 211: 148–9. Also printed in *CEM* 10 (1888): 29–30.

'Lucem dare.' Words by Wilson; music by Mrs Edgar Jarvis. In *Varsity*, 24 December.

'Notice of St Margaret's Chapel, Edinburgh Castle.' *PSAS* 21: 291–316.

'Our Native Languages.' *CEM* 9: 168–74. Reprinted from *PTRSC* for 1886.

'Some Stone Implements from Lake St. John, Que.' *PCI*, 3rd ser., 5: 124. Abstract.

Words to 'The Undergraduate's Lament,' 'Alma Mater,' 'Commencement,' and 'Our New Degree.' In *The University of Toronto Song Book*, 57, 90, 82–3. Toronto: I. Suckling & Sons, publishers. Numerous reprints under various publishers' and

music dealers' names, some with a preface dated 1891. The revised and
enlarged edition published in 1918 contains only one of Wilson's songs, 'Commencement.'

'The University of Toronto and University College.' In *The Year Book of the University of Toronto ... 1886–87*, ed. J.O. Miller and F.B. Hodgins, 18–30. Toronto:
Rowsell & Hutchison.

1888

*Address at the Convocation of the University of Toronto and University College, October 19,
1888.* Toronto: Rowsell & Hutchison, printers. Also published as 'University
College: President Sir Daniel Wilson's Address' in *CEM* 10: 337–42, 379–84.

'Sonnet' and 'Our Ideal.' In *The High School Reader*, Ontario Readers, 383.
Toronto: Rose Publishing Co.

1889

*Address at the Convocation of Faculties of the University of Toronto, and University College,
October 1st, 1889.* Toronto: Rowsell & Hutchison, printers.

'English at Junior Matriculation.' *CEM* 11: 81–5.

'Learned Linguistics. Annual Meeting of the Modern Language Association.' *Toronto Mail*, 3 January. Abstract of an address by Wilson on 'History as Embodied
in Language.'

'Trade and Commerce in the Stone Age.' *PTRSC* 7, section 2: 59–87. Reprinted in
The Lost Atlantis (1892), 81–129.

William Nelson: A Memoir. Edinburgh: T. Nelson and Sons. 'Printed for private circulation.'

1890

Address at the Convocation of the University of Toronto, October 1, 1890. Toronto: Rowsell
& Hutchison, printers. Also published as 'Education' in *CEM* 12: 321–6.

'Addresses by the President of the University, the Hon. the Minister of Education,
and Profs. Osler, Welch, Minot, Vaughan, and Wright.' In *University of Toronto:
Formal Opening of the New Building of the Biological Department, December 19,
1889*, 1–2. Toronto: J.E. Bryant Co. 'Reprinted from "The Canadian Practitioner."'

'The Book of Nature ... "All Research into the Book of Nature Has Not Discovered
an Erratum."' *CEM* 12: 41–4. Address given at the centenary celebrations of the
American Philosophical Society in Philadelphia.

*A Letter to the Hon. G.W. Ross, LL.D., Minister of Education, with Resolutions and Letters
from the Board of Trustees, the Faculty, Heads of Universities, Graduates, &c., in
Approval of College Residence.* Toronto: Rowsell & Hutchison, printers.

'Queen Mary and the Legend of the Black Turnpike.' *PSAS* 24: 415–35.

'The Vinland of the Northmen.' *PTRSC* 8, section 2: 109–25. Reprinted in *The Lost Atlantis* (1892), 37–80.

1891

Address at the Convocation of Faculties of the University of Toronto and University College, October 5th, 1891. Toronto: Rowsell & Hutchison, printers.

'Degrees Conferred. University of Toronto Special Convocation. Graduates in Medicine and Dentistry ...' *Toronto Daily Mail,* 7 May. Includes the text of Wilson's address.

'John Knox's House, Netherbow, Edinburgh.' *PSAS* 25: 154–62.

Memorials of Edinburgh in the Olden Time. 2d ed. 2 vols. Edinburgh: Adam and Charles Black. Also issued in a large paper edition of 150 copies signed by the author and the publisher. A reference to 'your first number of the 2^d edition ... published two days ago' in a letter from Peter Miller to Wilson dated 24 July 1890 suggests that this edition, like the first, appeared in parts before the book publication (see TRL, S65, vol. 4: 37).

The Right Hand: Left-Handedness. Nature Series. London and New York: Macmillan and Co.

1892

'Canadian Copyright.' *PTRSC* 10, section 2: 3–17.

The Lost Atlantis and Other Ethnographic Studies. Edinburgh: David Douglas. Also published in New York by Macmillan and Co.

Medical Education in Ontario: A Letter to the Hon. G.W. Ross, LL.D., Minister of Education. Toronto: Rowsell & Hutchison, printers.

1897

Private Letters of Sir Daniel Wilson respecting James Mosman's House at the Netherbow, Edinburgh. Edinburgh: Printed for private circulation.

1924

Letters to P.A. Munch, 1850–6. In *Lærde Brev fraa og til P.A. Munch,* edited by Gustav Indrebo et al., 1: 404, 438; 2: 2, 54, 90, 101, 172. Oslo: H. Aschehoug & Co., 1924–55.

1982

Edinburgh: Times Past. Newtongrange: Lang Syne Publishers. Contains facsimiles of thirty plates from the '1847 edition' [i.e., the part publication?] of *Memorials of Edinburgh in the Olden Times,* but without Wilson's name.

Secondary Sources

Ainley, Marianne Gosztonyi, ed. *Despite the Odds: Essays on Canadian Women and Science.* Montreal: Véhicule Press, 1990.

Allen, D.E. *The Naturalist in Britain.* London: A. Lane, 1976.

Allen, James. *Facts concerning Federation.* [Toronto:] Victoria University Alumni Association, 1889.

Altick, Richard D. *The English Common Reader: A Social History of the Mass Reading Public, 1800–1900.* Chicago: University of Chicago Press, 1957.

Anderson, James E. *The Human Skeleton: A Manual for Archaeologists.* Illus. by Tom Munro. Rev. ed. Ottawa: National Museums of Canada, 1969.

Ash, Marinell. '"A Fine, Genial, Hearty Band": David Laing, Daniel Wilson and Scottish Archaeology.' In *The Scottish Antiquarian Tradition: Essays to Mark the Bicentenary of the Society of Antiquaries of Scotland and Its Museum, 1780–1980,* ed. A.S. Bell, 86–113. Edinburgh: John Donald Publishers, 1981.

– 'New Frontiers: George and Daniel Wilson.' In *The Enterprising Scot: Scottish Adventure and Achievement,* ed. Jenni Calder, 40–51. Edinburgh: Royal Museum of Scotland, 1986.

– 'A Past "Filled with Living Men": Scott, Daniel Wilson and Scottish and American Archaeology.' In *Scott and His Influence: The Papers of the Aberdeen Scott Conference, 1982,* ed. J.H. Alexander and David Hewitt, 432–42. Occasional Paper no. 6. Aberdeen: Association for Scottish Literary Studies, 1984.

– '"So Much That Was New to Us": Scott and Shetland.' In *Essays in Shetland History: Heiðursrit to T.M.Y. Manson, 1904 9th February 1984,* ed. Barbara E. Crawford, 193–207. Lerwick: The Shetland Times, 1984.

– *The Strange Death of Scottish History.* Edinburgh: Ramsay Head Press, 1980.

Barkan, Elazar. *The Retreat of Scientific Racism: Changing Concepts of Race in Britain and the United States between the World Wars.* Cambridge: Cambridge University Press, 1992.

Bender, Thomas. *New York Intellect: A History of Intellectual Life in New York City, from 1750 to the Beginnings of Our Own Time.* New York: A.A. Knopf, 1987.

Berger, Carl. *Honour and the Search for Influence: A History of the Royal Society of Canada.* Toronto: University of Toronto Press, 1996.

– *Science, God, and Nature in Victorian Canada.* Toronto: University of Toronto Press, 1983.

– *The Sense of Power: Studies in the Ideas of Canadian Imperialism, 1867–1914.* Toronto: University of Toronto Press, 1970.

– 'Wilson, Sir Daniel.' In *DCB,* 12 (1990): 1109–14.

Berman, Morris. *Social Change and Scientific Organization: The Royal Institution, 1799–1844.* Ithaca: Cornell University Press, 1978.

Bieder, Robert E. 'Albert Gallatin and the Survival of Enlightenment Thought in Nineteenth-Century American Anthropology.' In *Toward a Science of Man: Essays in the History of Anthropology*, ed. Timothy H.H. Thoresen, 91–8. The Hague: Mouton, 1975.

– *Science Encounters the Indian, 1820–1880: The Early Years of American Ethnology*. Norman: University of Oklahoma Press, 1986.

Biggar, C.R.W. 'The Reverend William Hincks, MA.' *University of Toronto Monthly* 2 (June 1902): 232.

Bissell, Claude T., ed. *University College: A Portrait, 1853–1953*. Toronto: University of Toronto Press, 1953.

Blackburn, Robert. *Evolution of the Heart: A History of the University of Toronto Library up to 1981*. Toronto: University of Toronto Library, 1989.

Blackie, John Stuart. *Notes of a Life*. Ed. A. Stodart-Walker. Edinburgh and London: William Blackwood & Sons, 1910.

Bothwell, Robert. *Laying the Foundation: A Century of History at the University of Toronto*. University of Toronto, Department of History, 1991.

Bourinot, John George. *Bibliography of the Members of the Royal Society of Canada*. [Ottawa?]: The Society, 1894.

Bovell, James. *Outlines of Natural Theology for the Use of the Canadian Student, Selected and Arranged from the Most Authentic Sources*. Toronto: Printed by Rowsell & Ellis, 1859.

Bowker, Alan Franklin. 'Truly Useful Men: Maurice Hutton, George Wrong, James Mavor & the University of Toronto, 1880–1927.' PhD thesis, University of Toronto, 1975.

Bowler, Peter J. 'From "Savage" to "Primitive": Victorian Evolutionism and the Interpretation of Marginalized Peoples.' *Antiquity* 66 (1992): 721–9.

– *Theories of Human Evolution: A Century of Debate, 1844–1944*. Oxford: Blackwell, 1989.

Bradford, Alexander W. *American Antiquities and Researches into the Origin and History of the Red Race*. New York: Dayton and Saxton, 1841.

British Association for the Advancement of Science. *Report of the Fourth Meeting ... Held at Edinburgh in 1834*. London: John Murray, 1835.

Britnell, Albert. *Catalogue of Books from the Library of the Late Sir Daniel Wilson, LL.D., F.R.S. ...* Toronto Second Hand Book Circular, no. 12, March–April 1897. [Toronto].

Brown, Iain Gordon. *The Hobby-Horsical Antiquary, a Scottish Character, 1640–1830: An Essay*. Edinburgh: National Library of Scotland, 1980.

Brown, John. 'A Retrospect – The Class of '92.' *Canadian Lancet and Practitioner* 81, no. 6 (December 1923): 164–7.

Browne, Janet. *The Secular Ark: Studies in the History of Biogeography*. New Haven: Yale University Press, 1983.

Bruce, George. *Some Practical Good: The Cockburn Association, 1875–1975*. Edinburgh: The Cockburn Association, 1975.

Bryson, Gladys. *Man and Society: The Scottish Inquiry of the Eighteenth Century.* Princeton: Princeton University Press, 1945.

Buckle, Henry T. *History of Civilization in England.* Vol. 1. London: J.W. Parker, 1857.

Bunyan, Ian, Jenni Calder, Dale Idiens, and Bryce Wilson. *No Ordinary Journey: John Rae, Arctic Explorer, 1813–1893.* Montreal: McGill-Queen's University Press, 1993.

Burrow, J.W. *Evolution and Society: A Study in Victorian Social Theory.* Cambridge: Cambridge University Press, 1966.

Burwash, Nathanael. *A Review of the Founding and Development of the University of Toronto as a Provincial Institution.* Toronto: Copp Clark, 1905.

Campbell, Sandra. 'Introduction' to *Sister Woman* [1919], by J.G. Sime, vii–xxviii. Ottawa: Tecumseh Press, 1992.

Canada, Province of. Acts relating to the University of Toronto, including 13 & 14 Victoriae, cap. 49, sec. 1 (10 August 1850); University of Toronto Act, 16 Victoria, cap. 89 (1853).

Cannon, Susan Faye. *Science in Culture: The Early Victorian Period.* New York: Science History Publications, 1978.

Cant, Ronald G. 'David Steuart Erskine, 11th Earl of Buchan: Founder of the Society of Antiquaries of Scotland.' In *The Scottish Antiquarian Tradition: Essays to Mark the Bicentenary of the Society of Antiquaries of Scotland and Its Museum, 1780–1980,* ed. A.S. Bell, 1–30. Edinburgh: John Donald Publishers, 1981.

Careless, J.M.S. *Brown of The Globe.* 2 vols. Toronto: Macmillan, 1959–63.

– *The Union of the Canadas; the Growth of Canadian Institutions, 1841–1857.* Toronto: McClelland and Stewart, 1967.

Carrithers, Michael. *Why Humans Have Cultures: Explaining Anthropology and Social Diversity.* Oxford: Oxford University Press, 1992.

Cawood, John. 'The Magnetic Crusade: Science and Politics in Early Victorian Britain.' *Isis* 70, no. 254 (1979): 493–518.

Chambers, Robert. *Traditions of Edinburgh.* Edinburgh: Printed for W. & C. Tait, 1825.

Chartrand, Luc, Raymond Duchesne, and Yves Gingras. *Histoire des sciences au Québec.* Montréal: Boréal, 1987.

Cockburn, Henry, Lord Cockburn. 'A Letter to the Lord Provost on the Best Ways of Spoiling the Beauty of Edinburgh.' In *Journal of Henry Cockburn; Being a Continuation of the Memorials of His Time, 1831–1854,* 2: 317–38. Edinburgh: Edmonston and Douglas, 1874. Reprinted in Bruce, *Some Practical Good,* 77–95.

Cole, Douglas. 'The Origins of Canadian Anthropology, 1850–1910.' *Journal of Canadian Studies* 8 (1973): 33–45.

Connor, J.T.H. 'Of Butterfly Nets and Beetle Bottles: The Entomological Society of Canada, 1863–1960.' *HSTC Bulletin* 6 (1982): 127–50.

– 'To Promote the Cause of Science: George Lawson and the Botanical Society of Canada, 1860–63.' *Scientia Canadensis* 10 (1986): 3–33.

Cook, Ramsay. *The Regenerators: Social Criticism in Late Victorian English Canada.* Toronto: University of Toronto Press, 1985.

Cooke, W. Martha E. *W.H. Coverdale Collection of Canadiana: Paintings, Water-colours and Drawings (Manoir Richelieu Collection).* Ottawa: Public Archives Canada, 1983.

Court, Franklin. *Institutionalizing English Literature: The Culture and Politics of Literary Study, 1750–1900.* Stanford: Stanford University Press, 1992.

Crawford, Robert. *Devolving English Literature.* Oxford: Clarendon Press, 1992.

Creet, Mario. 'Sandford Fleming and Universal Time.' *Scientia Canadensis* 14 (1990): 66–89.

Croal, A.G. 'The History of the Teaching of Science in Ontario, 1800–1900.' DPaed thesis, University of Toronto, 1940.

Crosby, Alfred W. *Ecological Imperialism: The Biological Expansion of Europe, 900–1900.* Cambridge: Cambridge University Press, 1986.

Cunningham, Andrew, and Nicholas Jardine, eds. *Romanticism and the Sciences.* Cambridge, New York: Cambridge University Press, 1990.

Cursiter, Stanley. *Scottish Art to the Close of the Nineteenth Century.* London: George G. Harrap, 1949.

Daiches, David, Peter Jones, et al., eds. *A Hotbed of Genius: The Scottish Enlightenment, 1730–90.* Edinburgh: University Press, 1986.

Dall, Caroline Healey. 'Sir Daniel Wilson.' *Journal of Social Science* (American Social Science Association) 30 (October 1892): xxiii–xxix.

Dallas, James. 'On the Primary Divisions and Geographical Distribution of Mankind.' *JAI* 15 (1886): 304–30.

Daly, Robert, and Paul Dufour. 'Creating a "Northern Minerva": John William Dawson and the Royal Society of Canada.' *HSTC Bulletin* 5 (1981): 3–14.

Daniel, Glyn. *The Idea of Prehistory.* Harmondsworth: Penguin, 1962.

– 'One Hundred Years of Old World Prehistory.' In *One Hundred Years of Anthropology,* ed. J.O. Brew, 57–93. Cambridge: Harvard University Press, 1972.

Darnell, Regna. 'The Uniqueness of Canadian Anthropology: Issues and Problems.' In *Proceedings of the Second Congress, Canadian Ethnology Society,* ed. J. Freedman and J.H. Barkow, 399–416. National Museum of Man, Mercury Series, Canadian Ethnology Paper, no. 28. Ottawa, 1975.

Darwin, Charles. *The Descent of Man.* 2d ed. London: John Murray, 1906.

Davis, J. Barnard, and John Thurnham. *Crania Britannica ... With Notices of Other Remains.* London: Taylor & Francis, 1865.

Dawson, John William. *Archaia; or, Studies of the Cosmogony and Natural History of the Hebrew Scriptures.* Montreal: B. Dawson; London: S. Low, 1860.

Dendy, William, and William Kilbourne. *Toronto Observed: Its Architecture, Patrons, and History.* Toronto: University of Toronto Press, 1986.

Desmond, Adrian J. *Archetypes and Ancestors: Palaeontology in Victorian London, 1850–1875.* Chicago: University of Chicago Press, 1984.

– *The Politics of Evolution: Morphology, Medicine, and Reform in Radical London.* Chicago: University of Chicago Press, 1989.

de Vecchi, Vittorio. 'The Dawning of a National Scientific Community in Canada, 1878–1896.' *Scientia Canadensis* 8 (1984): 32–58.

– 'Science and Scientists in Government, 1878–1896.' Parts 1–2. *Scientia Canadensis* 8 (1984): 112–43; 9 (1985): 97–113.

Dick, Maxwell. *Description of the Suspension Railway Invented by Maxwell Dick.* Irvine: E. MacQuistan, 1830.

Dickens, Charles. *American Notes for General Circulation.* Ed. John S. Whitley and Arnold Goldman. Harmsmondsworth: Penguin Books, 1985.

Dictionary of Canadian Biography. Vols. 11–13. Toronto: University of Toronto Press, 1982–94.

Dobyns, Henry F. *'Their Number Become Thinned': Native American Population Dynamics in Eastern North America.* Knoxville: University of Tennessee Press, 1983.

Drummond, A.T. 'Observations on Canadian Geographical Botany.' *Canadian Naturalist and Geologist* 1 (1864): 405–13.

Dunn, John. *Western Political Theory in the Face of the Future.* 2d ed. Cambridge: Cambridge Univerity Press, 1993.

Eagan, W.E. 'Reading the *Geology of Canada.*' *Scientia Canadensis* 16 (1992): 154–64.

Edinborough, Arnold, ed. *The Enduring Word: A Centennial History of Wycliffe College.* Toronto: University of Toronto Press, 1977.

The [Edinburgh] Post-Office Annual Directory ... 1808–9 to 1853–4. Various publishers.

Edinburgh Town Council. *Address from the Town Council of Edinburgh, on the Subject of the New Buildings for the High School, of Which the Foundation Was Laid on 28th July, 1825.* [Edinburgh, 1825].

– *Minutes of the Town Council, and Report of the Committee, respecting the Proposed New High School.* [Edinburgh, 1823].

Eiseley, Loren C. *Darwin's Century: Evolution and the Man Who Discovered It.* Garden City, NY: Doubleday, 1958.

Ellis, W. Hodgson. *Application and Testimonials of W. Hodgson Ellis, Candidate for the Chair of Chemistry in University College, Toronto.* 1879.

– 'Edward John Chapman, PhD, LLD.' *University of Toronto Monthly* 2 (June 1902): 229–31.

Epp, Henry, and Leslie E. Sponsel. 'Major Personalities and Developments in Anthropology in Canada, 1860–1940.' Paper presented to the annual meeting of the Canadian Sociology and Anthropology Association, Toronto, 23–26 August 1974.

Ewing, J. Franklin. 'Current Roman Catholic Thought on Evolution.' In *Evolution after Darwin*. Vol. 3. *Issues in Evolution*, ed. Sol Tax and Charles Callender, 19–28. Chicago: University of Chicago Press, 1960.

Fairclough, H.R. 'Sir Daniel Wilson.' *University of Toronto Monthly* 2 (February 1902): 118–21.

Fasti. 1, no. 1 (31 October 1884). Student newspaper, University of Toronto; only issue known.

Ferguson, Adam. *An Essay on the History of Civil Society.* 2d ed., corr. London: A. Millar and T. Cadell [etc.], 1768.

Forbes, Edward. 'On the Connexion between the Distribution of the Existing Fauna and Flora of the British Isles and the Geological Changes Which Have Affected Them.' Geological Survey of England and Wales, *Memoirs* 1 (1846): 336–432.

Ford, Anne Rochon. *A Path Not Strewn with Roses: One Hundred Years of Women at the University of Toronto, 1884–1984.* Toronto: University of Toronto Press, 1985.

Geikie, Walter B. 'An Historical Sketch of Canadian Medical Education.' Reprint from *Canada Lancet*, January–February 1901.

Gifford, John, Colin McWilliam, David Walker, and Christopher Wilson. *Edinburgh.* The Buildings of Scotland. Harmondsworth: Penguin Books, 1984.

Godenrath, Percy F. *Catalogue of the Manoir Richelieu Collection of Canadiana.* Montreal: Canada Steamship Lines, 1930.

Goudie, Gilbert. *David Laing, LL.D.: A Memoir of His Life and Literary Work.* Edinburgh: Printed for private circulation by T. and A. Constable, 1913.

Grand Procession at the Opening of the New High School, Calton Hill, Edinburgh, on Tuesday 23d June, 1829 ... from the Old High School. [Edinburgh, 1829].

Graves, Charles L. *Life and Letters of Alexander Macmillan.* London: Macmillan, 1910.

Gruber, Jacob W. 'Horatio Hale and the Development of American Anthropology.' *Proceedings of the American Philosophical Society* 111 (1967): 5–37.

Guillet, Edward C. *In the Course of Education: Centennial History of the Ontario Educational Association, 1861–1960.* Toronto: University of Toronto Press, 1960.

Hale, Horatio. *The Iroquois Book of Rites.* Philadelphia: D.G. Brinton, 1883.

– 'Sketch of Sir Daniel Wilson.' *Popular Science Monthly* 4 (December 1893): 256–65.

Halkett, Samuel. *Testimonials in Favour of Mr. Samuel Halkett.* [Edinburgh? 1848].

Hannah, Hugh. 'Sir Daniel Wilson, the Man and His Work.' *The Book of the Old Edinburgh Club* 17 (April 1930): 1–16.

Harper, J. Russell. *Early Painters and Engravers in Canada*. Toronto: University of Toronto Press, 1970.

Harris, Lawren. Foreword. In *Catalogue: Group of Seven Exhibition of Paintings*. Toronto: Art Gallery of Toronto, 1920.

Harris, Marvin. *The Rise of Anthropological Theory*. New York: Thomas Y. Crowell, 1968.

Harris, Robin. *English Studies at Toronto: A History*. Toronto: University of Toronto Press, 1988.

Hayes, Alan L., ed. *By Grace Co-workers: Building the Anglican Diocese of Toronto, 1780–1989*. Toronto: Anglican Book Centre, 1989.

– 'The Struggle for the Rights of the Laity in the Diocese of Toronto, 1850–1879.' Canadian Church Historical Society, *Journal* 26 (1984): 5–17.

Henderson, Elmes. 'Bloor Street, Toronto, and the Village of Yorkville in 1849.' Ontario Historical Society, *Papers and Records* 26 (1930): 445–56.

Herrmann, Luke. *Turner Prints: The Engraved Work of J.M.W. Turner*. Oxford: Phaidon, 1990.

Hind, Henry Youle. *Narrative of the Canadian Red River Exploring Expedition of 1857 and of the Assiniboine and Saskatchewan Exploring Expedition of 1858*. 2 vols. London, 1860; reprint, Edmonton, 1971.

Hodgins, J. George, ed. *Documentary History of Education in Upper Canada* ... 28 vols. Toronto: Warwick Bros. & Rutter, 1894–1910.

Hoebel, Edward A. 'William Robertson: An 18th-Century Anthropologist-Historian.' *American Anthropologist* 62 (1960): 648–55.

Hoff, Tory. 'The Controversial Appointment of James Mark Baldwin to the University of Toronto in 1889.' MA thesis, Carleton University, 1980.

Hooker, J.D. 'Outlines of the Distribution of Arctic Plants.' Linnean Society, *Transactions* 23 (1862): 251–310.

Horsman, Reginald. *Race and Manifest Destiny: The Origins of American Racial Anglo-Saxonism*. Cambridge: Harvard University Press, 1981.

– 'Scientific Racism and the American Indian in the Mid-Nineteenth Century.' *American Quarterly* 27 (1975): 152–68.

Howard, Richard B. *Upper Canada College, 1829–1979: Colborne's Legacy*. Toronto: Macmillan, 1979.

Hrdlička, Aleš. 'Physical Anthropology in America: An Historical Sketch.' In *Anthropology in North America*, by Franz Boas et al., 135–81. New York: Steckert, 1915.

Hubert, Henry A. *Harmonious Perfection: The Development of English Studies in Nineteenth-Century Anglo-Canadian Colleges*. East Lansing: Michigan State University Press, 1994.

– 'The Vernacular in Nineteenth-Century Anglophone Colleges.' *Canadian Literature* 131 (winter 1991): 114–25.

Hughes, Thomas. *Memoir of Daniel Macmillan.* London: Macmillan, 1883.

Humboldt, Alexander von. *Cosmos: A Sketch of a Physical Description of the Universe.* Trans. E.C. Otte. 5 vols. London: Bohn, 1848–58.

– *Personal Narrative of Travels to the Equinoctial Regions of America, during the Years 1799–1804.* Trans. and ed. Thomasina Ross. 3 vols. London: H.G. Bohn, 1852–3.

Hunter, Andrew Frederick. 'The Semi-Centennial of "Prehistoric Man."' *University Monthly* 13 (1912–13): 12–20.

Hutcheson, Francis. *A System of Moral Philosophy in Three Books.* 2 vols. London: A. Millar and T. Longman; Glasgow: R. and A. Foulis, 1755.

Irving, John A. 'The Development of Philosophy in Central Canada from 1850 to 1900.' *Canadian Historical Review* 31 (1950): 252–87.

Jasen, Patricia Jane. *Wild Things: Nature, Culture, and Tourism in Ontario, 1790–1914.* Toronto: University of Toronto Press, 1995.

Jay, Elisabeth. *Mrs Oliphant: 'A Fiction to Herself' – A Literary Life.* Oxford: Clarendon Press, 1995.

Johnson, Alexander. *Science and Religion: An Address Delivered at the Convocation of McGill University, May 1st, 1876, to the Bachelors of Applied Science.* Montreal: Dawson, 1876.

The Jubilee Volume of Wycliffe College. Toronto: Wycliffe College, 1927 [i.e., 1937].

Kaplan, Louise J. *The Family Romance of the Imposter-Poet Thomas Chatterton.* New York: Athenaeum, 1988.

Keane, David Ross. 'Rediscovering Ontario University Students of the Mid Nineteenth Century: Sources for and Approaches to the Study of the Experience of Going to College and Personal, Family and Social Backgrounds of Students.' 4 vols. PhD thesis, University of Toronto, 1981.

Keen, Benjamin. *The Aztec Image in Western Thought.* New Brunswick: Princeton University Press, 1971.

Kehoe, Alice B. 'The Invention of Prehistory.' *Current Anthrolopogy* 32 (1991): 467–76.

– *The Land of Prehistory: A Critical History of American Archaeology.* New York and London: Routledge, 1998.

– 'Vestiges of the Natural History of Man: The Ideology of Archaeology.' Paper presented at the Archaeology of Ideology Conference, Calgary, 9 November 1990.

Kelly, Linda. *The Marvellous Boy: The Life and Myth of Thomas Chatterton.* London: Weidenfeld and Nicolson, 1971.

Kern, Stephen. *The Culture of Time and Space, 1800–1918.* Cambridge: Harvard University Press, 1983.

Killan, Gerald. *David Boyle: From Artisan to Archaeologist.* Toronto: University of Toronto Press, 1983.

King, John. *McCaul: Croft: Forneri: Personalities of Early University Days.* Toronto: Macmillan, 1914.

Klindt-Jensen, Ole. *A History of Scandinavian Archaeology.* London: Thames and Hudson, 1975.

Langton, Hugh Hornby. *James Loudon and the University of Toronto.* Toronto: University of Toronto Press, 1927.

– 'Sir Daniel Wilson.' *Review of Historical Publications Relating to Canada* 5 (1900): 199–217.

– *Sir Daniel Wilson: A Memoir.* Edinburgh, Toronto, London: Thomas Nelson & Sons, 1929.

Langton, William Alexander, ed. *Early Days in Upper Canada: Letters of John Langton.* Toronto: Macmillan, 1926.

– 'Sir Daniel Wilson as an Artist.' *University of Toronto Monthly* 2 (1901–2): 180–3.

Leacock, Stephen. 'Laus Varsitatis: A Song in Praise of the University of Toronto.' In *The Varsity Magazine Supplement*, December 1916, 115–16.

– *Professors, or My Fifty Years among the Chalk Dust: The Voice of Stephen Leacock. Recordings from 1938 & 1943.* Intro. Peter Gzowski. Orillia, Ont.: The Stephen Leacock Museum, 1995. Cassette tape.

Letter to the Right Hon. the Lord Provost of the City of Edinburgh, regarding the System of Education Pursued at the High School. Edinburgh: Adam Black [etc.], 1829.

Levere, T.H. 'The Most Select and the Most Democratic: A Century of Science in the Royal Society of Canada.' *Scientia Canadensis* (forthcoming, 1998).

– *Research and Influence: A Century of Science in the Royal Society of Canada.* Ottawa: Royal Society of Canada, 1998.

Lindsay, Debra. *Science in the Subarctic: Trappers, Traders, and the Smithsonian Institution.* Washington: Smithsonian Institution Press, 1993.

Logan, William Edmond, et al. *Geology Survey of Canada: Report of Progress from Its Commencement to 1863 ...* Montreal: Dawson Brothers, 1863.

Loudon, William James. *Sir William Mulock: A Short Biography.* Toronto: Macmillan, 1932.

– *Studies of Student Life.* Vol. 6. Toronto: Macmillan, 1930.

Lubbock, John. *The Origin of Civilisation and the Primitive Condition of Man.* London: Longmans, Green, 1870.

– *Pre-historic Times, as Illustrated by Ancient Remains, and the Manners and Customs of Modern Savages.* London: Williams and Norgate, 1865.

– *Pre-historic Times.* 2d ed. London: Williams and Norgate, 1869.

– *Pre-historic Times.* 4th ed. New York: D. Appleton & Co., 1887.

– Review of *Prehistoric Man.* In *Natural History Review,* no. 9 (1863): 26–30.

Macallum, A.B. 'Huxley and Tyndall and the University of Toronto.' *University of Toronto Monthly* 2 (December 1901): 68–76.

McCardle, Bennett. 'The Life and Anthropological Works of Daniel Wilson (1816–1892).' MA thesis, University of Toronto, 1980.

McIlwraith, T.F. 'Sir Daniel Wilson: A Canadian Anthropologist of One Hundred Years Ago.' *PTRSC,* 4th ser., 2 (1964), section 4: 129–36.

McKillop, A.B. *Contours of Canadian Thought.* Toronto: University of Toronto Press, 1987.

– *A Disciplined Intelligence: Critical Inquiry and Canadian Thought in the Victorian Era.* Montreal: McGill-Queen's University Press, 1979.

– *Matters of Mind: The University in Ontario, 1791–1951.* Toronto: University of Toronto Press, 1994.

MacLaren, Ian S. 'The Metamorphosis of Travellers into Authors: The Case of Paul Kane.' In *Critical Issues in Editing Exploration Texts: Papers Given at the Twenty-Eighth Annual Conference on Editorial Problems, University of Toronto, 6–7 November 1992,* ed. Germaine Warkentin, 67–101. Toronto: University of Toronto Press, 1995.

Maclean, John. *The Indians – Their Manners and Customs.* Toronto: Briggs, 1889.

MacMechan, Archibald. *Reminiscences of Toronto University.* [n.p., n.d.]

McRae, Sandra F. 'The "Scientific Spirit" in Medicine at the University of Toronto, 1880–1910.' PhD thesis, University of Toronto, 1987.

Meek, Ronald L. *Social Science and the Ignoble Savage.* Cambridge: Cambridge University Press, 1976.

Meikle, W. Duncan. 'And Gladly Teach: G.M. Wrong and the Department of History at the University of Toronto.' PhD thesis, Michigan State University, 1977.

Memorials of Chancellor W.H. Blake, Bishop John Strachan, Professor H.H. Croft and Professor G.P. Young Presented to the University of Toronto Library, January 31, 1894. Toronto: Rowsell & Hutchison, 1894.

Michasiw, Kim Ian. 'Nine Revisionist Theses on the Picturesque.' *Representations,* no. 38 (spring 1992): 76–100.

Millar, John. *The Origin of the Distinction of Ranks; or, An Inquiry into the Different Circumstances Which Give Rise to Influence and Authority, in the Different Members of Society.* 3d ed., corr. and enl. London: J. Murray, 1779.

Miller, William Frederick. *Memorials of Hope Park, Comprising Some Particulars in the Life of Our Dear Father, William Miller, and Notices of His More Immediate Ancestors; Together with a List of His Engravings.* London: Printed for the compiler by Simmons and Botten, 1886.

Mills, Eric L. 'A View of Edward Forbes, Naturalist.' *Archives of Natural History* 11 (1984): 365–93.

Miner, Muriel Miller. *G.A. Reid: Canadian Artist.* Toronto: Ryerson Press, 1946.

Mitchell, Sir Arthur, and C.G. Cash. *A Contribution to the Bibliography of Scottish Topography.* Vol. 1. Edinburgh: Scottish History Society, 1917.

Morgan, Lewis H. *League of the Ho-dé-no-sau-nee, or Iroquois.* Rochester, NY: Sage, 1851.

Moriarty, Catherine. *John Galbraith, 1846–1914: Engineer and Educator, a Portrait.* University of Toronto, Faculty of Applied Science and Engineering, 1989.

Morton, Samuel George. *Crania Americana; or, A Comparative View of the Skulls of Various Aboriginal Nations of North and South America; to Which Is Prefixed an Essay on the Varieties of the Human Species ...* Philadelphia: J. Dobson, 1839.

Morton, W.L. *Henry Youle Hind, 1823–1908.* Canadian Biographical Studies, 7. Toronto: University of Toronto Press, 1980.

Mulock, William. *Address of William Mulock, M.A., M.P., Vice-Chancellor of the University of Toronto at the Annual Commencement, June 7th, 1889.* Toronto: T. Hill & Son, Caxton Press, 1889.

– *To the Senate of the University of Toronto.* [Toronto? 1892]

– *'The University Act' (Toronto) R.S.O. cap. 279: A Review of University Legislation and Some of Its Results: An Address Delivered at the Annual Banquet of the Ottawa Branch of the Alumni Association at the Chateau Laurier, Friday, March 21, 1924.* Ottawa: Ottawa Branch of the Alumni Association of the University of Toronto [1924?]

Munch, Peter Andreas. *Lærde Brev fraa og til P.A. Munch.* Ed. Gustav Indrebo et al. 3 vols. Oslo: I Kommisjon hjaa Aschehoug, 1924–71.

Murray, Heather. 'The Appointment of W.J. Alexander.' In *Working in English: History, Institution, Resources,* 17–45. Toronto: University of Toronto Press, 1996.

Needham, H.G. 'The Origins of the Royal Ontario Museum.' MA thesis, University of Toronto, 1970.

Newsboys' Lodging and Industrial Home, Toronto. *Annual Reports.* Toronto, 1870–89.

Nicholson, Malcolm. 'Alexander von Humboldt and the Geography of Vegetation.' In *Romanticism and the Sciences,* ed. Andrew Cunningham and Nicholas Jardine, 169–88. Cambridge: Cambridge University Press, 1990.

Noble, W.C. 'One Hundred and Twenty-Five Years of Archaeology in the Canadian Provinces.' *Canadian Archaeological Bulletin* 4 (1972): 1–78.

Oliphant, Margaret Oliphant (Wilson). *The Autobiography and Letters of Mrs M.O.W. Oliphant.* Arranged and ed. by Mrs Harry Coghill. Edinburgh and London: William Blackwood and Sons, 1899; reprint, Leicester: Leicester University Press, 1974.

O'Malley, Michael. *Keeping Watch: A History of American Time.* New York: Viking, 1990.

Ontario. Legislative Assembly. *Sessional Papers.* 1878–92. Toronto. Annual reports of the Council of University College and the University of Toronto (when printed) and the School of Practical Science, some of which are contained in the report of the minister of education.

Ontario. Royal Commission on the University of Toronto. *Report of the Royal*

Commission on the University of Toronto. Toronto: Printed by order of the Legislative Assembly of Ontario by L.K. Cameron, 1906.

Orgel, Stephen. 'Introduction.' In *The Tempest*, by William Shakespeare, 1–87. Oxford: Oxford University Press, 1987.

Owram, Doug. *Promise of Eden: The Canadian Expansionist Movement and the Idea of the West, 1856–1900*. Toronto: University of Toronto Press, 1980.

Pagden, Anthony, *The Fall of Natural Man: The American Indian and the Origins of Comparative Ethnology*. Cambridge: Cambridge University Press, 1982.

Palliser, John. *The Journals, Detailed Reports, and Observations Relative to the Exploration, by Captain John Palliser, of That Portion of British North America ... during the Years 1857, 1858, 1859, and 1860*. London: Printed by G.E. Eyre and W. Spottiswoode, 1863.

Peake, Frank. 'Unity and Discord: A Study of Anglican Tensions in 19th Century Ontario.' In *Some Men and Some Controversies*, 101–27. Erin, Ont.: Press Porcépic, 1974.

Piggott, Stuart. *Ruins in a Landscape: Essays in Antiquarianism*. Edinburgh: University Press, 1976.

– and Marjorie Robertson. *Three Centuries of Scottish Archaeology: George Buchanan to Lord Abercromby*. Edinburgh: Edinburgh University Press, 1977.

Prichard, James Cowles. *Researches into the Physical History of Man*. London: John and Arthur Arch, 1813; reprint, Chicago: University of Chicago Press, 1973.

Pringle, Allen. 'A Little Afraid of His Own Logic.' *Canadian Bee Journal*, 1888, 932–3.

– 'Those Bee Glands and Evolution.' *Canadian Bee Journal*, 1888, 1031–2.

Ramenofsky, Ann F. *Vectors of Death: The Archaeology of European Contact*. Albuquerque: University of New Mexico Press, 1987.

Rawlinson, William George. *The Engraved Work of J.M.W. Turner, R.A.* 2 vols. London: Macmillan 1908–13.

Reaney, James. *The Dismissal; or, Twisted Beards and Tangled Whiskers*. Erin, Ont.: Press Porcépic, 1976.

Redgrave, Samuel. *A Dictionary of the English School*. London, 1878; Bath: Kingsmead Reprints, 1970.

Rehbock, Philip. *The Philosophical Naturalists*. Madison: University of Wisconsin Press, 1983.

Reid, Dennis. *Lucius O'Brien: Visions of Victorian Canada*. Toronto: Art Gallery of Ontario, 1990.

Reid, Thomas. *An Inquiry into the Human Mind, on the Principles of Common Sense*. 2d ed., corr. Edinburgh: A. Millar; London: A. Kincaid and J. Bell, 1765.

Reid, W. Stanford, ed. *The Scottish Tradition in Canada*. Toronto: Published by McClelland and Stewart in association with the Multiculturalism Program, Department of the Secretary of State of Canada, 1976.

Reimer, Howard J. 'Darwinism in Canadian Literature.' PhD thesis, McMaster University, 1975.

Rendall, Jane. *The Origins of the Scottish Enlightenment*. London: Macmillan Press, 1978.

Richardson, Douglas. *A Not Unsightly Building: University College and Its History*. Oakville, Ont.: Mosaic Press for University College, 1990.

Richardson, W. George. *Queen's Engineers: A Century of Applied Science, 1893–1993*. Kingston: Queen's University, Faculty of Applied Science, 1992.

Robertson, William. *The History of America*. 2 vols. London: W. Strahan, T. Cadell, and J. Balfour, Edinburgh, 1777.

Robson, Albert H. *Canadian Landscape Painters*. Toronto: Ryerson Press, 1932.

Roome, P. 'The Darwin Debate in Canada: 1860–1880.' In *Science, Technology and Culture in Historical Perspective*, ed. Louis A. Knafla, Martin S. Staum, and T.H.E. Travers, 183–205. Calgary: University of Calgary, 1976.

Ross, George W. *Speeches Delivered to the Legislative Assembly of Ontario ... on Moving the Second Reading of the Bills Respecting the Federation of the University of Toronto with Other Universities, the Endowment of the University of Toronto and the Reorganization of Upper Canada College, 12th April, 1887*. [Toronto, 1887]

Ross, Murray G. *The Y.M.C.A. in Canada: The Chronicle of a Century*. Toronto: Ryerson Press, 1951.

Royal Commission on the Ancient Monuments of Scotland. *An Inventory of the Ancient and Historical Monuments of the City of Edinburgh, with the Thirteenth Report of the Commission*. Edinburgh: HMSO, 1951.

Ruskin, John. *Modern Painters*. 4 vols. London: Blackfriars Publishing Co. [n.d.]

Russell, Alexander. *The Light That Lighteth Every Man: Sermons by Alexander Russell, B.D., Late Dean of Adelaide*. With an introd. by E.H. Plumptre. London: Macmillan, 1889.

Schoolcraft, Henry Rowe. *Narrative Journal from Detroit Northwest through the Great Chain of American Lakes to the Sources of the Mississippi River in the Year 1820*. Albany, NY, 1821.

Schull, Joseph. *Edward Blake*. Vol. 1, *The Man of the Other Way (1833–1881)*; vol. 2, *Leader and Exile (1881–1912)*. Toronto: Macmillan, 1975–6.

Scott, Sir Walter. *The Journal of Sir Walter Scott from the Original Manuscript at Abbotsford*. 2 vols. Edinburgh: David Douglas, 1891.

– 'Memoir of His Early Years, Written by Himself.' In *Life of Sir Walter Scott, Bart.*, by J.C. Lockhart, abr. ed., 1–56. Edinburgh: Adam & Charles Black, 1871.

– *The Minstrelsy of the Scottish Border*. 2 vols. Kelso: James Ballantyne; London, Edinburgh, 1802.

– *Northern Lights: or, A Voyage on the Lighthouse Yacht to Nova Zembla and the Lord*

Knows Where in the Summer of 1814. Ed. William F. Laughlan. Hawick: Byway Books, 1982.

– *Waverley; or, 'Tis Sixty Years Since*. Ed. Claire Lamont. Oxford: Clarendon Press, 1981.

Should Victoria University Join the Proposed Federation of Colleges? [n.p., n.d.]

Sime, Georgina, and Frank Nicholson. 'Recollections of Mrs. Oliphant.' In *Brave Spirits*, 25–55. [London]: Distributed by Simpkin Marshall & Co. [1952].

Simpson, John M. 'Scott and Old Norse Literature.' In *Scott Bicentenary Essays: Selected Papers Read at the Sir Walter Scott Bicentenary Conference*, ed. Alan Bell, 300–13. Edinburgh: Scottish Academic Press, 1973.

Simpson, W. Douglas. 'Sir Daniel Wilson and the *Prehistoric Annals of Scotland*: A Centenary Study.' *PSAS* 96 (1962–3): 1–8.

Slotkin, James S., ed. *Readings in Early Anthropology*. Chicago: Aldine, 1965.

Smellie, William. 'An Historical Account of the Society of Antiquaries of Scotland.' *Transactions of the Society of Antiquaries of Scotland* 1 (1792): iii–xiii.

Squair, John. *Admission of Women to the University of Toronto and University College; and Rectification of a Passage in 'Alumni Associations in the University of Toronto' (1922)*. Toronto: University of Toronto Press, 1924.

– *The Autobiography of a Teacher of French ... Being a Contribution to the History of the University of Toronto*. Toronto: University of Toronto Press, 1928.

– *Forty Years Ago*. Toronto: University of Toronto Press, 1924.

Stacey, Robert. 'Frances Anne Hopkins and the Canoe-Eye-View.' In *Frances Anne Hopkins, 1838–1919: Canadian Scenery*, 44–63. Thunder Bay, Ont.: Thunder Bay Art Gallery, 1990.

Stanton, William. *The Leopard's Spots: Scientific Attitudes toward Race in America, 1815–59*. Chicago: University of Chicago Press. 1960.

Steven, William. *The History of the High School of Edinburgh*. Edinburgh: Maclachlan & Stewart, 1849.

Stevenson, R.B.K. 'The Museum, Its Beginnings and Its Development. Part I, To 1858: the Society's Own Museum.' In *The Scottish Antiquarian Tradition: Essays to Mark the Bicentenary of the Society of Antiquaries of Scotland and Its Museum, 1780–1980*, ed. A.S. Bell, 31–85. Edinburgh: John Donald Publishers, 1981.

– 'The Return of Mons Meg from London, 1828–1829.' In *Scottish Weapons and Fortifications, 1100–1800*, ed. David H. Caldwell, 419–21. Edinburgh: John Donald Publishers, 1981.

Stocking, George W., Jr. 'From Chronology to Ethnology: James Cowles Prichard and British Anthropology, 1800–1850.' In J.C. Prichard, *Researches into the Physical History of Man*, ed. G.W. Stocking, ix–cx. Chicago: University of Chicago Press, 1973.

– 'Scotland as the Model of Mankind: Lord Kames' Philosophical View of Civilization.' In *Toward a Science of Man: Essays in the History of Anthropology*, ed. Timothy H.H. Thoresen, 65–89. The Hague: Mouton, 1975.

– 'What's in a Name? The Origins of the Royal Anthropological Institute (1837–71).' *Man*, n.s., 6 (1971): 367–90.

Stouffer, Allen P. *The Light of Nature and the Law of God: Antislavery in Ontario, 1833–1877*. McGill-Queen's Studies in Ethnic History. Montreal: McGill-Queen's University Press, 1992.

Supplement to the Report of the Minister of Education, 1892. University Extension: Report of a Meeting Held in the Public Hall of the Education Department, November 5th, 1891. Toronto, 1892.

Thomas, Morley. *The Beginnings of Canadian Meteorology*. Toronto: ECW Press, 1991.

Tilson, Alistair. 'Who Now Reads *Spalding*?' *English Studies in Canada* 17 (December 1991): 469–80.

Toronto (Diocese of). Synod. *Proceedings* ... Toronto, 1851–89. Later published as *Journal of the Incorporated Synod of the Church of England in the Diocese of Toronto*.

'The Trade of the Artists' Colourman.' In *Paint and Painting: An Exhibition and Working Studio Sponsored by Winsor & Newton to Celebrate Their 150th Anniversary*. London: Tate Gallery, 1982.

Trigger, Bruce G. 'Daniel Wilson and the Scottish Enlightenment.' *PSAS* 122 (1992): 55–75.

– *Natives and Newcomers: Canada's 'Heroic Age' Reconsidered*. Montreal: McGill-Queen's University Press, 1985.

– 'Sir Daniel Wilson: Canada's First Anthropologist.' *Anthropologica*, n.s., 8 (1966): 3–28.

Tylor, E.B. 'American Aspects of Anthropology.' In *Readings in the History of Anthropology*, ed. R. Darnell, 218–34. New York: Harper & Row, 1974.

University College, Toronto. *Calendar*. 1857/8–1891/2. Toronto.

University College YMCA. *Annual Report ...*, 1888–89. Copy in AO, F 980, H.J. Cody Papers.

University of Toronto. *Return to an Address to His Honour the Lieutenant Governor ...* Toronto: C. Blackett Robinson, 1881.

– *The Year Book of the University of Toronto* ... 1886–87. Ed. J.O. Miller and F.B. Hodgins. Toronto: Rowsell & Hutchison, 1887.

The University of Toronto and Its Colleges, 1827–1906. Toronto: University of Toronto Library, 1906.

Varsity. 1 (1880–1)– . Student newspaper, University of Toronto.

Vaughan, Alden T. 'From White Man to Red Skin: Changing Anglo-American Perceptions of the American Indian.' *American Historical Review* 87 (1982): 917–53.

– and Virginia Mason Vaughan. *Shakespeare's Caliban: A Cultural History*. Cambridge: Cambridge University Press, 1991.

Walden, Keith. 'Male Toronto College Students Celebrate Hallowe'en, 1884–1910.' *Canadian Historical Review* 68 (1987): 1–34.

Wallace, W. Stewart. *A History of the University of Toronto, 1827–1927.* Toronto: Macmillan, 1927.

– *The Macmillan Dictionary of Canadian Biography.* 4th ed., rev. W.A. McKay. Toronto: Macmillan, 1978.

–, ed. *The Royal Canadian Institute Centennial Volume, 1849–1949.* Toronto: Privately printed, 1949.

Watt, K. Jane. 'Passing Out of Memory: Georgina Sime and the Politics of Literary Recuperation.' PhD dissertation, University of Alberta, 1997.

Weber, Gay. 'Science and Society in Nineteenth Century Anthropology.' *History of Science* 12 (1974): 260–83.

Wedd, W. 'The Rev. John McCaul, LLD.' *University of Toronto Monthly* 2 (October 1901): 2–5.

White and Blue. 1 (1879–80). Student newspaper, University of Toronto; only one volume published; superseded by the *Varsity.*

Williams, Merryn. *Margaret Oliphant: A Critical Biography.* Basingstoke: Macmillan, 1986.

Williams, Stephen. *Fantastic Archaeology: The Wild Side of North American Prehistory.* Philadelphia: University of Pennsylvania Press, 1991.

Wilson, Daniel, vicar of Islington. *Two Sermons, Preached on Sunday, December 19th, 1875, at St Peter's Church, Islington, on the Occasion of the Death of the Rev. Joseph Haslegrave, M.A., Vicar of St Peter's, Islington, for 40 Years.* London: William Macintosh [1875].

Wilson, George. *The Grievance of the University Tests, as Applied to Professors of Physical Science in the Colleges of Scotland: A Letter Addressed to the Right Honourable Spencer H. Walpole, Secretary of State for the Home Department.* Edinburgh: Sutherland and Knox; London: Simpkin, Marshall & Co., 1852.

– and Archibald Geikie. *Memoir of Edward Forbes.* Cambridge: Macmillan and Edmonston, 1861.

– and James M. Russell. *Poems: Memorials of Cousins.* Edinburgh: Printed for private circulation [n.d.].

Wilson, Jessie Aitken. *Memoir of George Wilson, M.D. F.R.S.E. ...* Edinburgh: Edmonston and Douglas; London: Macmillan, 1860.

Wilson, Robert A. *A New History of the Conquest of Mexico.* Philadelphia: J. Challen, 1859.

Wood, B. Anne. *Idealism Transformed: The Making of a Progressive Educator.* Kingston: McGill-Queen's University Press, 1985.

Wrong, George M. 'Sir Daniel Wilson.' *Arbor* 3 (January 1912): 150–60.

Yeo, Richard. 'An Idol of the Market-Place: Baconianism in Nineteenth-Century Britain.' *History of Science* 23 (1985): 251–98.

Young, C.R. *Early Engineering Education at Toronto, 1851–1919.* Toronto: University of Toronto Press, 1958.

Young, Robert M. 'Natural Theology, Victorian Periodicals, and the Fragmentation of a Common Context.' In *Darwin's Metaphor: Nature's Place in Victorian Culture,* 126–63. Cambridge: Cambridge University Press, 1985.

Youngson, A.J. *The Making of Classical Edinburgh, 1750–1840.* Edinburgh: University Press, 1966.

Yuille, George, ed. *History of the Baptists in Scotland from Pre-Reformation Times.* Glasgow: Baptist Union Publications Committee [1926].

Zeller, Suzanne. 'Classical Codes: Biogeographical Assessments of the Great Northwest in Victorian Canada.' *Journal of Historical Geography* 24 (1998): 20–35.

– 'Environment, Culture, and the Reception of Darwin in Canada.' In *Disseminating Darwinism: The Role of Place, Race, Religion, and Gender,* ed. Ron Numbers and John Stenhouse. Cambridge: Cambridge University Press, in press.

– 'George Lawson: Victorian Botany, the Origin of Species, and the Case of Nova Scotian Heather.' In *Profiles of Science and Society in the Maritimes Prior to 1914,* ed. Paul A. Bogaard, 51–64. Fredericton: Acadiensis Press, 1990.

– *Inventing Canada: Early Victorian Science and the Idea of a Transcontinental Nation.* Toronto: University of Toronto Press, 1987.

– *Land of Promise, Promised Land: The Culture of Victorian Science in Canada.* Canadian Historical Association Booklet, no. 56. Ottawa: Canadian Historical Association, 1996.

– 'Mapping the Canadian Mind: Reports of the Geological Survey of Canada, 1842–1863.' *Canadian Literature* 131 (1991): 157–67.

– 'Nature's Gullivers and Crusoes: The Scientific Exploration of British North America, 1800–1870.' In *North American Exploration,* vol. 3, *A Continent Comprehended,* ed. John Logan Allen, 190–243. Lincoln: University of Nebraska Press, 1997.

– 'The Spirit of Bacon: Science and Self-Perception in the Hudson's Bay Company, 1830–1870.' *Scientia Canadensis* 8 (fall 1989): 79–101.

Contributors

Marinell Ash, a graduate of the University of California at Santa Barbara and the University of Newcastle, lectured in Scottish history at the University of St Andrews and was a radio producer with the educational department of BBC Scotland before establishing her own historical research bureau in 1983. The author of *The Strange Death of Scottish History* (1980) and numerous articles on historiography and archaeology, she discovered Daniel Wilson in the course of researching the history of the Society of Antiquaries of Scotland. Dr Ash died in 1988.

Harold Averill, originally from rural Manitoba, has a background in Commonwealth and Canadian history. He is currently Assistant University Archivist at the University of Toronto. As a volunteer, he has been active in the Toronto archival community and has contributed to the growth of the Canadian Lesbian and Gay Archives for the past two decades. His current research interests include the early history of the University of Toronto.

Kitty Cruft, immediately after graduating from the University of Edinburgh, joined the Scottish National Buildings Record to establish the national archive of drawings, prints, photographs, and manuscripts relating to Scottish architecture (now including archaeology); she retired in 1991. With Andrew Fraser, she edited *James Craig, 1744–1795: The Ingenious Architect of the New Town of Edinburgh* (1995), to which she contributed the biographical sketch of Craig's life. She is currently researching the Borders volume in the Buildings of Scotland series published by Penguin Books.

Elizabeth Hulse has been a rare books librarian at the University of Toronto, a manuscript editor with the Dictionary of Canadian Biography, and archivist of the Art Gallery of Toronto. Her publications include a study of the book trades in nineteenth-century Toronto. She currently works as a freelance researcher and editor.

Gerald Keith grew up in central British Columbia and was educated at the University of Toronto, where he received two degrees in physics. He is currently training at the Gestalt Institute of Toronto, and in his spare time he writes articles and short stories. Co-authoring an essay on Daniel Wilson fanned his interest in historical writing, and he is pursuing further research on the University of Toronto in the nineteenth century.

Bennett McCardle is the author of a master's thesis on the life and anthropological works of Daniel Wilson, completed for the Department of Anthropology, University of Toronto. She has worked as a researcher and director of research for the Indian Association of Alberta and as an archivist at the Archives of Ontario. She is currently with the Tourism Policy and Research Branch of the Ontario Ministry of Economic Development, Trade and Tourism.

Margaret A. Mackay was born and raised in Saskatchewan and is a graduate of University College, Toronto. She is currently Director of the School of Scottish Studies at the University of Edinburgh, which houses the national archive of oral testimony and tradition. Together with James Macaulay, she edited Marinell Ash's *This Noble Harbour: A History of the Cromarty Firth* (1991) after the author's death.

Heather Murray is Associate Professor of English at the University of Toronto. She is the author of *Working in English: History, Institution, Resources* (1996) and is currently completing a study of literary societies in nineteenth-century Ontario.

Robert Stacey, a graduate of University College, is a Toronto-based writer, art historian, exhibition curator, and editor with a special interest in Canadian art, design, illustration, photography, architecture, and cultural geography. Among his recent publications are *J.E.H. MacDonald: Designer* (1996) and *Massanoga: The Art of Bon Echo* (1998). *Figures in a Landscape: The Art of Robert Reginald Whale (1805–1887)*, which he guest-curated for the Art Gallery of Hamilton, toured Canada in 1997.

Bruce G. Trigger, Professor of Anthropology at McGill University, is the author of numerous books and articles on the Native peoples of eastern Canada and the history of archaeology. He is now working on a comparative study of early civilizations.

Suzanne Zeller is Associate Professor of History at Wilfrid Laurier University. She is the author of *Inventing Canada: Early Victorian Science and the Idea of a Transcontinental Nation* (1987), *Land of Promise, Promised Land: The Culture of Victorian Science in Canada* (1996), and related articles. Her research interests concern the social, cultural, and environmental impact of ideas of science.

Index